Exploring World History Curriculum Package

From Creation to the 21st century, *Exploring World History* presents ancient, medieval, and modern history from the perspective of faith in God and respect for His Word. In addition to reading the history narrative about events, issues, and people from around the world and across the centuries, students read the words of people who made history in original documents, speeches, poems, and stories. The course offers a thorough survey of Western civilization with significant coverage of Latin America, Africa, and Asia. The lessons feature hundreds of full-color photographs and illustrations.

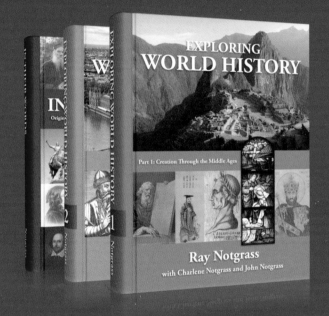

Exploring World History is designed to be easy-to-use for parent and student. Each of the 30 weekly units has an introduction that features a summary of the unit with the Bible memory work, books used, and suggested writing assignments and hands-on projects. Each of the 150 daily lessons (five lessons per week) includes the history text and the reading assignments for that day. A focused student can direct his own study, and the parent can offer assistance as needed.

The full curriculum package includes:

- *Exploring World History Part 1*
- *Exploring World History Part 2*
- *In Their Words*

Completing the full course provides your child with a year's high school credit in three subjects: World History, English, and Bible. The curriculum includes the instructions, lessons, and assignments for completing the course over one school year. As part of the English credit, the course also assigns twelve literature titles that go along with the history lessons (see page xvi of *Part 1*).

The *Exploring World History Student Review Pack* is an optional additional resource. This pack includes three additional resources. The *Student Review Book* includes lesson review questions, literature review questions, literary analysis, and Bible commentary. The *Quiz & Exam Book* has weekly quizzes and six exams. The *Answer Key* has all of the answers for the parent to use in grading.

For more information, visit notgrass.com or call 1-800-211-8793.

Exploring World History
Part 1

Creation Through the Middle Ages

For all those who have in any way shared the sacred and imperishable gospel
with those from every tribe and tongue and people and nation (Revelation 5:9).
You have helped to fulfill God's plan for mankind and have offered hope where there was none.

Exploring World History Part 1
Ray Notgrass with Charlene Notgrass and John Notgrass

ISBN 978-1-60999-061-9

Previous Page: Noah's Ark (English, 15th Century)

Front Cover Images: Machu Picchu, Peru (funkz / Flickr / CC-BY-2.0), Moses (Library of Congress), King Tang of Shang Dynasty, Julius Caesar (Skara kommun [Stifts- och landsbiblioteket i Skara] / Flickr / CC-BY-2.0), Stained Glass Window in the Cathedral of St. Paul, Minnesota (Sharon Mollerus / Flickr / CC-BY-2.0), Alfred the Great. *Back Cover Image:* Temple of Zeus, Athens, Greece (psyberartist / Flickr / CC-BY-2.0).
Author Photo: Mary Evelyn McCurdy.

Unless otherwise noted, scripture quotations taken from the New American Standard Bible,
Copyright 1960, 1962, 1963, 1971, 1972, 1973, 1975, 1977, 1995
by the Lockman Foundation Used by permission.

Cover design by Mary Evelyn McCurdy
Interior design by John Notgrass

Printed in the United States of America

Notgrass Company
975 Roaring River Road
Gainesboro, TN 38562

1-800-211-8793
www.notgrass.com
books@notgrass.com

Iguazu Falls on the Border of Brazil and Argentina

Table of Contents

How to Use This Curriculum vii

Advice on Writing x

Assigned Literature xvi

1 Introduction to World History 1

1 - It Begins With God 3
2 - Understanding Our World 7
3 - Your Place in the World 11
4 - Religion in History 15
5 - Bible Study: Eternity Before Creation 20

2 The Beginning 25

6 - Creation 27
7 - Sin 31
8 - Early People Groups 36
9 - Questions from Genesis 40
10 - Bible Study: The Existence of God 44

3 Early Civilizations 49

11 - Sumer 51
12 - Egypt 56
13 - Key Concepts: Ancient Science
        and Mathematics 61
14 - Key Person: Hammurabi and
        His Code of Laws 65
15 - Bible Study: The Land Between
        the Rivers 68

4 Abraham and His Descendants 73

16 - Abraham, Isaac, and Jacob 75
17 - Key Concept: The Faith of Abraham 81
18 - Everyday Life: Nomads 85
19 - Key Event: The Destruction of
        Sodom and Gomorrah 89
20 - Bible Study: "God Meant It for Good" 94

5 God Chooses Israel 99

21 - Israel Becomes a Nation   101
22 - Key Event: The Exodus   105
23 - Key Person: Moses   109
24 - Everyday Life: The Story of Ruth   115
25 - Bible Study: The Law   122

6 Israel and Her Neighbors 127

26 - Israel United and Divided   129
27 - Nations of the Ancient Near East   134
28 - Key Person: David   139
29 - Everyday Life: The Time of
          King Solomon   145
30 - Bible Study: Amos,
          the Unlikely Prophet   152

7 Persia 157

31 - The Rise of a New Kingdom   159
32 - Key Concept: Persian Religion   163
33 - Key Person: Cyrus   169
34 - Everyday Life: Babylon
          During the Time of Daniel   173
35 - Bible Study:
          "For Such a Time as This"   177

8 Ancient Asia and Beyond 185

36 - Ancient India   187
37 - Ancient China   193
38 - Everyday Life: Chinese Government,
          Culture, and Science   199
39 - Ancient Africa, America,
          and Europe   205
40 - Bible Study:
          God's Love for the Nations   213

9 Greek Civilization 217

41 - Survey of Greek History   219
42 - Key Concept: Philosophy and
          the Pursuit of Knowledge   225
43 - Key Event: The Peloponnesian War   232
44 - Everyday Life: Ancient Athens   237
45 - Bible Study: God's Wisdom vs.
          Man's Wisdom   242

Pillar of Ashoka, Vaishali, India (Third Century BC)

10 Roman Civilization 247

46 - The Rise of Rome   249
47 - Key Person: Augustus Caesar   255
48 - Key Concept: Roman Law   259
49 - Everyday Life: The Roman Empire   263
50 - Bible Study: The Kingdom of God   269

11 The Central Event in History 273

51 - Introduction to the Gospel of Luke   275
52 - The Revolution Jesus Brought   282
53 - Unlikely Heroes   289
54 - Major Themes in Luke   297
55 - Bible Study: Jerusalem   304

12 The Church Age 311

56 - The Church Begins   313
57 - Key Event: The Conversion of
          Cornelius   320
58 - Key Person: Paul   325
59 - Everyday Life: The First Century
          Mediterranean World   331
60 - Bible Study: How to Study
          a New Testament Letter   338

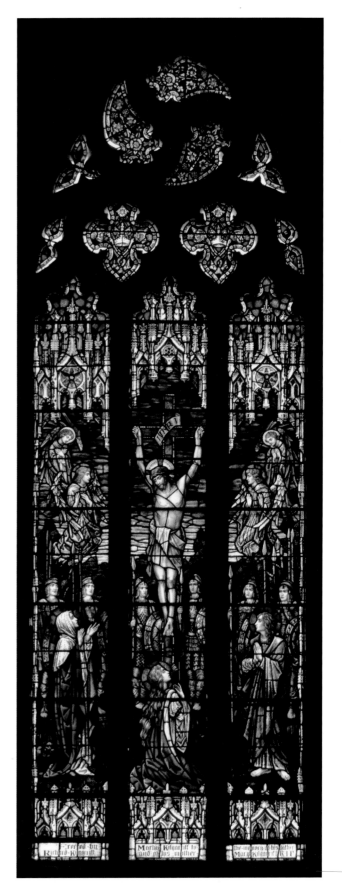

*Stained Glass Window in the
Cathedral of the Assumption, Tuam, Ireland*

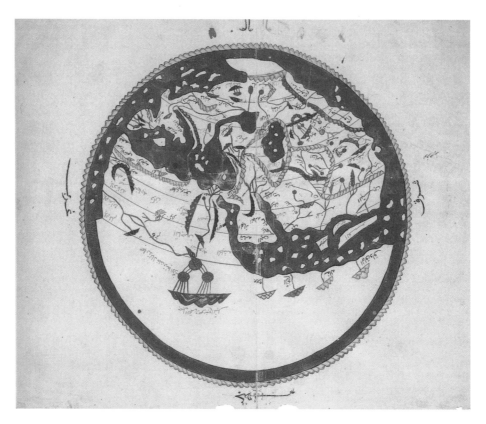

World Map Created by Muslim Scholar Muhammad al-Idrisi for Silician King Roger II (12th Century)

13 Changes in Rome and in the Church   343

61 - The Decline of Rome   345
62 - The Way of Christ: Attacked, Then Accepted   351
63 - Changes in Church Practice   356
64 - Key Person: Constantine   363
65 - Bible Study: The Inspiration and Authority of Scripture   369

14 The Early Middle Ages   373

66 - Europe After the Fall of Rome   375
67 - Key Event: The Rise of Islam   382
68 - Key Person: Alfred the Great   389
69 - Everyday Life: The Vikings   393
70 - Bible Study: Methods and Motives in Evangelism   398

15 The Late Middle Ages   403

71 - A Changing World   405
72 - Everyday Life: Feudalism and the Rise of Cities   412
73 - Key Event: The Crusades   419
74 - Key Person: Thomas Aquinas   425
75 - Bible Study: Obeying God, Obeying Men   430

Credits   C-1

How to Use This Curriculum

You are about to embark upon an exciting journey. You will go to fascinating places and meet amazing people. You will hear stories of faith, courage, endurance, and victory over seemingly impossible odds. You will wrestle with challenging ideas that could change your life. You are about to begin a study of the story of mankind.

Our Goals

We have several goals for this curriculum. First, we want to honor God. To Him be all praise.

Second, we want to help you understand world history. The story of our world is the story of what God has done and what people made in His image have done. To tell the story we have provided 150 lessons. Part 1 has 75 lessons to be completed in the first semester. Part 2 has 75 lessons to be completed in the second semester. You will also learn the history of the world from the words of people who lived it when you read the assignments in *In Their Words*.

Third, we want to open your heart to good books and to help you enjoy reading. The twelve full-length works of literature we have chosen to go along with this course are uplifting and worth reading.

Fourth, we want to help you understand the Bible better. We have placed a great emphasis on the story of the Bible, from Old Testament times through the period of the early church. The Bible studies included with the units are intended to help you see how relevant the Bible is to the study of history and to our lives today. The more you get into the Word, the more God will change your life.

Fifth, our prayer is that you will be a better person and a better Christian for having invested your time in this material. You will only get out of it what you put into it, so give it your best and you will receive great blessings from it.

How It Works

This curriculum provides credit in three high school subjects: world history, English, and Bible. The 150 lessons are divided into thirty units of five lessons each. Since a typical school year has thirty-six weeks, you have some flexibility in completing the course. You can take two weeks to complete a unit when you find a topic particularly interesting or when your schedule is especially busy. Families are free to choose how they want to schedule the course, but many families choose to begin a unit on Monday and finish it on Friday.

On the first day of a unit, you and a parent should read the unit introduction. Here you will find a brief overview of the unit; a list of lessons for that unit; a Bible passage to memorize; a list of books used with that unit; choices for a project for that unit; and, when a literature title is begun, an introduction to that book.

After reading the introduction, choose a project to complete by the end of the unit and make a schedule for how to complete it. Find the memory work for the week in the Bible translation of your choice.

Complete the following each day:

- Read the lesson for the day.
- Complete each of the Bible, *In Their Words*, and Literature assignments for the lesson.
- If you are using the optional *Student Review*, complete the assignment(s) for that lesson.
- Work on your Bible memorization and on your chosen project.

On the last day of each unit, you will recite or write your memory work and complete your project for the unit.

An assignment checklist is available as a free download on our website (notgrass.com/ewlinks).

Student Review

We offer an optional *Student Review* pack with daily review questions; a quiz for each unit; and comprehensive exams in history, English, and Bible every five units. Reminders to do these are included in the list of daily assignments. The *Student Review* also has Bible commentary for many Bible readings and literary analysis for the twelve full-length works of literature.

Tips on Memorization

Each unit of *Exploring World History* gives a Bible passage to memorize. Here are some tips on memorization. Pay attention and internalize what the verses mean. It will be much easier to memorize thoughts that you understand than a string of words

that have no meaning to you. Write the verses on an index card or divide them between several index cards. Keep these handy to use when you have a spare moment. Copying out the verses is a good exercise, especially if you learn visually.

Draw pictures illustrating the verses. Ask another person to read the verses to you. Ask another person to listen to you and correct your recitation. Working on memorization consistently in small chunks of time over several days works much better than last-minute cramming.

Unit Projects

Each unit has three choices for a project. Your choices always include a writing assignment. Discuss with a parent how many writing assignments you need to complete to fulfill the English requirement as you study *Exploring World History*. We recommend that you choose the writing assignment as your project a minimum of six times throughout the course. The other project choices include a wide variety of activities: building models, cooking, field trips, volunteer opportunities, and more, all of which will enhance and expand what you are learning in the course.

The projects relate to the material in the unit. Where applicable, the lesson from which the project is drawn is noted. You should choose your project at the beginning of the unit and work on it throughout the unit. Don't wait until the end of the unit or until you reach the lesson noted. You may need to look ahead at the relevant section of the lesson to get started on your project.

As you choose your project unit by unit, take the opportunity to try new things and expand your skills. If you have never made a model out of STYROFOAM™, or seldom do any cooking, or don't know how to make a video, this is your chance!

You are expected to complete each project at a high school level. Some of these assignments could be given to an elementary school student and the results would be on an elementary school level. Your work should be performed with care and research and with attention to accuracy, creativity, and excellence. Throwing something together in a haphazard fashion is not appropriate. Whether you spend your time writing an essay or building a model, use your mind and hands to create something you can be proud of.

Lesson Illustrations

We have carefully chosen historic illustrations and modern photographs to help you get a glimpse of the people and places you read about in this curriculum. Many of the illustrations are works of fine art from around the world. You will notice that artists often represented scenes from the Bible using clothing and buildings that were contemporary to the artist. We included some of these paintings for their artistic value, even though they are not accurate from an historical perspective.

How We Present Scripture

The most important material in this course are the studies from God's Word. Understanding world history and literature is important, but how we live before God is the most important issue before each one of us. We want to help you as you do that.

We emphasize the Bible a great deal, especially in the first half of the course. The events of the Bible took place in history, so we should look at the historical context of the Bible. At the same time, the Bible, Old Testament Israel, and Christianity have had a huge influence on world history, and we would not do justice to world history if we downplayed this influence. The Bible is central to our understanding of world history.

We believe in the inspiration and authority of the Bible, and our desire is to present the Bible in all of its truth, wisdom, and power. We strive in all we do simply to be Christians. We are on a quest to understand the truth that God has provided in His Word. We believe that eternal truth does exist, but we do not claim to know it all.

In this curriculum we have sought to present a fair analysis of church history, highlighting various people, viewpoints, and denominations. If you read something in this curriculum that differs from what your family believes, take the opportunity to discuss the issue and search the Scriptures together. We welcome your feedback. If you believe that we have written something in error, please e-mail us so that we can learn together the truth that will set us free.

Thanks

This has been a family project for us. I wrote most of the lessons and guided the overall project. My wife, Charlene, and our son, John, each contributed several lessons. John did a fantastic job developing this new edition with a new format, color pictures, and many new documents in *In Their Words*. Our daughter Bethany and I developed the unit activities and the assignments at the end of the lessons. Our daughter Mary Evelyn designed the beautiful covers. All of us along with our son-in-law Nate did the proofreading.

As we have worked on this curriculum, time and again we have seen God's wisdom, power, and love displayed in the story of mankind. We are convinced anew that Jesus really is the answer for every individual and for human society. We see this curriculum as an opportunity for us to help and encourage other homeschooling families and to explore together the wonderful story of world history. May God bless you.

Ray Notgrass
Gainesboro, Tennessee
ray@notgrass.com
January 2014

Advice on Writing

Composition is part of most high school English courses. It usually involves learning how to express ideas, write themes, and do research papers. Practicing writing helps you to develop your style and skill, just as practicing any activity will help you to be better at it. I make my living by writing, so I appreciate the importance of this skill.

One goal of high school composition is to prepare you for college composition. I have taught college students who never learned to construct a good sentence, let alone a good paragraph. However, learning to write just for high school and college composition assignments is a limited goal. Life does exist beyond school.

You will probably have many occasions to engage in research and to prepare your thoughts on a vital subject such as abortion or capital punishment. You will have numerous opportunities to write: letters to friends and family, journals, letters to the editor, advertisements for your business, and reviews and articles for periodicals, to mention just a few. The Internet has created new possibilities for sharing your ideas in written form. Desktop publishing has made getting a book published within the reach of many people who might not get a contract from a big-name publisher.

Writing helps you express what you understand about a subject. If you can't explain something to another person, you probably don't understand it well yourself. The writing assignments in this course will help you learn to pull your thoughts together.

Good writing style is important in getting your ideas across to other people. Writing skills will be helpful in your job or in conducting your own business. You will bless your spouse and children if you write thoughtful letters to them often. You can help others by expressing yourself well in writing.

Three ways to improve your writing are to read good writing, to write often yourself, and to receive criticism of your writing with humility and a desire to do better. Reading and applying the guidance in good books on writing will also help you refine your technique. I recommend *The Elements of Style* by William Strunk Jr. and E. B. White.

Writing Assignments in This Course

Each week you do a writing assignment (instead of one of the other suggested projects), you will have two or three possible topics from which to choose. Some of the assignments ask you to imagine you were living at the time and write a journal entry, speech, or article to express your perspective on something related to that unit. The other assignments ask you to write an essay about a particular person, idea, or other topic.

A basic way to compose an essay is to write five paragraphs: an opening paragraph that states your purpose, three paragraphs that develop three different points or arguments, and a closing paragraph that summarizes your position or topic. If you are floundering on a particular assignment, using this outline can get you started.

The usual target length of your writing projects for this course is 300 to 500 words, which is about two or three typed, double-spaced pages.

Writing Tips to Implement

Here are some tips I have learned that have helped my writing.

Write with passion. Believe in what you are saying. People have plenty to read, so give them something that will grip them. If you don't believe deeply in what you are saying, you give others no reason to do so either. This raises an issue that is related to many writing assignments. Assigned writing is like assigned reading: we often approach it as a chore. Deep emotion and a passion for convincing others are difficult to express in a theme on "The American Interstate System" or "How I Spent My Summer Vacation."

If a writing assignment in this curriculum does not excite you, change it or select one about which you can write passionately. If you ever do write about the American Interstate system, approach it in a way that makes it personal and compelling.

Writing with passion means that you should not soft-pedal what you say. Phrases such as "It seems to me," "I think that it would be good if," or "My personal opinion, for what it is worth," take the fire out of your message. It is your piece, so we know it is your opinion. Just state it. Related to this is the common use of quotation marks to highlight a word. Save quotation marks for when you are actually quoting something.

Develop your paper in an orderly and logical way. Using an outline helps me to structure what I am writing. Identify the major points you want to make, the order in which you need to make them, and what secondary points you want to include to support your major points. Be sure that each paragraph has one main point, expressed in a topic sentence, with the other sentences supporting that point. In a narrative, tell what happened first before you tell what happened later. In an essay, make your points in the order of their importance to your overall theme.

Don't try to put everything you believe into one piece. Trust that you will have the opportunity to write again, and stay focused on your topic. Your challenge is to narrow your topic sufficiently to be able to cover it completely.

Use short, simple sentences. Longer sentences do not necessarily show greater intelligence or convey ideas more effectively. You are trying to teach or convince a reader who perhaps has not been thinking about the topic the way you have. He or she will need to see your ideas expressed simply and clearly. Shorter sentences generally stay with people longer: "These are the times that try men's souls." "The only thing we have to fear is fear itself."

Writing Habits to Avoid

Avoid these habits that weaken your writing.

Do not begin sentences with "There is" or "There are." Find a more forceful way to cast the sentence. Compare "Four score and seven years ago our fathers brought forth upon this continent a new nation" to "There was a country begun by our ancestors 87 years ago."

Do not habitually begin sentences with "and" or "but." This practice has become a trendy habit in informal writing, but the grammar books tell you never to do this.

Avoid the word "would." Such usage is an attempt to soft-pedal, to indicate customary behavior, or to describe something that is not a reality. "That would be a good idea" is less powerful than "That is a good idea." "Americans would often violate the terms of treaties made with Native Americans" is not as sharp as "Americans often violated the terms of the treaties."

Don't imitate someone else's style. That person didn't become a good writer by copying someone else's style; he or she developed his or her own style. You might become enamored with the writing of a favorite author and want to write the way he or she does. Learn from that author, but be yourself.

Additional Suggestions

C. S. Lewis had good suggestions about writing (*Letters of C. S. Lewis*, edited by W. H. Lewis, first published in 1966; this edition New York: Harcourt Brace, revised edition 1988; pp. 468-9, 485):

- Write with the ear. Each sentence should read well aloud.

- Don't say something is exciting or important. Prove that it is by how you describe it.

- Turn off the radio (in our day, he might say the iPod and television).

- Read good books and avoid nearly all magazines.

A key to good writing is rewriting. Writing is hard work, and you shouldn't let anyone tell you otherwise. You will not get every word and phrase just right the first time you put them down on paper or type them on the computer. Great, famous, well-paid writers have to rewrite their work and often have editors who revise and critique what they write. Don't be impatient, and don't wait until the last minute. Write something; then go back and rewrite it; then go back a day or two later to consider it again. This is where another pair of loving and honest eyes is helpful. People who have read my writing and who were willing to point out the faults in it have often helped me (although I admit that I have winced inside when I heard their criticism).

Find someone who is willing to take a red pen to your work; a favorite uncle or grandparent might not be that person. You might know exactly what you mean by a particular statement, but someone else might not understand what you said at all. I have often found that when someone doesn't understand a statement I have written, it is because I have tried to say something without really saying it. In other words, I have muddied what should have been a clear statement; and that fuzzy lack of commitment showed through.

Your writing will improve with practice, experience, and exposure to good writing. I hope that in ten years you will not write the same way you do now. The only way you can get to that point is to keep writing, keep learning, and keep reading. I hope that this course helps you on your journey.

Writing a Research Paper

We recommend that you write a research paper of eight to ten typed double-spaced pages (about 2,000-2,500 words) over a four-week period of your choice while you are studying *Exploring World History*. Waiting until the second semester would give you time to prepare and to practice writing shorter papers for your weekly special projects.

This section guides you step-by-step through the process. You and your parents should discuss whether you think a research paper assignment is appropriate for you. Also discuss with your parents whether you should reduce or eliminate the special projects for each unit during the time you are working on your research paper.

When you are ready to begin, refer to this section. If you feel a need for more detailed guidance, we recommend the section on research papers in *Writer's Inc.* by Great Source. You can also find sample research papers online. The Purdue University Online Writing Lab (OWL) has a sample. (Visit notgrass.com/ewlinks for more details.)

Research Paper Basics

A research paper combines the work of investigation with the task of writing. Choosing your topic is the first step. When you write a research paper, you must define your topic as clearly as possible. You might have to do some general research before you can define your topic. Topics such as "The British Empire" or "The Impact of Roman Civilization" are too broad for a research paper. "Commerce within the British Empire" or "The Architecture of Rome" are more defined and manageable.

Next comes research. Research involves finding legitimate, authoritative sources on the subject and gathering information from those sources. The modern researcher has a wealth of material available to him, some good and some worthless. Sources include books, periodicals, encyclopedias, scholarly articles, and original sources. Original or primary sources are materials written or developed at the time of history you are investigating. A diary written by a sailor on a trading vessel during the Victorian Era is an example of an original source. You probably will not be able to hold the actual document in your hands, but many transcriptions of original source materials can be found in print and online. Secondary sources are materials written later about the subject in question.

Use caution with online sources, as many are not authoritative. A comment by a reader on a blog about the Roman Empire is not necessarily based on fact, and you cannot use information gathered from such a source in a research paper. It might give you an idea about something to research yourself, but just because someone posted it online doesn't

make it accurate or relevant. Wikipedia is the classic example of a non-authoritative source for research. A great deal of the material found on Wikipedia is accurate; but because of the way in which the articles are created and edited, Wikipedia cannot be relied upon as an authoritative source. Websites maintained by universities, government entities, and reputable publishers of reference materials are good sources for online research. Google Books and Project Gutenberg have many historic books available in their entirety online.

Do not neglect print resources for information. A good old-fashioned one-hour visit to the library might provide much more valuable material than hours of sifting through material online. However, you need to be sure that your print sources are reliable also. Encyclopedias and books published by large publishers are your best sources.

The researcher must give proper credit to her sources. Plagiarism is using someone else's words or ideas without giving proper credit to that source. The Internet contains information that you could simply copy and paste into your paper. Though this might be tempting, it is absolutely wrong. Plagiarism is at once lying, stealing, and cheating. You do not have to cite a source for basic information, such as the fact that Columbus sailed across the Atlantic in 1492. However, you do need to cite sources for detailed information and for unique perspectives about a topic. As you take notes while doing research, indicate clearly what is a direct quote and what is your paraphrase of another person's writing. Do not copy another person's exact words into your paper without showing that you are quoting and giving credit to the source.

A research paper is a big project that can seem overwhelming. Divide the project into manageable steps. We have provided a schedule that will help you do this. You might need extra time on some steps while you breeze quickly through others. You must stay on track to meet your deadline. Look ahead to the finished product and take it step-by-step.

Your paper should be based on historical fact and should not primarily be an opinion piece. Sometimes differentiating between the two is difficult. A simple list of facts that can be found elsewhere is not interesting. Your paper should have a point, and you should bring your own thoughts to bear on the facts you gather in your research. Your paper will be dull if you do not draw interesting conclusions.

Noting how Roman architecture expressed Roman ideals and impacted the concept of beauty and form centuries later is excellent; on the other hand, listing reasons why you like Roman architecture is irrelevant to this paper. Your task for your research paper is to provide information, make observations, and draw conclusions on the topic in an interesting, readable format that is worth someone's time to read.

Four-Week Schedule (see further explanation for each day below)				
Day 1	**Day 2**	**Day 3**	**Day 4**	**Day 5**
Investigate possible topics.	Choose a topic and write a purpose sentence.	Research sources, make preliminary outline.	Learn how to give credit.	Make a research plan.
Day 6	**Day 7**	**Day 8**	**Day 9**	**Day 10**
Begin research.	Continue research.	Continue research.	Finish research.	Finalize outline.
Day 11	**Day 12**	**Day 13**	**Day 14**	**Day 15**
Begin writing.	Work on first draft.	Work on first draft.	Work on first draft.	Finish first draft.
Day 16	**Day 17**	**Day 18**	**Day 19**	**Day 20**
Work on final draft.	Work on final draft.	Work on final draft.	Finish final draft.	Polish and turn it in!

Day 1: Read "Research Paper Basics" (on the previous two pages) and all daily assignments below. Make a list of at least seven ideas for topics. Discuss ideas for topics with a parent. Select topics that you would like to spend the next few weeks studying and writing about. The index of this curriculum is a source for possible topics.

Day 2: Investigate possible sources for your top three topic ideas to make sure you will be able to find enough material. Choose your topic and write a one-sentence summary of your purpose for the paper. Don't say, "This paper is about how the British Empire transformed international relations." Instead, state the substance of your paper: "The

British Empire transformed international relations in trade, politics, economics, and science."

Day 3: Gather possible sources for research. Make a list of places to look. You can bookmark websites, visit the library, and look through relevant periodicals. Develop a preliminary outline for your paper.

Day 4: Learn how to cite your sources properly. Your research paper should follow MLA (Modern Language Association) guidelines for source citations. Your paper needs to have footnotes or in-text citations for your sources of information and a separate Works Cited page at the end of your paper. Look online for the most up-to-date MLA guidelines. We recommend Purdue University's Online Writing Lab (OWL).

Practice some example citations. Whether you use note cards, copy and paste to a computer document, or a combination of these approaches, be consistent and accurate in your in-text and bibliography citations. Look over the guidelines and your examples with a parent to make sure you are on the right track.

Day 5: Make a general outline for your paper to help guide your research. Make some notes about what you want to say in your paper, questions you hope to answer in your research, and ideas for the main point of your paper. This plan will enable you to make the most of your research time. You want to immerse yourself in the topic you will be writing about. Your final paper will not include every bit of information you read, but you want to write from a position of overflow instead of scraping together just enough facts to fill up your paper.

Day 6: Begin your research. Develop a system to stay organized, keeping track of the source for every quote or fact. For example, if you are using the book, *Tea for the Queen*, note which facts and quotations come from that specific work and the relevant page numbers. You need to know clearly where every item of information came from: book, website, article, etc. Use a minimum of six different sources for your paper.

Day 7: Continue your research.

Day 8: Continue your research.

Day 9: Finish your research. Where do you want this paper to go? What do you want to say? Decide what information you gathered in your research is relevant and what isn't. Highlight key findings in your research. Set aside (but don't throw away) information that does not seem relevant to what you want to say. Talk about your general ideas for your paper with a parent.

Day 10: Work on the final outline for your paper. Jot down the points you want to make in the introduction, the main sections of your paper, what you want to include in each section, and what you

want to emphasize in the conclusion. Organize these into an outline. Your research might have shown you that you need to emphasize a point that you had not previously realized was important, or you might not be able to find much information about what you thought was a main idea.

Look through the information you gathered in your research to make sure you didn't leave anything important out of your outline. Finalize your outline and talk about it with a parent. A good, detailed outline will ease your writing process significantly.

Day 11: Re-read "Advice on Writing" on pages x-xii of this book. Begin writing your paper, starting with your introduction and conclusion. Your introduction should give a general idea of what your paper is about and the main points you will make. Your conclusion will re-emphasize your main points. Include proper citations as you go, both in-text and on your Works Cited page.

Day 12: Continue work on your first draft.

Day 13: Continue work on your first draft.

Day 14: Continue work on your first draft.

Day 15: Finish the first draft of your paper. Check your in-text source citations and Works Cited page against your research notes and make sure your formatting is correct. Proofread your paper and make corrections. Give your paper a title. Ask a parent to read and correct your paper and make suggestions for improvement.

Day 16: Discuss the paper with your parent. Think about improvements that you can make. Begin working on the final draft of your paper. Fix mistakes and polish your style.

Day 17: Continue working on your final draft.

Day 18: Continue working on your final draft.

Day 19: Finish writing your final draft. Read your paper carefully for spelling and grammatical errors.

Day 20: Read your paper aloud. Make any final corrections. Save it, print it off, and turn it in. Good work!

Detail from Interior with Poppies and Reading Woman (Lizzy Hohlenberg), *Anna Ancher (Danish, 1905)*

Assigned Literature

Units 3-5	*The Cat of Bubastes*	G. A. Henty
Unit 8	*The Art of War*	Sun Tzu
Unit 10	*Julius Caesar*	William Shakespeare
Units 13-14	*The Imitation of Christ*	Thomas à Kempis
Units 16-18	*Here I Stand*	Roland Bainton
Units 19-20	*A Tale of Two Cities*	Charles Dickens
Units 21-22	*North and South*	Elizabeth Gaskell
Units 23-24	*The Hiding Place*	Corrie ten Boom
Unit 25	*Animal Farm*	George Orwell
Units 26-27	*Bridge to the Sun*	Gwen Terasaki
Units 28-29	*Cry, the Beloved Country*	Alan Paton
Unit 30	*The Abolition of Man*	C. S. Lewis

1

Introduction to World History

Summary   A study of the world begins with God, its Maker. The history of mankind helps us to understand our world today because every person has a place in the world and is affected by the strands of world history. We cannot understand world history accurately without a grasp of how religion has played a crucial role in it. The story of God extends even before the creation of the world, into all eternity.

Lessons
1 - It Begins With God
2 - Understanding Our World
3 - Your Place in the World
4 - Religion in History
5 - Bible Study: Eternity Before Creation

View of Earth from Space

Memory Work

Learn Deuteronomy 10:12-14 by the end of the unit. The first two units have daily reminders to work on your memory work. After those units, you will need to remember to do this each day. You will be reminded to recite or write your memory work on the last day of the unit.

Books Used

The Bible

Project (choose one)

The first two units have daily reminders to work on your project. After those units, you will need to remember to do this each day. You will be reminded to complete your project on the last day of the unit.

1) Write 300 to 500 words on one of the following topics:

- What is your connection to the world? Maybe one of your parents was born in another country, you know a missionary, or you have traveled internationally. What everyday things do you use that come from other countries? You might think of other connections to the world that you would like to discuss. Write an essay about your connection to the world. See Lesson 3.

- Write an essay about how one of the following events might have been seen differently in another country from the way it was seen in the United States: (1) the September 11, 2001, terrorist attacks on the United States, (2) a U.S. presidential campaign and election, (3) a Super Bowl football game. See Lesson 2.

2) Create a large poster on poster board that illustrates visually the influence of other cultures on America culture and the influence of American culture on other cultures. Include a minimum of twenty-five cultural influences (incoming and outgoing combined).

3) Memorize John 1:1-18 (in addition to the memory work for the unit).

Lesson 1

It Begins With God

The story of our world must begin with God, its Maker. God is eternal. He has always existed and will always exist. God is spirit, so He is not limited by space and time. In His love and by His creative power, God made the finite, material universe in which we live. Within this physical universe, God created humans on the planet Earth. The story of mankind, which covers the span of a few thousand years within the context of eternity, is what we call world history.

Our Spiritual Quest

The most important part of human history is mankind's relationship with God. Humanity began when God created man in His own image. Man had fellowship with God in the Garden of Eden. Soon, however, man rebelled in sin and was separated from God; and the great quest for reconciliation began. As mankind scattered over the face of the earth, some people continued to worship God, while others believed in various substitutes for God. Then God reached out to mankind in love by sending Jesus Christ to be our Redeemer and Reconciler. The Bible is the story of God's work to bring people back into a relationship with Him.

God is our Creator and Sustainer. However, most of the people who have lived in the past and most of the people who are alive today have not known the one true God nor had a relationship with Him. Mankind has by and large resisted knowing and submitting to God. Many cultures have developed alternative religious systems. Some people (a relatively small number of those who have ever existed) have refused to believe in any supernatural being at all. Jesus Christ—King of Kings, Lord of Lords, Savior of the World, and the One by whom the world was created—is not known or believed in by most people in the world today; so the spiritual quest continues.

Why The Spiritual Quest Is Central

The quest to know God is mankind's most important task because God defines who we are as human beings. Since we are created by God in His image, we have a responsibility to fulfill His purposes for us.

More important than the story of wars, conquerors, politics, and technology, then, is the fact that Jesus Christ came and died for you and me. People have a fundamental need to live in a right relationship with God through Jesus Christ. This is the one way that a person can live his or her life on the basis of what is true. This right relationship with God will enable a person to live in God's will now and live with God forever.

Without a grasp of this fundamental need to know God, the study of world history, though wonderful and fascinating, is ultimately a meaningless and pointless exercise. To be sure, the story of mankind even apart from this spiritual quest deserves our best intellectual abilities and engages all of our emotions. We learn of heroes who saved lives (sometimes at the cost of their own) and of villains who caused the death of millions. We read of inventors and thinkers who have changed the way human life is lived. We are amazed that, out of the billions of people who have ever lived, some individuals are remembered even thousands of years after they walked this earth. We are overwhelmed to think about the billions of people who have lived here. The story of human history helps us to understand how today's world got to be the way it

is. We can be inspired to try to make a difference for good in our own lives, and perhaps we can learn enough about yesterday's mistakes to keep from making them again tomorrow.

However, fifty years from now it will make little difference whether you knew anything about Mesopotamia or the Holy Roman Empire or Communist Russia if you do not have a right relationship with God and seek to honor Him with your life. It will make all the difference, both here and for eternity, if you do know the Lord, live for Him, learn how to serve Him better by knowing human history, and pass this knowledge on to the next generation. This puts the study of world history into perspective.

World History and Your Purpose

We have many good spiritual reasons for studying world history. First, human history sheds light on our identity and purpose. The building of the Pyramids in Egypt, the conquests of Genghis Khan, tribal wars in Africa, the accomplishments of the Scientific Revolution, the spread of the British Empire, and recent advances in computer technology all contribute in some way to defining who we are and where we are going. The development of different cultures, the exploration of this world and of outer space, and the lives of people who lived in the past all have an impact on how and where you live, what you believe, and why you believe it.

Second, we can learn lessons from world history. Ancient China, medieval Africa, and 19th century Australia might not appear at first glance to have much to do with us today; and, admittedly, not all the strands of world history affect us equally. However, humans have always had to deal with issues of spiritual identity and purpose, power and control in society and politics, relationships in communities and in families, and how best to use our lives. None of the basic issues human beings face today—war, poverty, the environment, marriage and family, and so forth—are new. Today's problems, such as how

Market in Can Cau, Vietnam

The Palace of the Parliament in Bucharest, Romania, is the largest civilian administrative building in the world, second in size only to the Pentagon, the military headquarters of the United States. The building is 282 feet tall above ground and extends 302 feet underground. Construction began in 1980 under Nicolae Ceauşescu, the last Socialist dictator of the country. It is now home to both houses of the Romanian Parliament.

much of the world can be blown up at one time, how many innocent people a terrorist can kill at once, and how much information we can know about the world and how fast we can know it, are only current manifestations of age-old questions.

Third, world history helps us understand the world in which we live and in which we seek to honor God. The story of mankind is made up of strands that are interwoven throughout the tapestry of history. Today's Islamic terrorism and the situation in the former Communist countries of Europe, for instance, are directly influenced by events of the mid-20th century. Events of the mid-20th century were influenced by what happened earlier in the century. What happened in the early 20th century was the result of events of the 19th century. What happened in the 19th century was influenced by the events of the 18th century, and so forth. What took place a long time ago in one country can have an impact on events in another country today. For example, the Protestant-Catholic conflict over three hundred years ago in England has an influence on what happens in Northern Ireland today. You will probably not hear an historical analysis of current events on the evening news, but you will not fully understand the world in which you live unless you learn these strands of history and how they are related to each other.

Conclusion

World history begins with God. It will ultimately end with God when we all appear before His judgment seat. Between those two points, each of us lives his or her life on the same planet where every other human being has lived. We are connected to other people because we share the same human condition and because we have been given life for the same purpose—to honor God. By knowing something about the story of human life on this planet, we can live our lives in a way that will make a difference now and into eternity.

This is why we study world history.

The earth is the Lord's, and all it contains,
The world, and those who dwell in it.
Psalm 24:1

Assignments for Lesson 1

A checklist of assignments is available on our website (www.notgrass.com/ewlinks).

Bible   Read John 1:1-18. Commentary available in *Student Review.*

                  Start memorizing Deuteronomy 10:12-14.

Project   Choose your project for this unit and start working on it.

Student Review   Optional: Answer the questions for Lesson 1.

Lesson 2

Understanding Our World

Pedro is a boy of eleven. He lives in a small village in the country of Honduras in Central America. No one in his village has running water or indoor plumbing. Pedro attends a school in the village, but they have few books or other resources. School is sometimes interrupted by heavy rains and is dismissed for the harvest season.

Pedro might go to the capital city of Tegucigalpa once or twice in his life, but he will rarely travel more than a few miles from his home and almost certainly will never leave his country during his entire lifetime. His father barely makes enough to support his family by farming and by selling wood crafts in the village marketplace. When Pedro is older, he will work the same ground and probably make wood crafts to support his family.

As insignificant and distant as all of this might seem, Pedro's life reflects several of the strands that make up the tapestry of world history.

Pedro speaks Spanish because Spanish explorers came to Central America hundreds of years ago. Pedro's ancestors are both Spanish and Central American Indian because people from these two groups intermarried.

Pedro is Roman Catholic; the conquering Spanish were Catholic, and that became the dominant religion in Honduras. But Pedro's beliefs are also strongly influenced by native traditions. His name, the Spanish form of Peter, shows Spanish and Catholic influence. Catholic dominance in Spain is the result of the spread of the Roman Catholic Church in the centuries after Christ. Peter was one of the apostles of Christ in the first century AD. The poverty in Honduras today stems in part from the Honduran government's history of mismanagement and inconsistent relations with other countries.

Village in Honduras

Pedro's story, with local variations, can be told billions of times over about boys and girls and men and women around the world, from Nels in Norway to Ashok in India to Nguyen in Vietnam. For instance, the reasons why many people in Canada are of French ancestry, why many people in Germany are (or used to be) Lutheran, why millions of people in India and Africa live in poverty, and why the Italian and Spanish languages are related to each other all have to do with world history. To understand today's world, we have to understand how life came to be the way it is for the people who live and work and marry and believe and fight and love and die in today's world.

Magazine Rack in Tokyo, Japan

The Complexity of Our World

Humans have developed many types of communities that are vastly different from each other. They range from villages made up of grass huts in Africa to high-rise apartment and office buildings in Singapore and Tokyo. People spend their days in many kinds of work, from farmers working the soil in order to feed their families to global investment specialists who use the latest computer technology to finance a wide range of business activities around the world. How cultures, forms of work, musical styles, political systems, and other realms of human interaction have developed are part of world history.

The various cultures of the world influence each other. The culture of Great Britain influences the culture of the United States, for instance, and the culture of the United States influences the culture of Great Britain (although most Brits probably won't admit it). The histories and cultures of European nations influence each other. Western culture was influenced by the culture of India in the 1960s when, of all things, George Harrison and the Beatles became enamored with Indian beliefs and practices (ask your grandparents about transcendental meditation, the sitar, and Nehru jackets). Japan fought against America in World War II; but after the war, Japan absorbed American business techniques and became better at them in some ways than Americans were.

This kind of influence has always taken place in history. Because ancient Israel's neighbors had kings, the people of Israel decided that they wanted a king, too. Wealthy medieval Europeans wanted silks and spices from the Orient. Many African peoples have been influenced by European culture even as they fought against it. The histories and cultures of the various nations of the world are distinct in some ways and have blended together in other ways. This is what makes the study of world history fascinating and at times complex.

The World Is Not America

One of the most difficult things for Americans to do as we study world history is to keep from looking at it through American lenses. World history is not defined by American history.

Just because people in another country do something differently from the way it is done in the United States does not mean that they are wrong. People in almost every nation believe that their way of doing things is right and best. Swedes think that the ways of Sweden are best. Egyptians think that Egypt is the heart of the world. The Chinese have long thought of themselves as the Middle Kingdom, the center of the world; to them, everybody else is "off-center" to some degree. As Americans, however, we need to be especially aware of our tendency to think of our country as the norm to which other countries should measure up.

The United States did not exist as a country until 1776 AD. It was not until the Spanish-American War of 1898 that the United States became a major player on the world stage. Only after World War II did America come to be seen as a world superpower. This means that human history had been taking place for thousands of years before our nation began, and much human history has taken place apart from us since our country has existed. Jews in first-century Israel, for instance, were not people who thought like Americans do and just happened to live in a different time and place. People in the nations of Africa do not have the same expectations of life that Americans have. The issues that mankind faces today are the same issues that mankind faced two and three thousand years ago, but various cultures have different perspectives on those issues.

Americans have often tried to impose their culture on other people. Americans might see our government's foreign policy as benevolent and helpful, while people in other countries might see us as a bully. Christian missionaries have sometimes wanted churches in other lands to look like American churches, which didn't always make sense

BBC Broadcasting House, London

to the people of those lands. Church gatherings and buildings in other parts of the world do not have to follow American traditions.

Many major events and trends in world history, such as the international trade routes of the Phoenicians, the rise of Islam, and the development of the European Renaissance, had nothing to do with America at the time. Even today, events often take place in other countries that make major headlines there but which we never hear about in the United States. If you listen to the BBC World Service for a few days, you will see that not everything newsworthy happens in the United States or involves the U.S.

This does not deny the fact that America is a major world power and that our country is involved with many things that happen outside of this country. The mixing of American interests and world interests is illustrated by one statistic from September 11, 2001. When terrorists brought down the World Trade Center on American soil, people from some sixty-two foreign countries died.

Stepping Outside of Ourselves

In this course, we will try to step outside of ourselves and our country to understand and appreciate the bigger picture of world history. We will try to look through the lenses of God's Word, not through the lenses of our cultural norms, to see what is right and wrong. We will try to be fair in describing what has been helpful and what has been harmful in our world's past. Above all, we will try to see what God has been doing as the human drama has unfolded.

But you, why do you judge your brother? Or you again,
why do you regard your brother with contempt?
For we will all stand before the judgment seat of God.
Romans 14:10

Assignments for Lesson 2

Bible   Read John 3:1-21. Commentary available in *Student Review.*

Work on memorizing Deuteronomy 10:12-14.

Project   Work on your project.

Student Review   Optional: Answer the questions for Lesson 2.

Lesson 3

Your Place in the World

It might seem like a huge step to go from your one individual life to an understanding of the whole world and its history. However, that huge step is actually made up of many smaller steps. You are connected to the world in many ways every day. To help you understand that connection, we'll start with you as an individual and move outward.

Who You Are

You are a distinct, individual person. You live within your own body. You think, you move, and you have responsibility for yourself.

However, you do not live by yourself. You are a member of a family. Your family members have relationships with each other. Members of your family share the responsibility for jobs that your family needs to have done: some provide income for the family, some cook, some do laundry, some clean the house, and some buy groceries or work in the garden. Your family might hire people to do other jobs such as mowing the lawn, repairing the plumbing, or providing you with Internet access.

You are part of an extended family whose members might live in several different places. To a significant degree, you are who you are as an individual because of your immediate family and

your extended family. Someone in your family decided to live where you are now living, which probably involved a decision to move from where they had been living. You are who you are in great measure because of decisions that your parents made: how to train you, what to teach you, how they demonstrate God's significance in your family's life, and so forth. Your family might have been Christian for many generations, or someone might have recently gone through a dramatic conversion and started your family on God's path.

Where You Live

Think about where you live. It might be a house with a yard, an apartment, or a farm. The things in your life come from various sources. You might make or grow some of them, but you probably buy most of them at a store. Your home might contain heirlooms that have been handed down for generations and that hold an honored place in your family's life.

You live in or near a town or city, and you have connections to that city. The city and county maintain the streets and roads that you use. The government uses tax dollars to maintain a library. You shop, buy license plates for your car, and

11

transact other business in the city. You get water and electricity from utility companies that are operated or overseen by local governments. Your parents vote for elected representatives.

The geography where you live is significant. Your weather is affected by such factors as how close you are to an ocean or to mountains, your elevation above sea level, and your latitude. You might live in a place where you see many people from other countries, such as a seaport or a university city, or you might live in a small town to which people from other countries seldom come.

In the United States, you live in a state. The state was formed decades or centuries ago as the result of people moving there from other places. A constitution was written, a government was formed, and the identity of statehood began for the people there.

You live in a country. The United States became a country when thirteen British colonies declared their independence as the United States of America in 1776. The Americans, with assistance from France, used military force to defeat the British attempt to end the revolution. The United States can be divided into several regions and sub-cultures. These sub-cultures have been influenced by millions of people who came to America from other countries. Whether your family is Native American, European, African, Hispanic, Asian, or Pacific Islander, people in a previous generation moved from where they were to live in this land. Your country, like yourself, is distinct but is also influenced by other countries.

Your World

Finally, you live in the world and you are affected by the world. The English language developed on the island of Britain. It was influenced by invasions of other peoples, such as the Saxons and the Normans. Today English is the most commonly used language in the world. One hundred years ago, French was the accepted language of international diplomacy.

A Polish migrant farm family in Maryland, 1909

McDonald's Restaurant in Beijing, China

Today, even though more people speak a dialect of Chinese as their native tongue than English, English is the language of the world. People in other countries learn English much more commonly than people in the United States learn a foreign language.

You might wear clothes made in Mexico, eat food processed in South America, drive a car built in Japan and powered by fuel from Saudi Arabia, use electronic devices made in Korea, and own other consumer goods that were made in China. When you go to the doctor, he or she might be from India. When your family goes out to eat, you might choose from among restaurants that specialize in food from Mexico, Italy, Thailand, Australia, Japan, Germany, or some other country.

Most houses in the United States have a sloping roof. English colonists brought this style with them from their homeland, where the sloping thatch roofs (often a foot or more thick) allowed the frequent rainfall to run off. Flat roofs are cheaper, but they are more practical in arid lands with little rainfall. Flat roofs in America frequently develop leaks from all the rain that is not able to run off.

The influence of culture has not all been imported into this country. Americans have gone to other parts of the world for various reasons and taken our culture with them. Someone in your extended family might be a missionary. Americans have gone as soldiers to fight wars in far-flung places or as workers in humanitarian causes. Increasingly, Americans work in other countries as experts in agriculture, finance, architecture, engineering, or computer technology. American products and culture have been exported to many other countries. You can find McDonald's restaurants in major cities all over the world, and an ever-growing number of citizens of the world dress the way Americans do.

Not a Western Civ World

The United States stands in the cultural tradition that is known as Western Civilization. The roots of our culture extend back into the ancient Greek and Roman civilizations, with significant influence from Old Testament Israel. Our culture also draws on western Europe and the culture that has existed there since the Middle Ages. The cultural tradition of Western Civilization influences us more than traditions in Africa or in Asia (which is known as the East). Western Civilization emphasizes such features as belief in the God of Israel, the rule of law (as opposed to the rule of individual men and their whims), the value of the individual, the importance of education, the pursuit of technological progress, and the belief that the world is headed toward a final day of reckoning (as opposed to the world passing through a cycle that repeats endlessly).

However, the cultures of Africa, the Middle East, and Asia have had an increasing worldwide influence in the last century. Conflicts between Arabs and Jews in Israel demand that we try to understand their cultures for our peace as well as for theirs. Japan has been a major player on the world scene since the early 1900s. China has significant and growing influence in world politics and economics. Christianity has experienced tremendous growth on the continent of Africa in the last few generations. The influence of Islam in the West has grown as Muslims live in greater numbers in Western nations.

We cannot completely know and understand every culture of the world. Starting with a foundational knowledge of our own cultural heritage is important. But we will be better equipped world citizens and world Christians when we have some grasp of the major trends in history that affect our world today. Many of those trends do not come from Western Civ. We focus on Western Civilization in this study, but we explore other world cultures as well. Understanding the cultural heritage of others will help us as we live in this world together and as we attempt to reach out to those who do not know the Creator we serve.

Holy, holy, holy is the Lord of hosts,
The whole earth is full of His glory.
Isaiah 6:3

Assignments for Lesson 3

Bible Read John 17 and 19:17-20. Commentary available in *Student Review.*

Work on memorizing Deuteronomy 10:12-14.

Project Work on your project.

Student Review Optional: Answer the questions for Lesson 3.

Mosque in Mali, West Africa

Lesson 4

Religion in History

Hordes of warriors advance toward enemy lines.

Huge pyramids rise from the sands of Egypt.

The pope calls upon Europeans to mount a crusade to Jerusalem.

People in India starve while cows are considered sacred.

A boatload of pilgrims approaches the shore of the New World.

Volunteers distribute medical supplies in the Philippines after a natural disaster.

Mobs attack and burn churches in Nigeria.

One thread that runs through all of these events is that each one has a religious motivation. Understanding world history means understanding the importance that religion has played and continues to play in world events. In the United States and other Western nations today, many political leaders and special interest groups try to keep religion out of the public forum and especially out of government. However, this separation between religion and government has not always been the case, nor is it the case in much of the world today.

Religious Motivations

Religion has dominated world cultures because religion has dominated the thinking of people. The vast majority of people who have ever lived has seen life in spiritual terms.

Most ancient peoples believed that their nation was formed by some divine cause. Ancient Egyptians, for example, believed in an elaborate system of spiritual powers. This belief system provided an explanation of why the Nile flooded, guided their governmental policies, and gave them motivation to go to war.

The people of Israel saw no separation between their religion and their government. To them the state was part of their religion and their religion gave them their identity as a state. The Law of Moses outlined religious duties but also regulated personal behavior and civic life.

Israel was a nation not because the people voted on it or because their representatives signed a Declaration of Independence from Egypt, but because God called them to Himself and made them His chosen people. Their national identity had a spiritual basis.

We are spiritual beings, and most people have religious beliefs of one form or another. Government action cannot eradicate deeply held religious beliefs. Communist governments are officially atheist and have tried to stamp out religious practice. However, when Communism fell in the Soviet Union and Eastern Europe around 1990, a huge outpouring of religious interest emerged.

Religion, especially Christianity, has been the motivation for much good. Christians build hospitals and distribute food and medical supplies around the world. Missionaries meet the physical needs of the people among whom they live. Government-sponsored programs such as the Peace Corps seek to do good without a spiritual motivation; but the impact of such programs pales in comparison to what religiously-motivated people have done.

Religious motivation has not always been good. Warriors have brutally and mercilessly killed their enemies for the glory of their god. The Japanese who invaded Manchuria and later attacked Pearl Harbor wanted to honor their emperor—whom they believed to be divine—by their actions. Muslim terrorists kill themselves and innocent people out of a deeply felt religious motivation.

Religion has at times been a thin veil to hide the ambitions of a king or a nation. When the Spanish sought to conquer the Western Hemisphere, they claimed to do so in the name of God; but national pride and the desire for economic gain lay just below the surface. In the Old Testament, when Assyria invaded Judah to expand its empire, the Assyrian king saw it as a contest between the god of Assyria and the God of Judah. In the eyes of the king, the outcome would reveal which god was stronger.

The Thirty Years' War (1618-1648) began with conflict between Catholics and Protestants in the Holy Roman Empire. Other countries became involved, and the fighting caused extreme devastation in Central Europe.

These meals in Haiti were provided by Christians who want to demonstrate God's love.

It was probably difficult for both ancient Assyrians and medieval Spaniards to distinguish between religious motivation and political motivation because to them these motivations were not separate. Both political and religious motivations were part of who they were as a people.

On the other hand, religion has sometimes been conveniently overlooked when political or economic motivations seemed more urgent. So-called Christian nations were busily engaged in the slave trade for well over two hundred years. England was callous toward the plight of the Irish in the early 1800s. Anglican religious prejudice toward Catholics prevented a humanitarian response to the needs of the Irish. In these cases, the people's professed religion did not influence them enough.

Religious Faith in America

Religion played an important role in America's founding. Many of the colonies were founded to provide religious freedom. Religion even influenced this country's move toward representative government. The divine right of kings, a common idea in the 1600s and 1700s, held that kings were put in place by God and that therefore their authority was not to be challenged. However, their authority was challenged by philosophers such as John Locke, who described the unwritten but very real social contract that exists when people agree among themselves to live together and to govern themselves in a certain way. God does raise up leaders, but he can do that through the expression of the will of the people.

The founding document of the United States, the Declaration of Independence, states that all men "are endowed by their Creator with certain unalienable rights" and that people have the right to alter or abolish government that becomes destructive of the proper purposes of government. Thus, the divine right of kings was replaced in American thinking by the divine right of the people. Based on the Declaration of Independence, the official foundation of government in America is God.

The accepted norm in our country today is that religion is to be kept separate from government activities. This is based on an interpretation of the First Amendment to the United States Constitution and on a statement in a letter by Thomas Jefferson regarding what he called a "wall of separation" between church and state. The First Amendment says, "Congress shall make no law respecting an establishment of religion." This means that the American government must not establish one church or one religion as the official religion of the country, the way that the Church of England is the official religion of Great Britain or that Islam is the official religion of Saudi Arabia. An established or state religion might receive revenue from the government and have other privileges as a result of this official recognition.

The concept of not having an established religion arose during the Enlightenment period in Europe and America during the 1700s. Philosophers and political leaders looked at the religious wars that had taken place in Europe (often Catholics versus Protestants), the religiously-motivated Crusades of the Middle Ages (when Catholics took up arms to drive the Muslims from the Holy Land), and the position of power and privilege that established churches enjoyed; and they wanted no part of it. People should be free to worship as they choose, Enlightenment thinkers said, without coercion by the government and without special advantages given to any one expression of faith. Faith is good, they admitted; but religion that gains political and economic power can become a hindrance to freedom. When people are forced to accept a certain religious faith, they might not truly believe it at all; thus faith can become a meaningless outward ritual instead of an inner, life-changing reality.

We have come to accept the wisdom of some degree of separation between church and state. Few Americans want the Baptist Church or the Episcopal Church to receive money from the government or want clergymen from only one denomination always officiating at government functions. We like the freedom to worship how, where, and with whom we choose. Most Western nations today do not claim to have religion as a basis for their policies.

The Soviet Union was officially an atheist country that discouraged and often persecuted religious activity. Bezbozhnik was a monthly Soviet magazine published from 1922 to 1941 by the League of Militant Atheists. This 1929 cover image shows industrial workers dumping an icon of Jesus out with the trash.

However, even in our country, where this official separation exists, our spiritual nature shows through. The First Amendment also forbids laws "prohibiting the free exercise" of religion, and this includes expressions of religion by government officials. Our national motto, printed on our money, is "In God We Trust." Both Houses of Congress employ chaplains who open every session with prayer. The government gives tax exemptions to religious bodies and groups.

The exact nature of this separation between religion and government is the subject of an ongoing debate in the United States, but at least the presence of religion in public life is still accepted to some degree.

Religion and Government

History has shown that a healthy respect for religion by government is good. When government sees religion as the enemy, the results have been bad. Governments that have actively opposed religion include the revolutionary government in 18th century France, Nazi Germany, and Communist states. When government officials do not submit to the moral limits that Christianity places on people, they tend to do bad things with the power they hold. Without a moral foundation for life based on the truths that God exists and that He matters, a secularized people are liable to support what is evil and take innocent lives as official policy—which is precisely what has happened and continues to happen in places around the world.

Even in officially secular countries religion plays a significant role because secularism is a religion: a system of beliefs that influences the actions of a people. Secularism holds that divinity does not exist or that it does not or should not influence public policy. The result is that the state is considered the ultimate authority. This is a belief system that accepts certain ideas as true without evidence. We simply cannot escape the fact that beliefs influence people's lives and world events.

As you study world history, keep in mind the religious motivations that were behind what you read about. Do not try to separate political and military events from the religion of the people because more than likely they were not separated at the time. We can examine whether the people so motivated did right or whether their religion was true; but we cannot do justice to the story of mankind by separating the faith that people have had from what they did.

Now, Israel, what does the Lord your God require from you,
but to fear the Lord your God, to walk in all His ways
and love Him, and to serve the Lord your God with all your heart
and with all your soul, and to keep the Lord's commandments and His
statutes which I am commanding you today for your good?
Behold, to the Lord your God belong heaven and
the highest heavens, the earth and all that is in it.
Deuteronomy 10:12-14

Assignments for Lesson 4

Bible   Read Genesis 1-4. Commentary available in *Student Review*.

                   Work on memorizing Deuteronomy 10:12-14.

Project   Work on your project.

Student Review   Optional: Answer the questions for Lesson 4.

Lesson 5 - Bible Study

Eternity Before Creation

As we discussed in Lesson 1, the history of the world is just one part of God's eternal story. What occurred before the world was created had a major impact on the story of our world.

God Has Always Existed

God is eternal and has always existed (Psalm 90:2). We understand that everything has to have a cause that brings it into existence: the hen lays an egg, an inventor builds a bicycle, an author writes a book. The egg, bicycle, and book did not just happen; they were caused. When we trace back the story of the world, we get to a First Cause, behind which we cannot go. We understand this First Cause to be God. If God had been created, that creator would be superior to Him, which would only beg the question another step. We believe that the eternal God lies behind everything else that exists.

The Bible says that Jesus was equal to God and was with God in the beginning (John 1:1-2). Genesis 1:2 tells us that the Spirit of God was moving before the world was created. Thus we have the three manifestations of God—Father, Son, and Spirit—described as being eternal and present at Creation.

We must try to remember that eternity has no measurement of time. Time is only a measurement used in this Creation. It is not that eternity is so long that we cannot grasp the amount of time it covers; it is that time is not a factor in eternity at all. We are wrapped up with time measurements in our world, but eternity is so different from our world that it does not involve time. We say that eternity has always existed and always will, which is true; but perhaps a more accurate statement is simply to say that eternity is.

God's Plan for the World

God had a purpose for the world before He created it, a purpose that included redemption. God knew Jesus to be the unblemished Lamb "before the foundation of the world" (1 Peter 1:19-20). God knew beforehand that mankind would need redemption, and He provided for it in Jesus before the first human was created.

A second part of God's plan was that those who were redeemed in Christ would become a people, God's children. God wanted His people to live holy and blameless lives before Him. The plan that God had for His people was to result in "the praise of the glory of His grace" (Ephesians 1:6; see similar phrases in Ephesians 1:12, 14). In other words, the plan that God had in mind, even before the world began, for people to be redeemed in Christ and for those people to live holy and blameless lives was intended to result in praise to God for His glorious grace. We can praise God for His will and for the grace He had in mind for us even before we were born.

Third, Ephesians 3:10-11 speaks of God's manifold wisdom being made known through the church to the heavenly realms, in keeping with "the eternal purpose which He carried out in Christ Jesus our Lord." God wanted to prove something to the spiritual world. He wanted to show that sinful human beings who were different from each other and who had once been enemies (namely Jews and Gentiles) can get along together in the church. This is possible when Christians realize that the grace they have received from Christ gives them life from the dead (Ephesians 2:1-16).

This sarcophagus from about 350 AD has one of the earliest known representations of (from left to right) the Holy Spirit, the Father, and the Son together.

This representation of Christ as the Lamb of God is from the Euphrasian Basilica in Croatia.

Revelation 13:8 speaks of something that was planned before the foundation of the world, but interpreters differ on what it is. The grammar of the verse indicates that Jesus was the Lamb slain from the creation of the world and that He has a book of life in which are written the names of the saved. An alternate reading is that the names have been written in the book of life from the foundation of the world. Regardless of how Revelation 13:8 is understood, Revelation 17:8 does clearly speak of names written in the book of life from the foundation of the world. Even though this is the case, we still have to decide whether we are going to follow Jesus. The way a person knows that his or her name is written in the book of life is by becoming a Christian.

Jesus/Wisdom as the Agent of Creation

John 1:3 says that everything came into being through Jesus, or the Word (the Greek word is *logos*) as He is called in this passage. Colossians 1:16 says that everything was created by Jesus: "all things have been created through Him and for Him." These verses teach that Jesus was in some way the agent for God's creative work. We can understand this to mean that the entire universe has one purpose: to give glory to Jesus. Everything that exists came into being through the glory of Christ, and the accurate way for us to understand and appreciate everything in our world is by seeing it in this light. Christ is the purpose for the world. Thus all of world history, before and after the cross, should be seen in the light of this reality.

Proverbs 8:22-31 says that wisdom was God's agent of creation. The passage is saying that wisdom is so important it is bound up in the very creation of the world. This does not contradict what we said above about Jesus as the agent of creation. The Greek word *logos* can be understood to mean wisdom. Jesus as God's *logos* is the ultimate expression of God's wisdom. In this sense, wisdom (in the person of Jesus) was the handmaiden of God's creative work.

The Presence of Satan

The Bible is not explicit about where Satan came from. We understand that he was created. He is not co-equal and co-eternal with God. If he were, then both good and bad would have the same eternal

This illustration of the devil is from the Codex Gigas, a 13th-century Latin manuscript that contains the Bible plus a collection of other documents.

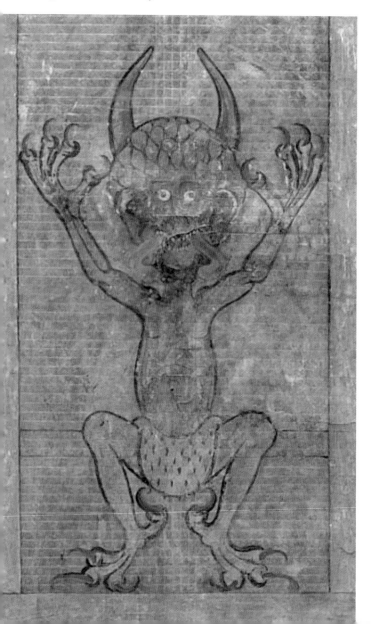

value and following one would be just as valid a choice as following the other. Satan is portrayed in Scripture as clearly a lesser power, who is allowed by God to have a limited realm of operation.

The most common understanding about Satan is that he is a fallen angel who rebelled against God and was cast out of heaven. First Timothy 3:6 might indicate that the devil became conceited and was condemned by God. Jude 6 mentions angels who did not remain in their proper abode and whom God has kept in eternal bonds under darkness. These are the most explicit statements in Scripture about Satan's past. Some people believe that Isaiah 14:12-15 and Ezekiel 28:12-19 describe the downfall of Satan. However, in their contexts these passages refer to the kings of Babylon and Tyre, respectively (Isaiah 14:4, Ezekiel 28:12). Perhaps the downfall of these kings was similar to what happened to Satan. The portrayal of Satan as a fallen angel might have been made most clearly in John Milton's epic poem *Paradise Lost*, but we must guard against letting human literature form our understanding of eternal truth.

Jesus said that Satan was a murderer from the beginning and that he is the father of lies (John 8:44). The devil has been sinning from the beginning (1 John 3:8). We believe that Satan is capable of choosing what to do and that he developed an evil nature because of his choices to do wrong. Apparently some other angelic beings rebelled against God also (see Jude 6 and possibly Revelation 12:4). Jesus said that an eternal fire had been prepared for the devil and his angels (Matthew 25:41).

Satan has taken opposing God as his purpose. We can see this in the events described in Genesis 3 and in Job 1-2. First Peter 5:8 describes the devil as the adversary, always seeking whom he may devour. As God is light, Satan is darkness; as God is truth, Satan is a liar; as God is love, Satan engenders hatred. God influences us to choose to do good; Satan tempts us to choose to do evil.

A Creation Before Creation?

As the description of Creation in Genesis 1 begins, it describes the earth as being formless and void and the Spirit of God moving over the face of the darkened deep. This seems to say that something was present before the creative activity described in the rest of the chapter took place. Some have speculated about a previous creation that descended into chaos before God created the world that we know. However, this injects a great deal of speculation into the space between verse 1 and verse 2. Genesis 1:2 is saying that whatever was present (which God created) was empty and without identity or significance before God spoke the Creation into existence.

With these thoughts about what existed before Creation, the stage is set for the beginning of world history. It is a story that is overseen by God and has as its purpose the honoring of Christ. The story of world history involves everyone who lives, has lived, and ever will live on the face of this planet.

The First Sentence of Genesis from a 1932 Illustrated Polish Torah

This was in accordance with the eternal purpose
which He carried out in Christ Jesus our Lord.
Ephesians 3:11

Assignments for Lesson 5

Bible   Read Genesis 5-7. Commentary available in *Student Review*.

Recite or write Deuteronomy 10:12-14 from memory.

Project   Complete your project for the unit.

Student Review   Optional: Answer the questions for Lesson 5 and take the quiz for Unit 1.

2

The Beginning

Summary

The Bible says that God made the world in six days. Soon after His creative work was over, Satan influenced Adam and Eve to sin. The rest of the story of the Bible deals primarily with God's plan for redeeming man from sin. Mankind divided into language and ethnic groups and spread out across the face of the earth. The last two lessons in this unit address some common questions that arise from studying Genesis and present logical proofs for the existence of God.

Lessons

6 - Creation

7 - Sin

8 - Early People Groups

9 - Questions from Genesis

10 - Bible Study: The Existence of God

Sunrise Over the Atlantic Ocean

Memory Work

Learn Genesis 1:26-27 by the end of the unit. This unit has daily reminders to work on your memory work. After this unit, you will need to remember to do this each day. You will be reminded to recite or write your memory work on the last day of the unit.

Books Used

The Bible
In Their Words

**Project
(choose one)**

This unit has daily reminders to work on your project. After this unit, you will need to remember to work on your project each day. You will be reminded to complete your project on the last day of the unit.

1) Write 300 to 500 words on one of the following topics:

- Each person must choose to believe that human beings were created by God or that they evolved by chance. Discuss the difference this choice makes in how we live our lives. See Lesson 6.

- Explain one of the questions about Genesis discussed in Lesson 9 (or another common question about Genesis) in your own words.

2) Interview someone who is learned in theology (such as a minister, evangelist, or elder) about his belief in the existence of God. Compose at least ten questions ahead of time. You can conduct your interview by phone or in person. Be respectful of your interviewee's time and keep the interview within an hour. If possible, make an audio recording of the interview. See Lesson 10.

3) Write a song or poem of at least sixteen lines about sin and redemption. See Lesson 7.

Lesson 6

Creation

The story of mankind begins with the creative act of God. This momentous beginning prepares the way for the rest of the Biblical narrative. The creation of man as described in Genesis sets important patterns for how God interacts with people. When people have followed God's pattern, good has resulted. When they have not, problems have occurred.

Man: A Spiritual Being

God made man in His image as the culmination of His Creation (Genesis 1:26). Being made in God's image means that man is a spiritual being, distinct from the earth, the firmament, the plants, and the animals, none of which has a spiritual nature. When people have denied their spiritual nature, they have treated each other as mere material objects. On the other hand, when people have believed that the physical world has a spiritual nature, they have gone into religious error.

Genesis 1:26 says that God created man "in Our image," the plural pronoun probably referring to Christ as His agent of creation. We understand this image or likeness to be God's spiritual nature, not any physical characteristics. As a spiritual being, God does not have literal physical characteristics.

Genesis 2:7 says that God formed man from the dust of the ground and breathed into him the breath of life. This describes the two physical aspects of man. Man has a physical body, and he also has the "breath of life" or physical life (breath, mental activity, heart function, etc., that end at death).

The common phrase "body and soul" describes the physical and the spiritual natures of man. First Thessalonians 5:23 refers to the "spirit and soul and body," but this three-part division merely separates the physical body from the physical life. In this verse, spirit is *pneuma*, the eternal, God-like part of man; soul is *psuche*, physical life; and body is *soma*, the tangible aspects of a person's body.

God gave man the authority to rule over the rest of creation (Genesis 1:28). When people have taken care of the physical world as a responsibility given to them by God, they have enjoyed health and abundance. When people have abused the physical world, they have caused pollution and scarcity.

Mankind began with one man and one woman. This means that all humans are related and share common ancestors. The divisions that people have created based on skin color are sinful; they ignore our common ancestry.

The creation of man is described twice, in Genesis 1 and in Genesis 2. It is the same story, but the two versions have different purposes. The account in Genesis 1 leads up to man as the high point of Creation. Genesis 2 describes the creation of man, then of the animals, and finally of woman. The second account emphasizes the garden that God created for man, which shows God's love and provision for man, as well as the husband-wife relationship that began with Adam and Eve. God gave the woman to the man to make man complete and so that they could create a family. Genesis 2:18-25 describes the process God followed to impress upon man the significance of His making woman for man. As woman was taken out of man, man and woman are joined together in marriage to be one. This tells us that God intended the family to be the cornerstone of human life and society.

Life in the Garden of Eden

Genesis 2:10-14 describes the Garden of Eden as having a river flowing out of it that separated into four rivers. We do not know the identity or location of the Pishon and Gihon Rivers; but since the Tigris and Euphrates are known today, some conclude that the Garden of Eden was in the area of Babylon (modern Iraq). The Tigris and Euphrates region is called the Cradle of Civilization. This is also the general area from which Abraham's family emigrated much later.

In the Garden of Eden, God provided everything that man needed. However, He did impose some limits on man. God forbade man from eating from the tree of the knowledge of good and evil (Genesis 2:17). This is another essential teaching from the Creation account, that man is subject to God. When people have remembered this, their lives have been blessed. When they have not, problems have arisen.

Genesis: Literal or Poetic?

Some see the account of Creation in Genesis as a broad, non-literal sketch that portrays Creation in poetic form. The six days of Genesis 1 do have a beautiful pattern, as indicated below (adapted from *Genesis* by John T. Willis, Austin, Texas: Sweet Publishing Company, 1979, page 78):

Day 1 - Light (1:3-5)	⟩	Day 4 - Lights in the expanse (1:14-19)
Day 2 - Sky, separation of waters (1:6-8)	⟩	Day 5 - Birds and fish (that live in the sky and waters; 1:20-23)
Day 3 - Dry land and vegetation (1:9-13)	⟩	Day 6 - Animals and man (that live on dry land; 1:24-31)

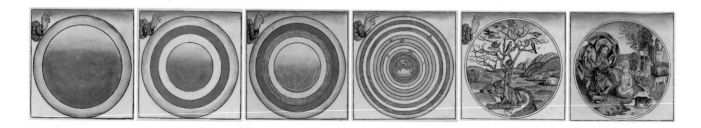

The Nuremberg Chronicle, published in 1493, is an illustrated paraphrase of the Bible and history of the world. These images depict the first six days of Creation.

The Garden of Eden *by Thomas Cole (1828)*

However, this pattern does not mean that the Creation account is not literal. Major problems result from seeing Genesis 1 as merely poetic and not literal. If Genesis 1 is not to be taken literally, when does the Genesis narrative become literally true? Is the account of sin also not to be taken literally? Is the flood story only figurative? How do we decide at what point to take Genesis as history? It is best to take Genesis as a literary whole and to understand it all to be literal.

Other Creation Accounts

Most cultures of the world have stories that attempt to describe the creation of the world. None of these are like the account in the Bible, which tells of the one God simply speaking the world into existence from nothing. The other stories are much more fanciful and sound like something that people would make up.

One of the better-known ancient creation stories is the *Enuma Elish* account from ancient Babylon. In *Enuma Elish* (the first two words of the Babylonian text), many gods fight one another, and elements of the physical universe come into existence as the by-products of these battles. Man is created to serve the gods. People care for the gods by providing sacrifices for them to eat.

Enuma Elish combines myths, polytheism, and nature religion to create a fantasy story. It has some similarities in form to the account in Genesis 1, in that light pierces the primordial darkness, various elements of the world come into being, man is created, and then the gods rest and celebrate. However, this does not mean that Genesis 1 and *Enuma Elish* are simply two roughly equivalent attempts to describe Creation. The Genesis 1 account clearly shows an inspired understanding of the truth about the world, while *Enuma Elish* comes across as a corruption of the original story.

With Creation, the story of man begins. God created man as the culmination of His creative work. However, man is not God. In the next lesson we see what happens when mankind transgresses those limits and succumbs to the temptation to want to be like God.

In one Maori creation story, Rangi is the sky father and Papa is the earth mother. Their children live in darkness until one of them pries Rangi and Papa apart. This carving was made around 1870 on a food storehouse in New Zealand.

Then God said, "Let Us make man in Our image,
according to Our likeness; and let them rule
over the fish of the sea and over the birds of the sky
and over the cattle and over all the earth,
and over every creeping thing that creeps on the earth."
Genesis 1:26

Assignments for Lesson 6

Bible   Read Genesis 8:1-11:10. Commentary available in *Student Review*.

Start memorizing Genesis 1:26-27.

In Their Words   Read the excerpt from "Ko Nga Tama a Rangi" (pages 1-2).

Project   Choose your project for this unit and start working on it.

Student Review   Optional: Answer the questions for Lesson 6.

Lesson 7

Sin

A friend of the author once summarized the story of the Old Testament as, "Creation, sin, and trouble, trouble, trouble!" That quick phrase does a pretty fair job of describing what happens in the Biblical narrative.

Genesis tells us that the world had its origin with God, who created it. Man is the pinnacle of Creation, since he is created in the image of God and rules over the physical world. Man is a spiritual being and is intended to have communion with his Maker, who is Spirit. However, the first humans chose to break that fellowship and committed spiritual failure, which we call sin. Through their misdeeds, sin entered the world and has plagued mankind ever since. We cannot adequately understand world history unless we have a grasp of the role that sin has played in it.

Sin is real. It is not merely what is considered to be socially unacceptable at a given time and place. Sin is real because evil is real. Since evil exists, men do evil deeds, which are sin. Sometimes sin involves the actions of only one person, such as lying or stealing. At other times, sin consumes an entire people, as when racial discrimination is practiced throughout a society.

Sin has consequences. Those who do wrong will be punished, whether in this life or in the next or both. Sin has consequences for the other people who are affected by one person's sin. When a person in a position of power sins, millions of people can be affected.

Genesis does not say that the fruit which Adam and Eve ate was an apple. This idea developed in medieval art and has come to be a common part of the telling of the story. Eve took the fruit of the forbidden tree; no further description is given. For centuries artists have attempted to portray Biblical stories such as these four of Adam and Eve. The image at the top of the page is a detail from Adam and Eve in Paradise (The Fall) *by Lucas Cranach the Elder (German, 1533) The top image at left is from a Persian medical manuscript called* The Benefits of Animals, *written about 1300. The center image is from a stained-glass window in the Saint-Julien cathedral in France, restored in the 19th century. The bottom image is from a church in Ethiopia, carved out of the rock around 1000. This and other paintings were added around 1700.*

Trouble in the Garden

Despite God's abundant blessing and provision, Adam and Eve rebelled against God's authority. Satan (embodied in the serpent on this occasion) suggested to Eve that the limits God had placed on the humans were not good. Eve gave in to the serpent's temptation and then led Adam into sin. Adam failed in his role as male leader since he did not protect Eve from evil influences.

The cycle of sin and its aftermath plays out in Genesis 2-3 the way it has played out countless times since. Man and woman rebelled against God's authority, wanting to decide for themselves what to do or not do. Sin is a selfish desire that shows a lack of trust in God. Sin thus originates in the heart, and this leads to wrong actions.

The sins of Adam and Eve caused their loss of innocence. After their sin, Adam and Eve were stricken with guilt and wanted to hide from God. When God confronted them, they tried to shirk the responsibility for their actions. God pronounced curses (consequences) upon Adam, Eve, and the serpent. Even with all of this, God showed His mercy and blessing to the sinners. He did not destroy them, and He even provided clothes for them to wear.

Further Accounts of Sin

The first people continued to face troubles by giving in to sin. Cain killed his brother Abel out of jealousy. When God confronted Cain, he made excuses. God meted out consequences on Cain but also showed him mercy.

As mankind spread out over the face of the earth, people continued to sin. God was grieved at the situation and resolved to start over. He commanded Noah to build an ark (probably a huge rectangular box, not a small, rounded ship as is often imagined) to preserve his family and pairs of animals through a flood. The flood lasted for over a year, and all humans and animals on the earth were destroyed except for those that were preserved on the ark. God then promised never again to destroy the earth by a flood. He set the rainbow in the sky as a sign of that covenant.

Stories of a massive flood in which a few people are saved are found in cultures around the world. The *Epic of Gilgamesh*, a Mesopotamian poem compiled around 1800 BC, contains one such example.

The serpent became a common symbol in many religious systems throughout history and around the world. The 17th-century image at left illustrates the Hindu god Krishna dancing on the head of his enemy Kaliya Naga, a poisonous snake.

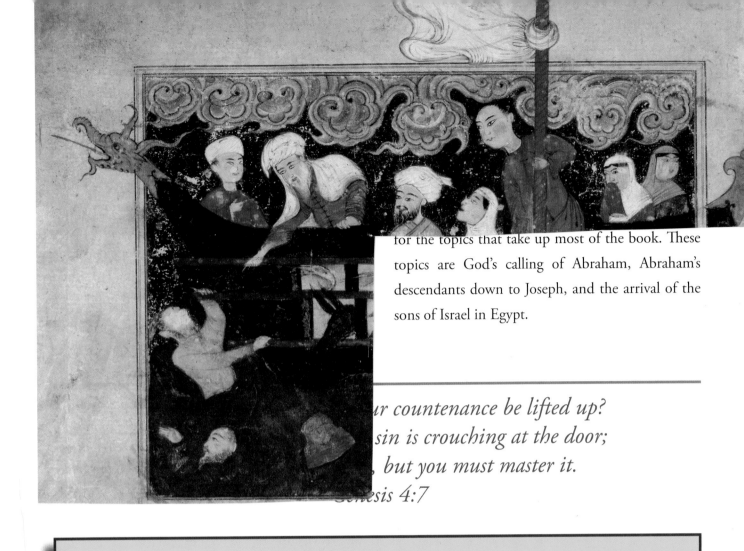

for the topics that take up most of the book. These topics are God's calling of Abraham, Abraham's descendants down to Joseph, and the arrival of the sons of Israel in Egypt.

...ur countenance be lifted up?
...sin is crouching at the door;
...but you must master it.
Genesis 4:7

Assignments for Lesson 7

Bible Read Genesis 11:11-15:21. Commentary available in *Student Review*.

Work on memorizing Genesis 1:26-27.

In Their Words Read the Australian Aboriginal Flood Story (pages 3-5).

Project Work on your project.

Student Review Optional: Answer the questions for Lesson 7.

Lesson 8

Early People Groups

As the population of the earth grew, mankind spread out from the place of its beginning. People lived as tribes or nations, each of which had a notable ancestor. Genesis tells us about some of the more significant developments in human culture.

Civilized Life

People developed cities early in history. Cain built a city and named it after his son, Enoch (Genesis 4:17). Several generations later, three sons of Lamech contributed to the further development of civilization. Jabal was the first of the nomads, who lived in tents and kept livestock. Jubal was the originator of musical instruments. Tubal-cain

Several caves in southern France feature wall paintings. In 1940 a group of teenagers discovered the Lascaux cave, which brought worldwide attention to the paintings. Lascaux has hundreds of images of animals, people, and abstract designs. To protect the original artwork, the cave has been closed to the public since 1963. However, portions of the artwork have been reproduced in a nearby cave called Lascaux II, as shown in the photo above.

began the practice of working with bronze and iron (Genesis 4:20-22).

The developments mentioned in this part of Genesis reveal two major contrasts which characterize human civilization. First, settled community life developed at the same time as the nomadic lifestyle. Later historical evidence supports this. Among the early tribes in North and South America, large cities developed in some places while other groups followed herds of wild game. A second contrast is portrayed with Jubal and Tubal-cain. They show us the development of the creative talents of man and the industrial pursuits of man. Both are essential parts of human civilization.

Notice what is not present in these accounts. Genesis makes no mention of early man evolving through various stages of ever-greater mental and physical capabilities. Instead, human beings, specially created by God, had significant abilities and employed them early on. Only the eyes of evolutionists see mankind as slowly developing civilization after evolving from lower forms of life. The evolutionary view is a theory fabricated to support certain presuppositions about man, while God inspired the account in Genesis to teach us what really happened.

Spiritual Developments

Eve bore another son, Seth. She recognized that God had given Seth to her and Adam because Abel had been killed. To Seth was born Enosh. Then Genesis tells us that people began to call upon the name of the Lord (Genesis 4:26).

This statement marks a spiritual turning of at least some of mankind, although scholars debate its exact significance. Some believe that it notes the beginning of a widespread worship of God. Now, apparently, people remembered their Maker and began giving Him honor. On the other hand, some Bible scholars see the significance in the particular use here of the name of the Lord, YHWH, the covenant name by which God revealed Himself to Moses (Exodus 3:14). It could be that Moses is noting that at this point in human history, people began to recognize God for who He really is and began worshiping Him on that basis.

Either way (and the significance of the statement might involve both factors), the worship of God at this time was significant. Some scholars note that the descendants of Cain were involved in the development of worldly pursuits while the descendants of Seth practiced the worship of God.

Ancestors do set patterns that are followed for many generations.

In the listing of the descendants of Adam through Seth in Genesis 5, Moses makes particular mention of Enoch, the father of Methuselah. Whereas the other people listed "lived," Enoch "walked with God" (Genesis 5:22, 24). Whereas the others in the list are said to have "died," Enoch "was not, for God took him" (Genesis 5:24). Apparently God took Enoch from this world in a way that might have been similar to the way in which Elijah was taken many years later (2 Kings 2:11). It is sad to note how quickly human beings left off walking closely with their Maker. The ways of the world and the rise of false religions took their toll on the souls of men.

The Descendants of Shem, Ham, and Japheth

After the flood, Noah's sons became the originators of nations that spread over the face of the earth. Generally speaking, the descendants of Japheth moved out to the north and west of what we know as the Middle East. As best we can determine, these gave rise to the European ethnic groups. The sons of Ham moved southward and are associated mostly with Africa. The offspring of Shem became the Middle Eastern people we call Semites, a term which uses a variation of the name Shem. The Semites are not mentioned last because Shem was the youngest son. Rather this order leads most naturally into the account of one family of Semites

Isidore (c.560-636 AD) was a Church leader and scholar in Spain. He compiled the Etymologiae, *a massive twenty-volume encyclopedia of science, law, agriculture, household goods, geography, and theology. This map, published in a 1472 edition of Isidore's work, divides the world known to Europeans into three sections: Asia, settled by Shem's descendants; Europe, by Japheth's; and Africa, by Ham's.*

that begins in the next chapter, namely Terah and his son, Abram (later called Abraham).

The geographical areas in which the descendants of Shem, Ham, and Japheth lived are not clear-cut, since descendants of more than one son are described as living in the same regions. Also, the different languages of these groups are mentioned in Genesis 10, even though the account of the Tower of Babel, which comes later (Genesis 11:1-9), states that until that time all men spoke the same language. This is not a contradiction in the Biblical narrative. Moses simply noted that the languages of the ethnic groups were different, and then related the story of how they became different.

Differences Among People

At some point, physical differences among people began to emerge. However, mankind has placed much greater emphasis on these than God does in His Word. One might wonder how such variation developed from one family, but in many families different children have lighter or darker features when compared to each other. As descendants of either Shem, Ham, or Japheth lived together and intermarried, those variations could have easily become more pronounced.

For many years, Caucasians divided humans into three racial groups: white (Caucasian), black (Negro), and yellow (Oriental). However, this is a

Ota Benga

The belief that some people are superior to others has led to tragic results throughout history. The 1904 Louisiana Purchase Exposition (World's Fair) in St. Louis, Missouri, featured exhibits showing the supposed progress of humans from primitive to advanced. The poster at right, used at the fair, illustrates the assumption that different people groups represented different stages on an evolutionary journey clockwise from "prehistoric man" at bottom right to the Caucasian at top right. In addition to collections of artifacts, members of tribes from around the world were put on display in their native dress and home environments.

One man brought to the fair was Ota Benga, a member of the Mbuti people from the Congo. Samuel Verner, a representative of the Exposition, had purchased him from a slave trader in Africa. For a few months in 1906, Benga was featured as an attraction at the Bronx Zoo (as shown below).

An African-American clergyman, James Gordon, led a protest against Benga's treatment, and Gordon found a place for Benga to live. Benga eventually moved to Virginia, where he attended school and got a job in a tobacco factory. As the years went by, his desire grew to return to Africa. However, the outbreak of World War I prevented him from traveling to the Congo. Benga took his own life in 1916 at age 32.

serious and erroneous oversimplification of skin color. It makes no provision for Hispanics and southern Europeans, for instance, whose skin is darker than that of northern Europeans but lighter than sub-Saharan Africans. It is much more accurate to understand that humans have a continuum of skin shades and other features. It is also important to understand that such external characteristics are of no consequence to God, who loves all people regardless of their physical appearance. Differences in appearance have been used by people (including but not limited to Caucasians) as an excuse to treat others as inferior, but such racism and prejudice are not from God. In Christ all ethnic divisions are insignificant (Galatians 3:28, Ephesians 2:11-16, Colossians 3:11).

The accounts in the first eleven chapters of Genesis give us a sweeping overview of about 2,000 years of history. These narratives and genealogical lists provided the people of Israel with the background information they needed to understand their identity as a nation specially chosen by God. From Genesis 12 on, Moses focuses on Abraham and his descendants. Other nations are mentioned in detail only as they come in contact with Abraham and later with the nation of Israel.

This is the book of the generations of Adam.
In the day when God created man, He made him in the likeness of God.
He created them male and female,
and He blessed them and named them Man
in the day when they were created.
Genesis 5:1-2

Assignments for Lesson 8

Bible   Read Acts 17:24-28 and Genesis 16-18. Commentary available in *Student Review*.

Work on memorizing Genesis 1:26-27.

In Their Words   Read the excerpt from *Antiquities of the Jews* (pages 6-7).

Project   Work on your project.

Student Review   Optional: Answer the questions for Lesson 8.

Grand Canyon National Park: View from Hermits Rest

Lesson 9

Questions from Genesis

Since the inspired account of Genesis does not contain a complete record of everything that happened in the early years of the world, we do not have conclusive answers to all of the questions about that period that people commonly raise today. What Moses wrote is accurate, and we assume that the first readers of Genesis understood the significance of what was written there. However, we do not have their same knowledge base, so we must do some detective work and draw the best conclusions we can about some of the matters discussed in the first part of Genesis.

When Did Creation Take Place?

The Bible describes the Creation as taking place in six days, accomplished by the word of God (Gen. 1; Ex. 20:11, 31:17). The Lord spoke, and it was so. The Genesis account gives no indication of the passage of any significant length of time.

One theory that appears to challenge the idea of a relatively young earth is uniformitarianism. This holds that the processes we see in the physical world today (such as the formation of minerals) have always taken place at roughly the same rate. If uniformitarianism is true, the earth would have to be very old for it to have developed to its current state.

However, uniformitarianism is an assumption, not an established fact. Geological features such as the Grand Canyon in the United States provide evidence for catastrophic changes during earth's history rather than consistently uniform development. Also, the quick recovery of the area around Mount St. Helens in Washington State after the 1980 volcanic eruption there suggests that we do not fully understand how the physical world reacts to catastrophes.

If we dismiss a strict uniformitarianism and admit that catastrophic events such as the flood of Noah's time have caused major changes to the earth's surface, then no geological evidence necessitates the idea that the earth was formed millions or billions of years ago. Since we believe God made the world, it is within reason to believe that He could make it in six days.

Archbishop James Ussher of the Church of England published an extensive study of world history between 1650 and 1654. He concluded that the earth was created in 4004 BC and assigned other dates to subsequent events in the Bible. Because of Ussher's influence, his dating calculations were printed in the margins of many editions of the King

James Version of the Bible. However, the Hebrew manuscripts from which the Old Testament is translated do not include such marginal dates.

Ussher's name has been most prominent, but he was not the only one to study the age of the earth. According to historians, some people in the ancient cultures of Persia, Babylon, Egypt, China, India, and Axum dated Creation between 6204 and 5369 BC. The traditional Jewish date for Creation is 3761 BC. Alphonso X of Spain went as far back as 6984 BC. Josephus proposed 5481 and 5402. Bede said 5199. Martin Luther suggested 3961. Astronomer Johannes Kepler calculated 3993.

These dates reflect variations, but they are nothing like the millions or billions of years proposed by modern scientists. Some ancient people believed that the universe had always existed or that it went through long cycles, but historical calculations and records suggest a young earth of a few thousand years. We might not be able to determine a precise date for Creation, but we can be confident that the Biblical record is accurate. The geological evidence supports the historical evidence for a young earth.

Whom Did Cain Marry?

Cain is described in Genesis 4:17 as having a wife, but no explanation is given of where she came from. She was evidently his sister, or perhaps his niece. When God gave the Law to Moses hundreds of years later, he prohibited marriage between close relatives (Leviticus 18). This might have been in part because genetic deterioration made such marriages more likely to produce children with genetic problems. Soon after Creation, however, this would not have been an issue.

Why Did People Live So Long Then?

We are amazed when we read in Genesis 5 of people living for hundreds of years. Methuselah, the oldest person on record, lived 969 years! (According to the years of the list in Genesis 5, Methuselah died

in the year in which the flood occurred.) Plausible explanations have been offered for this longevity.

God might have given these people long lives to enable them to have many children and so increase the population of the earth rapidly. Another possibility is that the earth was purer and not as harmful to human life then. Fossil evidence indicates that some plants and animals grew larger in the past than they do now. The theory of evolution holds that plants and animals become more fit over time, but evidence indicates that at least some growing things have become smaller and less fit over the years.

This idea of a purer earth might also help explain the dinosaur species that existed long ago. They might have grown large because they lived many years in a better environment than exists on earth today. Scientists take fossil evidence, add assumptions and presuppositions, and create theories. Too often these theories are presented as established facts.

The Indroda Dinosaur and Fossil Park in Gujarat, India, features fossilized dinosaur eggs.

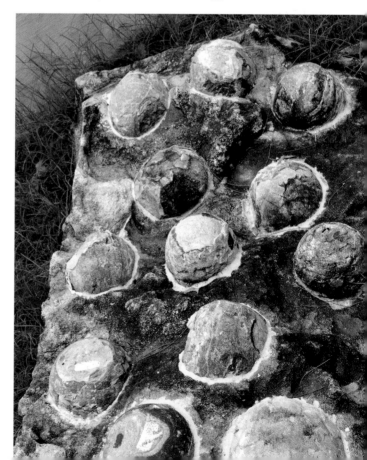

The Myth of Human Evolution

The Bible teaches that all human beings are descended from Adam and Eve. The idea that different groups of humans or human-like creatures developed independently does not fit the Biblical account.

Archaeologists have unearthed various fossils (often a single bone or tooth) and given them different scientific names in an effort to create an evolutionary link between apes and humans. Thomas Huxley was a strong proponent of Charles Darwin's theory of evolution. He used the illustration below in his book Evidence as to Man's Place in Nature *(1863) to show how apes and humans share similar skeletal structures. However, similarities in skeletal structure do not require the conclusion that apes and humans descended from a common ancestor. Since the same Creator designed all living creatures, we should not be surprised to find similarities among them.*

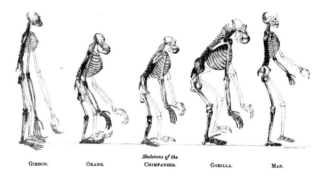

What Were the Sins of Lamech?

Lamech, a descendant of Cain, took two wives (Genesis 4:19). This is the first recorded instance of polygamy in the Bible. Several men in the Biblical record had more than one wife, including Jacob, David, and Solomon. We understand these occurrences to be in violation of God's plan of one man and one woman for life. The fact that the Bible records these instances of polygamy does not mean that God endorses them. The Bible tells of many events that are in violation of God's will.

Lamech is also quoted as telling his wives that he has killed a man in revenge for striking him and that he would kill many times again to avenge himself (Genesis 4:23-24). His violent nature is similar to that of Cain, his ancestor. This shows the extent of sin in the world. It reminds us of the consequences of the example of sin entering into the life of mankind in general and of a particular family.

Who Were the "Sons of God"?

This common question about Genesis 6:1-4 requires careful analysis and thinking. First, the tenor of the passage indicates that the sons of God taking daughters of men was not a good thing. Verse 2 suggests that the sons of God were selfish and arrogant for taking the daughters of men. God says that He was striving against the ways of man (verse 3). Verse 5 summarizes man's wickedness.

Second, we understand that the offspring of these unions were the mighty men of old that Moses' audience had heard about (verse 4). The Nephilim were on the earth at that time, and verse 4 might be saying that the Nephilim were the offspring being described. When the spies who went into Canaan reported back to the people of Israel, they said that some of the people living in the land were Nephilim and suggested that they were giants (Numbers 13:33).

Bible scholars have suggested four possible identities for the sons of God:

- angels, based on the use of the phrase in Job 1:6 and Psalm 29:1;

- children from aristocratic families, based on the use of the phrase for a king in 2 Samuel 7:14, Psalm 2:7, and elsewhere;

- godly men who walked with the Lord, based on the use of the phrase in such passages as Proverbs 3:12 and Isaiah 1:2; and

- the descendants of Seth, with the daughters of men being the descendants of Cain, based on the genealogies immediately preceding this paragraph.

The idea of the "sons of God" being angels has the least basis in Scripture. Angels having sexual relations with humans is foreign to all of the rest of Scripture. God's wrath is described as being directed against the sins of humans, not angels.

The identity of the sons of God as aristocratic children is possible, but Genesis does not make distinctions between royalty and commoners in this section. It is also unclear why such marriages would corrupt mankind.

It seems best to understand the "sons of God" as humans, probably men who had been godly (and perhaps who were the descendants of Seth) who wrongly wanted to take materially-minded women as their wives. Their children, the mighty men, might have devoted their efforts to increasing their own power and prestige instead of honoring the Lord. Marriages that are wrongly begun and have worldly purposes often leave a bad legacy for future generations.

The Lord was sorry that He had made man on the earth,
and He was grieved in His heart.
But Noah found favor in the eyes of the Lord.
Genesis 6:6, 8

Assignments for Lesson 9

Bible   Read 2 Peter 3:1-9 and Genesis 19-21. Commentary available in *Student Review*.

Work on memorizing Genesis 1:26-27.

In Their Words   Read the excerpt from *The Annals of the World* (pages 8-10).

Project   Work on your project.

Student Review   Optional: Answer the questions for Lesson 9.

Detail from The Creation of Adam, *Michelangelo (Italian, c. 1511)*

Lesson 10 - Bible Study

The Existence of God

The existence of God is a fundamental question that we must consider. If God does not exist, the world and our lives are the product of merely materialistic forces, and our existence has no purpose. If God does not exist, right and wrong are simply human concepts, and we have no destiny beyond the grave. If God does not exist, a faithful Christian and a mass murderer share the same end.

Since God does exist, we need to understand how He works in the world. We want to know His nature and His expectations for us. We want to know the right way to approach and worship Him. We want to know which of the beliefs about divinity are correct, incorrect, or partially correct. We want to know the Bible, His inspired Word. In short, we want and need to know all we can about Him.

The Bible assumes that God exists. Many modern scientists and others assume that God does not exist (or at least does not really matter); they try to explain everything that happens as having purely natural causes.

Over the centuries people have developed logical arguments that attempt to prove God's existence. We will examine three of the most common classical arguments. Remember that a relationship with God does not just involve knowledge. It requires faith, or trust. No amount of evidence (even someone rising from the dead) will force someone to believe if he does not want to. Each of us must decide to take a step of faith, as we read in Hebrews 11:3, 6:

> By faith we understand that the worlds were prepared by the word of God, so that what is seen was not made out of things which are visible. . . . And without faith it is impossible to please Him, for he who comes to God must believe that He is and that He is a rewarder of those who seek Him.

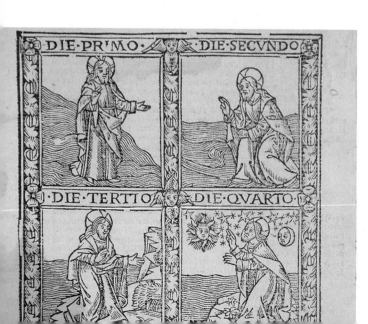

16th-Century Woodcut Illustrations of the First Four Days of Creation

The Argument from First Cause

Thomas Aquinas is perhaps the best-known advocate of the argument from first cause. Everything in our world has a cause: a chicken lays an egg, which hatches a chick; atmospheric winds and temperature changes cause storms; water erodes soil, and so forth. Everything that is in motion has been set in motion by something else.

The fact that everything in our physical world has been caused means that everything is in some way dependent on something else. One can trace these causes back through time and space. An oak tree, for instance, is the result of an acorn being planted and nourished. However, at some point one comes to the first cause for everything else, that which is not itself caused, that which is not dependent on anything else. This first cause, Thomas said, is God. God was not caused. He is not the product of some other force or motion.

Genesis 1:1 gives a statement of First Cause: "In the beginning God created the heavens and the earth." God is the beginning point, the force or cause

Thomas Aquinas (1225-1274) was an Italian priest. His writings have had a profound influence on modern theology and philosophy.

for everything else. He is the explanation for how everything came about and for all of the processes of causation in the universe.

This scanning electron microscope image shows red blood cells, different types of white blood cells, and platelets.

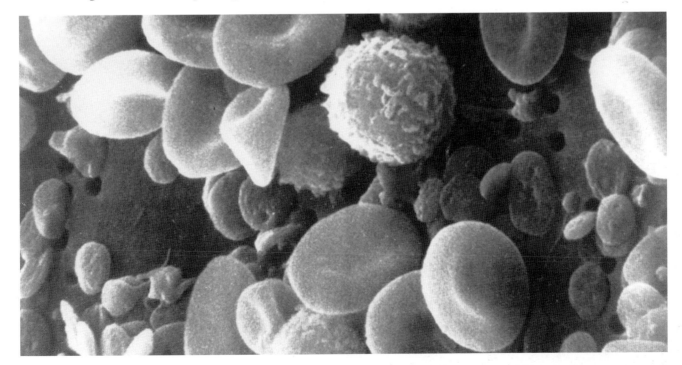

The Argument from Design

A second logical proof of God is based on the fact that design exists in the world. Spring always comes, corn seed always produces corn, the moon orbits the earth and the earth orbits the sun, and the water cycle (precipitation-evaporation-condensation) always works. The human body is filled with intricate design. Did all of this order and design just happen by chance, or does some intelligence lie behind the order we see in the universe?

The classic statement of this proof uses a watch as an example. If you take the back off of an old-fashioned watch and see all of the parts moving and working to keep time, you logically assume that the watch had a maker. A watch implies a watchmaker. Design implies a designer. The designer of the universe must be an intelligence outside of the universe itself. That designer is God.

C. S. Lewis presents the case for design in his book *Miracles*. How, he asks, could our rational world and our rational minds be the product of an irrational process? He concludes that they cannot. It takes more "faith" (trusting in the unseen and unproven) to believe that our world just happened than to believe that an Intelligence lies behind it and guides it all.

Psalm 19:1 states, "The heavens are telling of the glory of God; and their expanse is declaring the work of his hands." To the ear of faith, the psalmist is saying, the created world speaks of God. After looking outward in Psalm 19, David looks inward in Psalm 139 and concludes, "I am fearfully and wonderfully made" (Psalm 139:14).

The Moral Argument

Lewis makes the moral argument for God in the first part of *Mere Christianity*. All people have a moral oughtness within them, Lewis notes; but he adds another important factor. Although everyone has this standard (we usually call it a conscience), nobody lives up to it. This moral standard does not come from society or from individuals themselves. It comes from outside of society and outside of

This image of two galaxies was created using the Hubble Space Telescope.

individuals. The only logical source from which such a standard could come is God.

Paul speaks of this moral oughtness in Romans 1:18-21. Mankind should have known better than the way they have behaved. They have rejected what they should have known about God; and as a result God gave them over to sin, and His wrath awaits them.

Psalm 14:1 says, "The fool has said in his heart, 'There is no God.'" The word fool in the Bible does not refer to a court jester or someone who embarrasses himself. A fool is a moral failure, one who has rejected God and who has therefore thrown away his life morally. It is not only foolish intellectually to say that there is no God; it is also morally destructive to reject God and His standards for human living.

A Needed Statement of Truth

We might think that Moses' description of Creation in Genesis 1 was an unnecessary reminder to his original audience. After all, God had freed Israel from bondage in Egypt; He was guiding them through the wilderness; and He was going to give them the land that He had promised their ancestors. Surely Israel, of all people, would have known that God was the Creator of the heavens and the earth.

However, what Moses wrote was an important statement of fact that the Israelites needed to remember. The Israelites were coming out of Egypt where many false gods were worshiped. They showed a lack of faith in God many times during the wilderness years. They needed to understand at the very beginning of God's revelation to them that it was the one true God, *YHWH*, who created the heavens and the earth. They needed to know this in order to have truth as the basis for their lives.

The need for the statement made in Genesis still exists today. We hear many religious notions discussed. The theory of evolution has carried the

This illustration of Moses and Aaron before Pharaoh is from a Syriac version of the Bible probably produced in the 600s.

day in scientific circles and in the media. Our world had its origin in the spoken, creative word of the one true living God; this declaration needs to be made loudly and clearly today. It was not a random, mindless Big Bang; it was God. It was not a process of evolutionary change over millions and millions of years; God spoke the universe into existence.

The fact that God exists and that He created us should make a difference in how we see ourselves and in how we live. Since we are God's creation and are made in His image, since we will one day face the alternatives of eternal life with God or eternal punishment apart from Him, then what we do and how we treat others matters tremendously. If the peoples and governments of the world worked from the assumption that every person is valued by God and is His handiwork, then world history, current events, and our future on this earth would be quite different.

*For we must all appear before the judgment seat of Christ,
so that each one may be recompensed for his deeds in the body,
according to what he has done, whether good or bad.*
2 Corinthians 5:10

Assignments for Lesson 10

Bible   Read Romans 1:16-31 and Genesis 22-24. Commentary available in *Student Review*.

Recite or write Genesis 1:26-27 from memory.

In Their Words   Read the excerpt from *Summa Theologica* (pages 11-13).

Project   Complete your project for the unit.

Student Review   Optional: Answer the questions for Lesson 10 and take the quiz for Unit 2.

3

Early Civilizations

Summary Archaeology tells us about some remarkable and highly-advanced civilizations that emerged thousands of years ago. Mankind did not crawl out of a cave or descend from monkeys. Instead, people have used their God-given abilities to create amazing things, even though their thought-world had become pagan. We highlight early scientific discoveries and the code of laws that Hammurabi developed. Finally, we look at the land between the Tigris and Euphrates from ancient times until today.

Lessons 11 - Sumer
12 - Egypt
13 - Key Concepts: Ancient Science and Mathematics
14 - Key Person: Hammurabi and His Code of Laws
15 - Bible Study: The Land Between the Rivers

Wall Painting from a Tomb in the Valley of the Kings, Egypt

49

Memory Work	Learn Job 42:1-6 by the end of the unit. Remember to work on it each day.
Books Used	The Bible *In Their Words* *The Cat of Bubastes*

Project (choose one)

1) Write 300 to 500 words on one of the following topics (work on it each day):
   - Explain the physics and geometry the Egyptians used in building the pyramids. See Lesson 13.
   - Write a speech directed at common people explaining how the people of Babylonia will benefit from having the Code of Hammurabi, as if you were living at the time. See Lesson 14.
2) Create a collection of photos showing the influence of ancient mathematicians on our world today. Compose your photos intentionally and artistically. Your finished project should be in the form of a slideshow on an electronic device or prints of the photographs displayed on a poster or in book form, with a minimum of fifteen photos. See Lesson 13.
3) Find an authoritative chart with ancient Egyptian hieroglyphs. Make a clay tablet from homemade or purchased clay. With a sharp tool, copy a few symbols onto the tablet and led it harden. See Lesson 12.

Literature

The Cat of Bubastes by G. A. Henty was published in 1888. This historical novel tells the story of Amuba, prince of the nation of Rebu beside the Caspian Sea. The story takes place when the Israelites were slaves in Egypt, which Henty places during the reign of Pharaoh Thotmes III. In the book, an Egyptian army conquers Rebu and Amuba is taken prisoner. He and his servant Jethro are taken to serve in the household of Ameres, the high priest of Osiris. There Amuba becomes friends with Chebron, the son of Ameres. In the story Amuba meets a Hebrew girl, Ruth. The plot centers on the accidental killing of a sacred cat and what this means for the main characters.

Through the book we learn a great deal about life in ancient Egypt, including its religious practices and beliefs and the way society was structured. Henty suggests in the book that paganism mistakenly attributes qualities of the one true God to various deities. The plot demonstrates how evil leaders can capitalize on fear and ignorance to manipulate people.

G. A. Henty's life (1832-1902) closely paralleled the Victorian Era in Great Britain, where Queen Victoria reigned from 1837 to 1901. Henty was a foreign correspondent for British publications in many places around the world. He began telling stories to his children that utilized the knowledge he gained in his travels. A friend suggested that he write the stories down for publication. Henty eventually published 144 novels in addition to numerous magazine articles. He had assistance in doing research for his books, and he often dictated his novels to stenographers. The typical plot line in his books involves a boy hero in a particular period in history. The boy often meets a famous historical person during the story. In *The Cat of Bubastes*, Amuba has an encounter with Moses, who was serving Pharaoh at the time.

Lesson 11

Sumer

Row upon row of employees record the business transactions of the day.

International trade is a key part of the economy.

Single-family dwellings that look very much alike fill the areas outside of the central city.

Children learn the elementary lessons of reading and writing in school.

A father writes in a letter that he is frustrated with his son's laziness.

A bride writes a poem that celebrates her love for her new husband.

All of these statements describe life in ancient Sumer. Despite the many ways in which we are different from the Sumerians, in some ways thousands of years and thousands of miles do not separate us much at all from one of the earliest known civilizations.

The Emergence of Civilizations

What is civilization? The idea of civilization includes cultural and technological development, written language and the keeping of written records, specialized skills and occupations, social classes, and complex government and religious practices.

Civilization flourished in the Middle East before the flood. After the flood, Noah's descendants began to rebuild civilization, and following their attempt to build a tower to the heavens, they began to spread out across the world.

What might be surprising, given the common assumptions of many people today, is the way in which the Sumerian civilization emerges in history. First, we have no evidence of cave dwellings giving way to constructed housing. Second, we have no evidence that the Sumerians moved there from another location or that they were nomads at first

Many people think that prehistoric man was much more primitive in his abilities and knowledge than modern man. However, this makes certain assumptions that are not supported by logic or evidence. First, people commonly assume that prehistoric man had a limited understanding of his world; but prehistoric man, by definition, did not leave a history of his life, so we cannot know what he understood or did not understand. Second, the term prehistoric man, while common, is something of a misnomer. We have a history of man from his origins in the Garden of Eden; so in one sense there is no prehistoric man. It is just that some groups did not record their history in a way that we can know it today. Third, the theory of evolution assumes long periods of slow development from pre-human or humanoid forms to what we call modern man. This is guesswork by scientists who have already decided what they want the evidence to show.

This is what we do know. Historic and archaeological records indicate that nomad and settled populations existed at the same time (as they do today). Human beings displayed remarkable skills and knowledge from the earliest recorded times. They could express deep sensitivity and profound consideration toward others. At the same time, those people were capable of maintaining slaves and committing terrible atrocities in war. This should not surprise us. Slavery was practiced in what some would call the most advanced nation of the world—the United States—until the 1860s. The 20th century saw many atrocities committed by one group upon another. In other words, if what the ancients did could be barbaric, people today can be barbaric also. In terms of art, the sculptures of ancient Sumer show much more skill (to this observer) than some expressions of what is called modern art today.

It is too easy—and too easily disproved—to say that the skills of early man were clumsy and primitive at first and more adept later. It is more accurate to say that people throughout history have demonstrated great ability to think, plan, and create because they are created in the image of God.

The Sumerians

The area around the lower Tigris and Euphrates Rivers (what is now southern Iraq) was once known as Sumer. The Greeks called the general region Mesopotamia, a name made from words that mean "between the rivers." The arc of land from the Persian Gulf across modern Iraq to Syria, Jordan, and Israel has also been called the Fertile Crescent. The land is relatively moist and fertile compared to the surrounding desert. This area has also been

These mosaics of shell, red limestone, and lapis lazuli were discovered in a royal cemetery in the ancient city of Ur. The wooden backing of the mosaics had decayed, so they were carefully removed from the ground and reconstructed.

The top panel shows a Sumerian king with his army of foot soldiers and chariots along with captured prisoners. The bottom panel shows the king presiding over a banquet with people leading animals and bringing bags, perhaps providing food for the banquet.

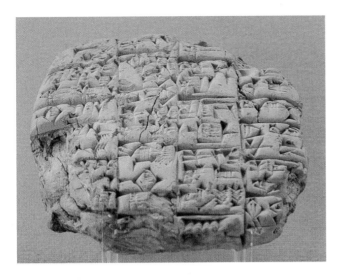

This cuneiform tablet is a letter from a Sumerian priest to a king. It tells the king that his son has been killed in battle.

culturally fertile for thousands of years as settlers, warriors, and traders have moved across it.

Sumerians lived in city-states. This means that each city functioned as its own country, with its own king, nobility, and army. City-states and local kings were common in that region and period. This is why Genesis 14:1-2 mentions several kings who ruled in a relatively small area. Most people in Sumer probably thought of themselves as citizens of a particular city and not as Sumerians. The largest and most important city-state in Sumer was Ur.

Most people in Sumer were farmers. Some were skilled workers and businessmen. Sumerians used the wheel, which made their work easier. They also had a yoke that allowed two oxen to pull a plow, thus enabling more effective farming. Sumerians dug canals and irrigation ditches to bring water to their fields of crops. Sumerian farmers grew a variety of vegetables and raised animals such as goats, pigs, and sheep. They also grew flax, which produced the fibers that were woven into linen cloth.

As a coastal people, the Sumerians developed a large sea trade. Their ships traveled to places such as Egypt and India. The raw materials that traders

brought back, including wood and precious stones (both of which were rare in Mesopotamia), were used by Sumerian craftsmen and artisans to make jewelry, dishes, and other items. Craftsmen also made pottery and colorful fabrics to sell.

The Sumerians were a religious people. They believed in many gods, but the citizens of each city had special loyalty to the god that they believed ruled them. The god of Ur was the moon god Nanna. Their worship involved the use of temples elevated toward heaven on flattened pyramid-like bases called ziggurats. Ziggurats were commonly several stories high. The Sumerians offered prayers, sacrifices, and rituals to their gods in the hope of having good crops and good results in business. Priests were highly respected and exerted much influence in Sumerian society.

This Sumerian figurine depicts a man praying. His shaven head might indicate that he is a priest.

A Written Language

We know as much as we do about the Sumerians because they developed a written language to record information. They wrote by pressing a pointed stick or stylus into soft clay tablets or cylinders to make characters. The clay could then be hardened and preserved. We call this written language cuneiform, from the Latin word *cuneus* meaning wedge. Most of the characters were combinations of wedge-shaped indentions into the clay. Written Sumerian had hundreds of characters, some of which stood for words and some for syllables. Schools taught a relatively few young men how to read and write so that they could become scribes.

A written language is a great help to a society. For instance, it enables the keeping of business and government records. Large numbers of clay tablets found in the area of Sumer were devoted to these purposes. In addition, writing also enables the recording of laws so that life is not subject to the whims and faulty memories of judges and rulers. The Sumerians were also able to record their thoughts and reflections on life in letters, diaries, and other literature. Written records enable later researchers to know what life in Sumerian cities was like.

Later History of Mesopotamia

The city-states of Sumer eventually declined in power while the city of Akkad to the north, situated on the Tigris River, grew in power. Sargon was a military leader who rose from humble origins to lead the Akkadian army. He established the first known empire that controlled several people groups. Sargon's empire stretched from the eastern Mediterranean to Sumer.

The people known as the Amorites built the city of Babylon on the Euphrates (south of modern Baghdad), and the early Babylonian Empire developed. We will say more about one ruler of Babylon, Hammurabi, in a later lesson.

Naram-Sin was the grandson of Sargon. This inscription from his reign describes the construction of a temple.

The Babylonian Empire weakened through rebellion, poor leadership, and invasions from without. The Kassites invaded from the east, and a few years later, the Hittites moved in from present-day Turkey and took control of Mesopotamia. The Hittites were fierce warriors who developed the use of iron weapons. Later, the Assyrians invaded the Mesopotamian region as part of their designs for world conquest. The Assyrians were fierce and cruel warriors. These developments indicate that military commanders sometimes took the place of religious priests as leaders of society.

Conclusion

The Sumerian civilization was similar to our own in some ways but vastly different in other ways. Understanding Sumer helps us to see the accuracy of the Bible and gives us information about early developments in the story of mankind. Knowledge of Sumer also reminds us of the great potential with which God created mankind and the great tragedy of lives that are lived without faith in God.

And Terah took Abram his son, and Lot the son of Haran,
his grandson, and Sarai his daughter-in-law,
his son Abram's wife; and they went out together
from Ur of the Chaldeans in order to enter
the land of Canaan; and they went as far as Haran,
and settled there.
Genesis 11:31

Assignments for Lesson 11

Bible Read Genesis 25-27. Commentary available in *Student Review*.

In Their Words Read the excerpt from *The Chronology of Ancient Kingdoms Amended* (pages 14-15).

Literature Begin reading *The Cat of Bubastes*. Plan to finish it by the end of Unit 5.

Student Review Optional: Answer the questions for Lesson 11.

Lesson 12

Egypt

The central reality of Egypt is the Nile River. It runs like a silver thread surrounded by a narrow green ribbon down the length of the country. Within its watershed, Egypt is rich and productive. Beyond the reach of the Nile, Egypt is mostly desert.

The Nile is the longest river in the world (though the Amazon basin is twice as large and carries much more water). This lifeline of Egypt starts in the region of Lake Victoria in Central Africa and flows for about 4,132 miles to the Mediterranean—roughly the distance between Chicago, Illinois and Paris, France. The Nile is unusual in that it flows from south to north.

Egypt has two distinct sections, each identified in terms of the Nile. Upper Egypt (further south, closer to the river's origin) is a valley, while Lower Egypt (nearer the Mediterranean) is more flat. About a hundred miles before it reaches the coast, the Nile fans out into the delta, formed by the silt that the river carries with it.

The land surrounding the Nile is rich farm land. Before the completion of Aswan High Dam in 1970, the Nile flooded Egypt every summer as a result of rains and mountain snows farther south. The floods are now controlled, but the water still enriches the fields and helps produce more abundant crops. The floods on the Nile were more regular and predictable than those on the Tigris and Euphrates.

The Nile provides water and food (fish and irrigated crops) and enables trade and transportation. The ancient Egyptians believed that the god Osiris ruled the Nile, so he was an important deity in the minds of the people. It is significant that the plagues sent by God on the Egyptians showed that He, not Osiris, controlled the Nile.

Religious Beliefs

The Egyptians were a deeply religious people. Worship was central to their lives. They believed in many gods, but some were more important to them than others. The Egyptians saw many powerful forces working around them, such as the river and the sun. Sometimes these forces came into conflict. The people identified these forces as manifestations of individual gods instead of creations of the one true God (G. A. Henty's book *The Cat of Bubastes* tells how some Egyptians came to understand the reality of one God). The pharaoh was seen as a god himself.

At times the worship of gods became a political battle. Around 1375 BC, Pharaoh Akhnaten and Queen Nefertiti established the monotheistic worship of the sun god Aten (sometimes called Re or Ra). However, during the reign of Tutankhamen a few years later, the young pharaoh's advisers re-instituted polytheistic worship. As with the plagues that involved the Nile, God showed in the ninth plague that brought darkness on the land that He ruled even the sun.

The Egyptians had a well-developed belief system about life after death. They spent a great deal of time preparing for it. They believed that, after death, each individual was judged by Osiris according to their good or bad deeds. The condemned were eaten by a monster, but the righteous entered into a happy existence. People believed that they needed provisions for the after-life, so Egyptians were buried with food, furniture, and other items from this life. Wealthier people got to take more with them, but even poor Egyptians were buried with some supplies.

They also believed that the soul of a person needed a body in the after-life. This is why the Egyptians developed the practice of embalming or mummification to such an advanced degree. They wanted to be sure that the bodies of the deceased were prepared for the life after this life.

The Power of the Pharaoh

Because he was seen as a god, the pharaoh's power was absolute. The government of Egypt closely regulated the lives of the people. No law code was needed since the word of the pharaoh was law. The Egyptian people generally accepted this, and as a result Egypt endured relatively few upheavals in its government. All land was seen as belonging to the pharaoh as a gift from the gods. Genesis 47:20 says that Joseph bought all the land of the Egyptians for Pharaoh. We don't know exactly how this transaction was carried out, but it does reflect the idea that the pharaoh owned all of the land. The pharaoh's vizier, or second in command, carried out the pharaoh's will and oversaw the day-to-day administration of the country. Joseph probably held this position (Genesis 41:37-44).

In Egypt's earliest period, the villages along the Nile functioned as city-states much as the communities of Sumer did. Menes of Upper Egypt conquered the lower Nile Delta and unified Egypt under one government. Menes established his capital at Memphis near the delta, where it remained for nine hundred years. This period is called the Old Kingdom.

Menes introduced the first of some thirty dynasties that ruled Egypt until about 332 BC. Although the country had some periods of instability, the Egyptian system of government under a single pharaoh or king endured for almost two thousand years, longer than any other system of government in history. It makes the United States' existence of just over 200 years seem brief by comparison.

Many years after Menes, a series of weak pharaohs plunged the country into turmoil. Then a new dynasty re-established order. These rulers moved the capital up the Nile to Thebes and began the Middle Kingdom. Internal dissension and foreign threats brought another period of instability until another dynasty ushered in the New Kingdom.

Dating Ancient Civilizations

Assigning specific dates to events before 2000 BC is difficult because the records are unclear and contradictory. Isaac Newton, in his Chronology of Ancient Kingdoms Amended, *points out that ancient civilizations tended to exaggerate their early history. Modern scholars often give credence to the historical records from Egypt, Assyria, and Babylon, while denying the reliability of the Jewish records maintained in the Bible. Instead of changing the Bible to fit data from other sources, we should start with the Bible and use that as a basis for interpreting other data.*

According to the Bible, everyone on earth except Noah and his family was destroyed by the flood (1 Peter 3:20). This probably took place about 2500 years before Christ (2348 BC according to Ussher's chronology). Some small artifacts might have survived the flood, but large structures would have been destroyed. Therefore the pyramids and other existing structures must have been built after the flood.

Mizraim was a son of Ham and grandson of Noah. Mizraim is to this day the Hebrew name for the land of Egypt; the Arabic name for Egypt is Misr. Evidently Mizraim or his descendants settled in Egypt fairly soon after the flood. Historical sources also place the founding of Babylon, Greece, and China in the early 2000s BC.

Hieroglyphics Carved on a Wall at Luxor, Egypt

Advances in Writing

As a complex and busy civilization, Egypt developed a way to communicate and to record information in written form. At first they wrote pictures to represent objects, but this did not allow for the expression of ideas and abstract nouns. Egyptians later began using pictures or symbols to represent sounds. This form of writing is called hieroglyphics, which means sacred carvings. Two forms of hieroglyphics developed. The earlier form is known as hieratic and was used primarily by priests. The simpler form that developed later and was used more widely is called demotic.

The meaning of hieroglyphic symbols was lost around the fourth century AD and not rediscovered for about 1500 years. Napoleon's troops found a large rock slab in 1799 while working on a building project near the Egyptian city known to Westerners as Rosetta. The slab had on it an official decree dating from about 200 BC. It was written in three forms: Greek, hieratic, and demotic. Scholars worked for twenty years using the known Greek to translate the unknown hieroglyphic scripts. The Rosetta

Stone (now on display in the British Museum) was the breakthrough that enabled modern experts to understand hieroglyphic writing.

Egyptians also made a contribution to writing materials. The papyrus plant grew along the Nile. From this plant, the Egyptians cut long strips about one inch wide. The strips were laid side by side to make sheets, then dried and smoothed into scrolls for writing. Such documents could be carried and stored more easily than clay tablets. Papyrus sheets do decay over time; but they last longer in hot, dry climates such as Egypt's. With a written language and the availability of inexpensive writing materials, the Egyptians produced a large body of literature.

Writing materials eventually came to be made from wood products, but the papyrus sheets gave us the name we still use: paper.

The Book of the Dead is a collection of Egyptian religious writings related to their understanding of the afterlife. This papyrus page is from around 1050 BC.

ry, but Hatshepsut
prosperous reign.
d, Thutmose II,
ssumed power for
lished trade routes
ies and initiated
ruction projects.
r about 22 years

ame pharaoh at
he 1300s BC. He
ineteen. His main
the fact that his elaborate tomb filled with riches was
tact in 1922. The artifacts from "King Tut's Tomb" have
around the world. His burial mask is shown at left.

So Pharaoh said to Joseph, "Since God has informed you of all this,
there is no one so discerning and wise as you are.
You shall be over my house, and according to your command
all my people shall do homage; only in the throne I will be greater than you."
Genesis 41:39-40

Assignments for Lesson 12

Bible Read Genesis 28-30. Commentary available in *Student Review*.

In Their Words Read "The Autobiography of Aahmes" (pages 16-18).

Literature Continue reading *The Cat of Bubastes*.

Student Review Optional: Answer the questions for Lesson 12.

Sphinx and Pyramids at Giza, Egypt

Lesson 13 - Key Concepts

Ancient Science and Mathematics

Discovery is a great experience. To realize something that no one has realized before brings a unique feeling. This is a major difference between mankind and the animal world. We have no indication that deer or dogs understand a circle or a computer, or that they even know that they know anything. Human beings understand, discover, and know that they do both.

The Sumerian and Egyptian civilizations achieved significant scientific breakthroughs which we still admire and use today. God equipped them with minds and with the powers of observation and analysis. People in those ancient societies used their abilities to understand and affect the world in which they lived. History is more than just dynasties and wars. The history of science is one fascinating part of the story of mankind.

Sumerian Contributions

The old saying that necessity is the mother of invention is true. The challenges and opportunities of life present us with the motivation to advance and invent. So it was in Sumer. The opportunities of trade and business and the need for improved farming techniques, coupled with a curiosity about the world in which they lived, encouraged the innovations that the Sumerians developed.

The Sumerians are credited with developing the sailing ship for travel by sea. This was a great advance over rowing. As an agricultural people, Sumerians developed the yoke and the wheeled cart. They displayed considerable engineering prowess with the system of irrigation they developed using the Tigris and Euphrates Rivers to water their fields.

Sumer also saw the use of metal tools and weapons, particularly those made of bronze. Copper had been in use for some time, but around 1600 BC Sumerians discovered that blending tin with copper to make bronze created a much more durable material. The prominence of bronze continued until the development of iron implements beginning about 1200 BC. Perhaps Tubal-cain's developments in the use of metals had been lost after the flood and had to be rediscovered by the Sumerians (see Genesis 4:22).

Sumerians were interested in numbers and time. They used a base-10 counting system, but they also used a base-60 system which influences us even today. You can see the practicality of a base-60 system by considering how many numbers divide into sixty evenly: 1, 2, 3, 4, 5, 6, 10, 12, 15, 20, and 30. The scholars of Sumer divided the hour into sixty minutes and the minute into sixty seconds. The basic measure of weight was the shekel. Sixty shekels made one mina (about one pound), and sixty minas made one talent.

Mathematicians in Sumer divided the circle into 360 degrees and learned how to calculate the area of a rectangle (an important skill for building ziggurats with rectangular bases). They determined how to find the length of the hypotenuse of a right triangle and developed the concepts of the square root and the cube root. Multiplication tables also existed in ancient Mesopotamia.

The Sumerians and their successors took note of the starry firmament above them. They followed a lunar calendar that had seven-day weeks. Sumerian astronomers learned how to predict eclipses accurately. Observers in Hammurabi's time charted the movement of prominent heavenly bodies.

Sumerian and later Mesopotamian architecture was good, but builders were limited to some degree by the lack of stone in the region. They used the arch, the vault, and the dome in their construction; but mud bricks did not work as well in these features as the stone used much later in Roman buildings.

Contributions of Egypt

The Egyptians also took note of the skies. They developed a calendar with 365 days: twelve months with 30 days each and five extra days at the end of the year, but with no provision for a leap year. Each month had three cycles of ten days each, and the days were 24 hours long. Egyptians also developed the sundial to be able to tell the passage of time from the movement of the sun's shadow. They are credited with using water clocks by the time of the Exodus.

Residents of the Nile had a great interest in medicine. Their practice of embalming the dead led to their investigation of the human body. The frequent illnesses caused by parasites in the Nile River led to attempts to find cures. Egyptians had a great concern about cleanliness. Joseph observed that shepherds, whose occupation was not clean, were loathsome to the Egyptians (Genesis 46:34).

No doubt the best known scientific advance in Egypt was the building of the pyramids. These burial vaults were intended to be permanent, and the four-sided shape was recognized as the most durable. Stone was plentiful in Egypt, and the huge blocks were cut at the quarries and apparently rolled over log roads to the work site. Earthen ramps provided the scaffolding to raise the stones into place as the pyramids were built.

The largest pyramid, at Giza, is 476 feet high. Each side at the base is 760 feet long. By comparison, the Statue of Liberty is 151 feet high, with the base adding another 154 feet in height. The Giza pyramid is made of 2.3 million blocks, each weighing 2.5 tons. The sides were once covered with marble, but this material was stripped away by thieves long ago.

This Mesopotamian tablet (c. 1700 BC) shows a calculation for the square root of 2. The solution written on the tablet is expressed as a fraction. Rounded to eight decimal places, it is 1.41421296. The modern calculation rounded to eight decimal places is 1.41421356.

This page is from a document known as the Edwin Smith Papyrus. It provides diagnosis and treatment methods for 48 types of physical injury such as wounds to the skull, nose, neck, chest, and arm. The text shows a deep understanding of anatomy and medical care.

Ruins at Karnak

Another Egyptian contribution to architecture is the obelisk, a four-sided shaft sometimes made from a single stone. Obelisks were used to honor gods and rulers. The Washington Monument has the shape of an obelisk.

The temple of Amon at Karnak, constructed over a period of several hundred years, is the largest ancient religious site in the world. The temple is 1220 feet long and 340 feet wide, covering ten acres. It could contain four Gothic cathedrals from medieval Europe. The Great Hypostyle Hall has 134 huge columns, and the central worship area reaches seventy feet in height.

Conclusion

This lesson lists just a few of the many accomplishments and contributions of the Sumerian and Egyptian civilizations. Scientists, engineers, and mathematicians today benefit from the work of previous generations; but their counterparts in ancient Sumer and Egypt had fewer shoulders to stand on and fewer tools to use. The accomplishments of those ancient scientists are therefore even more remarkable and show what human beings can do.

As great as these works are, they are not as important in God's eyes as knowing Him. The pharaohs were laid to rest in impressive pyramids. By contrast, Moses as a child was laid in a simple basket covered with tar and pitch. We know whom God held in higher esteem. The pyramids are not even mentioned in Scripture.

[The children of Israel] built for Pharaoh
storage cities, Pithom and Raamses.
Exodus 1:11

Assignments for Lesson 13

Bible   Read Genesis 31-33. Commentary available in *Student Review*.

Literature   Continue reading *The Cat of Bubastes*.

Student Review   Optional: Answer the questions for Lesson 13.

Hammurabi and His Code of Laws

When Anu the Sublime, King of the Anunaki, and Bel, the lord of heaven and earth, who decreed the fate of the land, assigned to Marduk, the over-ruling son of Ea, god of righteousness, dominion over earthly man, and made him great among the Igigi, they called Babylon by its illustrious name, made it great on earth, and founded an everlasting kingdom in it, whose foundations are laid so solidly as those of heaven and earth; then Anu and Bel called by name me, Hammurabi, the exalted prince, who feared god, to bring about the rule of righteousness in the land, to destroy the wicked and the evil-doers; so that the strong should not harm the weak; so that I should rule over the black-headed people like Shamash, and enlighten the land, to further the well-being of mankind.

Hammurabi, the prince, called of Bel am I, making riches and increase, enriching Nippur and Dur-ilu beyond compare, sublime patron of E-kur; who reestablished Eridu and purified the worship of E-apsu; who conquered the four quarters of the world, made great the name of Babylon, rejoiced the heart of Marduk, his lord who daily pays his devotions in Saggil. . . . When Marduk sent me to rule over men, to give the protection of right to the land; I did right and righteousness . . . and brought about the well-being of the oppressed.

So begins the most famous legal document of ancient times outside of the Bible, the Law Code of Hammurabi, king of Babylon.

Hammurabi was king around 1790-1750 BC. His military exploits allowed him to gain control over the entire Mesopotamian region. The extensive records that his administration kept reveal him to have been an adept leader and successful warrior. Hammurabi established an effective civil service system that enabled him to administer a large area.

The law code that was published during Hammurabi's reign is an example of his administrative skills.

In an absolute monarchy such as ancient Babylon, the word of the king was the ultimate law. This was especially true when the king was seen as having been sent by the gods or seen as being a god himself. Since Hammurabi did not want to handle each legal case himself, he established a code for his kingdom that gave judges guidance in how to decide cases that came before them.

Hammurabi and the Babylonian god of justice, Shamash. Apparently Shamash is dictating the law to Hammurabi, which indicates the king's belief that the law was divinely inspired.

The Code of Hammurabi includes 282 specific provisions that cover matters related to social classes, property rights, trade, personal assaults, and marriage and family issues as well as justice and equity. Most are presented as case law; that is, if something happens, this is what should be done.

The code was not the earliest system of laws in ancient times. Laws had been developed and followed for centuries before his day. Hammurabi's code is significant for several reasons. First, it is the

---

"The Seven Laws of Noah"

Through Moses, God gave the Israelites 613 laws regulating their relationship with God and with each other. According to Jewish tradition, God had previously given seven laws that applied to all the descendants of Noah, Jews and Gentiles alike.

1. *Prohibition of Idolatry*
2. *Prohibition of Murder*
3. *Prohibition of Theft*
4. *Prohibition of Sexual Immorality*

5. *Prohibition of Blasphemy*
6. *Prohibition of Eating Flesh with Blood*
7. *Requirement to Maintain Courts*

The collection of Jewish commentaries known as the Talmud indicates that Gentiles who follow these laws will be considered righteous by God. Comparing this list to the conclusions of the Jerusalem council described in Acts 15 is interesting. The church leaders agreed that Gentiles did not need to follow the entire law. But they were instructed to abstain from food sacrificed to idols, from blood and things strangled, and from sexual immorality. Murder, theft, and blasphemy understandably violate the commands to love God and our neighbor.

All law codes recognize that there is a standard of behavior to which we should aspire. Paul talks about Gentiles who do by nature the things of the Law; they show that the work of the Law is written in their hearts (Romans 2). Since each person commits sin, no one can stand before God justified by his own behavior. Jesus provided a way for both Jews and Gentiles to find salvation through Him.

earliest and most complete law code that we know, even though portions of it are missing. Second, it provided a uniform system of justice for his entire kingdom. Third, the code was inscribed on a black stone pillar in a public place for all to see and to be warned. Fourth, the code created a society of laws and not of men, so that justice could be administered fairly.

For the Lord is our judge, the Lord is our lawgiver,
the Lord is our king; He will save us.
Isaiah 33:22

Assignments for Lesson 14

Bible   Read Genesis 34-36. Commentary available in *Student Review*.

In Their Words   Read the excerpts from the Code of Hammurabi (pages 19-21).

Literature   Continue reading *The Cat of Bubastes*.

Student Review   Optional: Answer the questions for Lesson 14.

Ruins of Dura Europos on the Euphrates River, Near Al-Salihiyah, Syria

The Land Between the Rivers

The land known in ancient times as Sumer, Mesopotamia, and Babylon, and now known as Iraq, has played a significant role in world history, Biblical history, and modern history. Both the Old and New Testaments give deep significance to the area. The land figures prominently in the first book of the Bible; and the name Babylon is used in the last book of the Bible.

As we study the Biblical record, we need to remember that Sumer, Babylon, Mesopotamia, and Iraq are not all the same exact land. They have not all had the same borders, although they have covered some of the same land area. In addition, other kingdoms, such as Assyria and Persia, once controlled parts of what is now Iraq; but again the borders of those kingdoms were not the same as those of Sumer, Babylon, Mesopotamia, or Iraq.

We should also remember that ethnic Arabs, who make up the majority of the population there today, are not the same people group that inhabited Sumer and Babylon in ancient times. The region has seen many people movements over the centuries.

To understand how such a change can happen, consider the changes in the ethnicity of the people who live in the area that is now the United States. Once all the people who lived here were Native Americans; but now, because of wars with European settlers, disease, migration, and other factors, only a small percentage of the people who live in the U.S. today are Native Americans.

The Tigris and Euphrates Rivers flow into the Persian Gulf (lower right on map). The yellow area shows the watershed area of the rivers. The map shows modern political boundaries, and the countries that are part of the watershed area are labeled.

Old Testament

The Tower of Babel, man's attempt to reach heaven by his own will and skill, was in the plain of Shinar (Genesis 11:2), which became Babylon. Abraham and his family moved from Ur of the Chaldees, the area that now includes southern Iraq. They settled for a time at Haran (Genesis 11:31-32), a city located in what is now Turkey. Abraham sent his servant to Nahor in Mesopotamia to find a wife for Isaac (Genesis 24:10). Isaac sent Jacob to get a wife in Paddan-Aram, which was also in Mesopotamia but is now in modern Turkey (Genesis 28:2).

During the time that Israel was in the wilderness following the Exodus, Balak king of Moab sent for the prophet Balaam at Pethor, which was "near the river" (that is, the Euphrates; Numbers 22:5). Balak wanted Balaam to prophesy against Israel. Balaam was willing to do so for a price, but the Lord inspired him instead to prophesy praise for Israel and doom for Balak (Numbers 23:1-24:25). Balaam is referred to several times in the Bible as an example of evil and error (for example, Nehemiah 13:2 and Revelation 2:14). Israelites killed Balaam during the conquest of Canaan (Joshua 13:22).

In the period of the Judges, one of the defeats Israel suffered because of her sin was at the hands of Cushan-rishathaim, king of Mesopotamia. I served him for eight years until the Lord the judge Othniel, who defeated the (Judges 3:8, 10).

Jonah preached aga Nineveh, capital of the Assyrian emp eh is located in what is now Iraq. Nineveh repented at the preaching of Jonah, but apparently their repentance did not stick. Later, Nahum preached against the sins of the city and predicted its downfall. The Assyrians defeated the Northern Kingdom of Israel and carried many of its people into captivity (2 Kings 17:6-26).

Assyria fell to the Babylonian Empire. The Babylonian king Nebuchadnezzar defeated the Southern Kingdom of Judah, and many from Judah were carried into exile (2 Kings 25:1-12). The prophet Habakkuk agonized over the sins of Judah, but he also agonized over the idolatry of the Babylonians (also called the Chaldeans).

During the time of the exile, Daniel showed great faith in God as an exile in Babylon. The book of Daniel is set in Babylon and also tells of the faith of the exiles Shadrach, Meshach, and Abednego. Ezekiel prophesied to the exiles in Babylon. Psalm 137 is a lament by an exile who longs to see Jerusalem again and who prays for God's revenge against Babylon.

The Persian Empire arose and defeated Babylon. The book of Esther describes events that took place during the Persian Empire in its capital of Susa. Susa (or Shushan) is in modern Iran, but much earlier it was ruled by Hammurabi. The stone column on which is inscribed the law code of Hammurabi was found in Susa.

The lamassu was an Assyrian deity represented by the body of a bull or lion with a human head and the wings of an eagle. This one was found in the palace of Dur Sharrukin in modern Khorsabad, Iraq.

The New Testament

The New Testament has fewer references to Mesopotamia, since the dominant power in that day was the Roman Empire. "Residents of Mesopotamia" were present on the Day of Pentecost when the Holy Spirit was poured out and the Lord's church began (Acts 2:9). These Mesopotamian Jews were apparently descendants of exiles who had continued to live in Mesopotamia even after the Jews had been allowed to return to Judah following the exile.

The two main references to Babylon in the New Testament occur in Revelation and 1 Peter. John had a vision of a woman on a scarlet beast, clothed as royalty but bearing a cup of abominations and immorality. On her forehead was written, "Babylon the Great, the mother of harlots and of the abominations of the earth" (Revelation 17:3-5). A clue to the woman's identity is given in verse 9, where she is described as sitting on seven hills or mountains. The city of Rome sits on seven hills. This image was apparently portraying the pagan Roman Empire as the great, immoral enemy of the church at that time. It was called Babylon because, to people of Jewish background, Babylon was the great pagan enemy that had carried their forefathers into

This is a 19th-century Russian illustration of Babylon as described in Revelation.

captivity centuries earlier. Peter also apparently uses this term to describe Rome when he says in 1 Peter 5:13, "She who is in Babylon, chosen together with you, sends you greetings." This was probably a veiled reference to the fellowship of believers in Rome.

Later History of the Area

According to tradition, the apostles Thomas and Thaddeus brought the gospel to Mesopotamia in the first century AD. Persian empires controlled the area for several hundred years, with a brief period of control by the Romans.

Arab believers of Islam conquered the region in the seventh century, then the Mongols took control in the 13th century. The Ottoman Empire, based in what is now Turkey, ruled the region beginning in 1638. Following the period of British control during and after World War I, the country of Iraq endured a long period of instability. A coup in 1968 gave power to the Baath political party. The original Baath leader was succeeded in 1979 by Saddam Hussein.

Under Saddam Iraq fought a long and indecisive war with Iran (1980-1988) and crushed an attempted rebellion by the Kurds in northern Iraq. Saddam invaded the tiny but wealthy country of Kuwait, south of Iraq, in 1990. A coalition of forces led by the United States pushed the Iraqis out of

Mongol forces under the command of Hulagu Khan laid siege to the city of Bagdad in 1258 and captured it. This illustration is from a 14th-century Mongol history of the world.

Lesson 15 - Bible Study: The Land Between the Rivers

This image shows American, British, and Australian planes during Operation Iraqi Freedom. Poland sent soldiers during the initial invasion, and local Kurdish forces also participated. After the initial invasion, thirty-six other countries sent military personnel to help.

Kuwait the next year. For the next decade, Iraq and the United Nations waged a continuing diplomatic battle over Iraq's development of atomic, biological, and chemical weapons (together called weapons of mass destruction). Iraq denied having such weapons but refused to let UN inspectors have full access.

Following the September 11, 2001, terrorist attacks on the United States, President George W. Bush identified Iraq as a main supporter of world terrorism. After Iraq continued to refuse to change its policies, a coalition of forces led by the United States invaded Iraq in early 2003 and toppled Saddam's regime in Operation Iraqi Freedom. Saddam himself was later captured and executed.

Elections for a new parliament in Iraq were held in March of 2010, and all coalition combat troops left the country by the end of 2011.

Conclusion

The number of Christians in Iraq has been relatively small (less than 3%) for many years. After the American invasion, perhaps as many as half of the Christians fled to Syria, Jordan, and Lebanon because of sectarian violence and persecution.

The land which saw early developments of civilization has often been led by aggressive and ungodly leaders. God's people have frequently suffered at the hands of those in power in Mesopotamia. God loves the people of Iraq, and we can pray that the gospel of Christ will make a difference in the hearts and lives of the people and leaders in the land between the rivers.

Dhief Muhsen (left), a guide and caretaker at the site of ancient Ur in Iraq, met with American soldiers from the South Carolina National Guard in 2009. Here he poses with Chaplain (Major) Steve Shugart.

By the rivers of Babylon,
There we sat down and wept,
When we remembered Zion.
Psalm 137:1

Dair Mar Elia was established around 600 AD. Known in English as Saint Elijah's Monastery, it flourished for centuries as a religious center. The existing buildings date from the 1500s. A Persian leader ordered the destruction of the monastery in 1743.

Assignments for Lesson 15

Bible   Read Genesis 37-39. Commentary available in *Student Review*.
Recite or write Job 42:1-6 from memory.

Literature   Continue reading *The Cat of Bubastes*.

Project   Complete your project for the week.

Student Review   Optional: Answer the questions for Lesson 15 and take the quiz for Unit 3.

4

Abraham and His Descendants

Summary   God chose Abram from Ur to create a nation that belonged to Him. One trait that Abram (or Abraham) is best known for is his faith in God. Abraham lived the life of a nomad, which some people still live today. We see what God did to the evil that was present in Sodom and Gomorrah, and we see the good that God brought out of the amazing story of Joseph.

Lessons   16 - Abraham, Isaac, and Jacob
17 - Key Concept: The Faith of Abraham
18 - Everyday Life: Nomads
19 - Key Event: The Destruction of Sodom and Gomorrah
20 - Bible Study: "God Meant It for Good"

Detail from Jacob's Dream, *James Thornhill (English, 1705)*

Memory Work

Learn Genesis 12:2-3 by the end of the unit.

Books Used

The Bible

The Cat of Bubastes

Project (choose one)

1) Write 300 to 500 words on one of the following topics:

- How would your life be different if your family were nomads? What would be better? What would be harder? See Lesson 18.

- Write about one or more characteristics you admire in either Abraham or Joseph. See Lesson 17 or Lesson 20.

2) Design and create a board game for your family to play about the lives of the patriarchs Abraham, Isaac, and Jacob and their families. Use questions and answers from Genesis 11-50 as part of the game. See Lesson 16.

3) Write a play based on one or more events and/or one or more people discussed in this unit. Your play should be at least seven pages long, but can be as long as you like. Recruiting family and/or friends to perform your play might be fun but is optional.

Lesson 16

Abraham, Isaac, and Jacob

When God confused the language of the people who attempted to build the Tower of Babel, He "scattered them abroad over the face of the whole earth" (Genesis 11:9). Soon a small people movement began in Mesopotamia, one that would take a man and his household to Canaan on the Mediterranean coast. This man began a nation that impacted the entire world.

Terah was a Semite (a descendant of Shem) who lived in Ur of the Chaldeans. He was the father of Abram, Nahor, and Haran. Terah moved with Abram,

Abram's wife Sarai, and Lot, the son of Haran, to the city of Haran in northern Mesopotamia. Haran was on a major trade route. There Terah settled and later died.

The Calling of Abram

God had many individuals and people groups to choose from, but He chose Abram of Ur to be the founder of the nation that would be known as Israel. Joshua 24:2 says that Terah served other gods, so Abram's family background was pagan. Acts 7:2-4 tells us that God appeared to Abram before he came to Haran and called him to Canaan.

Abram's response to this call is a demonstration of his faith in the one true God. Just as He did with Noah and the flood, God was starting again, this time with Abram the Semite. God had a plan for people to leave idolatry and worship Him. His plan included a Savior for all the world who would come centuries later to the people of Israel.

After Abram arrived in Canaan, God told him that this was the land He would give to his

Abraham's Journey from Ur to Canaan
József Molnár (Hungarian, 1850)

75

descendants. Abram built altars to God and called upon His name. God showed Abram that He was not just a local god of Ur or Haran. He was present wherever Abram was because He was God of the whole world. Abram committed himself to God by worshiping Him there. This is significant since the Canaanites were living in the land, and they were definitely not worshipers of God.

God's Covenant with Abraham

God told Abram that his descendants would be as numerous as the stars and committed Himself to Abram in a dramatic covenant scene. Following God's instructions, Abram cut animal carcasses in half, and the Lord passed between the pieces as a flaming torch. This ceremony was a common way to confirm an agreement between two parties. The one who passed between the pieces of carcass was saying, "May I wind up like these pieces if I do not keep the agreement I am making today." God showed Abram how serious He was about His plan for Abram.

Abram faltered in his faith when Sarai became impatient about having a child. She urged Abram

This 17th-century engraving by Czech artist Wenceslaus Hollar depicts Abraham and Lot separating.

to father an heir through her handmaiden Hagar. This type of surrogacy was known and accepted at the time, but it was not part of God's stated plan. The child produced through this union was Ishmael, from whom the Arab people are descended; thus both Jews and Arabs consider Abram their forefather.

God reconfirmed His covenant with Abram, revealing a new name for Himself: El Shaddai, God Almighty (Genesis 17:1). The confirmatory sign of the covenant was to be the circumcision of male children, indicating the total commitment of the people to God. Circumcision was practiced by other (though not all) Middle Eastern nations, but it was often performed at puberty and not soon after a boy's birth.

The Lord also gave Abram and Sarai new names. In this way, God was putting all of Abram's past behind him and giving him a new future as the bearer of God's covenant of promise. God changed Abram's name from Abram (exalted father) to Abraham (father of a multitude). Sarai became Sarah (both names mean princess; the difference is just in the spelling). Despite their incredulity, God assured the couple that a child born to their union would be the fulfillment of God's promise to make a great nation.

Abraham and Sarah both laughed at the thought of becoming parents at their advanced ages. Appropriately enough, God said their son's name would be Isaac, which means "he laughs." The name could be something of a dig at Abraham's skepticism, but what a joyful thought that the child of one's old age would be named Laughter!

Isaac and Jacob

When Abraham was one hundred and Sarah was ninety, Sarah did indeed give birth to Isaac as God had promised. The child grew to be a man, and the happy family had about thirty-seven years together.

Lesson 16 - Abraham, Isaac, and Jacob

The Meeting of Isaac and Rebecca
Giovanni Benedetto Castiglione (Italian, c. 1640)

A few years after Sarah's death, when Isaac was forty, Abraham instructed his servant to find a wife for Isaac among their own people in Mesopotamia, not from among the Canaanites. God led the servant to Rebekah, Abraham's great-niece, the granddaughter of Abraham's brother Nahor.

God reconfirmed to Isaac the promise He had made to Abraham that Isaac would have many descendants. Isaac and Rebekah were the parents of twins, Jacob and Esau. The two brothers had a tumultuous relationship from before birth through manhood.

Esau married two Hittite women, which brought grief to Isaac and Rebekah. Esau later took an Ishmaelite wife as well. Isaac instructed Jacob to find a wife among their family, as Abraham had done for him. Jacob went to the household of his uncle Laban in Paddan-aram (in Mesopotamia),

The Cave of Macpelah

When Sarah died, Abraham negotiated with Ephron the Hittite for a cave in which to bury her, as recorded in Genesis 23. The arrangement that was made reflected the Hittite customs of the day. Ephron's offer in verse 11 to give the land to Abraham was a common bargaining maneuver to make the seller look generous. Abraham wanted to buy only the cave because the purchaser of an entire piece of property was expected to follow certain requirements. When Abraham agreed to buy the property, he wanted to make it clear that title was transferred completely to him. Verse 17 mentions the trees on the tract of land that Abraham purchased. Hittite land contracts customarily made specific mention of the trees on land being sold, perhaps to make clear the timber rights associated with a piece of property in a region where trees were precious commodities. (By the way, no archaeological record of the Hittites was known until about 1900. Before then, skeptics wondered if such a people really existed. The discoveries confirmed again that the Bible is true.)

About 30 years before Jesus was born, Herod the Great ordered the construction of a large rectangular structure over a cavern in the town of Hebron (in the modern West Bank). The tombs in the cavern were believed to be those of Abraham, Sarah, Isaac, Rebekah, Jacob, and Leah. The site has since been a place of pligrimage for Jews, Christians, and Muslims. The exterior, as shown at right, remains largely as it was built originally except for the two minarets on the corners, built by Muslims under Saladin in the time of the Crusades. The interior decorations have been modified extensively over the centuries as control of the location changed hands.

who turned out to be a trickster equal to Jacob. Jacob wound up marrying two daughters of Laban and having children by handmaidens of the sisters as well.

In a dramatic and somewhat mysterious scene, Jacob wrestled with a man at night. At the end of their struggle, the man gave Jacob a new name, Israel, which means striven with God. Jacob was given an intimacy with God that sometimes took the form of a struggle, but God worked through him in a mighty way to create a nation that would be His chosen people. The sons of Jacob became the founders of the tribes of Israel.

Lessons from the Patriarchs

Abraham, Isaac, Jacob, and Jacob's sons are called the patriarchs (the term is from the Greek and means father-leader). A patriarch was the unquestioned leader of his family and household. The patriarch saw to the choosing of a wife for his son (hence Esau's selection of his own wives is especially rebellious). The oldest male child inherited the position of family leader, and the patriarch bestowed upon the oldest son his special blessing. This tradition made Jacob's supplanting of Esau especially shocking.

This fresco (c. 1293) by Italian painter Giotto Di Bondone depicts Isaac rejecting Esau after Jacob stole the blessing.

Polygamy

The pattern for marriage in the Bible is one man and one woman for life (Genesis 2:24). Some men in the Bible practiced polygamy, which is the marrying of more than one woman. The Bible does not directly condemn polygamy, but it speaks of it in a way that shows God's disapproval of it.

Men have practiced polygamy to show their power and prestige to other men. Wrong as polygamy is, God can still work through it, as He did in the case of Jacob to create the nation of Israel.

Rachel Hiding the Idols, *Giovanni Battista Tiepolo (Italian, 1728)*

The Biblical patriarchs give us a good illustration of how the man as husband and father is to lead his family today. God's plan is for the man to lead in his home. One great temptation that men face is to fail to carry out this role, either by abandoning it or by assuming an unloving and dictatorial posture. In any system, when things are not right with the leadership, the entire system breaks down, as we can see in many homes today.

We must be aware, however, that the Biblical patriarchs were not perfect, cardboard-cutout heroes. They had both strengths and weaknesses. Abraham let Sarah push him around. Abraham and Isaac lied about the identity of their wives. Jacob took advantage of his brother by deceit, and his sons committed a variety of serious wrongs. We must not use the patriarchs in Genesis as justification for non-Biblical ideas about male leadership in the family, but we can learn something of God's intention for the family from them. The important thing about them was how they made themselves available to God and how God in His sovereignty worked through them.

The story of Abraham and his descendants shows how a nation is formed. One man makes a new start. Often he moves to a new place. In Abraham's case, the new nation was God's idea; and God worked with this nation for centuries to bring forth the Savior of the world.

Do not fear, Abram, I am a shield to you;
Your reward shall be very great.
Genesis 15:1

Assignments for Lesson 16

Bible Read Genesis 40-42. Commentary available in *Student Review*.

Literature Continue reading *The Cat of Bubastes*. Plan to finish it by the end of Unit 5.

Student Review Optional: Answer the questions for Lesson 16.

Mosaic of the Twelve Tribes of Israel from
the Givat Mordechai Synagogue in Jerusalem

Lesson 17 - Key Concept

The Faith of Abraham

In Romans 4, Paul cites Abraham as an example of what faith in God means. James uses Abraham as an example of faith that is demonstrated by action (James 2:21-24). In the roll call of the faithful in Hebrews 11, the author describes both Abraham and Sarah as living by faith; that is, by "the assurance of things hoped for, the conviction of things not seen" (Hebrews 11:1). Obviously, the faith of the Old Testament figure Abraham was an important example for the New Testament church.

The faith of Abraham made a difference in world history. Abraham led a people movement because of his faith in God. Later, Abraham's descendants, the children of Israel, took over the Promised Land on the same basis of faith. The faith of Abraham serves as a model for Christians, who are part of the most significant religious movement in world history. One of the main concepts in the Bible, the most important book in world history, is faith in God. To understand the Biblical concept of faith, we should examine the faith of Abraham.

Examples of Abraham's Faith

Abraham demonstrated faith when he followed God's call and left his homeland and his extended family to move to Canaan. God was unseen, and the culture in which Abraham lived did not believe in Him. Abraham chose to trust the word that God spoke to him as authoritative for his life, and he showed his faith by obeying God and moving to a new land. Abraham was literally trusting his life, his fortune, and his destiny to the unseen God who had called him.

The Lord promised that Abraham's descendants would become a great nation (Genesis 12:2). Abraham wondered how this could be since he had no children. Abraham had either adopted or designated one of his servants, Eliezer of Damascus, to be the heir of his fortune. God promised Abraham that a son he would beget would be his heir. The Lord promised that Abraham's descendants through this son would be as numerous as the stars (Genesis 15:1-5).

At this point, Abraham faced a choice. He could either reject the word of God, continue to question it, or decide to believe it. Abraham had already shown a willingness to trust God's word. Continuing to question God would only delay the decision he had to make. So Abraham decided to believe. In response, God credited Abraham's faith as righteousness (Genesis 15:6). As good as he was, Abraham's actions did not qualify him to be considered righteous (or justified; the word is the same in Greek) in God's eyes. God accepted Abraham's faith as the substitute for good actions and declared him to be justified.

Abraham showed faith in God by accepting circumcision as the sign of the covenant as God commanded (Genesis 17:9-14, 23-27). Circumcision is no small matter, but God wanted Abraham and all of the adult men in his household to undergo the painful procedure. Abraham could have chosen not to do it, or he could have not insisted that the men in his household submit to it. However, Abraham wanted his obedience to be complete; so he obeyed the commandment of circumcision.

Abraham demonstrated faith when he pleaded with the Lord on behalf of Sodom and Gomorrah (Genesis 18:22-33). Abraham no doubt was concerned about his nephew Lot and hoped that God would not destroy him. But in a larger sense, the patriarch was also troubled by the prospect of God sweeping away righteous people while He was destroying the two wicked cities. As Abraham put it, "Shall not the Judge of all the earth deal justly?" (Genesis 18:25). Abraham believed that God would always do right, and the destruction of undeserving people did not fit into Abraham's definition of dealing justly. Abraham's faith in God was proved to be well-placed. God promised that He would not destroy the cities if even as few as ten righteous people were found there. Sadly, God could not even find that many righteous people to justify sparing the cities. God is not only just, He is merciful.

The Sacrifice of Isaac

The greatest test of Abraham's faith occurred when God told him to offer Isaac as a sacrifice on an altar on a mountain of Moriah (Genesis 22). How shocking and seemingly not in keeping with God's character this commandment must have seemed to Abraham, who had come to trust God deeply. It seemed to wipe out the promise that God had made that Isaac would enable the fulfillment of God's promise to Abraham. Abraham could have doubted God, or doubted the message, or doubted whether he could actually do the deed. Nevertheless, Abraham continued to show his trusting faith when he took all the steps necessary to complete the painful task and raised the knife to slay his son.

God was still in charge. He kept Abraham from taking his son's life because He had a greater purpose than to have Abraham engage in child sacrifice. God wanted to see whether Abraham trusted the gift God had given him (namely, Isaac) or God Himself, the Giver. Isaac was a great blessing to Abraham, but the old man showed that he trusted God more. We can be deeply appreciative of the good gifts of God but then come to be dependent on having good things and good times in order to trust God. When difficult times come and God's blessings are stripped away from us, we are still called to trust God.

According to Hebrews 11:19, Abraham believed that God could raise men from the dead. Despite God's command to sacrifice Isaac, Abraham still

Two depictions of Abraham and Isaac: 12th-century Italy at right; 18th-century Ethiopia below.

The Dismissal of Hagar, *Pieter Lastman (Dutch, 1612)*

trusted that God would keep His promise through Isaac; and resurrection from the dead was the only way Abraham saw that it could happen if he carried through with the sacrifice. God gave Abraham an even better blessing by keeping him from killing his son at all. Abraham drew no line on his faith in God. He did not say that he would trust the Lord thus far but no further. His preparations for sacrificing Isaac show how strong Abraham's faith was.

Abraham's Failings of Faith

Exemplary as it was, however, Abraham's faith was not perfect. He stumbled at times in his trust of God. On two different occasions Abraham misled others to protect his own life. He feared that first Pharaoh and then Abimelech would do away with him in order to take Sarah as a wife (Genesis 12:10-20, 20:1-18). Abraham allowed Sarah's impatience to push him into lying with Hagar in order to produce an heir. This was after God had promised to give him a son by Sarah (Genesis 16:1-5). Abraham laughed when God promised that he would have a son (Genesis 17:17).

No one's faith is perfect. These stories about Abraham's failings show that (1) the Bible tells the truth, even including the weaknesses and failings of its heroes; and (2) God can work through someone who has imperfect faith. When we fail in our faith, God is still in charge and can bring about His will. Abraham and all of the other heroes of the Bible had their failings; but in the last analysis they trusted God, and as a result God was able to use them. Our call is to do the same: not to have a flawless faith but to be available to God so He can accomplish His will through us.

Faith in a Faithless World

Abraham's trust of God was remarkable. Although God created the world, mankind repeatedly turned away from Him and failed to follow Him. Despite His blessings and His warnings, the civilizations that developed in the early years of mankind did not know or honor God. Out of the pagan city of Ur in the Chaldeans, and away from the pagan family with whom he lived, Abraham responded with faith to the call of the one true God. God's purpose was not just to create a new nation through Abraham, but to create a nation that would honor Him and live as the light of truth to a world darkened by idolatry and unbelief. Through many twists and turns in the story, God accomplished His purpose in the nation of Israel. From Israel came Jesus, the Savior of all the world.

The world in which we live does not, for the most part, believe in God. God calls us to put our faith in Him without drawing a line about how much we will believe. He wants His people to be a shining example of faith so that others will be drawn to saving faith in the Lord Jesus. We don't have to be perfect, just available. If we are available, even in times of trial, difficulty, and questions, God will accomplish great things through us.

So then those who are of faith are blessed with Abraham the believer.
Galatians 3:9

Assignments for Lesson 17

Bible Read Genesis 43-46. Commentary available in *Student Review*.

Literature Continue reading *The Cat of Bubastes*.

Student Review Optional: Answer the questions for Lesson 17.

Lesson 18 - Everyday Life

Nomads

Omar is a nomad. In many ways his life is similar to the life that Abraham, Isaac, and Jacob knew thousands of years ago. Throughout history some people groups have chosen a nomadic life while others have chosen to live in a settled location. Still others have chosen a semi-nomadic life. Omar is a Bedouin, a nomadic ethnic group that has traditionally herded camels, goats, and sheep in the deserts of the Middle East and North Africa.

Desert Dwellers and Their Descendants

The word *bedawi* means "desert dweller" in Arabic, which is the language of the Bedouins. The traditional Bedouin home is a tent. A tent houses one family. Families belonging to the same clan camp together. Several clans make up a tribe, which can have as few as fifty members or as many as several hundred. The head of a tribe is a shaykh (or sheikh). He is assisted by a council of elders.

Desert survival skills have been passed down from one generation to another for centuries. According to a Bedouin proverb, "The elderly are the books of the young."

Bedouin men are responsible for making the important decisions necessary to survive in the harsh desert environment. They do not wander aimlessly following their herds, but use their knowledge of the desert to lead them to water and the best grazing areas.

The Bedouin people migrate with the seasons. During winter when there is rain, they go deep into the desert. During the hot, dry summers, they gather in large numbers near water sources which are often near towns and markets. Here they sell or barter with sedentary people to obtain foods they need in

Some of the Sami people of Scandinavia continue to live a semi-nomadic life herding reindeer. This photo was taken around 1896 in Norway.

addition to the meat and dairy products obtained from their herds.

Animals are central to Bedouin culture. In addition to caring for their herds, the Bedouin have a tradition of capturing wild falcons and training them for hunting. The birds became almost a member of the family. After the long process of training, the falcon's master would use it for hunting for a period of time and then return it to the wild. Falconry continues as a popular sport among the Bedouins. They also breed and train saluki hunting dogs. Bedouins have bred and trained Arabian horses for centuries. Their original purpose was for war.

Older men pass down stories and traditions to the younger generations. Young men feel honored to be able to listen to their parents and grandparents tell the stories of the past. Arabian horses were such an integral part of Bedouin culture that the family history of the horses, along with tales of bravery by particular horses, were passed down in much the same way as the stories of the people themselves.

At Home Among the Bedouins

In Bedouin culture, women do most of the physical labor, including making the tent. They gather animal hair, use a wooden spindle to spin it into thread, and weave long narrow rugs which they sew together to make the outside wall and the top of the tent. Women enjoy the social activity of weaving, which they do in groups. They also weave rugs, cushions which are stuffed with wool from their sheep, and other furnishings. When it is time to move on, the women are responsible for taking the tent down, loading it on camels, and setting it back up when the group reaches its next destination.

The tent has a men's section and a women's section. These are divided by a beautifully decorated curtain. In addition to leading their families, clans, and tribes, Bedouin men also spend time socializing with one another and practicing hospitality to visitors. Male guests gather around the hearth in the men's section to enjoy the generous hospitality

The International Festival of the Sahara in Douz, Tunisia, attracts thousands of attendees each year. It highlights traditional nomadic life with music, poetry reading, a Bedouin wedding ceremony, and camel races.

which Bedouins have practiced for centuries. Note when Abraham entertained visitors in Genesis 18:1-8. See also Jesus' parable of the friend at midnight in Luke 11:5-8.

Guests are welcomed with tea and a special meal. After dinner the host prepares coffee on the fire in the hearth. It is sometimes spiced with cardamom. He and his guests share news and talk about their herds. One man sings or recites poetry, an art form that has been important to the Bedouins for many generations. The evening's entertainment may also include music. The main musical instruments of the Bedouin are the voice and clapping hands, but the entertainment sometimes includes the music of a metal flute or a one-string type of violin.

Women sleep in the women's section. Here they care for the children, who also sleep in this section. Boys remain with their mothers until they are about seven years old. Another responsibility of a Bedouin woman is caring for the elderly.

The women's section of the tent includes a kitchen and a storage area. Women gather fuel for cooking and they prepare meals. The women prepare stone-ground wheat flour and use it to bake round loaves of unleavened bread, sometimes using an outdoor sand oven. Dates found in desert oases are common desserts. They make yogurt from the milk of camels and goats. From goat milk, they also make cheese and a type of butter called ghee, which is sometimes served over rice.

Bedouin Clothing

Women make traditional Bedouin clothing from the wool and hair of camels, sheep, and goats or from cotton. Men wear a long, loose, light-colored tunic. It is topped with a sleeveless cloak, sometimes made of silk. The loose fit allows air to circulate. This keeps sweat from evaporating too quickly, which helps the Bedouins keep from dehydrating in the hot, dry air of the desert. Bedouin men wear a leather belt and also a headcloth called a kufiyya. The kufiyya helps to keep the wearer warm and serves as a shield from wind, sun, and sand. It is held in place by an agal made of wool ropes. The style of the ropes indicates the man's status within the tribe.

Women wear loose garments. Black is common in many tribes. The front of a Bedouin woman's garment is often highly decorated with embroidery. They also wear expensive jewels. Their headcovering covers their heads and faces. When a Bedouin dies, it is customary to leave the deceased person's clothes on top of his or her grave, so that a passerby in need can use them.

Relations Between Tribes and With The Outside World

Nomads almost by definition do not own land. They need to access land, however, to feed their animals, so the issues of land ownership and usage are real. Tribes respect the traditional land used by other tribes. As nomads in the ancient world moved around, they had to be aware of the various jurisdictions of kings (border issues among modern nations are similar). When Sarah died, Abraham had to buy property that included a cave. Abraham was treated by the Hittites as a wealthy resident who didn't own land (or at least not the kind of land that he needed).

Nomads in the ancient world lived in extended families with a few servants or hired workers. A small number of people was vulnerable to attack, while a huge number was difficult to feed. The large number of people and animals overseen by Abraham and Jacob were exceptional and showed their great wealth. Abraham and Lot were both blessed with abundance, but they had to divide because they were not able to use the same land (Genesis 13:5-12).

We might tend to think that nomads were isolated from the currents of life, but this was not always true. Nomads have tended to live near major trade routes, and they visit cities to buy needed supplies. A trading caravan passed by when Joseph's brothers were wondering what

About one-fourth of the population of Mongolia continues to live a nomadic lifestyle, using horses to move their yurts (some on wheels) to different locations.

wanted to expand the territory they controlled. Many, however, have sought to live peacefully with their neighbors.

The nomadic lifestyle of Bedouins is threatened by the modern world. After World War II, modern country boundaries became more important in their part of the world than they had been in the past. Nomads are no longer as free to travel from place to place. Many of their young people want the conveniences of the modern world.

Hebrews 11:9 says that Abraham, Isaac, and Jacob dwelled in tents and lived as aliens in the land. The author says that Abraham was looking for the city with true foundations, "whose architect and builder is God" (Hebrews 11:10).

The way of the nomad is an illustration of the life of God's people. We are not to settle down in this world. We are passing through on our way to the heavenly city, whose architect and builder is God.

to do with him (Genesis 37:25-28). Because they came in contact with people in many areas, ancient nomads actually contributed to trade and the exchange of inventions, ideas, and cultural practices among nations. Some nomadic people, such as the Huns, Turks, and Mongols, have been warriors who

By faith [Abraham] lived as an alien in the land of promise, as in a foreign land, dwelling in tents with Isaac and Jacob, fellow heirs of the same promise.
Hebrews 11:8-9

Assignments for Lesson 18

Bible   Read Genesis 47-50. Commentary available in *Student Review*.

Literature   Continue reading *The Cat of Bubastes*.

Student Review   Optional: Answer the questions for Lesson 18.

Detail from Lot Leaves Sodom With His Family,
Peter Paul Rubens (Flemish, c. 1615)

The Destruction of Sodom and Gomorrah

Time and again, mankind has broken God's heart. The sin of Adam and Eve, Cain's murder of his brother, the sinfulness that led to the flood, and the arrogance shown by the builders of the Tower of Babel are all examples of how deeply sin runs in the hearts and minds of men and women.

As we have observed before, we cannot properly understand world history unless we recognize and identify sin. Sin is not an old-fashioned concept that has no relevance or meaning today. Sin has impacted the world in Soviet Russia, Nazi Germany, American and South African racial discrimination, the September 11 terrorist attack, corporate abuse of workers, and many other ways. As Christian people, we cannot be neutral or non-committal concerning the reality of evil. The Bible spends a great deal of time talking about sin. It is why Jesus came to die on the cross. We cannot properly evaluate our individual lives if we do not address the reality of our own sin.

We can be thankful that we do not have to stop with merely the recognition of sin. We know the answer to it! God is merciful and just. He is not like sinful man, nor is He like the cruel and unjust

Canaanite gods. God has provided in Jesus the way out of bondage to sin. We must admit the bad news about sin, but we must also understand the significance of God's good news: the answer for sin is Jesus Christ.

God's Heavy Burden

The Lord and two angels visited Abraham and Sarah to tell them that they were going to have a child. This was shocking but joyful news. Sarah was going to become a mother in her old age. God was fulfilling His promise to Abraham in a wonderful and miraculous way.

When the visitors arose to leave, they looked toward Sodom. The time for sharing good news with Abraham and Sarah had passed, and the time had come to deal with the bad news of the sin of Sodom and Gomorrah. Abraham was to teach his family and household to keep the way of the Lord by doing righteousness and justice. They had to understand sin and God's hatred of it. They needed to see that the destruction coming upon Sodom and Gomorrah was not a chance event or the action of another god. It was God's judgment upon the unrighteousness of those cities.

Abraham's Appeal to God

As the two angels departed to go to Sodom, the Lord remained with Abraham. Abraham dared to discuss with God the destruction He planned to bring upon the cities. It seemed incredible to Abraham that God would destroy righteous people along with the wicked who were there. Perhaps Abraham was thinking specifically about Lot and his family, but more generally Abraham was concerned about what was right. Far be it from God, Abraham said, to treat the righteous and the wicked alike. "Shall not the Judge of all the earth deal justly?" (Genesis 18:25). Abraham believed (as we also should) that God will always do what is right. He is trustworthy, and we can count on Him.

Just as God's call to sacrifice Isaac tested Abraham, so this scene of negotiation caused Abraham to grow in his relationship with God. The Lord knew His own mind, but He wanted to help Abraham understand what was happening. Abraham started at fifty righteous people and worked his way down to ten. This reveals God's merciful heart, that He would preserve the lives of ten righteous people instead of destroying two wicked cities. Abraham could see this trait in God. However, the scene also shows how wicked the cities were since they did not contain even ten righteous people. Abraham needed to understand this.

The Visitors in the City

When the two angels arrived in Sodom, Lot urged them to spend the night in his house. He knew that this would be better for them than staying in the city square. Word got out among the men of Sodom, and they came to Lot's house and asked that the visitors be brought outside so that they could have homosexual relations with them (Genesis 19:1-5).

Homosexual activity is consistently and firmly condemned in Scripture (Leviticus 18:22 and 20:13,

Romans 1:26-27, 1 Corinthians 6:9, and 1 Timothy 1:10). It violates God's plan and order. However, the sins of Sodom and Gomorrah were many. Isaiah said that they committed injustice (Isaiah 1:10-17, 3:9). Jeremiah accused them of adultery, lying, and wickedness (Jeremiah 23:14). Ezekiel said they were guilty of selfish pride and neglect of the poor (Ezekiel 16:49). The cumulative sins of Sodom and Gomorrah had become so great that God in His justice had no recourse but to destroy the cities completely.

Then we consider Lot. The Apostle Peter calls him righteous Lot and says that his soul was tormented by what he saw around him (2 Peter 2:7-8). Lot was indeed more righteous that the others who lived in Sodom, but Lot had major failings. When Abraham and Lot separated because the same land could not support both of their households, Lot chose the well-watered valley of the Jordan for himself. He moved his tents to Sodom, but even when he knew the wickedness of the city he did not leave. He offered his two virgin daughters to the men of the city for them to lie with instead of the two visitors. He had allowed his daughters to become engaged to men of the city who did not respect him. Lot hesitated when the angels urged him to leave the city to escape

---

The illustration below shows an angel leading Lot and his daughters away from the city. Lot's wife has been turned into a pillar of salt near the gate. The image is taken from the Nuremberg Chronicle, published in 1493.

the coming destruction. After the destruction of the cities, Lot's daughters conspired to get him drunk and to lie with him. Both Lot and his daughters committed sins in this matter.

The Destruction of the Cities

God rained fire and brimstone from heaven on Sodom and Gomorrah. Some have tried to give a naturalistic explanation for this, such as the explosion of a volcano; but the Bible says that God made it happen, and that is what matters. The destruction of the cities was complete. Besides losing his home and his way of life, Lot also lost his wife. In violation of the angels' warning, she looked back one last time and was turned into a pillar of salt. In a sad conclusion to the event, the next morning Abraham went out to the place where he had stood with the Lord before the destruction took place and saw the smoke rising from the valley as from a furnace.

The site of Sodom and Gomorrah is likely under or near the southern end of the Dead Sea. When Lot moved to Sodom, the area was "well watered, like the garden of the Lord, like the land of Egypt" (Genesis 13:10). The entire region is now barren, and a large crystalline salt mountain sits on the western side of the sea. Moses warned the Israelites that if they disobeyed the Lord, they would face the same consequences. Their land would be "a burning waste of salt and sulfur—nothing planted, nothing sprouting, no vegetation growing on it" (Deuteronomy 29:23). Historical records indicate that people were active in this area until around 1900 BC. This suggests that the destruction of the cities occurred about that time.

The Legacy of Sodom and Gomorrah

Sodom and Gomorrah are referred to repeatedly in Scripture as examples of sin. They have become a symbol for wickedness and for utter destruction

On the western shore of the Dead Sea in Israel, a huge mass of halite, or rock salt, has been growing for centuries. It is called Mount Sodom. No plants can grow on it. People in the area refer to the formation shown above as Lot's Wife.

in literature and speech. Unfortunately, when the example of Sodom and Gomorrah is forgotten, sin returns. The godless mind basks in sin and relegates the story of Sodom and Gomorrah to the status of a fairy tale or a mythical illustration used by religious bigots. The godly mind, by contrast, sees the lesson of the incident and seeks to avoid sin and thus avoid its punishment.

We also see in Sodom and Gomorrah the powerful influence of the world on Lot and his family. The Bible gives no indication that Lot's family engaged in homosexual activity, but their lives were negatively affected by the sin around them. Lot allowed his daughters to be engaged to men from Sodom.

It is hard to imagine how troubled those marriages might have been (since neither the men nor Lot's daughters were sterling characters). Lot also gave in to the dangerous tendency of thinking that certain sins (such as his daughters engaging in immorality) were not as bad as other sins (the men of Sodom having relations with the visitors). If our goal is just to be a little better than the world, we will simply slide into destruction a little more slowly.

What Else Was Happening? (2000-1500 BC)

1. Large cities flourished along the Indus River in and around modern Pakistan. The people built advanced drainage systems, used regular weights and measures, engaged in trade over long distances, and had a written language. Seals from this Indus Valley civilization are pictured at right.

2. Settlers probably arrived in Australia during this period. Some were nomadic, while others settled in villages. Australia is home to many unusual animals, and fossil evidence indicates that some of these animals grew larger in the past than they do now.

3. The Norte Chico civilization in modern Peru built large terraced pyramids (see examples at right). Their cities did not have defenses, suggesting that their culture was able to develop in peace. No remnants of pottery have been found, and their diet seems to have consisted largely of seafood.

4. People living along the Mississippi River in what became Louisiana and Mississippi constructed large earthworks. This culture, named Poverty Point after the plantation where artifacts were discovered, seems to have procured food through hunting and gathering rather than agriculture. Archeological evidence indicates that they were part of a large trading network.

5. The Chinese were manufacturing silk from the cocoons of mulberry silkworm moths. Originally used for clothing, silk was eventually used for musical instruments, fishing line, and paper. The Chinese kept the production process secret for hundreds of years, allowing them to maintain a monopoly on the material.

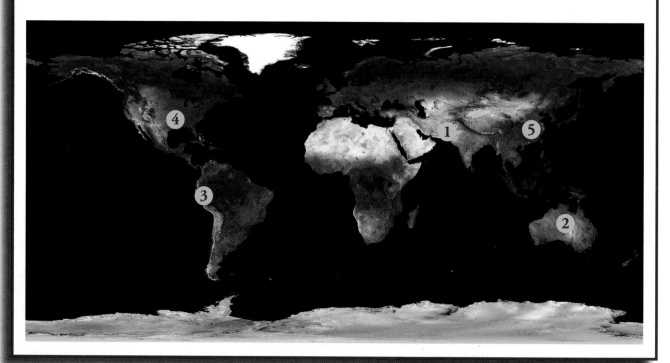

Unless the Lord of hosts
Had left us a few survivors,
We would be like Sodom,
We would be like Gomorrah.
Isaiah 1:9

Assignments for Lesson 19

Bible   Read Job 1-3. Commentary available in *Student Review*.

Literature   Continue reading *The Cat of Bubastes*.

Student Review   Optional: Answer the questions for Lesson 19.

Joseph Made Known to His Brethren, *F. Hartwich (German, c. 1840)*

Lesson 20 - Bible Study

"God Meant It for Good"

He was a spoiled, self-absorbed young man; but he became an effective public servant who was generous toward others. His life saw many ups and downs, but through it all he could see God working for a good purpose.

The story of Joseph is one of the most dramatic narratives in all of the Bible. No novelist or Hollywood screenwriter could produce a more gripping tale with its plot twists, family intrigues, and satisfying conclusion. God has given us not only a good story but also a demonstration of His power to bring good out of bad. In addition, we see how the life of Joseph furthered God's plan for Israel and ultimately the world.

Besides being effective and intriguing, the account is also historically accurate. The Egyptian officials mentioned in the story bear titles that have been found in documents and inscriptions. The names of Egyptian people are real Egyptian names. The lifestyle and customs alluded to are accurate. Perhaps the most dramatic aspect of the story of Joseph is that it is true. It occurred around 1700 BC.

Hated By His Brothers

Jacob loved Rachel and wanted her to be his wife, but the union was fraught with difficulties and complications. Laban made Jacob marry his older daughter, Leah, first. Both Rachel and Leah had Jacob lie with their maids to produce offspring. Finally, when Jacob was ninety-one, Rachel bore a son, Joseph. She later died while giving birth to another son, Benjamin.

In this large and complicated family, the patriarch Jacob loved Joseph more than any of his other sons because Joseph was the son of his old age. Jacob showed this favoritism by giving Joseph a beautiful, varicolored coat. Such a garment would be worn by someone who was not expected to work, since work clothes were plainer. This, along with the fact that Joseph brought a bad report to Jacob about his brothers, caused the other sons of Jacob to hate Joseph with a passion. Joseph added to their hatred by telling them of his two dreams that indicated they would one day bow down to him. He could have kept the dreams to himself, but instead he chose to tell them.

One day Jacob sent Joseph to see about his brothers while they were with the flock (notice that Joseph was at home, not out working in the pasture). As he was coming, the brothers saw a chance to be rid of Joseph without having to answer to their father. Reuben convinced them, however, to put him into a dry cistern, from which Reuben planned to rescue him later. Then while Reuben was away, a caravan of traders passed by. Judah suggested selling Joseph into slavery to be rid of him instead of killing him, so they sold him to the traders. Reuben was grieved when he found out what his brothers had done. As a cover-up, the brothers dipped Joseph's colorful coat into goat's blood to make it appear that the young man had been attacked and killed by a wild animal. Jacob wept for his apparent loss, while Joseph was taken to Egypt and sold to Potiphar, captain of Pharaoh's bodyguard.

In Potiphar's Household

The Lord was with Joseph and made him prosper in all he did. Potiphar made Joseph his household manager, and God blessed Potiphar's house while Joseph was there. Joseph was able and handsome. Potiphar's wife found him attractive and tried to seduce him multiple times, but he consistently refused. Once when he escaped from her clutches, he left his garment behind. Potiphar's wife used this as evidence to say that he had tried to seduce her. Potiphar believed this false accusation and had Joseph thrown into prison. God was with Joseph even in prison, however, and the chief jailer put Joseph in the position of trust over the other prisoners.

Joseph and Zulaikha, *Kamāl ud-Dīn Behzād (Persian, 1488). Zulaikha is the name given to Potiphar's wife in Jewish and Muslim tradition.*

Joseph Interpreting Pharaoh's Dream
Peter von Cornelius (German, 1817)

While Joseph was in prison, Pharaoh's cupbearer and baker offended the ruler, who had them put in prison—the same prison which held Joseph. Joseph interpreted their dreams and told them that their dreams bode well for the cupbearer and ill for the baker. Joseph asked the cupbearer to remember him to Pharaoh so that he could get out of prison, but the cupbearer forgot about him.

Two years later, Pharaoh had some dreams which his magicians could not interpret. The cupbearer then remembered Joseph. Pharaoh called for him, and Joseph interpreted the dreams. In response, Pharaoh named Joseph to the position of vizier, second only to Pharaoh himself in power. Joseph oversaw the stockpiling of grain during the seven years of plenty to prepare for the seven lean years.

Jacob Sends His Sons to Egypt

While the famine was spreading and Joseph was busy keeping a nation alive, Jacob's other sons apparently were standing around and staring at one another, wondering what to do. Jacob told them to go to Egypt to buy grain, but their father did not allow Benjamin to go. In other words, it appeared that his other sons were expendable; but Benjamin was not. When they arrived in Egypt, Joseph recognized his brothers but they did not recognize him. They did not expect to see him in a position of authority, and the grooming techniques used in Egypt would have greatly changed Joseph's appearance.

Joseph had some fun with his brothers, accusing them of being spies. He demanded that one brother remain as a hostage while the others returned to Canaan to bring Benjamin, Joseph's only full brother. As they were leaving, Joseph ordered that their money be hidden with their grain. The brothers discovered the money and wondered what it meant.

Jacob did not want to let Benjamin go to Egypt, but he finally relented and instructed the brothers to take gifts, double the money for an additional grain purchase, and the money they had earlier found in

Joseph's Brothers on the Road to Egypr
Lambert Jacobsz (Dutch, 1632)

Joseph and Asenath
Anonymous (Flemish, c. 1500)

their sacks. When they returned to Egypt, Joseph's steward gave God the credit for their finding the money in their sacks of grain.

After sharing an emotional reunion with Benjamin and eating a meal with them, Joseph ordered their grain sacks to be filled, their money to be returned as before, and the silver cup he used to help interpret dreams to be put in Benjamin's sack. After they departed, Joseph ordered them to be brought back. Terrified and bewildered, they offered everything they could to get out of trouble. Finally Joseph revealed himself to his brothers, who were overwhelmed and amazed.

Israel Comes to Egypt

Joseph gave God the credit for his being in Egypt. He said that God had brought him there to preserve life, which Joseph had done for both Egypt and for his family. Joseph said that God had made him "a father to Pharaoh". This is an expression found in Egyptian writing from the time to refer to the person who looked after Pharaoh as Joseph did. Joseph made arrangements for his father and all of the household to come to Egypt to live in the land of Goshen. Seventy people made the trek, and then they all had a joyful reunion. Pharaoh welcomed them and approved of the arrangements Joseph had made. While the Egyptians were paying Pharaoh all they had for grain, the sons of Israel acquired property and lived successfully.

Jacob's dying wish was that he be buried in Canaan. When Joseph brought his two sons to Jacob so that he might bless them, Jacob pulled one last surprise to show how God would work. He crossed his hands and gave the primary blessing to Ephraim, Joseph's younger son, instead of the older son, Manasseh. The patriarch then prophesied for good or ill about his sons and their descendants. Joseph was able to take the body of Jacob back to Canaan to bury him in the cave of Machpelah, where Abraham, Sarah, Isaac, Rebekah, and Leah had been buried years before.

Now that Jacob was out of the picture, the brothers feared that Joseph would seek revenge on them for what they had done to him. They meekly went to Joseph and said that Jacob had told them to apologize to Joseph and to beg him for mercy for their wrongs. In doing this they fell down before him, just as Joseph had predicted!

The brothers likely made up the story of their father's message as a desperate plea for clemency. Joseph's reply was full of the faith, grace, and maturity that he had learned through what he had endured. "Am I in God's place?" he asked. "You meant evil against me, but God meant it for good in order to bring about this present result, to preserve many people alive" (Genesis 50:19-20). Joseph assured them that he would do all the good he could for them.

The last paragraph of the book summarizes Joseph's life. Joseph expressed his faith that God

Jacob Blessing the Children of Joseph
Rembrandt (Dutch, 1656)

would return his father's family to the land He had promised to give their ancestors. He charged them to carry his remains with them so that he could be buried there also.

Conclusion

Joseph was turned on by his brothers, lied about by Potiphar's wife, and forgotten by Pharaoh's cupbearer. He was lowered into a pit expecting to die, sold into slavery, and thrown into jail. Yet none of these circumstances prevented Joseph from doing God's will. On the other hand, Joseph was a favored son, a favored servant, and the second most powerful man in one of the ancient world's greatest kingdoms. Through all of the failures and successes of Joseph's life, God worked for the good of Joseph and of those around him.

The extended family of Jacob entered Egypt under favorable circumstances, but after several years things turned sour for them. Because of their unhappy situation, God brought about good for them: their deliverance from bondage. In the Exodus, God brought the descendants of Israel (Jacob) to Himself and made them His chosen people. From that chosen people came the Savior of the world.

God is able to bring good things out of bad because He is God. His overriding sovereignty accomplishes His will despite the circumstances that arise in our lives. We do not want bad things to happen, and yet the experience of countless individuals is that the place of trial is the place where we grow the most. Joseph's brothers did not have the trials that Joseph faced; in fact, they had blessing after blessing heaped upon them. To the end, however, they were only looking out for their own skins. Joseph, meanwhile, discovered through his trials the meaning of faith and thus became a better person. We can be encouraged through this Bible story to face our own lives with faith and to believe that even when times are hard God is at work for our good.

You meant evil against me,
but God meant it for good.
Genesis 50:20

Assignments for Lesson 20

Bible   Read Job 38-42. Commentary available in *Student Review*.
            Recite or write Genesis 12:2-3 from memory.

Literature   Continue reading *The Cat of Bubastes*.

Project   Complete your project for the unit.

Student Review   Optional: Answer the questions for Lesson 20 and take the quiz for Unit 4.

5

God Chooses Israel

Summary

God brought Israel out of slavery and made them His chosen people. The Lord raised up Moses, who led Israel, despite their frequent grumbling and lack of faith, into the Promised Land. The period of the Judges was marked by everyone doing what was right in his own eyes. During this period, however, Ruth, an ancestor of David, showed great faith and was rewarded for it. The Law of Moses gave structure to the life of Israel and taught the people what it meant to worship the one true holy God.

Lessons

21 - Israel Becomes a Nation
22 - Key Event: The Exodus
23 - Key Person: Moses
24 - Everyday Life: The Story of Ruth
25 - Bible Study: The Law

Miriam's Dance, from a 14th-century Bulgarian Psalter

Memory Work

Learn Psalm 78:5-7 by the end of the unit.

Books Used

The Bible (You will read the book of Ruth while you are reading Lesson 24.)
In Their Words
The Cat of Bubastes

**Project
(choose one)**

1) Write 300 to 500 words on one of the following topics:

- Write journal entries from the Exodus through the wilderness as if you were an Israelite. Record your observations, fears, and faith. See Lesson 22.

- Write a character study of Moses: his strengths, his weaknesses, his successes, his failures, and how God helped him grow. See Lesson 23.

2) Make a video documentary of the early history of Israel as told in this unit. Your documentary should be at least five minutes long.

3) Create a painting that celebrates the law that God gave to Moses. See Lesson 25.

View from Mount Carmel, Israel

Lesson 21

Israel Becomes a Nation

During the second half of the second millennium BC (1500-1000 BC), the Shang dynasty exercised control of China. The Hindu religion was growing in India. Phoenician ships were trading and exploring around the Mediterranean Sea and even into the Atlantic Ocean. The city of Mycenae was built in southern Greece. The Trojan War took place. Stonehenge was already a landmark in England. Mayan tribes were living in villages in Central America.

Meanwhile, along the southeastern coast of the Mediterranean, a nation that had begun as one large family underwent a people movement that took them from being slaves in Egypt to possessors of a land on the eastern Mediterranean coast. Many nations settled new lands during this period. What was unique about this particular group is that their identity, their move, and their new land were all specially guided by God.

Affliction and Deliverance

The extended family of Jacob's sons and their children had come to Egypt in peace and with the approval of Pharaoh. Jacob's son Joseph had been Pharaoh's vizier and had arranged for his family to move to Egypt during the famine. They lived in the land of Goshen and prospered.

After several years, however, a different pharaoh came to the throne who did not remember Joseph and the agreement by which the sons of Israel had been allowed to live in the land. This new pharaoh feared the growing number of Israelites. Desiring to show his authority, he subjugated the Israelites to forced labor, requiring them to make bricks for his many building projects. However, the more they were oppressed, the more the Israelites grew.

Pharaoh next tried a policy of ethnic cleansing by selective infanticide. He ordered Hebrew midwives to kill all male Israelite children and only let the girls live. This, he might have thought, would give the Israelites fewer potential soldiers. The girls could be intermingled with other slaves and the potential threat diffused. But the midwives feared God and refused to kill the male children, and God blessed the midwives for what they did.

Deliverance for the Israelites came from within Pharaoh's own household. A woman of the tribe of Levi hid her baby boy in a basket and put it into the Nile, where it was found by Pharaoh's daughter. The princess named the boy Moses and raised him as her own son. When Moses was about forty years old, he killed an Egyptian who was beating a Hebrew.

Pharaoh heard about it and tried to kill Moses, but Moses escaped into the land of Midian. There Moses married Zipporah, daughter of Jethro, and tended his father-in-law's flocks.

About forty years later, God called Moses from a burning bush to return to Egypt and tell the new Pharaoh to release the descendants of Israel from bondage so that they could go into the wilderness and worship Him. Moses was reluctant to do so at first, but he eventually agreed and returned to Egypt. Pharaoh stubbornly refused to let this large band of workers and potential enemies leave his control. God sent a series of plagues on Egypt, which finally convinced Pharaoh to release them. God parted the Red Sea so that the Israelites could escape. When Pharaoh and his army chased them, God sent the waters of the sea back over the pursuers and drowned them.

Chosen People and the Promised Land

In the wilderness, God initiated a covenant in which He declared that He would be the God of the Israelites and called them to be His people. They were to set themselves apart from the world as a holy nation, dedicated to worshiping and serving only the one true God. The Lord set forth His Law for them to observe and gave instructions for building a large tent or tabernacle as the place they were to worship Him. The people agreed to the covenant, but their commitment to it was shaky. Almost immediately they began worshiping a golden calf that Aaron, Moses' brother, made for them.

The Israelites showed lack of faith many times, but especially when they listened to the faithless report of spies who had searched out the land of Canaan which God had promised to give them. Ten spies said that the Israelites could never overcome the people who were living in the land. Joshua and Caleb believed that God would bring them victory,

Detail from Worshipping of the Golden Calf
Lucas van Leyden (Dutch, c. 1530)

but the people listened to the ten fearful ones. As a result, God made them wander in the desert for forty years, until that adult generation had died off.

Moses led them to the border of the Promised Land, but God did not allow him to enter it because of his own disobedience. Joshua took up the role of leader and led the Israelites across the Jordan, which God divided for them just as He had divided the Red Sea for the previous generation. Since Canaanite tribes already lived there, Israel had to fight them in order to capture their cities and take control of the land. The Israelites defeated the Canaanites, but some pagan people continued to live in the land and became an influence on the Israelites that caused them to disobey God, even to the point of worshiping idols. Joshua oversaw the allotment of land to the various tribes of Israel. Some had chosen to live east of the Jordan but had promised to serve God and to help capture Canaan for their brothers.

The Period of the Judges

God always wanted the Israelites to look to Him and not to any human as their true leader. In a stirring farewell speech, Joshua challenged the Israelites to put away the gods they had known in Egypt and the gods their forefathers had known in Mesopotamia and to turn aside from the gods of the Canaanites. "Choose for yourselves today whom you will serve . . . as for me and my house, we will serve the Lord" (Joshua 24:15).

Joshua's generation did not do a good job of teaching their children about the Lord. When they died out, a generation arose that did not follow the God of their fathers. The Israelites forsook the Lord and began to worship the gods of the people around them. The Hebrew word for master is *ba'al*. It came to be used for the chief Canaanite god (Ba'al) and for other gods as well (the Ba'als). They also worshiped the goddess Ashtoreth (plural, Ashtaroth).

A cycle of events repeated itself several times during this period in Israel's history. Because of Israel's unfaithfulness, God turned them over to enemies and plunderers. The people cried out to the Lord for help, and God raised up a judge to deliver them. Under the judge the Israelites routed the enemy and peace was restored. Then the people forgot their blessings, returned to following Ba'al and other gods, and the cycle began again (see Judges chapter 2).

Detail from Samson with the Philistines, *Carl Heinrich Bloch (Danish, 1863)*

The term judge brings to our minds the hearing of court cases; but only one judge, Deborah, is described as settling disputes (Judges 4). The term judge as used in the book of Judges is best understood as referring to someone who brought the judgment of God against Israel's enemies in battle. Deborah, by the way, does not disprove the Biblical pattern of male spiritual leadership. She actually filled a vacuum caused by the lack of responsible male leadership on the part of Barak.

The stories recorded in the book of Judges tell of gross unfaithfulness and immorality committed during this time. Instead of enjoying the new land that God had given them and the abundant provision God had promised, the Israelites wandered spiritually and did not live up to their identity as God's holy people. The last verse of Judges says it well: "In those days there was no king in Israel; everyone did what was right in his own eyes" (Judges 21:25).

Conclusion

The children of Israel did not build pyramids or other structures that still stand today. They did not contribute significant scientific or mathematical advances to mankind's knowledge. Israel did not command a vast territory in a way that served as the model for governing an empire.

Instead, the legacy that Israel gave to the world was the knowledge of what it means to live for the one true God—and what it means when an individual or a nation does not live this way. As we will see later in this unit, the Law that God gave to Moses has had a significant impact on Western legal practices. The inspired writings of the Hebrews have had an influence on our thought and literature that cannot be measured. God's working with Israel is an important building block in His providing a Savior for all the world. These are the reasons why a study of Israel is important, not just for religious history but for world history in general.

"Have I not commanded you? Be strong and courageous!
Do not tremble or be dismayed, for the Lord your God
is with you wherever you go."
Joshua 1:9

Assignments for Lesson 21

Bible   Read Exodus 1-5. Commentary available in *Student Review*.

Literature   Continue reading *The Cat of Bubastes*. Finish it by the end of this unit.

Student Review   Optional: Answer the questions for Lesson 21.

Lesson 22 - Key Event

The Exodus

In the Exodus, God fulfilled His promise to Abraham by making a nation of his descendants and giving them the land of Canaan. The Exodus is the most significant single event in the history of Old Testament Israel. It brought independence for Israel, showed God's willingness to act on their behalf, and gave them their identity as God's people.

First Kings 6:1 says that Solomon began the temple 480 years after the sons of Israel left Egypt. We are fairly certain that the temple was begun around 966 BC, which would put the Exodus around 1446 BC.

From Oppression to Hope

God brought good out of bad when He led Joseph through many trials to become vizier of Egypt. Through God's mercy, Jacob's household was able to come to Egypt and live in prosperity. However, this good thing turned bad when a different pharaoh feared the Israelites and made them perform hard labor. God heard their groaning; remembered the covenant He had made with Abraham, Isaac and Jacob; and acted to end their suffering.

The Lord called Moses to lead His people out of bondage. Pharaoh's first response to Moses' call to let God's people go was to accuse the Israelites of being lazy and to increase their work load. Rather than thanking Moses for being their deliverer, the Israelites called down God's judgment upon him for making their lives more difficult.

Plagues and Deliverance

To convince Pharaoh, God initiated a series of plagues on Egypt. God used the plagues to show that He was more powerful than the gods of the Egyptians and their magicians. Pharaoh was unmoved by the first plague, even though it showed God's power over the Nile River. Pharaoh's magicians reproduced it. After the second plague, which the magicians also reproduced, Pharaoh agreed to let the people go to sacrifice to God in the wilderness; but after the plague passed, he hardened his heart and changed his mind. The Egyptian magicians could not reproduce the third plague and recognized it as the finger of God, but Pharaoh's heart continued to be hardened; he still was not willing to admit that the Lord was indeed God.

The Lord protected Israel from the fourth plague as a further demonstration of His working on their behalf. Pharaoh again gave them permission to go and even asked that they pray for him; but when the plague passed he hardened his heart again.

Aaron Changes the Water of the Nile into Blood, *Jan Symonsz Pynas (Dutch, 1610)*

God continued to press his case by sending plague after plague, but stubborn Pharaoh responded by continuing to refuse Moses' request. The plague of darkness was especially humiliating to the Egyptians, who worshiped the sun-god as a chief deity. The Hebrews, meanwhile, had light.

The tenth plague was the death of the first-born in every Egyptian house. God said that Israel was His first-born son. The price that Pharaoh paid for refusing to let God's first-born son go was that his first-born son would be killed. As part of the institution of the Passover meal, God instructed the Israelites to spread sheep's blood on their doorways so that the Lord would pass over their houses. As

The Departure of the Israelites Out of the Land of Egypt, *David Roberts (Scottish, 1830)*

Pharaoh mourned the death of his own first-born child, he finally agreed to let the people of Israel go; and they left before he changed his mind.

As the Israelites fled eastward to the Red Sea, Pharaoh once again had a change of heart and set out with his army to bring the Israelites back. Seeing the advancing army, the Israelites became frightened and accused Moses of bringing them out to the wilderness to die. God parted the waters so that the Israelites could walk to the other side. When Pharaoh and his army tried to follow, the Lord closed the sea over them and they were drowned.

The Covenant at Sinai

Three months after leaving Egypt, the Israelites came to Mount Sinai. There Moses met with God, who offered a covenant to Israel. The Lord offered the covenant on the basis of the grace He had already shown in bringing Israel out of slavery to Him. All the earth is His, God noted; but if the Israelites would obey His voice and keep His covenant, Israel would be His special, chosen people, a kingdom of priests and a holy nation.

The people agreed to do whatever the Lord said. Following an elaborate preparation, the Lord then spoke the words of the Law to Moses, beginning with the Ten Commandments.

God's Blessings, Israel's Grumbling

The people of Israel had a difficult time recognizing God's blessings and living in the faith that God was trustworthy and good. When Moses stepped forth as their deliverer, at first they didn't rejoice at their newfound hope but instead grumbled because Pharaoh increased their work load. When God brought them out to the Red Sea, they didn't trust that God would carry through with their deliverance but instead bewailed the fact that Pharaoh's army was following them.

God provided amply for the people, even though they complained frequently. When the people grumbled about the lack of fresh water, God gave them water. When the people grumbled for lack of food, God sent them manna. When they complained that all they had to eat day after day was the same manna from heaven, God gave them quail.

When God spoke from Mount Sinai, they were afraid and did not want God to speak to them directly. When Moses took a long time conversing with God on Mount Sinai, the people lost faith and had Aaron make a golden calf as a pagan idol. When ten of the spies who went into Canaan returned with fearful reports, the people did not rejoice at the land God was giving them but instead gave up hope.

The people of God, shown grace upon grace and called into a covenant with the one true God, did not let the blessings they received change their hearts. Instead, they focused on the difficult things before them and complained even about their blessings. Rather than becoming a grateful people who trusted the God who had provided for them again and again, they became a grumbling people who doubted God and abandoned Him at the least difficulty. May God's people today learn from their example and resolve to thank God for His blessings and to trust God even through the hard times (see 1 Corinthians 10:6-12).

Significance of the Exodus

The Lord commanded Moses to take a census of Israel in the second year after they had come out of Egypt. The census revealed 603,550 men, not including the Levites (Numbers 1:2, 2:32). We can safely assume that most of these men were married and that many of them had children. It is not unreasonable to conclude that one to two million people came out of Egypt in the Exodus.

The Exodus made Israel into a nation and gave them their identity as God's holy people. It showed that God can be trusted. Hundreds of years had passed since God had made His promise to Abraham. The intervening years had brought many unlikely twists and turns in the story, but God was faithful. Numerous references in the Bible point to the Exodus as a demonstration of God's mercy (see, for example, Psalm 105 and Hosea 11:1-4).

The Gathering of the Manna
Dieric Bouts the Elder (Dutch, 1467)

Each year, even centuries later, the Passover reminded all Israelites of God's mercy and helped them feel as though they participated in the Exodus. The fathers in every generation were to say to their children, "With a powerful hand the Lord brought us out of Egypt, from the house of slavery" (Exodus 13:14). Jews around the world continue to observe the Passover each year. However, those who do not know Christ are missing the ultimate fulfillment of God's promise.

This pivotal event of the Old Testament has meaning for the Christian as well. Just as God brought Israel out of the bondage of slavery through the waters of the Red Sea into the freedom and blessing of being God's people, so God brings us out of bondage to sin through the waters of baptism into the freedom and blessing of being Christians (see 1 Corinthians 10:1-4). Paul describes Jesus as our Passover lamb (1 Corinthians 5:7). The wanderings of the Israelites in the wilderness have been compared to the hardships of the Christian life. Crossing the Jordan and reaching the Promised Land have become symbols of death and heaven in many hymns.

The story of Israel is unique in history. God wanted the Israelites to have a powerful sense of their special, divine calling so that they would live up to His will for them. They failed in this to a great degree, but the call still serves as a beacon for those who want to escape spiritual slavery and find the freedom of a new identity as God's people.

You yourselves have seen what I did to the Egyptians,
and how I bore you on eagles' wings, and brought you to Myself.
Now then, if you will indeed obey My voice and keep My covenant,
then you shall be My own possession among all the peoples,
for all the earth is Mine; and you shall be to Me
a kingdom of priests and a holy nation.
Exodus 19:4-6a

Assignments for Lesson 22

Bible   Read Exodus 13-15. Commentary available in *Student Review*.

In Their Words   Read Dayenu (page 22).

Literature   Continue reading *The Cat of Bubastes*.

Student Review   Optional: Answer the questions for Lesson 22.

Detail from The Finding of Moses, *Laurens Alma Tadema (Dutch, 1904)*

Lesson 23 - Key Person

Moses

Moses led the Israelites out of slavery in Egypt, through forty years of wandering in the wilderness, and to the brink of the land God had promised to give them. While in the wilderness, Moses was the messenger who gave God's Law to Israel; and he was the leader who guided them through many trials of faith.

Moses was a great leader, but he did not start out being bold and courageous. He grew into the position God gave him, and along the way he showed that he had his share of human failings.

Overview of Moses' Life

Moses was born in Egypt to Amram and Jochebed from the tribe of Levi. He was raised as the son of Pharaoh's daughter. We assume that he was brought up in the royal household and received an education in keeping with his status. However, he was aware of his Hebrew background, a fact which influenced a decisive moment in his life.

When Moses was about forty years old, he defended a fellow Hebrew by killing the Egyptian who was beating him. Word about his deed got out; and when Pharaoh tried to kill him, Moses escaped to the land of Midian on the Arabian

peninsula. There Moses met the family of Reuel, priest of Midian. Moses married Zipporah, one of the priest's daughters, and the couple had two sons. Moses' father-in-law is called by two names in the Bible. Reuel means friend of God and was probably his name (Exodus 2:18). Jethro, which means excellence, was probably his title (Exodus 3:1).

For the next forty years, Moses lived as a shepherd for Reuel, no doubt learning wilderness life and also learning the work of a shepherd, skills he would need when leading the people of Israel. Moses spent the first forty years of his life in the household of Pharaoh and the next forty years as a shepherd—quite a come-down in status.

At the age of eighty, Moses received God's call from the burning bush on Mount Horeb (also called Mount Sinai) to return to Egypt and lead His people out of bondage. Moses was reluctant to follow God's instruction, but he obeyed the call and went back to the land he had left as a wanted man. Pharaoh did not want to let the Israelites leave, but a series of plagues from God finally convinced Pharaoh to do so. Moses led the Israelites through the Red Sea and to Mount Sinai, where God initiated and established the covenant between Himself and the nation of Israel.

The Lord told Moses to send twelve spies into Canaan who would bring back reports on the land and its inhabitants. Ten of the spies returned with fearful reports and dire warnings about Israel's inability to take the land. Joshua and Caleb were convinced that God could make it happen, but the people believed the ten negative spies and bewailed their fate. God punished them by making the people of Israel spend the next forty years in the wilderness until that adult generation died out (except for Joshua and Caleb). So for the last forty years of Moses' life, he shepherded Israel in the wilderness and brought the new generation to the Jordan River in preparation for entering the Promised Land.

Moses himself, however, was not allowed to enter. Earlier Moses had struck a rock instead of speaking to it to bring forth water. Because of this act of disobedience, God forbade him from going into Canaan. After viewing the land from Mount Pisgah, Moses died at the age of 120. God buried him in the land of Moab.

Moses and the Burning Bush
Dieric Bouts the Elder (Dutch, 1467)

Guided by the Hand of God

The life of Moses was clearly guided by the hand of God. He was born under a death threat, as Pharaoh had ordered all male Hebrew children to be cast into the Nile. Moses' mother did cast her baby into the Nile, but she put him into a basket first; and the daughter of Pharaoh found him. Moses' sister arranged for their own mother to nurse him until he was weaned.

Forty years later, Moses fled from Egypt, again under a death threat. In Midian God led him to the family of a priest. When Moses returned to Egypt to free the Israelites, God gave him courage and the words to speak when he appealed to Pharaoh. God clearly had a purpose for Moses' life, and He saw to it that His will for Moses was fulfilled.

A Reluctant Leader

Moses did not accept the mantle of leadership willingly. When God called him at the scene of the burning bush, Moses gave a series of excuses to try to get out of the assignment, as recorded in Exodus chapters 3 and 4.

1. "Who am I to do this?" Moses asked. God's reply was that He would be with Moses (Exodus 3:11-12). It was not so much a question of who Moses was but who God was, and God was going to be with him.

2. "What shall I tell the Israelites about who sent me?" God was not commonly known by the Israelites, and of course they had heard much about Egyptian gods. With what divine authority would Moses go? God said that His identity is "I AM." The God who truly exists, as opposed to all the false gods, was his authority (Exodus 3:13-15).

3. "What if they don't listen to me? What if they deny that God has appeared to me?" Moses was not convinced that they would take his word for it, so God showed him two

miracles and gave him the promise of a third as proof that God had indeed spoken with him (Exodus 4:1-9).

4. "But I am not eloquent. I am slow of speech and tongue." Evidently Moses had some speech impediment or a great fear of speaking in public. He thought God should use someone more eloquent in the role. But God replied, "Who made the mouth? Who makes someone dumb or deaf?" In other words, God was in control of Moses' mouth. The Lord would be with his mouth and would give him the words to say (Exodus 4:10-12).

5. "Lord, send whomever you want," Moses said at last, which meant "anyone but me." The Lord was angry with Moses and said that Aaron would be Moses' mouthpiece. God indeed sent someone else—but only to accompany Moses (Exodus 4:13-16).

Sometimes we give excuses to God, but they really do no good. God knows the situation, and He knows us better than we do. Moses was reluctant, but God could still use him as long as he obeyed. Moses' weakness did not stop him from being God's servant. God wanted Moses in this role; and even though Moses was not all he could have been at the time, God trained him on the job.

Intercessor for Others

Moses spent his life interceding for others. He acted on behalf of a fellow Israelite when the latter was being beaten by an Egyptian. He helped the daughters of Reuel when shepherds drove them away from the water. Moses pleaded with God on behalf of Egypt during the plagues. Of course, Moses presented God's case to Pharaoh on behalf of the people of Israel.

In the wilderness, Moses appealed to God on behalf of the Israelites when God was ready to destroy them. On two occasions, God considered

Victory O Lord! by John Everett Millais (English, 1871) depicts Aaron and Hur helping Moses hold up his hands during battle with the Amalekites (Exodus 17).

wiping out Israel and starting over with Moses to build a nation (Exodus 32:9-10, Numbers 14:11-12). This was something God had done before in the case of Noah. Moses pleaded Israel's case, even though the people were ready to cast him off and select a new leader (Numbers 14:4).

On both of these occasions, Moses told God that the action He was planning to take would not look good to other nations. It would make it appear that God had brought Israel out of Egypt just to do away with them, Moses said. Other nations would think that God was not strong enough to bring the people into Canaan. In addition, Moses pointed out, God had made a covenant with Abraham, Isaac, and Jacob. He had given His word about giving the land to their descendants. In Numbers 14:17-18, Moses quoted God's own words to Him, the words

He had spoken to Moses in Exodus 34:6-7 about being compassionate, gracious, and slow to anger. God relented on both occasions, but He did punish Israel appropriately.

Close Relationship with God

"The Lord used to speak to Moses face to face, just as a man speaks to his friend" (Exodus 33:11; see also Numbers 12:6-8). Moses probably enjoyed a closer intimacy with the Almighty than anyone else who has ever walked this planet except for the Lord Jesus Himself. This intimacy changed Moses' life and helped him to become the leader that he was. God initiated the relationship at the burning bush, and neither He nor Moses ever moved away from this closeness. It is because of this intimacy that Moses was able to intercede for the Israelites as mentioned above.

After the incident of the golden calf, God declared to Moses that He would not go with Israel into the Promised Land. Moses again appealed to the Lord, saying that God's presence with them distinguished Israel from all the other nations on the earth. Moses asked to know God's ways so that he could find favor in His sight. God agreed to do this, and Moses asked to see God's glory. God allowed Moses to see His back (for no man can see the face of God and live), and the Lord declared to Moses His goodness and compassion.

The Tetragrammaton: YHWH

God revealed His name to Moses as "I AM" (YHWH, related to the Hebrew verb "to be," Exodus 3:14). God's identity is that He is the God who is, who really exists. God revealed who He is by the deeds He performed. The ancient Hebrew language did not have any vowels, only consonants; so God's name was rendered YHWH (the Greek word tetragrammaton means "four letters"). The translation into German was JHWH, the significance of which we will explain shortly. In an attempt to obey the third of the Ten Commandments — not to misuse God's name — the Israelites never pronounced YHWH at all. Instead, they used the word Adonai, which means Lord. In English translations of the Old Testament, when you see LORD in all capital letters, the word in Hebrew is YHWH. It is being translated the way the Israelites would have rendered it, using Adonai or Lord.

Many centuries later, when fewer people spoke Hebrew and the common pronunciations were becoming unfamiliar, Jewish scholars added vowel points, or symbols, to indicate how words were to be pronounced. For the word YHWH, they used the vowel points for Adonai. Thus the rendering in the Hebrew Bible became Y-a-h-o-w-a-h. The German rendering was J-a-h-o-w-a-h, which became Jehovah. But this word came about only in the Middle Ages. Jehovah was not used in the Hebrew Old Testament and was never used by Jews as a name for God. It is actually a combination of the consonants of YHWH and the vowels of Adonai.

The Mesha Stele (pictured at left, in The Louvre) is among the oldest known surviving written uses of the name YHWH. It was discovered in Palestine in 1868. Dating from about 800 BC, this monument was created by Mesha, king of Moab, to celebrate a victory against the king of Israel. Mesha is mentioned in 2 Kings 3.

Moses' face was changed by his conversations with the Lord. When he came down from talking with God on Mount Sinai, his face shone. The other people were afraid to come near him, so Moses began to wear a veil. He lifted the veil when he talked with the Lord, but he kept the veil in front of his face at other times. Paul wrote that Moses used the veil so that the people could not see that the shine of his face faded over time (2 Corinthians 3:13). Moses was not only transformed physically by his relationship to God, but inwardly as well.

Moses' Spiritual Growth

At first, as mentioned earlier, Moses was reluctant to do God's bidding. He feared that since the Israelites would not listen to him, neither would Pharaoh. However, Moses eventually went boldly to Pharaoh; and, as we have noted, he approached God Himself with great confidence.

As the Egyptian army was approaching the Israelites at the Red Sea, Moses assured the frightened people that God would act on their behalf. God said to Moses, "Why are you crying out to Me? Tell the sons of Israel to go forward" (Exodus 14:15). In other words, there is an appropriate time for prayer; but then comes the time for action. It is maturity to know when those times are.

Moses struggled deeply with the Israelites' lack of faith. At times he rebuked them, at times he complained about them to the Lord, and at other times he interceded to God on their behalf. It takes a person of great maturity to be able to separate the sin from the sinner, to rebuke sin when necessary but to pray for someone out of a heart of concern when prayer is needed.

Moses learned the art of delegation from his father-in-law. Jethro noticed that Moses was spending all day every day deciding issues between the people (knowing how they grumbled against God, we can only imagine how they complained about each other!). Jethro told Moses that he was in danger of letting the people wear him out with

This illustration, from a Frankish manuscript (c. 840 AD), depicts Moses receiving the Tablets of the Law and reading them to the Israelites.

this responsibility. Moses needed to appoint "able men who fear God, men of truth, those who hate dishonest gain" to serve as arbiters among smaller groups of Israelites. Moses himself needed to concentrate on being the people's representative before God and handling the major disputes. Moses followed Jethro's advice, and life among the people ran much more smoothly. This incident is an example of the wise delegation of responsibility and the value of recognizing godly men who can serve God's people (Exodus 18:13-26).

In spite of his growth and his years of faithful service, Moses was not perfect. At Meribah, the Israelites again grumbled about Moses, this time because they did not have water. God told Moses to speak to the rock and water would come forth. In his anger, however, Moses struck the rock. Because of this disobedience, God did not allow Moses to enter the Promised Land. God said that Moses did not believe God or treat Him as holy in the sight of the people. God could not let such obvious disobedience go unpunished. The consequences of doing so would have been too great for the people of Israel.

Choose Life

The book of Deuteronomy is a series of three sermons that Moses gave near the end of his life to the people of Israel as they were preparing to enter Canaan. He reviewed what had happened to them from the Exodus to that point, reiterated some of the Law that God had given through him, and made a final exhortation to the people to serve God faithfully, even though he knew they would not.

When Moses had outlined the choice they faced of following or rejecting God, he said, "I call heaven and earth to witness against you today, that I have set before you life and death, the blessing and the curse. So choose life in order that you may live, you and your descendants" (Deuteronomy 30:19).

Moses laid down his life to serve his people, even though they did not appreciate him and often complained about what he did. He showed that he was able to rise above such pettiness, and in so doing he set an example that many generations after him would appreciate and honor. God showed His wisdom in choosing Moses to be the leader of Israel at the most critical time in their history. The world is different because of what he did.

A Note on Terms: *Through the centuries, people have used several terms for the land area at the eastern end of the Mediterranean Sea. In this curriculum, we use the term Israel to refer to the nation of Israel, both ancient and modern. We use the historical term Palestine to refer to a larger area that includes Israel, especially during the period from the Roman occupation of ancient Israel to the establishment of the modern State of Israel.*

Now Moses was faithful in all His house as a servant,
for a testimony of those things which were to be spoken later.
Hebrews 3:5

Assignments for Lesson 23

Bible Read Deuteronomy 1-6. Commentary available in *Student Review*.

In Their Words Read the excerpt from *Geography* (pages 23-24).

Literature Continue reading *The Cat of Bubastes*.

Student Review Optional: Answer the questions for Lesson 23.

Lesson 24 - Everyday Life

The Story of Ruth

The book of Ruth tells the beautiful story of King David's ancestors. It shows how a few people were faithful to God during the unhappy period of the Judges when, generally speaking, "everyone did what was right in his own eyes" (Judges 21:25). The story is an example of how God works to accomplish good for His people. We also see the importance of fulfilling one's family responsibilities. *Before reading further in this lesson, stop and read the book of Ruth.*

As inspired literature, the book of Ruth is a masterpiece. Clear themes are woven through the narrative. The covenant name of God, YHWH, is used eighteen times in the book. The Hebrew word group that includes redeem and redeemer is used twenty times. One main idea in the book, then, is that as Boaz was the kinsman-redeemer for Ruth, God is the Redeemer of Israel. God's redemption is illustrated by His redeeming Ruth and Naomi from poverty through Boaz.

The word return is used fifteen times, twelve times in the first chapter. Naomi returned to Israel with her daughter-in-law, Ruth returned from the paganism of her people to the right path of serving God, and in the end the Lord returned blessing upon Naomi when Obed was born to Boaz and Ruth. Another key concept in the book is kindness.

God showed kindness to His people even during the time of the Judges, and the Israelites in the story demonstrate this same kindness toward each other.

The name of the author is not given in the book, which might have been written during or after the reign of David in honor of his forebears. Set in a particular time and place in history, Ruth gives us glimpses of everyday life during this period. We will take special note of these insights in this lesson.

Difficulty and Sadness

In the days of the Judges a famine struck Israel, probably as punishment for its unfaithfulness. Elimelech, of Bethlehem in Judah, took his wife Naomi and their two sons, Mahlon and Chilion, about fifty miles east to the land of Moab, hoping to be able to survive there as economic refugees. That Elimelech would go to Moab indicates his desperate circumstances, since Moab and Israel had long been enemies (see Judges 11:17 and Numbers 22-24).

Elimelech died in Moab. His sons took Moabite women, Ruth and Orpah, as wives, even though God had forbidden the Israelites from marrying foreign wives (Deuteronomy 7:3) and had forbidden a Moabite from entering the congregation of Israel (Deuteronomy 23:3-6). People do not always follow

God's Law. It could well be that Elimelech and his sons did not know the Law well, since copies of it were scarce and it was not faithfully taught and practiced during this time. More tragedy struck the family when the sons of Elimelech died, leaving the widowed Israelite Naomi with two widowed Moabite daughters-in-law.

In ancient Israel a woman was provided for by her father until she married, then by her husband until he died, and then by her sons. Naomi, in a foreign land because of a famine, now had no one to provide for her. When the Lord ended the famine in Israel, Naomi headed back to Judah. Her daughters-in-law accompanied her, but Naomi discouraged them from following her. She could promise no more sons to them as husbands to fulfill the requirement of levirite marriage (explained on page 118).

Amidst tears, Orpah followed Naomi's advice and returned to her home; but Ruth clung to Naomi and wanted to go on with her. Ruth made a conscious decision to turn away from her Moabite roots and religion and adopt Israel and Israel's God as her own. Naomi could see that Ruth was determined to continue with her, so she stopped trying to convince her to go back.

Return to Bethlehem

When the women arrived at Bethlehem, the people of the village were excited to see Naomi again after ten years. "Is this Naomi?" they asked. The heartbroken widow answered with a word play on her name. Naomi means pleasant, but Naomi saw her life as anything but pleasant. Instead, she said, "Call me Mara (which means bitter), for the Almighty has dealt very bitterly with me" (Ruth 1:20). Perhaps significantly, Naomi did not use the covenant name of God, YHWH, or even Adonai, Lord, but the less personal El Shaddai (Almighty). She felt distant from God's blessings.

God's blessings, however, were about to come upon Naomi in abundance. The word Bethlehem means house of bread. After the famine, it would

once again be a house of bread for Naomi and the people of Judah. Following her time of loss and grief, Naomi would receive more blessings from the Lord than she could imagine and would have much over which she could rejoice. Significantly, the narrative does not call her Bitter but continues to call her Naomi—Pleasant. Naomi's life would not be defined by the bitterness of the past but by the pleasant things which God had in store for her.

Naomi and Ruth had to find some way to survive since they did not have husbands to provide for them. The Law of Moses made provision for the poor in Israel. The Lord commanded the Israelites not to harvest every last sheaf of grain and every last grape in the vineyard. They were to leave the corners of the field and some of the grapes for the poor (Leviticus 19:9-10, 23:22). This private-sector work-relief program for the poor was intended to be a benefit "for the alien, for the orphan, and for the widow, in order that the Lord your God may bless you in all the work of your hands" (Deuteronomy 24:19). Naomi and Ruth certainly qualified to be gleaners.

Ruth and Naomi, *Nicolaas Verkolje (Dutch, 1744)*

Ruth and Boaz, *Barent Fabritius (Dutch, 1660)*

Harvesting Grain

Ruth went out to harvest what grain she could from the fields. Elimelech had a wealthy kinsman named Boaz living in the region, but apparently Ruth knew nothing about him. Ruth 2:3 literally says that Ruth's "chance chanced upon" the portion of the field that belonged to Boaz. The implication in the narrative is that she did not just happen to come to the field of Boaz. Instead, the Lord guided her path there. In so doing He provided for her physical needs and gave her the opportunity to find a permanent solution to her distressing life situation.

When Boaz came upon the workers in his field, they exchanged greetings that expressed faith in God (Ruth 2:4). Boaz noticed Ruth and wanted to find out who she was. He assumed that as a young woman, she would be under the protection of someone. When he learned that she was with Naomi and that the two of them were alone in the world, he

made special provisions to take care of them. Boaz was not going to treat Ruth as a poor vagrant gleaner.

Boaz had heard about the sacrifice Ruth had made in joining Naomi in Israel. He spoke a blessing upon Ruth, asking that she receive a full reward from the Lord, "under whose wings you have come to seek refuge" (Ruth 2:10-12). The image of baby birds or chicks under their mother's wings conveys the idea of security from attack and provision for one's need. Ruth had put her trust in the Lord. In his blessing, Boaz was asking the Lord that her trust be rewarded. A major part of the way the Lord took care of Ruth was through the kindness of Boaz himself.

Naomi was overjoyed when she learned that Ruth had worked in the fields of Boaz. She advised Ruth to stay with the female servants and to work only in the fields of Boaz. Being with the men would provide protection, while being with the young women would provide fellowship and keep her from being alone and possibly victimized. Working only in the fields of Boaz would show Ruth's trust in him and her thankfulness for his kindness. It would also allow her to continue to enjoy his protection and provision.

Planning the Proposal

Marriages in those days were arranged by the parents, so it was natural that Naomi would take steps to provide Ruth with a home and family security. Naomi found out Boaz's activities and knew when Ruth should approach him. The barley harvest being finished, he would be winnowing the crop at the threshing floor. Naomi instructed Ruth to prepare herself for meeting Boaz. When he lay down to sleep for the evening, she was to go in, uncover his feet, and wait for him to tell her what to do.

Ruth went to the threshing floor and hid until Boaz had gone to sleep. Boaz had enjoyed a successful harvest, had worked all day winnowing the barley, and had enjoyed a filling meal. Now he was ready for a good night's sleep, but he still had one more business task to perform. He needed to protect his

A group of people reenacted the story of Ruth and Boaz in Palestine around 1940. This is one of a series of photographs showing "Ruth" carrying grain, with the city of Bethlehem in the background.

harvest from robbers, so he slept at the end of the heap of grain. When he had gone to sleep, Ruth came to him, uncovered his feet, and lay down.

Uncovering his feet, probably by removing the cloak that he wore during the day and used as a blanket at night, was an indication that she wanted to marry him. At midnight Boaz awoke and was surprised to see a woman lying at his feet. Ruth asked Boaz to "spread your covering over your maid" (a euphemism for marriage used in Ezekiel 16:8), since he was a near kinsman to her late husband.

Family relationships were important in Old Testament Israel. The kinsman-redeemer was expected to buy back family property (Leviticus 25:25), purchase the freedom of a brother who had been enslaved (Leviticus 25:47-55), or avenge a murder (Numbers 35:19). The law of levirite marriage in Deuteronomy 25:5-10 called for the brother of a deceased Israelite to take his dead brother's widow and have children by her in the dead brother's name. Although it is not specifically called for in the Law, the practices described in Ruth indicate that the kinsman-redeemer was commonly expected to fulfill the levirite marriage requirement for a deceased relative. Ruth was asking Boaz to be her kinsman-redeemer, redeeming her from poverty, widowhood, and childlessness.

Boaz, however, went beyond mere legal expectations. He genuinely cared for Ruth and had great admiration and respect for her. Although Boaz had been extremely kind to Ruth, he expressed thanks to her for her kindness towards him in being interested in him as a husband. She had not pursued younger men in town, which suggests that Boaz was several years older than Ruth. Because of her virtuous behavior, which was well-known in the community, Boaz was honored to serve as her kinsman-redeemer.

However, one matter had to be resolved before he could fulfill the role of kinsman-redeemer. Although he was related to Elimelech, another man in town was a closer relative. The text does not indicate whether Naomi knew about this closer kinsman. Before Boaz could properly take the role of kinsman-redeemer, the other man had to decline it. Boaz promised to resolve the issue the next day.

Negotiating with the Relative

Boaz went to the town gate, the best place to find the nearer kinsman with whom he had to speak. When Boaz found him, he called ten elders of the city to be witnesses. By making these arrangements, Boaz showed his good character and his respect for the opinions of others. He wanted to talk with the relative in the open, and he wanted reliable witnesses to be present. The way in which Boaz handled the situation suggests that he was a person of considerable position and influence in the community.

The negotiations began in the indirect way that is still typical of the Middle East. Boaz mentioned a tract of land which once belonged to Elimelech that Naomi needed to sell. The parcel of land had to be redeemed by a relative. Boaz told the relative that he (the relative) had first right and obligation to buy the land, but that Boaz would do so himself if the relative were unwilling. The relative said that he was willing to redeem the land.

At this point, Boaz mentioned Ruth, as if to say, "By the way, there will be a wife involved." Apparently redeeming the land and redeeming the widow had to be done by the same kinsman-redeemer. This changed things for the relative, who said that he could not serve as the redeemer lest he ruin his own inheritance. If he married Ruth and she gave birth to a son, the field would revert to the son and the relative would lose his investment. In addition, the relative might also have been concerned that the expense of a family would cause him to lose the property he already owned. Boaz again showed his generous nature by not being concerned about such matters. Since the nearer kinsman declined to exercise his right to be the redeemer, Boaz was willing to do it.

The deal was confirmed by the relative giving his sandal to Boaz. This was a custom of the time to show that the giver was relinquishing all rights of possession. The nearest provision in the Law of Moses regarding such a practice is found in Deuteronomy 25:7-10, which interestingly enough deals with the law of levirite marriage. The law said that if a man refused to take his brother's widow and father a child by her in his dead brother's name, the woman was to take his sandal, spit in his face, and declare the shame of his refusal in the presence of the elders. The giving of the sandal to Boaz was not a matter of shame but of the relative merely handing over his rights as kinsman-redeemer. Apparently the Israelites' practice of the sandal had changed since the Lord had given the original provision.

The Connection with David

Boaz and Ruth were married, and they had a son. The women of Bethlehem rejoiced with Naomi over the complete reversal of her fortunes. They offered glowing praise of Ruth and expressed the prayer that Naomi's grandson would bring her joy in her old age. The women of the town (who apparently had an active and influential presence as a group in the community) are credited with giving the boy his name, Obed, which means "servant of the Lord" (Ruth 4:17). This is the only child mentioned from the union of Boaz and Ruth.

Obed was the father of Jesse, who became the father of David. The book ends with the genealogy from Perez, son of Judah, through Boaz and concluding with David. Ruth was David's great-grandmother. It is conceivable that David knew Ruth in his early years. The story of Ruth might well have been one of the favorite tales in David's family history.

During a period of instability in Israel, David took his parents to Moab, Ruth's homeland, for safety. While they were there, his parents stayed with the king of Moab (1 Samuel 22:3-4). Perhaps their connection with Moab through Ruth helped make this temporary move possible.

Michelangelo painted this image in the Sistine Chapel (1511-1512) as part of a series on the ancestors of Christ. Salmon is shown on the right and Ruth and Obed on the left.

What Else Was Happening? (1500 BC - 1100 BC)

(1) The Olmec civilization developed along the Gulf of Mexico. These people were creative artists, as evidenced by the many different types of sculpture that have survived. Among the most striking examples are the colossal heads (example at right).

(2) The Minoan Palace at Knossos, Crete, was a sprawling complex with hundreds of rooms. More likely a religious center than a palace, it had an elaborate water drainage system, including toilets, and extensive storage facilities. Discovered in the late 1800s, the site underwent excavation and attempts at reconstruction into the 1900s.

(3) The Battle of Kadesh took place about 1275 BC between Egyptian and Hittite armies. It involved some 30,000 men and a few thousand chariots. The Egyptians claimed victory, but they ended up retreating.

(4) The Vedas are foundational religious texts for Hinduism—hymns, sacrificial ceremonies, chants, and magical/medical rituals. The material evidently began to be collected during this period. Followers memorized the information and passed it down from one generation to the next. The middle image at right is from a 19th-century written copy.

(5) The Shang dynasty flourished in China. Tens of thousands of so-called oracle bones have been discovered. Questions were written on bones or shells in an appeal for dead ancestors to give guidance (example at right). The culture also practiced human sacrifice.

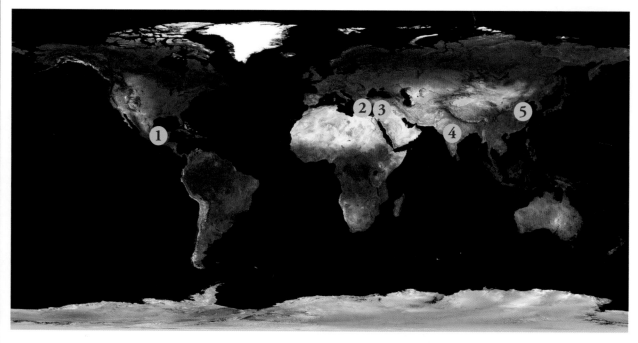

Then the women said to Naomi,
"Blessed is the Lord who has not left you
without a redeemer today,
and may his name become famous in Israel."
Ruth 4:14

Assignments for Lesson 24

Bible   Your reading of Ruth was your Bible assignment for today.

Literature   Continue reading *The Cat of Bubastes.*

Student Review   Optional: Answer the questions for Lesson 24.

Lesson 25 - Bible Study

The Law

While Israel was camped around the base of Mount Sinai in the desert, God gave to Moses a code of laws to regulate the national, personal, interpersonal, and worship activities of the people. This was not the first legal code that governed a nation in the ancient Near East. The Sumerians, Babylonians, Egyptians, and Hittites, as well as others, had written laws. God's Law did, however, have unique attributes that set it apart from other legal systems.

The Law of Moses served as the practical guide for the daily and yearly life of Israel. It has also influenced the development of Western legal systems in more recent times. This lesson will help you understand and appreciate the blessing of the Old Testament Law.

Covenant and Regulations

Any married couple can tell you the difference between a marriage and a marriage license. A marriage is a relationship between two people who have committed themselves to each other in a unique way for the rest of their lives. It is a bond shared by the persons involved. A marriage license is the legal document that shows the binding nature of the marriage. It stands for the many legal statutes that protect and support marriage. A good marriage is not held together by a piece of paper. It is held together by the love and commitment that the man and woman have for each other. Yet without a marriage license, that relationship would have no status before the law.

In the same way, the heart of the relationship between God and Israel was not the Law, but the covenant agreement that they entered into at Sinai. What held the relationship together was the heart-felt commitment that God had for Israel and that Israel had for God. When Israel's commitment was lacking, the relationship suffered. The Law was not the sum total of the covenant; the purpose of the Law was to provide form and content to the relationship between God and Israel. In other words, since the covenant existed, the Law stated what God expected from the people.

The structure of the covenant and Law is similar to the treaties used in the ancient Near East between a conquering ruler (called a suzerain) and the conquered people (called vassals). The suzerain stated what he would do for the vassals and what he expected from the vassals. The vassals were not in a position to negotiate the terms of the treaty. All they could do was either accept it or reject it. However, they did benefit from the arrangement because the suzerain promised to protect the vassals. In this vein, God called Israel to Himself and stated what He would do and what He expected Israel to do. Israel could not negotiate the terms of the covenant. They could only either accept it or reject it.

The nations around Israel tended to believe in multiple gods because they thought that no single god was all-powerful. God wanted Israel to know that He was their one God and that He was strong enough. He wanted their complete loyalty. God is a jealous God. He tolerates no competitors and no half-hearted allegiance. With YHWH, it is all or nothing. These are the terms on which He offered the covenant, and this is how He wanted Israel to respond to it.

A Covenant Based on Grace

Many people believe that the old covenant was based on law and the new covenant in Christ is based on grace. However, the old covenant was based on grace as well. God showed grace to the Israelites by bringing them out of slavery in Egypt, and then He offered the covenant to them on the basis of the unmerited favor He had shown them (Exodus 19:4-6).

God never wanted Israel just to obey the external requirements of the Law without any devotion to Him. God wanted the Israelites to love Him with all of their heart, soul, and strength. He wanted their heart-felt commitment to Him and to following His Word (Deuteronomy 6:4-9). God never wanted a rote, mechanical, or hypocritical going through the motions of keeping His commandments (Isaiah 1:10-15).

The Law must be understood in the context of the relationship between God and Israel. The first five books of the Old Testament are what are usually called the Law. These books of Moses are also known as the Pentateuch, from the Greek words for five books. However, not every verse in these books is a law. They contain many stories about God and His dealings with mankind and specifically with Israel. These stories are part of the Law, and that is the point. We must not try to separate the Law from the covenant. The stories in the Pentateuch give the context for the Law. The legal code came out of the entire covenant experience for Israel.

God wanted Israel to live as His holy people. He wanted Israel to follow His guidelines because He had done so much for them. However, many Israelites came to believe that being chosen by God meant that they were superior to other

The Books of the Torah

Torah is the Hebrew name for the first five books of the Old Testament (the Greek name is Pentateuch). In the Hebrew Bible, the name for each book is taken from the first few words of the book itself.

Genesis is about origins. Exodus concerns Israel's departure from Egypt but also includes many laws. Leviticus deals primarily with the regulations of the Levitical priesthood. Numbers is so named because

of the census that opens the book, but it provides us with most of the history of the wilderness wanderings of Israel. In Deuteronomy Moses repeats the Law for a new generation. The name Deuteronomy is from the Greek deutero-nomos, *meaning second law. The Torah scrolls above are from the Chesed-El Synagogue in Singapore.*

people. By the time of Christ, a group of Jews known as the Pharisees had added their own rigid interpretations of the Law that defined faithfulness and unfaithfulness as they saw it. The Pharisees lost the big picture of God's love in the details of their interpretations.

God was not a Pharisee who was converted to grace under Jesus! We should not equate the Old Testament Law with Phariseeism. Jesus said that He did not come to abolish the Law but to fulfill it (Matthew 5:17). Jesus tried to clear the fog brought on by the Pharisees, to help people see what God is really like. The Law provided training in what it meant to live for the one true and holy God. This way of living was brought to completion in Jesus Christ, who transforms us on the inside and gives us the ultimate motivation of love to live for God.

The Nature of the Law

The Law of Moses contains three kinds of legal provisions. The first are apodictic (a-poh-DIK-tic) laws, or laws of absolute obligation. These are the "Thou shalt/Thou shalt not" provisions. The Ten Commandments are good examples of these laws. Provisions dealing with ceremonial activities are apodictic laws. God simply stated how things were to be done.

The second kind of provisions are casuistic (kaz-you-IS-tic) or hypothetical laws. These usually begin with the phrase "If a man" or "When a man." In other words, these laws apply only when certain events take place. Exodus chapters 21 and 22 contain many casuistic laws.

The third kind of law is case law. These laws came about when new situations arose that had not been previously addressed. The Lord's word in these cases applied to all similar situations in the future. For example, Numbers 15:32-36 addresses what the penalty for Sabbath-breaking was. Numbers 27:1-11 describes how the inheritance laws were to be applied when a man had only daughters and no sons.

Laws were also given which dealt with the responsibilities of the priests, how sacrifices were to be made, the observance of annual feasts, personal cleanliness, dietary laws (clean and unclean foods), and interpersonal relationships. Themes that run through the law include fairness, holiness, and respect for life.

The Law revealed what is important to God and how the Israelites were to approach Him. Since God is clearly different from pagan deities, He was to

The Ten Commandments

The Ten Commandments stand as a preamble to the Law as a whole. The importance of the Ten Commandments is shown by the references to them in the Law (Exodus 34:28; Deuteronomy 4:13 and 10:4). Jesus does not use any of the list when He cites the two most important laws (Mark 12:28-31), but the ten address issues expressed by both of the greatest commands.

The Ten Commandments and the Law of Moses had an influence on Western legal systems. The Law showed that a standard outside of ourselves which came from God is what we ought to live by. Some things are holy by their very nature and must be respected as such (God, marriage, and the parent-child relationship, for instance). Since people are made in God's image, some things are wrong to do to people, such as lying, murder, and adultery. These concepts from the Law have influenced what secular legal systems have protected and what they have punished. The tablets above from the Philippines display the Ten Commandments in the Cebuano language.

This Hebrew text is from the Book of Numbers. The name of God is in the middle of the image.

be worshiped in a distinctly different way. Because people matter to God, they were to be treated in a godly fashion. Because holiness is important to God, God's way is distinctive from other religions. Since people are important to God and holiness is important to God, to be God's holy people was an especially significant calling.

The Meaning of the Law for Christians

The Law is just as inspired as the rest of the Bible. However, the Old Testament Scriptures are connected to the old covenant, which is no longer the way people are called to have a covenant relationship with God. This is available only in Jesus, and the New Testament Scriptures are connected to the new covenant and are thus the authority for Christians in their covenant relationship to God. The Law led us to Christ as a pedagogue led a child to his tutor in ancient Greece (Galatians 3:24-25; the Greek word in this passage, commonly translated tutor, is *pedagoge,* better translated child-conductor). Now

that we have Christ, we no longer need a child-conductor. The book of Hebrews explains how Christ set aside the old covenant with its regulations when He established the new covenant through His blood (Hebrews 7-10).

Some provisions of the Law deal with timeless issues, such as immorality and kindness. These principles apply to Christians because the one true holy God has called the church to be His holy people. We can grow in our understanding of the nature of God by seeing what He allows and forbids in the Law.

No one keeps the Old Testament Law perfectly. In the first place, no one can (Romans 3:19-20). Secondly, the Law cannot be followed completely because the temple does not exist and thus the ritual law cannot be kept. In addition, we do not need to keep the Law because the sacrifice Christ made of Himself for us was a once-and-for-all atonement (Hebrews 10:14). Thus, keeping the Law is not something we should pursue. Efforts in the early church to make Christians obey the Law were met with stiff apostolic resistance (Acts 15, Galatians 5:1-6).

Conclusion

God gave the Law for Israel to live by as His chosen and holy people. Israel lived under what is called the Law of Moses for about 1,500 years. After the Temple in Jerusalem was destroyed in 70 AD, many Jews tried to continue to live by as many laws as they could. However, much of the ritual code was impossible to keep with the loss of the Temple.

The Law that God gave to Israel through Moses was a blessing for those called to live by it (Psalm 19:7-11). In the Law, the Israelites had instructions from God about how they were to live and how they were to worship Him. They could see both that God is merciful and that God exacts appropriate punishment for transgression. God set high standards for justice and love, much higher than the standards of the pagan nations around them. The Law was not intended to be a list of burdensome regulations to keep people from enjoying life. It was God's way of guiding His people in the first steps of holiness, a gift that brought abundant blessings when they obeyed it, and the way that Israel could know how God wanted them to live in holiness and righteousness.

*For this commandment which I command you today
is not too difficult for you, nor is it out of reach. . . .
But the word is very near you, in your mouth and
in your heart, that you may observe it.
Deuteronomy 30:11, 14*

Assignments for Lesson 25

Bible Read Leviticus 19 and Deuteronomy 32. Commentary available in *Student Review.*

Recite or write Psalm 78:5-7 from memory.

Literature Finish reading *The Cat of Bubastes*. Literary analysis available in *Student Review.*

Project Complete your project for the unit.

Student Review Optional: Answer the questions for Lesson 25 and for *The Cat of Bubastes*; take the quiz for Unit 5; and take the first history, English, and Bible exams.

6

Israel and Her Neighbors

Summary

In this unit we look at the history of Israel from the beginning of the monarchy to the return of the Jews from captivity in Babylon. We will also survey the nations that existed around Israel during this period. Special attention is given to David, the man after God's own heart, and the beautiful temple that Solomon built in Jerusalem. Prophets played a major role in Israel's history as they pleaded, reminded, and warned their often spiritually deaf listeners. We look particularly at the prophet Amos.

Lessons

26 - Israel United and Divided
27 - Nations of the Ancient Near East
28 - Key Person: David
29 - Everyday Life: The Time of King Solomon
30 - Bible Study: Amos, the Unlikely Prophet

17th-Century Model of the Temple, Hamburg Museum, Germany

127

Learn Amos 5:8 by the end of the unit.

The Bible
In Their Words

1) Write 300 to 500 words on one of the following topics:
   • Write a psalm of praise to God. See Lesson 28.
   • Write a sermon in which you try to convict your hearers to change their ways. See Lesson 30.
2) Create a model of one of the temple furnishings as described in 1 Kings 7:15-44. See Lesson 29.
3) Memorize Psalm 8.

The Old Testament is a library of many different kinds of literature: history, genealogies, law code, wisdom writings, apocalyptic literature, songs, and poetry. We need to respect how God inspired the Bible and read these different forms of literature in appropriate ways. We would not read a poem the way we read a law code, nor would we read wisdom literature the same way we read history.

The books of Genesis through 2 Kings tell a fairly continuous narrative of Israel's history from Creation to the beginning of the Babylonian captivity of Judah. First and Second Chronicles repeat much of the history, but they emphasize David and the Southern Kingdom. Second Chronicles records the decree of the Persian king Cyrus that allowed the Jews to return to their homeland. Ezra, Nehemiah, and Esther tell about events that happened after the captivity. The books of Job through Song of Solomon are called the Writings and date from various times.

All of the books of the prophets are collected in one group from Isaiah to Malachi. Isaiah, Jeremiah and Lamentations, Ezekiel, and Daniel are called the Major Prophets because of the length of their books. The last twelve books of the Old Testament are called the Minor Prophets, but only because of the relative brevity of their books, not because their messages were of minor importance. Information in the prophetic books and elsewhere in the Old Testament helps us know when each prophet preached.

About forty percent of the Old Testament is written in poetic form. This includes individual passages in the histories, much of the prophetic books, and the book of Psalms. Hebrew poetry is not like English poetry. Rhythm is important, but rhyme is not. A key feature of Hebrew poetry is parallelism: the same thought expressed in different words. Every line in every Hebrew poem is not necessarily parallel to another line, but parallelism is common.

Some Hebrew poetry is written in the form of an acrostic, in which each succeeding line or stanza begins with the succeeding letter of the Hebrew alphabet. The description of the worthy woman in Proverbs 31:10-31 is an acrostic. The first four chapters in Lamentations are acrostics. The ultimate acrostic is Psalm 119, which was written in praise of God's Law. Each of its first eight lines begins with *aleph* (the first letter of the Hebrew alphabet), each of the second eight lines begins with *beth* (the second letter), each of the next eight lines begins with *gimel*, and so on through the Hebrew alphabet.

Detail from David and Jonathan, *Cima da Conegliano (Italian, c. 1508)*

Israel United and Divided

Looking at world history merely from a secular viewpoint, Israel was hardly a blip on the screen. It was not large, and it had few natural resources. For about two hundred years it was divided into two competing kingdoms. Surrounding nations often invaded it or demanded tribute, and Israel did little to defend itself. Both kingdoms of divided Israel were defeated by foreign nations, and thousands of people were taken into captivity.

However, the history of Israel is a central part of the story of the ancient world. God chose Israel to be His holy people out of all the nations of the earth. His hand at times protected and at other times chastened Israel because of His love for the people and because of His intention to accomplish His plan through them. Religions of other nations in the ancient Near East have faded into obscurity, but the worship of the God of Israel has spread around the globe.

An understanding of Israel is important for any student of world history because of its influence on later cultures. Understanding Israel helps us understand the New Testament and the gospel of Christ. In the history of Israel we can see most clearly God's work in the ancient world.

From Judges to a King

Israel struggled through the period of the Judges without clear leadership and with a tendency to adopt the practices of the pagans around them. God raised up the last judge, Samuel, to lead Israel into a new period of their history. When Samuel's sons failed to live up to their father's pattern of godliness, the people of Israel came to him and asked, "Now appoint a king for us to judge us like all the nations" (1 Samuel 8:5).

Samuel was hurt by the request, but God told him that they were actually rejecting Him, not Samuel. Samuel warned them that a king would be a burden to them, but the people would not listen. "There shall be a king over us that we also may be like all the nations, that our king may judge us and go out before us and fight our battles" (1 Samuel 8:19-20). God's purpose for Israel was for them to be different from the other nations, but instead Israel wanted to be like the other nations. They thought that they could be like the world in some things and still be God's holy people, but they were mistaken.

Samuel anointed Saul to be Israel's first king around 1042 BC. Saul fully looked the part. He stood head and shoulders taller than anyone else

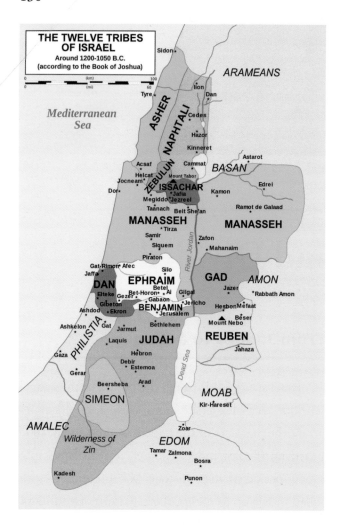

THE TWELVE TRIBES OF ISRAEL
Around 1200-1050 B.C.
(according to the Book of Joshua)

who extended Israel's control and enriched Israel's treasuries even more. The era of David and Solomon was ever after regarded in Israel as its golden age.

When Solomon's son, Rehoboam, ascended to the throne in 931 BC, the people asked him to ease the burden of forced labor that his father had placed on them. Rehoboam, however, listened to the advice of his younger counselors instead of the wisdom of the elders. He decided that he had something to prove to Israel, so he determined to make the people's labor even harder. Jeroboam led a revolt against Rehoboam and the Davidic dynasty. He led the ten northern tribes into a new alliance and became king over them in Samaria. Only the tribes of Judah and Benjamin remained loyal to the line of David.

The Divided Kingdom

In Scripture, the ten northern tribes are called Israel. They are also sometimes known as the Northern Kingdom. Judah and Benjamin are called Judah. We also call them the Southern Kingdom. Jeroboam wanted to discourage people in the North from going to Jerusalem to worship God, so he built

In the 1520s, Hans Holbein the Younger painted murals for the Great Council Chamber of the Town Hall in Basel, Switzerland. Only a few portions remain, including this depiction of Rehoboam comparing his little finger to his father's waist (1 Kings 12:10).

(1 Samuel 10:23). His impressive appearance, however, disguised his heart of rebellion. When Saul disobeyed the Lord's instructions, God rejected him and his descendants from sitting on the throne of Israel (1 Samuel 15:22-23). God led Samuel to a different kind of person, the shepherd boy David, to begin the dynasty that would reign continually on the throne of Israel. "God sees not as man sees, for man looks at the outward appearance, but the Lord looks at the heart" (1 Samuel 16:7).

The Dynasty of David

Saul died during a battle around 1010 BC. David became king first over Judah and then, after a short period of instability, over all of Israel. David was an effective leader whom God blessed with many victories over the surrounding nations. He was succeeded in 970 BC by his son Solomon,

ΘΕΣΤRVCCIO IHEROSOLIME

The Destruction of Jerusalem by the Babylonians, from the Nuremberg Chronicle *(1493)*

shrines in the North and fashioned, of all things, two golden calves as idols (1 Kings 12:25-31). This led the Northern Kingdom into continuous idolatry. Throughout its turbulent history of over two hundred years, Israel was officially pagan. It had a series of dynasties on its throne, and many of its kings met with violent ends. However, Israel became wealthy through trade and alliances with other countries.

The Southern Kingdom did better in its walk with the Lord, but not by much. Judah always had a descendant of David on the throne. Most of its rulers acknowledged God but also worshiped the false deities of the land. Only the occasional reformer, such as Josiah, tried to clean up the worship practices of Judah and restore the faithful worship of the one true God; but such reforms were always short-lived.

The kingdoms of Israel and Judah sometimes fought against each other and sometimes were allies against a common foe. The people had wanted a king so that they could be like the nations around them, and they got what they wanted. The political intrigues and military battles in which Israel and

Judah engaged sapped their strength and diverted their attention from pursuing God. Instead of being the distinct people of God, they took up the worship practices of the Gentiles. They did indeed become like the nations around them.

During the period of the Divided Kingdom, God sent many prophets to preach among the people. Most went either to the Northern Kingdom or the Southern Kingdom, while a few preached against the sins of the Gentile nations. Elijah and Elisha served the Lord in the Northern Kingdom during the reign of the wicked Ahab and Jezebel. We know little of what Elijah and Elisha spoke, but we know many stories about the miracles they performed. Isaiah and Jeremiah, on the other hand, prophesied to the Southern Kingdom. The Bible records many of their sermons in the books that bear their names.

The Fall of Israel and Judah

The foreign nations with which Israel and Judah had relations were interested in accomplishing their own national goals, not in respecting the people of

God. In 721 BC (or possibly 722) Assyria invaded and captured the Northern Kingdom and sent many of its people into exile. Second Kings 17 states clearly that this happened to Israel as punishment for their unfaithfulness to God. The king of Assyria brought people from Babylon and elsewhere to repopulate the area with those who would be more loyal to him. Few people from the Northern Kingdom ever returned to the land. They are sometimes called the Ten Lost Tribes of Israel.

Kingdoms rise and fall, and Assyria eventually fell to Babylon (or Chaldea). Then the sins of Judah became so great that God used the empire-building impulses of the Babylonians to punish the Southern Kingdom. In a series of raids between 606 and 586 BC, the Chaldeans took thousands of captives from Judah to Babylon. Second Chronicles 36 says that this happened because of the unfaithfulness of Judah.

Babylon eventually fell to the Medo-Persian Empire, and the Persian king Cyrus instituted a new policy allowing captive peoples to return to their homelands. Many Jews returned to Judah and Jerusalem, but a significant number remained in Babylon or wherever they had settled. This was the beginning of the Dispersion, the Jews who lived scattered among the nations instead of in the land that God had given their forefathers. The often uneasy relations between Jews and the other people of the nations where they live have continued to be a reality in world history and world politics to the present.

Restoration of the Jews to Israel

Jews returned from Babylon to the land of Israel over a period of years. Ezra oversaw the rebuilding of the temple, and Nehemiah led the reconstruction of the wall around Jerusalem. Their efforts were plagued at times by a lack of interest among the Jews and by harassment from nearby populations, but their work was eventually completed.

The Jews returned to Israel a chastened people. Idolatry was never again the issue that it had been in earlier generations. In addition, the Jews continued a new tradition that they had begun while they were in captivity. Since the Jews could not worship at the temple as God had instructed them, they had begun to gather on Sabbath days to hear the Scriptures read and expounded. The Greek word for these assemblies was *sunagoge* (coming together), rendered in English as synagogue. The Jews who returned to Israel maintained the synagogue tradition even after the temple was rebuilt, and Jews around the world continue to meet in synagogues today.

During the early 1900s, many Jews fled from persecution in Russia to Shanghai, China. The Ohel Moshe Synagogue, pictured below, was built in 1927 to serve the growing Jewish community there. Shanghai was the only major city in the world that allowed Jews to immigrate to it during the Holocaust. Several thousand Jews arrived in the city between 1937 and 1941. Ho Feng-Shan, a Chinese diplomat in Austria, risked his career and personal safety to help hundreds, perhaps thousands, of these Jews to leave Europe.

The Significance of Israel

Small as it was, Israel contributed significantly to world history. Through Israel, the world came to know the one true God. Israel was monotheistic (believing in one God) while most other cultures were polytheistic. The righteous character of God stood in stark contrast to the vengeful and capricious gods of other nations. Israel also provided an example of ethical religion, in which a person's faith was to influence how he lived. Most other cultures made little connection between religious practice and personal morality.

Israel did not make significant contributions to the world in terms of science or architecture, but its inspired literature towers above everything else that has been written. Cultures around the world have been enriched by stories from the Old Testament, which have served as the basis for literature and art centuries later. The Law of God given to Israel through Moses was clearly more enlightened and humane than any law code ever produced by the mind of man. The greatest gift that came from Israel is the Messiah, Jesus. Because of Him and through His followers, the world has been forever changed for the better.

Give thanks to the Lord, for He is good,
For His lovingkindness is everlasting.
Oh let Israel say,
"His lovingkindness is everlasting."
Psalm 118:1-2

Assignments for Lesson 26

Bible Read 1 Samuel 12-13 and 2 Kings 17. Commentary available in *Student Review*.

Student Review Optional: Answer the questions for Lesson 26.

Lesson 27

Nations of the Ancient Near East

Israel did not occupy the Promised Land in a vacuum. They were surrounded by several other nations, nations that were pagan and that often threatened the peace of Israel. The Bible and archaeology give us information on many of the nations that existed in the ancient Near East. This lesson highlights some of these peoples.

David and Goliath (Spanish, c. 1123)

The Philistines

Philistia was a group of city-states that occupied the coastal region southwest of Israel. Its five main cities were Gaza, Ashkelon, Ashdod, Ekron, and Gath. The Philistines were descendants of Ham who are thought to have come from the area of the Aegean Sea, perhaps when European tribes invaded and settled Greece (see Unit 9). The earliest archaeological reference to the Philistines occurs in a text from the Egyptian Pharaoh Ramesses III about 1185 BC.

Philistine warriors used iron weapons, which gave them a great advantage over the Israelites (see 1 Samuel 13:19-22). Their knowledge of iron reflects an important step in the transition from what is called the Bronze Age to the Iron Age.

The Philistines and the Israelites were constantly in conflict. For instance, after suffering many defeats at the hands of the Israelite judge Samson, the Philistines finally captured him and chained him between two pillars (Judges 16). In his last act, Samson pushed on these two middle pillars on which the house rested. This caused the house to collapse, killing Samson and the Philistines who were present. Archaeologists have found a Philistine architectural style in which a building was supported primarily by two central pillars.

Later, the showdown between the young David and the giant Goliath took place when the armies of Israel and Philistia were drawn up against each other (1 Samuel 17). In ancient warfare, armies would sometimes send forth their best warriors for a one-on-one battle. Whoever won this contest of champions led his army to victory in the war. David was an unlikely champion; but no other Israelite dared to take on Goliath, and David fought with complete trust in the Lord (1 Samuel 17:45-47). David later allied himself with the Philistines for a time when he was on the run from Saul. As king, David finally eliminated the Philistine threat with a decisive victory that God gave the Israelites (2 Samuel 5:22-25).

The Philistines believed in many gods. Their chief deity was Dagon, god of the harvest. Ashtoreth was their chief goddess. They also worshiped Baalzebub. The ark of the covenant made a mockery of Dagon and the Philistines when the Philistines captured it in battle and put it in the temple of Dagon (1 Samuel 5).

The legacy of the Philistines lives on today in place names. The name Palestine is generally thought to be derived from the word Philistine. The coastal area between modern Israel and Egypt is called Gaza.

The Hittites

Although the Bible contains fifty references to a nation known as the Hittites, nothing was known about them outside of Scripture for many centuries. Some scholars doubted whether they even existed. However, archaeological discoveries around 1900 showed once again that the Bible is true and that the skeptics were wrong.

Mythological Creatures from Hittite Culture

The Hittite civilization, which was centered in Asia Minor, flourished between about 1800 and 1200 BC. They were skillful in battle and expanded their territory by conquering neighboring peoples. Like the Philistines, the Hittites developed iron weapons through a smelting process that they attempted to keep secret. They also used a light, horse-drawn chariot that helped them achieve military victory. Enemies from the west defeated the Hittite Empire around 1200 BC, although their military skills continued to be feared for some time (see 2 Kings 7:6).

Many questions remain about the Hittite civilization. They are not known to have made great advances in literature or the arts, but the Hittite law code was more humane than the laws of the Mesopotamian region.

The Phoenicians

Phoenicia occupied the area to the north of Israel, largely what is now Lebanon. The origins of this nation are somewhat obscure, although they might have migrated from the Persian Gulf region. Phoenician life was centered in its two largest city-states, Tyre and Sidon. Other port cities were built as well.

The Phoenicians were a seafaring and trading people. They were known for their cedar wood (later known as the cedars of Lebanon) and for a rare purple dye called murex that came from snails. The dye was beautiful, but it was so expensive that usually only kings could afford it. As a result, purple came to be associated with royalty. The name Phoenicia is from the Greek word for purple.

Phoenician trading ships crisscrossed the Mediterranean and even ventured into the Atlantic,

A Phoenician Model of a Ship, Found in Byblos

going as far as England and the southern tip of Africa. Phoenician sailors learned how to use the stars to help them navigate. As their trade expanded, the Phoenicians established colonies as stopping points. Their colonies were located on Cyprus, at Gibraltar, and (by 800 BC) at Carthage on the North African coast. Foreign conquerors took control of Phoenicia from time to time, but the nation managed to survive and continued to prosper into Roman times.

The Black Obelisk (c. 825 BC) Depicts an Israelite Bowing Before Assyrian King Shalmaneser III

Pagan Gods

King Ahab of the Northern Kingdom married Jezebel of Sidon, a Phoenician city. Jezebel worshiped the Canaanite god called Ba'al (see figurine at right). Ahab agreed to do so also, and they influenced all of Israel to worship Ba'al. Since Ba'al means master, this worship was a direct rejection of the worship of God as their Lord. Ahab also erected an image of the goddess Asherah. The term was also used for the idol itself (see 1 Kings 16:29-33). The plural form of Asherah is Asherim.

King Ahaziah consulted Baalzebub, a Philistine god, when he became ill (2 Kings 1:1-6, 16). Baalzebub means "lord of the flies." The name was so odious to Jews that it later became a term for Satan (Mark 3:22-23).

The worship of Canaanite gods was despicable to the followers of YHWH. Pagan worship included the construction of altars on high places, where pagans took part in ritual immorality to encourage the gods to make the land fertile. The people occasionally practiced child sacrifice as well (2 Kings 16:3).

The Phoenicians were carriers of civilization as they transported goods. Because of their need for maintaining records, in the 1500s BC the Phoenicians developed a written alphabet with twenty-two consonants. The Greeks adapted the alphabet and added vowels, and this became the basis for the Western alphabet as we know it. The Phoenician port of Byblos was known for its trade in papyrus. The Greeks took their word for book from it: *biblion*. It is the origin of our name for the Book of Books, the Bible.

The Assyrians

The Assyrians were descendants of Asshur, son of Shem (Genesis 10:22). One of their oldest cities was called Assur. The Assyrian nation developed in northern Mesopotamia along a major trade route. They built a strong military, first to protect their own land but later to control trade and other peoples.

Assyrian rule eventually extended to Babylon, Syria, Palestine, and Egypt. The Assyrians were known as fierce fighters who used cruel methods against their opponents. The nation did not have enough soldiers to police their vast empire, so they employed terror as a means of control. Assyria conquered the Northern Kingdom of Israel in 721 BC and attacked but did not conquer the Southern Kingdom.

God showed His love for the people of Assyria by having Jonah preach in its capital, Nineveh. Amazingly, this war-like people repented even at the prophet's reluctant preaching. However, their repentance did not last. The prophet Nahum later predicted the downfall of Assyria, saying that the Assyrians would receive on themselves the cruelties they had inflicted upon others. Babylon destroyed Nineveh in 612 BC.

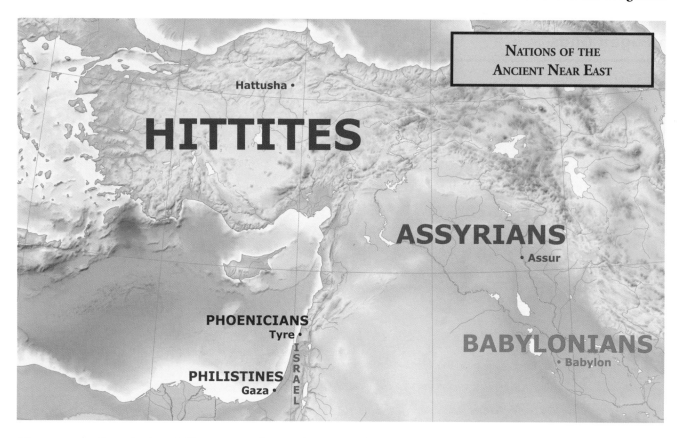

These nations flourished at different times during the 2nd and 1st millennia BC, but this map shows their relative areas of influence around Israel.

*And Elijah came near to all the people and said,
"How long will you hesitate between two opinions?
If the Lord is God, follow Him; but if Baal, follow him."
But the people did not answer him a word.
1 Kings 18:21*

Assignments for Lesson 27

Bible   Read 2 Samuel 8-9 and 1 Kings 17-19. Commentary available in *Student Review.*

In Their Words   Read the Inscription on the Sarcophagus of Eshmunazar II and the excerpts from Books IV and V in the *Histories* (pages 25-27).

Student Review   Optional: Answer the questions for Lesson 27.

Detail from The Transfer of the Ark *(Italian, c. 1625)*

Lesson 28 - Key Person

David

After Saul disobeyed the Lord's instructions concerning the destruction of Amalek, Samuel met him and rebuked him. Samuel told Saul, "The Lord has torn the kingdom of Israel from you today and has given it to your neighbor, who is better than you" (1 Samuel 15:28). That neighbor was David, son of Jesse, who through many trials went from being a shepherd boy to being a mighty king.

David was born in Bethlehem around 1040 BC. His father Jesse was the son of Obed, who was the son of Boaz and Ruth. David had seven older brothers and two sisters. He was a ruddy and handsome youth who developed his mind and body in the field as he kept the family's sheep. David distinguished himself through musical skill, courage, and prudence.

The Lord sent Samuel to Bethlehem to anoint a new king. Jesse's sons came before Samuel in turn, but the Lord had not chosen any of the first seven, despite their appearance and stature. David was still out tending the sheep, so Jesse had to send for him. When David arrived, the Lord identified him as the chosen one. Samuel anointed David in the midst of his brothers, and the Spirit of the Lord came upon him. Though he was the anointed king, David still had to face many tribulations.

Since Saul was afflicted with an evil spirit, his servants sought a harpist to come and sooth him. David came to attend Saul with refreshing music. Saul appreciated David and made him his armor bearer. David went back and forth between serving Saul and his job of tending Jesse's flock.

Facing the Giant

On one occasion, the Philistines gathered their armies for battle against Israel. The opposing armies camped on opposite sides of a valley. David's three eldest brothers joined Saul's army, but David was left behind.

The Philistine champion Goliath came forward forty mornings and evenings to taunt and challenge the Israelite army. The Israelites were terrified by his massive size and powerful weaponry. None of them was willing to accept Goliath's challenge.

One day Jesse sent David to the camp with food for his brothers and their commander. Goliath came out as usual, and David heard his taunt. David wondered why his countrymen allowed this mockery to continue. Though his brother Eliab belittled him, David told Saul that he would fight the Philistine. With a sling and a stone and the power of the living God, David killed Goliath. The Philistine army

A French breviary (liturgical prayer book) from 1296 features this illustration of Samuel anointing David at the top and David facing Goliath at the bottom.

broke and ran, and the Israelites pursued them. Thus David earned the respect of the people, the musical praise of the women, and the suspicion of Saul.

David and Jonathan, Saul's son, became fast friends after this. Both were brave and honorable young men, and they shared faith in the Lord and His power. Their souls were knit together, and they made a covenant with each other.

The Struggle with Saul

Saul was jealous of David's popularity and success. He tried to kill David himself and then wondered how he could get the Philistines to do the job for him. Saul offered his elder daughter Merab to David in marriage but ended up giving her to someone else. Saul learned that his daughter Michal loved David, so she became the first of David's many wives. Saul continued his furious attempts to rid himself of David. Saul's children Michal and Jonathan sided with David, helping him to escape.

While David was on the run, he ate the consecrated bread at Nob, played the fool before King Achish in Gath, became a mercenary for Achish, and defeated the Amalekites to rescue his captured wives. Twice he had the opportunity to kill Saul, but he refused to raise his hand against the Lord's anointed.

The end finally came for Saul and three of his sons during a battle with the Philistines. David chanted a lament for Saul and Jonathan and wanted the sons of Judah to learn it. "Your beauty, O Israel, is slain on your high places! How have the mighty fallen!" (2 Samuel 1:19).

David Becomes King

The Lord directed David to Hebron where the men of Judah accepted him as king. However, Saul's army commander Abner put forward Saul's son Ish-bosheth as king. This led to civil war between the house of Saul and the house of David. David's commander was his nephew Joab. David appreciated Joab's military prowess, but they had a rocky relationship.

The war dragged on, and eventually Abner decided to go over to David after Ish-bosheth offended him. David agreed to meet with Abner if his wife Michal, whom Saul had given to another man, was restored to him. David gave a feast for Abner and his men, and Abner encouraged the elders of Israel to recognize David as king.

Joab held a grudge against Abner for killing Joab's brother Asahel during an earlier battle. He told David that Abner was just trying to spy on him. Joab called Abner to meet with him privately and murdered him. David disclaimed responsibility for Abner's death and joined in his funeral procession.

Ish-bosheth lost heart when he heard of Abner's death. Two of his officers killed him, hoping to gain David's favor. David did not approve of this murder either, so he had those two men executed.

Finally David was recognized as king over all Israel. He captured the stronghold of Zion at Jerusalem, which became known as the City of David. He was about thirty-seven years old, and He reigned for thirty-three more years. David administered justice and righteousness for his nation.

The Family Man

While David reigned at Hebron during the civil war, his family began to grow. His first wife Michal had no children. His firstborn was Amnon, born by Ahinoam the Jezreelitess. Abigail, the widow of Nabal, bore him Chileab (or Daniel). Absalom was the son of Maacah, Adonijah was the son of Haggith, Shephatiah was the son of Abital, and Ithream was the son of Eglah.

In Jerusalem, David took more wives and concubines. These nine sons were added to his family there: Ibhar, Elishua, Elpelet, Nogah, Nepheg, Japhia, Elishama, Eliada, and Eliphelet. Bathsheba also bore David four sons, Shammua, Shobab, Nathan, and Solomon. Tamar is the only daughter whose name we know, but she was not David's only daughter (2 Samuel 5:13).

David's multiplication of wives directly disobeyed the Law of Moses (Deuteronomy 17:17), and we clearly see the result of his folly. His lust of the flesh led him into the sins of adultery and murder in the case of Bathsheba and Uriah. His difficulty in controlling himself gave him difficulty in controlling his children. We have the specific description in 1 Kings 1:6 that David never crossed (or displeased) his son Adonijah, and that likely describes David's relationship with all of his children.

David's son Solomon recognized children as a heritage from the Lord (Psalm 127:3); but children who are not properly trained become a curse, as seen in Proverbs. "A foolish son is a grief to his father and bitterness to her who bore him" (Proverbs 17:25). The grief caused by undisciplined children often spreads beyond the immediate household.

Devotion to God

Even in his youth, David was devoted to the God of Israel. Indeed, he was a man after God's heart (1 Samuel 13:14). David expressed his praise, his thanksgiving, his fears, and his struggles through the many psalms he wrote.

David and Bathsheba
Lucas Cranach the Elder (German, 1526)

The Psalms

Bible scholars have classified the Psalms into several categories depending on the subject matter and the approach used by the writer. Consider the descriptions of these categories. You will read several examples in today's Bible reading.

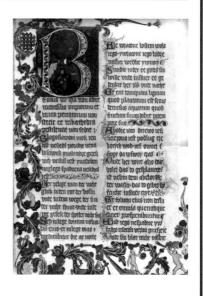

Psalms of Lament and Petition

This is the largest single category, comprising about one-third of the Psalms. The writer is in distress and makes a petition to God. This category has been divided into these three sub-categories:

- *psalms of innocence, in which the writer cannot understand why the distress is happening because he believes he is innocent*
- *psalms of penitence, in which the writer acknowledges his guilt that has caused the distress*
- *psalms of confidence, in which the writer expresses assurance that God will see him through the distress*

Some psalms of lament and petition are called imprecatory psalms because they ask God to bring harm on the one who is persecuting the writer as an expression of God's righteous judgment.

Psalms of Praise and Thanksgiving

This is the second largest category of psalms. These psalms are joyous celebrations of praise to God for His Creation, His work in history, His salvation, or His goodness.

Psalms of Teaching (or Didactic Psalms)

These psalms teach truths about God that the writer wants Israel to remember.

Royal Psalms

These psalms might fall into any of the categories above, but they are connected in some way with the king of Israel. They might have been composed for a king's coronation or other special event. In many cases the king is a foreshadowing of Christ.

Other Information about the Psalms

The headings that begin many of the psalms provide information about the author and the setting of the psalm. Seventy-three psalms are credited to David, twelve to Asaph, and eleven to the sons of Korah. Some do not have an author listed. The Psalms are divided into five books, probably to correspond to the five books of the Law (see the beginning of Psalms 1, 42, 73, 90, and 107). Psalms 120 through 134 are called Songs of Ascents. These might have been sung by pilgrims on their way to Jerusalem to celebrate the festivals prescribed in the Law. Jerusalem is geographically higher than the surrounding area, so people ascending to Jerusalem would sing Songs of Ascents.

The Florian Psalter (top right), created in Poland around 1400, had text in Latin, Polish, and German. Above left is King David Playing the Harp *by Gerard van Honthorst (Dutch, 1622).*

David brought the ark of God to Jerusalem (after a zealous but misguided initial attempt) and desired to build a house for the ark. However, that was not to be during his reign. Instead, God gave that job to David's son. Still, David made extensive preparations for constructing the temple.

David showed his faith through compassion on his enemies and friends. Even when Saul was hotly pursuing him, David did not desire to harm him. He did not seek revenge on Saul or his family. Indeed, King David desired to show kindness to Saul's house because of Jonathan. Saul's servant Ziba told him about Mephibosheth, the crippled son of Jonathan. David restored to Mephibosheth his family lands and welcomed Mephibosheth to his table as one of his own sons.

After sinning against Bathsheba and Uriah and God Almighty, David showed the importance of repentance. He humbled himself before the Lord and accepted God's righteous discipline. He desired a clean heart and a steadfast spirit (Psalm 51:10).

Final Years

The concluding years of David's life were full of trouble and strife. His son Amnon violated David's daughter (and Amnon's half-sister) Tamar. Tamar's brother Absalom killed Amnon. Absalom sought to take the throne from his father, and Joab killed him. The Benjamite Sheba led a revolt. A three-year famine afflicted the land. Battles continued with the Philistines, including more trouble with giants.

The Lord allowed Satan to tempt David into directing a census of the fighting men in Israel (see 2 Samuel 24 and 1 Chronicles 21). Joab was hesitant to follow David's instruction, but the king's word prevailed. Perhaps David's sin was pride in wanting to know his military strength. We know that his heart was troubled after the fact. God offered him a choice of punishments: a few years of famine, a few months of military defeat, or a few days of pestilence. David chose the pestilence, which afflicted the land from Dan to Beersheba.

When David was advanced in age, his servants found a beautiful girl, Abishag, to care for him. Adonijah resolved to be king, and Joab and the priest Abiathar supported his claim. Nathan and Bathsheba reminded David that he had promised the throne to Solomon. At David's command, Zadok the priest anointed Solomon to be king, and Adonijah and his followers dispersed.

Before he died, David charged Solomon to show himself a man and follow the Lord's commandments. He also provided plans for the temple. One of his final commands was for Solomon to punish Joab. "Then he died in a ripe old age, full of days, riches and honor; and his son Solomon reigned in his place" (1 Chronicles 29:28).

An Example for Us

David holds a prominent place in the story of God's work among men. He is the only person with that name in the Bible. His faith and virtue are models for us to follow. His folly and vice are warnings for our instruction. He was a key link in the chain from Abraham to Christ, and he spoke of the coming Messiah. "The Lord says to my Lord: 'Sit at My right hand until I make your enemies a footstool for Your feet'" (Psalm 110:1). David served the purpose of God in his generation.

Solomon watching as David is lowered into his tomb, from a medieval manuscript.

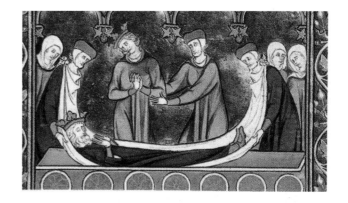

*"For David, after he had served the purpose of God in his own generation,
fell asleep, and was laid among his fathers and underwent decay;
but He whom God raised did not undergo decay."*
Acts 13:36-37

Assignments for Lesson 28

Bible   Read 2 Samuel 22-24 and Psalm 44 (a psalm of innocence), Psalm 51 (penitence), Psalm 23 (confidence), Psalm 8 (praise), Psalm 136 (thanksgiving), Psalm 19 (teaching), Psalm 110 (royal), and Psalm 119:1-16 (acrostic). Commentary available in *Student Review.*

Student Review   Optional: Answer the questions for Lesson 28.

Solomon's Court (Frankish, 9th century)

The Time of King Solomon

Solomon ruled over Israel from about 970 to 931 BC. Israel's wealth and international power were at their height during his reign. The son of David undertook the construction of the magnificent temple in Jerusalem as well as other building projects. Solomon gained a wide reputation for his insightful wisdom and knowledge of the world. He governed Israel with a firm hand and an efficient bureaucracy.

However, Solomon's glorious tenure ended in spiritual failure. His many foreign wives led him into the practice of idolatry. The harsh rule of his son and successor Rehoboam led to a division within the nation that resulted in tragic consequences for Israel, both spiritual and material, for centuries. In this lesson we will survey Solomon's reign and learn about life in Israel during that period.

Solomon's Faithfulness

At the beginning of Solomon's reign, the people of his kingdom were as numerous as the sand on the seashore. Each man in Israel and Judah enjoyed living in peace and prosperity "under his vine and his fig tree" (1 Kings 4:25). These were the glory days of the Israelite people. They were blessed to be ruled by the wise King Solomon, who became greater than all of the earth's kings in terms of riches and wisdom.

Solomon loved the Lord and walked in the statues of his father David, even though he participated in unauthorized worship on the high places. There Solomon burned incense and made sacrifices. Once he offered a thousand burnt offerings on the great high place in Gibeon.

In Gibeon the Lord appeared to Solomon, and Solomon made his famous request for an understanding heart. When Solomon awoke from his dream, he went to Jerusalem and stood before the ark of the covenant. There he offered burnt offerings and made peace offerings. Perhaps Solomon was showing that he was turning away from worship on the high places by leaving Gibeon and sacrificing before the ark of the covenant in Jerusalem.

Solomon's Wisdom and Learning

The Lord gave Solomon a wise and discerning heart. No other mortal has ever been like Solomon, either before he was born or since that time. The Lord also gave him riches and honor. God promised that He would also give him a long life if Solomon would be obedient.

Solomon's wisdom was greater than that of the sons of the east and greater than the wisdom of Egypt. He shared his wisdom with the many that came to listen to and learn from him. He spoke 3,000 proverbs and wrote 1,005 songs. In his book of Proverbs, he taught about wisdom, parenting, marriage, work, diligence, foolishness, righteousness, controlling the tongue, riches and poverty, paying attention, honesty, drunkenness, farming, and more. His Song of Solomon is a beautiful love story. In Ecclesiastes he wrote about the meaning of life. Solomon's breadth of understanding included knowledge about trees, animals, birds, creeping things, and fish.

One responsibility that King Solomon had was judging his people wisely. One time two prostitutes came to him with a question regarding a child. The women lived together in a house. Each gave birth to a child. One of the children died, and both women claimed to be the mother of the living child. King Solomon asked for a sword and commanded that the child be divided into two parts and that one part be given to each woman. One woman agreed with this decision, but the other (the real mother) was grieved at the idea and asked the king just to give the living child to the other woman. In this way King Solomon determined who the real mother was. This decision convinced the Israelites that Solomon's wisdom was from God.

Governmental Organization

Solomon's dominion extended from the Euphrates River to the land of the Philistines and on to the border of Egypt. The subject kings in these regions brought tribute to Solomon and served him.

Speculum Humanae Salvationis (Mirror of Human Salvation) *was a 14th-century work comparing New Testament events with related Old Testament events. This illustration of King Solomon on his throne is from a 1360 edition.*

His kingdom enjoyed peace with all of its neighbors. Domestically, Solomon oversaw a large body of government officials who worked for him. These included priests, secretaries, a recorder, the leader of his army, deputies and their leader, an official over Solomon's household, and an officer who oversaw the forced laborers.

The wealth of Solomon was overwhelming. He had 40,000 stalls of horses for his chariots and

King Solomon and the Queen of Sheba
Konrad Witz (German, 1435)

12,000 horsemen. Solomon built cities for his chariots and for his horsemen. He made 200 large shields of beaten gold with a large amount of gold on each and 300 other shields of beaten gold with three minas of gold on each.

Each of Solomon's deputies was responsible for provisions for the king and his household for one month of the year. Providing for the king was a major undertaking. The provisions for Solomon's court for one day included about 300 bushels of fine flour, about 600 bushels of meal, ten fat oxen, twenty pasture-fed oxen, one hundred sheep, deer, gazelles, roebucks, fattened fowl, and barley, as well as straw for the 40,000 stalls of horses.

Solomon was powerful in foreign relations. He made an alliance with the Egyptian pharaoh and married his daughter. Solomon received the city of Gezer as a dowry for her. When King Hiram of Tyre in Lebanon heard that Solomon had replaced David as king, he sent his servants to Solomon. Because the Lord gave wisdom to Solomon, there was peace between Hiram and Solomon. The two leaders made a covenant between them.

The king of Israel was famous in all the surrounding nations. All the earth came to hear the wisdom God had put in Solomon's heart. The visitors brought gifts of gold, silver, garments, weapons, spices, horses, and mules. When the queen of Sheba visited King Solomon, she was impressed by his wisdom, his prosperity, the abundance of his food, and the resplendence of his court.

Foreign Commerce and Sea Travel

Solomon made an agreement with King Hiram of Tyre to buy cedars of Lebanon for the building of the Temple. Solomon promised to send his servants to be with Hiram's servants and to give wages for Hiram's servants. King Hiram was to decide what the wages would be. Hiram agreed to provide cedar and cypress timber in exchange for food for his household. The king of Lebanon provided all the cedar and cypress timber that Solomon desired. He also provided gold. King Solomon provided King Hiram with 200,000 bushels of wheat and 200 bushels of beaten oil each year.

After Hiram had helped Solomon for twenty years while the Temple and royal palace were being constructed, Solomon gave Hiram twenty cities in Galilee. However, when Hiram went to see the cities, he was not pleased with them. They came to be called the land of Cabul, which means "as good as nothing."

King Solomon built a fleet of ships on the shore of the Red Sea. Hiram had sailors who knew the sea. These sailors went with the fleet along with servants of Solomon. The fleet brought back 420 talents of gold from Ophir. The ships also brought back almug trees and precious stones. King Solomon used almug wood to make harps and lyres. Solomon also had ships of Tarshish. Once every three years the ships of Tarshish brought gold, silver, ivory, apes, and peacocks. Solomon imported horses and chariots from Egypt that were paid for in silver. He also had merchants who got horses from Kue.

What Else Was Happening? (1100 - 750 BC)

1. During the Mumun pottery period in Korea, agriculture expanded. Probable crops were millet, barley, wheat, legumes, and rice, which later become more prominent. The name Mumun refers to the many undecorated cooking and storage vessels found (example at right).

2. The Sa Huynh culture in Vietnam developed trade networks with nearby people, evidently extending to the islands of Taiwan and the Philippines. They also practiced cremation.

3. The first known athletic festival held at Olympia, Greece, is dated at 776 BC. Various other athletic competitions were held in Greece and later in other parts of the Mediterranean, but the Olympic Games were the most prestigious. A stone from the starting line at the Olympic Stadium is shown at right.

4. Phoenician traders established hundreds of small settlements around the Mediterranean Sea. One that became prominent and powerful was Carthage, in modern Tunisia. It was likely founded in the 800s BC.

5. The Adena culture was developing in the Ohio Valley of North America. They built numerous earthen mounds, likely as burial places and as locations for ceremonies and gatherings. An example from Zaleski, Ohio, is shown at right.

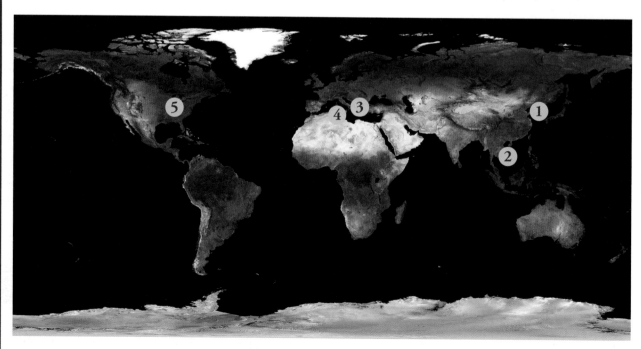

Building Projects

The two major building projects during the time of Solomon were the Temple and the royal palace. He also built a citadel called the Millo, the cities of Hazor and Megiddo, the wall of Jerusalem, storage cities, and other projects in Jerusalem, Lebanon, and the lands under his rule.

Building materials used for the Temple included stone, beams, cedar planks, cypress boards, olive wood, bronze, and gold. The stone used in the Temple was prepared at the quarry. No hammer, axe, nor any iron tool was heard in the Temple while it was under construction. The stone used in the building of Solomon's palace was sawed with saws. Bronze casting was done by King Hiram. He used the clay ground between Succoth and Zarethan in the plain of the Jordan for this purpose. The Temple was constructed in seven years.

By contrast, King Solomon spent thirteen years building his palace. Made of cedars from Lebanon, it included these architectural features: a foundation of expensive stones, cedar pillars, cedar paneling, rows of windows with frames, and a throne hall paneled with cedar. The great throne of Solomon was made of ivory, overlaid with refined gold. Six steps led up to the throne. The rear of the throne had a round top, and it had an arm on each side of the seat. Two lions stood beside the arms. A total of twelve lions stood on the steps, six on one side and six on the other. All of Solomon's drinking vessels were of gold. None were of silver because silver was not considered to be anything of value in the days of Solomon.

Isaac Newton included a detailed analysis of the temple that Solomon built in his book The Chronology of Ancient Kingdoms Amended. *This is his illustration.*

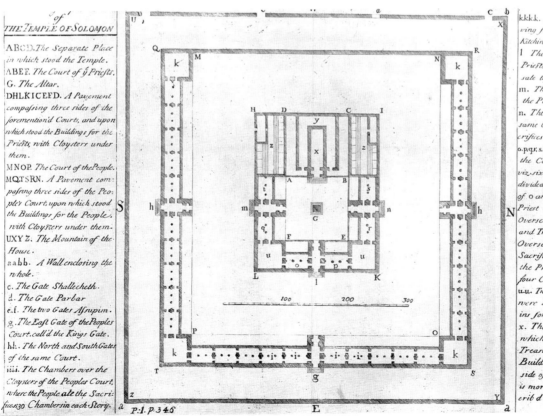

Solomon's Labor Force

King Solomon conscripted 30,000 laborers from all of Israel. Each month one-third of them would go to Lebanon to work. Then they would stay home for two months. Adoniram was over the forced laborers. Solomon did not make slaves of the Israelites. The forced laborers were descendants of the Amorites, Hittites, Perizzites, Hivites, and Jebusites that the Israelites had not destroyed when they entered the Promised Land.

Solomon had 3,300 chief deputies who supervised the building of the temple and the laborers. Seventy thousand transporters worked for Solomon. Eighty thousand men worked as hewers of stone. They quarried great costly stones to lay as the Temple foundation.

In addition to the Israelite workers, Gebalites and subjects of King Hiram of Lebanon cut stones and prepared timber and stones for the Temple. King Hiram was the son of a man from Tyre who had been a worker in bronze. Hiram was filled with wisdom, understanding, and skill about working with bronze; and he was brought to Israel to work with the bronze used in the temple. Hiram's mother was from the Israelite tribe of Naphtali.

Temptations in the Days of King Solomon

Wealth and physical magnificence, however, cannot buy a relationship with God. Sadly, Solomon loved many foreign women, including Moabites, Ammonites, Edomites, Sidonians, and Hittites; and he allowed them to lead his heart astray.

The Lord had commanded the Israelites not to associate with these other nations because He knew they would turn the Israelites' hearts to their pagan gods. The Lord God, who appeared to Solomon twice, told Solomon specifically not to go after other gods. However, Solomon accumulated 700 wives, princesses, and 300 concubines. As God had warned, these wives turned Solomon's heart after other gods. He pursued the Ashtoreth, goddess of the Sidonians, and Milcom, the idol of the Ammonites. He built a high place for Chemosh, the idol of Moab, and for Molech, the idol of Ammon. He did all of this for his wives.

The everyday people of Israel during Solomon's reign received mixed signals from their king. His early devotion to God, reflected in the building of the temple, was obvious. God's blessings on Solomon were equally apparent. Yet, while many enjoyed prosperity, thousands of Israelites were forced to work on Solomon's building projects. Solomon's spiritual downfall must have left many Israelites wondering what had happened to him. His marrying many foreign wives was a poor example for others to follow. The people of Israel were adversely affected by the political intrigues that followed Solomon's reign. How different the history of Israel might have been if Solomon had continued to serve the Lord faithfully and if he had continued to live by the wisdom that God had given him.

This 1525 carving illustrates Solomon worshipping an idol with one of his wives.

Yet I say to you that even Solomon in all his glory
did not clothe himself like one of these [lilies of the field].
Matthew 6:29

Assignments for Lesson 29

Bible Read Proverbs 1-3 and Ecclesiastes 1-3. Commentary available in *Student Review.*

Student Review Optional: Answer the questions for Lesson 29.

Shepherd in Israel

Amos, the Unlikely Prophet

A prophet is a spokesman for God. God called the prophets "My servants" (for example, in Jeremiah 29:19). A prophet received a personal and specific call from God to deliver His message to a specific audience. This role was needed because diviners and fortune tellers were at work in Canaan, and false prophets occasionally stepped forward on their own initiative. People needed the true word from God, especially when a political or spiritual threat confronted His people.

The prophets warned Israel of punishment that was coming because of their sins. They appealed to the people to return to God's way, especially in terms of obeying the Law and abandoning the worship of false gods. The prophets reminded Israel that blessings from God were conditioned upon their faithful adherence to the covenant. Their inspired messages came in several forms. In addition to addressing the people directly, prophets sometimes spoke in parables or allegories. At times a prophet acted out his message or had a vision that God interpreted for him. Some of the messages of the prophets were written down by inspiration, sometimes by the prophet himself and sometimes by another person.

Prophets delivered the messages that God wanted to convey to the people. Sometimes this involved recalling the past, while at other times the prophet pointed out the failings of the people at the time. On some occasions, a prophet predicted what was going to happen in the future. Predicting the future is the common meaning associated with the idea of prophesy today, but such messages were really only a part of what the prophets said.

Two other points about prophetic predictions are worthy of note. First, some predictions were conditional. In other words, if the people did certain things or repented of their sins, God would bless them. If they did not, God withheld His blessing. Second, most of the predictions that Old Testament prophets made have already been fulfilled. Some involved the restoration of the Jews to Israel after the exile, and some involved the coming of the Messiah. Just because a passage in the Bible contains a prediction, this does not automatically mean that we today should expect its fulfillment sometime in the future.

One recurring theme in Old Testament prophecies is the call to social and ethical righteousness. As we will see in our study of Amos in this lesson, God cares about how His people treat the poor, administer justice in the courts, and conduct business. God is not just concerned with whether His people worship Him in the manner

He prescribes. He expects faith in Him to make a difference in how people live.

Despite the prophets' emphasis on the failings of Israel and the punishment they were facing, God's spokesmen always had a word of hope to give to the people. The prophets spoke of better days ahead because God is a God of hope and promise. He does not leave His people in despair, even when their sins have been great. God "does not retain His anger forever, because He delights in unchanging love" (Micah 7:18). God wants to bless, not punish. Sometimes, however, He has to punish those who have abused His blessings.

The most important predictions that the prophets made involved the coming of the Messiah (or Anointed One; the Greek word is *Christos,* or Christ). He was to be Immanuel (God with us, Isaiah 7:14) and the Righteous Branch of Jesse (Jeremiah 23:5-6). The Messiah would suffer for the sins of others and thereby bring deliverance (Isaiah 53:4-6, 11). These Messianic prophecies gave the hearers the assurance that God would not forget His people. They give us today the assurance that the Scriptures are inspired and that Jesus was indeed the fulfillment of God's plan.

A study of the Old Testament prophets is worthwhile for many reasons. These were men of great faith and vision who boldly stood up for God in a society that had largely abandoned God. They relied totally on God and His word and were not concerned about being liked or accepted by their hearers. They were not successful preachers as many people define success today. They did not build large congregations, nor did they see a huge swing back to faithfulness. Usually they were largely ignored by those who heard them. The prophets were not "successful" in bringing many to repentance, but they were faithful in carrying out God's will for them. The prophets were excellent communicators, using clear language and vivid illustrations. They provided a superb picture of God and always pointed people back to God's love as the best motivation for obeying Him (Jeremiah 31:3).

Amos, the Shepherd-Prophet

Amos was not a full-time preacher. He was a shepherd (Amos 1:1) and a fig grower (Amos 7:14). He lived in Tekoa, about twelve miles south of Jerusalem. God called Amos to prophesy not against the Southern Kingdom but against Israel, the Northern Kingdom, about 750 BC. God wanted Israel to know that they were accountable for living under God's Law and were going to be punished because they had not done so. Rather than living as the people of God, Israel had become a decadent, corrupt, pagan nation that was full of sin. Amos delivered powerful and vivid messages that were ignored by the people of Israel to their own hurt. Read through the book of Amos and take note of the following comments.

This 13th-century German illustration is from a prayer book originally belonging to Sophie, Princess of Bavaria. Amos is represented at top left next to a depiction of the annunciation. Isaiah is pictured at bottom left next to an illustration of the birth of Christ.

Amos 1:1-2—Identification of the prophet, the time in which he spoke, and a reminder to pay attention to the word of the Lord.

Amos 1:3-2:16—Amos uses an effective device to make his point. He begins by denouncing the sins of the pagan nations around Israel. He uses a repeated structure, "For three sins and for four." Three sins would have been enough for God to destroy them; four made for overwhelming evidence. Amos condemns the Arameans of Damascus, the Philistines, and the people of Tyre, Edom, Ammon, and Moab. No doubt the people of Israel heartily agreed that all these other nations deserved punishment. Then Amos points out the sins of Judah (2:4-5). Now Amos is really telling it like it is! He has gotten the Israelites agreeing with him and giving him a loud "Amen."

Then Amos gets to his real point: "For three transgressions of Israel and for four I will not revoke its punishment" (Amos 2:6). He condemns his hearers for their own sins. His point is that they are just as deserving of God's punishment as all the other people he has mentioned. Israel was guilty of greed, taking advantage of the poor, ignoring those who were good, and engaging in cultic prostitution at pagan worship sites. Israel had lived this way despite the blessings God had given them, and now they are going to reap what they have sown.

Amos 3:1-15—The prophet reminds Israel of cause and effect. Because they had lived in sin, they were going to suffer the effect of punishment. Bethel (verse 14) was one site of Israel's false religion.

Amos 4:1-5—Amos condemns the lazy, indulgent women of Israel, "the cows of Bashan" as he so vividly phrases it. Their days of luxury would end in horror as they were dragged off to punishment. Go ahead and sin, God tells them, since you love to do it so; but be warned that you will pay dearly.

Amos 4:6-13—Amos uses another repeated phrase as a rhetorical device. God reminds them of the punishments He has already sent but then says, "Yet you have not returned to Me" (verses 6, 8, 9, 10, 11). They had failed again and again to repent

---

Around the site of ancient Tekoa are a Palestinian town named Tuqu (background) and a new Israeli settlement called Tekoa (foreground). According to tradition, Amos was buried in a nearby cave.

of their ways. As a result, God is going to inflict on them even harsher punishment.

Amos 5:1-3—Amos takes up a lament or funeral dirge for Israel. The Hebrew original reads with a three beat-two beat rhythm as a mourner would do if he broke down in sorrow:

Fallen!-Not to rise-Again,
Virgin-Israel!
Neglected-on her-land,
None-to raise her!

Amos 5:4-15—Despite Israel's failings and rejection of God, God appeals to the people to return to Him. "Seek Me that you may live" says the Lord repeatedly (verses 4, 6, and 14). However, they would not find Him in their pagan worship sites (verse 5). This is YHWH, the one true God who made the world (verses 8-9). But Israel was so far gone into sin that they had no respect for someone with integrity (verse 10). They increase their wealth at the expense of the poor (verses 11-13). If they practiced love and justice for their neighbor, perhaps God would be gracious to them (verses 14-15).

Amos 5:16-27—A reprieve was not to be, however. Their fashionable streets would be filled with mourning, and they could not escape the punishment of God. The "day of the Lord" would bring them doom, not gladness (verses 16-20). God takes no joy in vain worship of Him. Instead, He wants to see justice and righteousness flow forth in the lives of His people (verses 21-24). Their paganism had existed even from the time in the wilderness (verse 26).

Amos 6:1-14—"Woe to those who are at ease in Zion," warns Amos. In other words, be careful if you think you have it made. The Israelites were prideful about what they had achieved, but their material comfort would not deliver them from the Lord's punishment.

Amos 7:1-9—The Lord gives Amos three visions. The first two are of complete destruction coming from a locust plague and from a fire. Amos pleads to God on Israel's behalf, and God relents

During the Middle Ages, when manuscripts wore out and were replaced with new copies, the old pages were often used in the binding of other books. This Hebrew manuscript of Amos was used in this manner as so-called binding waste.

from bringing complete destruction. Then God shows Amos a plumb line. Many times in Scripture a measuring device is used to illustrate coming destruction so that the observer can be impressed with how great the destruction will be. Israel did not measure up; she had gotten off plumb. Now God would relent no longer but would bring destruction upon her.

Amos 7:10-17—The king of Israel does not want to listen to Amos. He tells the prophet to go back to Judah and prophesy there. Amos replies that he has no choice about what he does. He is not a professional prophet. He was minding his own business when God called him to prophesy against Israel. The king would pay the consequences of rejecting God's word.

Amos 8:1-14—God gives Amos another vision, this time of a basket of ripe summer fruit. The Hebrew word for summer sounds like the Hebrew word for end. The time is ripe, God says, for the end of Israel to come. God predicts an earthquake (verse 8), which occurred two years later (Amos 1:1). Israel could have seen the quake as a warning and changed their ways, but they did not.

Amos 9:1-10—The Lord continues to predict the calamity that would come upon Israel. God says that Israel was really no different from Ethiopia to Him. He made everyone, and Israel should not be prideful about being God's chosen people. God would destroy the sinful kingdom of Israel, but He would not totally destroy the house of Jacob (verse 8). God still had a plan to fulfill through Israel.

Amos 9:11-15—The promise of restoration. God says that one day He would restore the rule of David's line. Descendants of David did not resume the literal throne of Israel after the exile, so verse 11 might simply refer to the restoration of Israel to its land. It is probably a reference to the Messiah, who would come from the family of David. Life will be so great that the harvesters will still be working when the planters are ready to plant the next crop. This could be symbolic of the spiritual blessings that would be available in Christ. If the passage is a prediction of the restoration of Israel to the land after exile, it would be conditional upon Israel's future faithfulness.

The warnings of Amos were soon fulfilled. In 722 BC, about a generation after Amos preached, Israel was conquered by the Assyrians. Many of its people were taken into exile, never to return.

He who made the Pleiades and Orion
And changes deep darkness into morning,
Who also darkens day into night,
Who calls for the waters of the sea
And pours them out on the surface of the earth,
The Lord is His name.
Amos 5:8

Assignments for Lesson 30

Bible   You have already read the Book of Amos. Read 2 Kings 14-16 to get the historical context that led to the preaching of Amos. Commentary available in *Student Review*.

Recite or write Amos 5:8 from memory.

Project   Complete your project for the unit.

Student Review   Optional: Answer the questions for Lesson 30 and take the quiz for Unit 6.

7

Persia

Summary   The ancient kingdom of Persia built upon the civilizations that came before it. We will discuss its rise to power, its strengths, and its downfall. Several religions that were significant in the ancient world came out of Persia. We will focus on Cyrus, Daniel and his times, and the story of Esther to see how God used them to accomplish His purposes during the Persian era.

Lessons   31 - The Rise of a New Kingdom
32 - Key Concept: Persian Religion
33 - Key Person: Cyrus
34 - Everyday Life: Babylon During the Time of Daniel
35 - Bible Study: "For Such a Time as This"

Relief at the Apadana Palace in Persepolis (Iran, c. 500 BC)

Memory Work

Learn Daniel 2:20-21 by the end of the unit.

Books Used

The Bible
In Their Words

Project (choose one)

1) Write 300 to 500 words on one of the following topics:

- Write about a woman in history (famous or not) who was influential or who displayed admirable qualities.

- Write an account, either fictional or from real life, of someone who was in the right place at the right time and what happened to him or her.

2) Write and illustrate a children's book about the story of Daniel. Your book should be a minimum of fifteen pages. See Lesson 34.

3) Research some traditional foods that are part of the celebration of Purim and locate some recipes. Choose one or two Purim foods to make for your family. See Lesson 35.

Lesson 31

The Rise of a New Kingdom

One lesson you will learn in this survey of world history is that kingdoms and worldly power do not last forever, but people are always hoping to beat the odds and build an empire that will. Those who are in positions of power often attempt to find fulfillment and significance in controlling other people. They always learn, however, that either their kingdom ends or their life ends, or both.

Persian Conquests

The Persian people lived east of the Persian Gulf and Mesopotamia, in roughly the same area that is Iran today. Little is known about them before the seventh century BC. They were under the authority of the kingdom of Media, which occupied an area north and east of the Tigris River and whose people were ethnically related to the Persians.

The Lydians had begun minting coins in the 600s BC. Croesus (KREE-sus), king of Lydia, was known for his fabulous wealth. Sometimes people refer to a wealthy person as being "as rich as Croesus." This silver coin was issued by Croesus about 550 BC. The Persians copied the idea of using coins for currency.

In 559 BC Cyrus arose as the leader of one Persian tribe. He then successfully moved to rule all of the Persians, and he hoped to control the world. Perhaps he saw a need to acquire more land and wealth to support his people. Most assuredly, he envied the ways of empires and wanted one for himself. Cyrus easily gained control of the Medes in 550 BC and took over their capital, Ecbatana. Cyrus was generous to the Medes, which sent a signal that he was not going to rule with the harshness of the Assyrians.

This mosaic depicting a battle between the forces of Alexander and Darius III was found buried in a house in Pompeii. It is likely from the first century BC.

Cyrus then moved west from Media and defeated the kingdom of Lydia and its ruler Croesus in Asia Minor in 546 BC. Seven years later, Cyrus conquered the Chaldeans and added their large holdings to his empire. Thus, over a period of twenty years Cyrus extended his reign to include Asia Minor, the Middle East, and the land extending east to the borders of India. This gave him the largest empire in world history to that time. Cyrus died in 529 BC. His son Cambyses conquered Egypt and Libya in 525 BC, but then unrest at home forced Cambyses to return to Persia. He was murdered on the way, and the nobleman Darius gained control and ruled from 521 to 486 BC.

The Administration of the Empire

Persian kings tried to control their empire not by military force or terror but by administrative efficiency. They demanded absolute and unswerving loyalty from conquered peoples; but they allowed subject nations the continued use of local languages, the practice of their own national religions, and a fair amount of local control.

Cyrus and his successors ruled in resplendent royal palaces that set the standard for Oriental potentates. Those who had the privilege of entering into the king's presence were required to lay face down before him. The king's word was absolute and final law.

Cyrus divided his kingdom into satrapies or provinces. These administrative districts were overseen by governors called satraps, who were members of the royal family or other trusted officials. The satraps were civil authorities who had no military role. The king appointed a secretary for each satrapy who examined the satrap's mail and served as the king's personal representative. They were called the "Eyes and Ears of the King." The kingdom had four capitals to keep government administrators closer to the people. The four capitals were Shushan (the Greek form is Susa, north of the northern edge of the Persian Gulf), Ecbatana (north of Susa), Persepolis (to the east of the Gulf), and Babylon on the Euphrates River.

Archers from the Palace of Darius I at Susa

The Royal Road

This map shows the Persian empire at its height in the 300s BC, along with the approximate course of the Royal Road. The Persians maintained a message relay system along the road. According to Herodotus, "Now there is nothing mortal which accomplishes a journey with more speed than these messengers, so skillfully has this been invented by the Persians: for they say that according to the number of days of which the entire journey consists, so many horses and men are set at intervals, each man and horse appointed for a day's journey. These neither snow nor rain nor heat nor darkness of night prevents from accomplishing each one the task proposed to him, with the very utmost speed" (Book VIII.98).

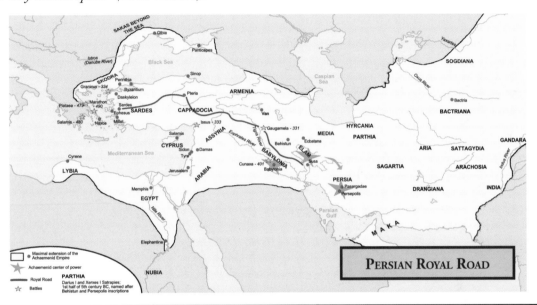

PERSIAN ROYAL ROAD

To help in the movement of troops and the administration of the empire, the Persians constructed the best system of roads in the world before the Romans. The centerpiece was the 1,500-mile Royal Road which stretched from Susa to Sardis in Asia Minor. Messengers could cover the distance in the amazing time of one week.

Accomplishments and Downfall

The Persians adapted many practices from the peoples they conquered. In addition to extending the use of coins in business transactions, the Aramaic language became the international language of commerce. It continued to be spoken in the Middle East until Jesus' day. The greatest structures that the Persians built were palaces, not temples.

Despite the Persian rulers' attempts at improved administration, their empire fell largely because of internal weaknesses. The king demanded tribute, taxes, and military service from conquered people; but as a rule he did not allow them to hold important positions in the governing of the empire. The realm was often shaken with revolts and turmoil, and rebellions by the satraps were one of the main sources of trouble. The Persian leaders wanted power and wealth, but they were unequal to the task of governing such a large empire.

Darius strengthened his control of the empire and improved the administration of government, but when he tried to extend Persian rule further he met defeat. Darius invaded Europe from Asia Minor. When he took control of the eastern Balkan Peninsula, he aroused the opposition of the Greeks. He was defeated in the resulting war with Greek city-states. This began the decline of Persia. The Persian Empire was weakened by instability within. Finally, it was taken over by the Greek conqueror Alexander the Great in 330 BC.

Persian Connections with the Old Testament

The Persian Empire controlled Palestine when the last books of the Old Testament were written. Cyrus allowed the Jews to return to Jerusalem and rebuild the temple, and he gave back to the Jews the articles that had been taken from the temple by the Chaldeans (2 Chronicles 36:22-23, Ezra 1:7-11).

The Biblical record clearly shows that Jews held important positions in the Persian Empire. Daniel was one of the exiles taken from Jerusalem to Babylon. He later served Darius the Mede after the Persians took control of Babylon (Daniel 5:31, 6:1-2, and other references). The story of Esther is set in Susa during the reign of Ahasuerus. Ezra 4:6-7 mentions Ahasuerus and his son Artaxerxes. Nehemiah was the cupbearer for King Artaxerxes. Artaxerxes allowed the Jewish leaders Ezra and Nehemiah to return to Jerusalem to rebuild the temple and the walls around the city.

Thus says the Lord to Cyrus His anointed,
Whom I have taken by the right hand,
To subdue nations before him,
And to loose the loins of kings . . . .
Isaiah 45:1

Assignments for Lesson 31

Bible Read Daniel 1-3. Commentary available in *Student Review.*

In Their Words Read the Book VII excerpt from the *Histories* (pages 28-30).

Student Review Optional: Answer the questions for Lesson 31.

Zoroastrian Fire Temple in Yazd, Iran

Persian Religion

The kings of Persia built the largest empire the world had known to that time, but it tottered for many years and fell about two hundred years after it began. A more enduring legacy from Persia was a new kind of religion. This religion continued to exist with adaptations beyond the time of Christ. It is helpful for us to understand this belief system that became a rival to Christianity so that we can see the differences between it and God's truth.

Zoroastrianism

Persian religious thinking had typical pagan roots, but a new approach to spiritual issues developed there shortly before the empire began. A man named Zoroaster (which is the Greek form of the Persian name Zarathustra) wanted to eliminate polytheism and animal sacrifices and make religion more spiritual and ethical. Zoroaster is generally thought to have lived in the 600s BC, although some scholars believe he lived much earlier, around 1000 BC.

Zoroaster believed in a good god called Ahura-Mazda (meaning wise lord), who created the world and does only what is right. Mazda is opposed by Ahriman (Destructive Spirit), a god of evil who does only what is bad. They are engaged in a struggle for the control of the universe which Ahura-Mazda will eventually win. Zoroaster believed that the earth is to exist for 12,000 years and that a messiah, Sashoyant, is to come at the end of that time.

In Zoroastrian thought, people are judged by how they have chosen to live. The righteous are rewarded while the sinful are punished. The world will end in a last battle which Ahura-Mazda will win. When evil is destroyed, those who have been condemned will be released and enter into bliss; thus all will eventually be saved.

This detail from The School of Athens *by Raphael (Italian, 1510) is thought to portray, from left to right, Zoroaster, Ptolemy, Raphael himself, and another painter, perhaps a friend of Raphael.*

163

Zoroaster emphasized being truthful, helpful, loving, and kind to the poor. He taught a negative form of the Golden Rule, similar to what many world religions have done ("That nature alone is good which shall not do unto another whatever is not good for its own self"). He condemned pride, wrathfulness, adultery, abortion, slander, and many other wrongs. A major sin was charging interest on a loan to a fellow believer. Zoroaster revered the cow and the work of farming ("He who sows corn sows holiness"). He taught against any self-inflicted suffering, including fasting, and excessive grief because they prevented farming and the begetting of children. Zoroastrians practiced simple daily rituals and occasional special days.

The writings sacred to Zoroastrianism are contained in the Avesta and in some other related documents. The Avesta includes doctrinal and ethical teachings as well as hymns or gathas to Ahura-Mazda. Parts of the original Avesta are not known to exist now. The Avesta was compiled between the third and seventh centuries AD from earlier materials.

Zoroaster introduced a dualistic system of belief: one god that was all good, another that was all bad. This differed from the polytheistic systems in which gods could do good or evil, and it differed from the monotheism of the Jews. It also claimed to be a revealed religion, with its doctrines given by the divine to a man.

In this carving at Naqsh-e Rustam, a royal Persian burial site, Ahura-Mazda (right) gives the ring of kingship to Ardashir I, a Sassanid Persian king of the third century AD.

These two images show two sides of a Mithraic altar piece (Roman, third century AD). On the left is a depiction of Mithras sacrificing the bull. On the right is a banquet scene with Mithras and Sol, the sun god.

Though it was an effort to purify the religious practices of Persia, Zoroastrianism itself became corrupted by pagan beliefs, superstitions, and magical practices. In time the three mystery religious cults described below developed as offshoots of Zoroastrianism.

Mithraism

In Persian thought, Mithras was Ahura-Mazda's chief divine helper in the fight against evil. He was supposedly born of a rock, tamed wild animals, and made a compact with the sun to help agriculture. The greatest accomplishment of Mithras was the capture of the divine bull. When he killed it, its blood and flesh brought forth herbs, grain, and other crops to grow from the earth. When Ahriman sent a flood upon the earth, Mithras built an ark and saved one man and representative animals.

Mithraism involved secret rituals and emphasized self-denial. Women were excluded from the cult. Sundays (for the sun) and December 25 (the birthday of Mithras and the celebration for the rebirth of the sun as the days started getting longer) were the most sacred days. The cult developed by the fourth century BC and spread into various places throughout the Near East. It entered the Mediterranean world by the first century AD, but it declined by 275 AD as the Christian faith turned people away from it.

Manichaeism

Mani was a priest in Ecbatana in the third century AD. He took dualism a step further by identifying a good god over the spiritual realm and an evil god that ruled the material world. Good was to be found only in the spiritual realm, and all material things were bad; thus the physical realm was to be avoided as much as possible in order to live in the good spiritual realm.

Since Mani realized that not all could live this way, he established two classes of followers. To liberate their spirits, the perfect class had higher standards, including celibacy, fasting, self-inflicted pain, and avoiding all physical pleasure and comfort. The secular class had lower expectations to meet. Women were seen as a force of darkness for men. The Manichaeans practiced baptism and observed a meal similar to the Lord's Supper.

Manichaeism spread east to India, Tibet, and China. This illustration from China shows Manichaean scribes (c. 800).

Mani was supposedly crucified by his opponents in 276 AD. Augustine was a Manichaean for nine years before his conversion to Christianity.

Gnosticism

A third cult that developed in the Near East around 100 AD was Gnosticism (from the Greek word *gnosis*, knowledge). Its greatest popularity was in the second century AD.

Gnostics believed that the highest spiritual goal was the attainment of secret inner knowledge possessed by only a few. This knowledge became available through participating in secret rituals and not by man's reason.

The savior for whom the Gnostics waited was to assume the form of a man but would not actually be a man, since the material world was entirely evil. He was sometimes called the Primal Man or the Son of Man. Some believed that Jesus was this savior but that He only appeared to suffer and die on the cross.

In 1945 near Nag Hammadi, Egypt, two brothers discovered a collection of documents from the early centuries AD that shed light on Gnostic teaching.

The Magi

The magi were originally a tribe of Medes who served as priests in the Persian Empire. Daniel uses the term more broadly to refer to wise men, astrologers, and interpreters of dreams (Daniel 2:27). The exact identity and homeland of the magi who visited the baby Jesus are subjects of debate, but they could have come from Persia. In Acts the term is used for those who practice magic arts (Acts 8:9; 13:6, 8). The word magi is the source for the English word magic.

The Adoration of the Magi
Bartolo di Fredi (Italian, c. 1388)

Assessment of These Beliefs

The most important fact to note about these belief systems is that they are wrong. Jesus is the way, the truth, and the life. No one comes to God except by Him (John 14:6). God created the physical world and declared it to be very good (Genesis 1:31). Our problem is not the physical world, but sin which tempts us. Knowledge of God's truth is not a secret available only to the few who have been initiated into an inner circle. It is an open secret that God has revealed to the world and wants proclaimed to everyone everywhere (Colossians 1:23-28).

We do not even know for sure when Zoroaster lived, but we do know when Jesus lived. Zoroastrianism and Mithraism obviously borrowed from pagan beliefs, and they had some influence from the teachings of the Hebrews as well. Manichaeism and Gnosticism obviously borrowed from Christianity.

Skeptics might point out the similarities between Christianity and these cults. We do need to practice kindness and we do need to be aware of the influence of the material world, but these truths do not make the entire system true. Most religions have elements of truth in them, but the fullness is in Christ (Colossians 2:9).

Perhaps 150,000 people worldwide still adhere to the Zoroastrian religion, especially in India and Iran. The Yazd province in central Iran was a major historical center of the religion, and it is still home to several thousand adherents. This glazed tile mosaic representing Ahura-Mazda is in the city of Taft.

The early church opposed the influence of Gnosticism. Gnostic teaching illustrates what can happen when people are not content with the revealed, inspired truth and instead go looking for something more (1 Corinthians 4:6).

These beliefs might not appeal to American Christians today, but they did have great attraction to many people in the Mediterranean and Middle Eastern cultures around the time of Christ. They arose during a time of great social and political change when people were looking for answers for their spiritual yearnings. We are enduring great social changes today; and many people are searching for deep, satisfying spiritual answers. Some believe they find answers in New Age cults or other man-made ideas, but Christians can help them see that the real answers they are looking for are in Christ.

These are matters which have, to be sure,
the appearance of wisdom in self-made religion and
self-abasement and severe treatment of the body,
but are of no value against fleshly indulgence.
Colossians 2:23

Assignments for Lesson 32

Bible Read Daniel 4-6. Commentary available in *Student Review.*

In Their Words Read the excerpts from *The Teachings of Zoroaster* (pages 31-32).

Student Review Optional: Answer the questions for Lesson 32.

Lesson 33 - Key Person

Cyrus

Cyrus was born around 580 BC. His father was Cambyses I, a descendant of Achaemenes. According to the Greek historian Xenophon, Cyrus was remembered as being handsome, generous, devoted to learning, and ambitious.

Cyrus came to power in Persia about 558 BC. In 550 BC he overthrew the Median Empire and established himself as a strong leader. By allowing Medes to serve in official positions, he encouraged a union of the peoples under his authority. Cyrus developed the system of satrapy. He appointed a governor (satrap) over each division of his empire and gave him significant freedom in administrating that district. Pasargade was Cyrus' capital city. It featured palaces, religious structures, and military defenses.

A Tolerant Ruler

Instead of crushing his enemies and forcing uniformity throughout his realm, Cyrus showed mercy to the nations he conquered and practiced religious and social toleration. Because of his generosity, the people of Babylon welcomed him as their ruler in place of their king in 539 BC. In the first year of his reign in Babylon, Cyrus sent a proclamation throughout his kingdom. He put it in writing:

Thus says Cyrus king of Persia, "The Lord, the God of heaven, has given me all the kingdoms of the earth and He has appointed me to build Him a house in Jerusalem, which is in Judah. Whoever there is among you of all His people, may his God be with him! Let him go up to Jerusalem which is in Judah and rebuild the house of the Lord, the God of Israel; He is the God who is in Jerusalem. Every survivor, at whatever place he may live, let the men of that place support him with silver and gold, with goods and cattle, together with a freewill offering for the house of God which is in Jerusalem" (Ezra 1:2-4).

This Biblical passage corresponds with a clay cylinder found in Babylon. On this cylinder, Cyrus congratulates himself on his successes and describes how he has, in his understanding, sent captive gods back to their proper homes.

As the Bible tells us, however, Cyrus was not motivated merely by his own goodwill. The Lord stirred up his spirit, as the Lord is more than able to

The Cyrus Cylinder praises the king, describes his royal genealogy, and highlights his policies after conquering Babylon.

do (Proverbs 21:1), to fulfill the prophecy given by Jeremiah. In addition to authorizing the return of the exiles to Judah, Cyrus returned the temple articles that Nebuchadnezzar had taken away and put in his pagan temples. His treasurer Mithredath counted out 30 gold dishes, 1,000 silver dishes, 29 duplicates, 30 gold bowls, 410 other silver bowls, and 1,000 other articles to the Jewish prince Sheshbazzar. Over 40,000 Jewish exiles took advantage of the king's decree and returned to the land of Israel. Priests and Levites, singers, gatekeepers, temple servants, and regular citizens took up residence in their ancestral homeland. They renewed their worship through sacrifices and feasts, and they prepared to rebuild the temple.

The Jewish leaders invoked the royal authority of Cyrus when enemies of the Jews tried to stop their work. The opponents did succeed in delaying the work. Years later, during a dispute about who authorized the reconstruction, another king, Darius, found in the royal archives in Ecbatana a copy of Cyrus' instructions regarding the temple. That settled the dispute, and it spoke well of the royal archive system.

The prophet Isaiah had spoken of Cyrus some one hundred years or more before his birth (Isaiah 44:28-45:25). God calls him "My shepherd" and says that he will work in the rebuilding of the temple in Jerusalem. Isaiah describes him as God's "anointed," whom God will use to subdue nations. God used Cyrus as part of His plan to let the nations know that the God of Israel was the one and only true God. As the nations bowed down and swore allegiance to Cyrus, so ultimately every knee will bow and every tongue will swear allegiance to the Holy One of Israel.

His Legacy

Cyrus died on a military expedition in 529 BC. His tomb, a small stone building on a raised platform, was built at Pasargade. His son took the throne as Cambyses II. The dynasty Cyrus established lasted in Persia for about two hundred years. Known as the Achaemenid dynasty, it was the most powerful empire of its day. Cyrus has long been honored in Iran (ancient Persia). Before the Islamic revolution in 1979, a large department store, many hotels, and two main streets in the capital were named after him.

What Else Was Happening? (750-500 BC)

1. The temple at Chavin de Huantar in what is now Peru was a center for the Chavin culture. The temple was surrounded by terraces and squares, and relief sculptures of animals adorn the buildings. The ruins of an entrance are shown at right.

2. Napata, a city along the Upper Nile, south of Egypt, became the early capital of the Kingdom of Kush. The Kushites controlled Egypt for several decades, and the kingdom continued until the 100s AD. (Cush is the spelling used in the English Bible.)

3. Hallstatt culture is the name given to the technology and art of Central Europe during this period, named after a town in Austria. Various tribes lived independent from the others, but they engaged in trade. Elaborate jewelry such as the necklace shown at right has been found from this period.

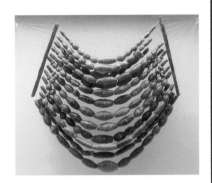

4. Lapita culture in the Pacific islands produced earthenware pottery. The people might have immigrated to the islands from Taiwan or mainland East Asia. They evidently raised pigs and chickens and harvested root crops and tree crops.

5. Jomon pottery in Japan was made with clay coiled up into the desired form. Influence from Korea became more prominent. The 1891 print at right portrays Jimmu, traditionally considered the first emperor of Japan (c. 660-585 BC).

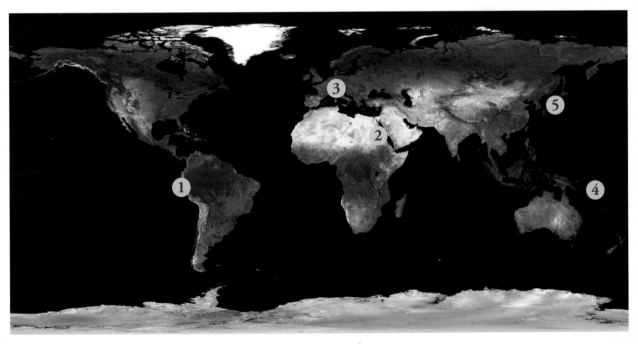

We do not know how much Cyrus came to know about the Lord. We do know that his empire, strong as it was, eventually faded away. The prophet Daniel, who lived during the reign of Cyrus and other Medo-Persian kings, had a vision about a future king of Greece who defeated the kings of Media and Persia (Daniel 8). This came to pass with the conquests of Alexander the Great.

The Cyrus Cylinder makes specific reference to Bel and Nebo, two Babylonian gods. Cyrus sought prayers for their favor. Just after the references to Cyrus in Isaiah, however, we read that "Bel has bowed down, Nebo stoops over; their images are consigned to the beasts and the cattle" (Isaiah 46:1). The Lord is God; there is no other.

The life of Cyrus vividly confirms how God can use anyone to accomplish His good purposes. Those of us who know the Lord should be thankful for that and show that we are thankful by how we live. We also see the benefits that come when mercy triumphs over judgment. Instead of the ruthless domination shown by many of his contemporaries, Cyrus showed compassion and leniency toward the nations he controlled. Finally, we must remember to devote ourselves first to the Lord's service, for the things of this world are passing away.

"For the sake of Jacob My servant, and Israel My chosen one,
I have also called you by your name; I have given you a title of honor
though you have not known Me."
Isaiah 45:4

Assignments for Lesson 33

Bible   Read Daniel 7-9. Commentary available in *Student Review.*

In Their Words   Read the excerpt from *Cyropaedia* (pages 33-35).

Student Review   Optional: Answer the questions for Lesson 33.

Lesson 34 - Everyday Life

Babylon During the Time of Daniel

The book of Daniel begins with the Lord giving Jehoiakim king of Judah into the hand of Nebuchadnezzar king of Babylon. All but the poorest people of Judah were taken captive (see 2 Kings 24:14). One of the captives was Daniel, who became an official in the Babylonian government. This lesson surveys information from the book of Daniel about everyday life in the Babylonian and Persian empires.

Government Policy

Nebuchadnezzar ordered his officials to choose some of the young captives from Judah and train them for service in his court. The Babylonians were not so prejudiced against the people of Judah that they could not recognize talent among them. The young men were to be physically and mentally fit, ready for an intense three years of training.

Among those chosen were Daniel, Hananiah, Mishael, and Azariah. Daniel requested that the Judeans be allowed to eat only vegetables and to drink only water. Perhaps he did not want them to become dependent on the pagan king, or perhaps he did not want them to eat food that was unclean as described in the Law.

After a training period, Daniel and other Israelite youths entered the king's service. They were recognized as having superior wisdom and understanding in all matters about which the king was concerned. Daniel, Hananiah, Mishael, and Azariah were Hebrew names. When they entered the service of King Nebuchadnezzar, they were given the names Belteshazzar, Shadrach, Meshach, and Abed-nego. Interestingly, most people through the centuries have referred to Daniel by his Hebrew name; but the other three named youths have been referred to by their Chaldean (Babylonian) names.

King Nebuchadnezzar made a large golden image and called his officials to come to its dedication. By this time Shadrach, Meshach, and Abed-nego administered the province of Babylon. The three Jewish officials refused to bow down to the image, and the king ordered them cast into the furnace. Death by burning had been used as a form of punishment in Babylon for many centuries; it is mentioned in the Code of Hammurabi. However, in this case the three men survived the furnace by the power of God.

Kings like to show off their power and prestige. When Belshazzar became the ruler, he held a great feast for a thousand of his nobles. During the feast, God sent a hand to write on the wall of the banquet

Illustration of the Fiery Furnace
Toros Roslin (Armenian, c. 1266)

hall. The queen advised Belshazzar to summon Daniel. When Daniel interpreted the handwriting, he reminded Belshazzar that the Most High God had granted sovereignty, grandeur, glory, and majesty to his father, Nebuchadnezzar. The same night that Belshazzar saw the handwriting, he was slain and Darius the Mede received the kingdom.

King Darius was the son of Ahasuerus and was of Median descent. He organized the kingdom under 120 satraps. The satraps were accountable to three commissioners. Daniel was one of the commissioners. King Darius planned to place him over the entire kingdom. Because they were jealous of Daniel's stature, the satraps and other commissioners looked for negligence or corruption in the way Daniel handled governmental affairs. They could not find any because Daniel was faithful. They decided they would have to accuse him about something related to the law of Daniel's God.

Daniel's enemies used a legal technicality to trap him. According to tradition, no law of the Medes and the Persians could be revoked. The jealous officials went to King Darius and told him that he should ban petitions to any god or man besides King Darius himself for a period of thirty days. If Darius did not agree, the officials warned, he would undermine his authority. Darius evidently did not consider the consequences of agreeing to their plan.

The officials knew that Daniel would disobey the decree because of his faithfulness to God. Sure enough, when Daniel heard about the law banning prayer to God, he went home and prayed about it! His enemies saw this and told the king. Darius was distressed, and until sunset he tried to rescue Daniel. The men reminded him again that according to the law of the Medes and Persians, no injunction or statute the king established could be changed.

Daniel was thrown into the lion's den. A stone was laid over its mouth, and the king sealed it with his own signet ring and the signet rings of his nobles. After Daniel was saved from the lions' mouths, Daniel told Darius that he had done no crime against the king. Darius had Daniel's accusers thrown into the lions' den.

Daniel Among the Lions, from Speculum Humanae Salvationis *(German, c. 1360)*

Music

The Babylonians used a number of musical instruments. The signal that everyone was to fall down before the golden image was the sounding of the "horn, flute, lyre, trigon, psaltery, bagpipe, and all kinds of music" (Daniel 3:5). The image at left is from the 1600s, but the stringed instruments are probably similar to those used at the time of Daniel.

Magic and Idolatry in Babylon

Daniel and his three fellow Jews were faithful to God in the midst of a strongly pagan nation. King Nebuchadnezzar had magicians, conjurers, sorcerers, and Chaldeans who advised him. The magicians might have been soothsayer priests and the Chaldeans might have been master astrologers. The king's Chaldeans said that their gods did not dwell with mortal flesh. Daniel and his fellow Jews, however, trusted in God to be with them.

The golden image that Nebuchadnezzar had erected on the plain of Dura in Babylon was sixty cubits high and six cubits wide—certainly an impressive figure. The servants of God, however, were more impressed with the power of God.

When Belshazzar gave a feast for the thousand nobles, he ordered that the gold and silver vessels from the temple be brought in. He wanted his nobles, wives, concubines, and himself to drink from them. They drank wine and praised the gods of gold, silver, bronze, iron, wood, and stone. Daniel, however, courageously told Belshazzar that those gods did not see, hear, or understand.

Pagans Recognize the Power of God

The working of God was so obvious in the lives of Daniel, Shadrach, Meshach, and Abed-nego that even the pagans recognized it time after time. After Daniel interpreted the first dream of Nebuchadnezzar, the king called Daniel's God a God of gods and Lord of kings.

When the fiery furnace had no effect on the bodies of Shadrach, Meshach, and Abed-nego, King Nebuchadnezzar blessed the God of Shadrach, Meshach, and Abed-nego. He made a decree that no one could speak anything offensive against their God. He declared to all people, nations, and tongues the signs and wonders which the Most High God had done for him.

After God humbled Nebuchadnezzar because of his pridefulness, Nebuchadnezzar blessed the Most High. He praised, exalted, and honored the King of heaven, saying that all His works are true, His ways are just, and He is able to humble those who walk in pride.

Before he cast Daniel into the lions' den, Darius told Daniel that the God whom Daniel constantly served would deliver him. He went to his palace where he fasted, had no entertainment, and could not sleep. At dawn he went to the lions' den and cried out to Daniel, a servant of the living God.

King Darius wrote to all the peoples, nations, and languages living in all the land. He decreed that in all his dominion men must fear and tremble before the God of Daniel. He said God is the living God, that He endures forever, that His kingdom will not be destroyed, and that His dominion is forever. He said that God delivers, rescues, and performs signs and wonders in heaven and on earth. He told them that God delivered Daniel from the power of the lions.

In the Babylonian and Persian empires of Daniel's day, the power of the king was the most important fact of life. A large government structure handled many administrative matters. The government bureaucracy included foreign captives and could be plagued by petty jealousies. Pagan beliefs dominated spiritual life, but a few people recognized and confessed the one true God. Even some of the pagans saw the workings of God and gave Him praise.

Now when Daniel knew that the document was signed, he entered his house (now in his roof chamber he had windows open toward Jerusalem); and he continued kneeling on his knees three times a day, praying and giving thanks before his God, as he had been doing previously.
Daniel 6:10

Assignments for Lesson 34

Bible   Read Daniel 10-12. Commentary available in *Student Review*.

Student Review   Optional: Answer the questions for Lesson 34.

Detail from Esther Denouncing Haman,
Ernest Normand (English, 1888)

Lesson 35 - Bible Study

"For Such a Time As This"

A beautiful young woman is placed by God in a position of influence. She risks her own life to save her entire ethnic group from a merciless holocaust. The villain behind the cruel plan is shown to be the king's trusted advisor. When the villain is exposed and executed, he is replaced by his nemesis, who is the kindly man that had reared the young woman after she had been orphaned.

The story of Esther is an account of selfless courage and of good triumphing over evil, but above all it is a demonstration of God's guiding hand of providence. It tells of Esther's brave action that prevented the killing of all the Jews in the Persian Empire. The deliverance of the Jews is the basis for the feast of Purim, which is celebrated in late February or early March of every year.

Cyrus, the king of Persia, conquered Babylon in 539 BC. The next year, he issued a decree allowing the Jews to return to their homeland. Many of them did so, but a significant number of Jews decided to continue living where they were. Darius was king of Persia a few years later (521 to 486 BC). The son of Darius was Ahasuerus (the Hebrew transliteration of his Persian name), also known as Xerxes (the Greek form of his name). He ruled the Persian Empire from 485 to 465 BC. We understand this to be the Ahasuerus in the story of Esther. The book tells of Jews who lived in Susa, the Persian capital.

The book of Esther is read every year at the feast of Purim. It has also provided comfort to Jews throughout the centuries whenever they have faced persecution. The girl in the photo at left was portraying Esther in a Purim festival in Tel Aviv, Israel, in 1934.

Because of its popularity with the Jews, more manuscript copies of Esther exist than of any other Old Testament book. It also received extensive treatment by the rabbis in commentaries on Scripture that were compiled around the first century AD. Esther is unusual in that the name of God is not mentioned; however, God's providence is suggested in 4:14 and the reference to fasting in 4:16 implies prayer. God is clearly the main character of the story.

Queen Esther, From a Series of Paintings of Illustrious People by Andrea del Castagno (Italian, c. 1450)

Read through the Book of Esther and refer to the commentary that follows.

Esther 1:1-12—Ahasuerus put on a great banquet for his officials and servants while Vashti, his queen, hosted a separate banquet for women. Men and women customarily dined together, so the reason for this separate event is not clear. Perhaps the size of the king's festivities necessitated the separate activity for women.

On the last day of the feast, the king ordered Vashti to come before his guests so that they could admire her beauty. Vashti refused. She might have been insulted by the king's intoxication, or perhaps she did not want to be made a public spectacle in what might have been an immodest way.

Esther 1:13-22—The infuriated king consulted his wise men on what to do, a common practice of eastern potentates. The phrase "who understood the times" might suggest that the wise men were astrologers, which they usually were; but here they were also experts in the law.

The wise men advised that Vashti should be dethroned as queen and another chosen in her place. This was to be the law of the Medes and the Persians, which could not be changed. Persian pride would suffer if the suggestion was made that their laws could be improved.

Esther 2:1-8—An undisclosed amount of time passed between the events of chapter 1 and the opening of chapter 2. The king's anger had subsided, and he is described as recalling what Vashti had done. Chapter 1 occurred in the third year of the reign of Ahasuerus, and Esther was selected in the seventh year (2:16).

The agents of Ahasuerus went throughout the realm and gathered attractive, unmarried young women for the king to consider as his new queen. The story now focuses on one such woman and her adoptive father. A Jew named Mordecai, of the tribe of Benjamin, lived in the fortified capital of Susa. The name Mordecai is the Hebrew form of the Babylonian name Mardukaya, which refers to Marduk, chief god of the Babylonians. Persia adopted the worship of Marduk when it conquered Babylon in 539 BC. Mordecai was obviously a faithful Jew, but his name suggests some degree of family adaptation to Persian culture.

The references to Mordecai's ancestors in Esther 2:5 are significant. One important fact about a person in Jewish eyes was the identity of his father and ancestors. This is why the Bible has several such references and genealogical listings. Who a person's father was said something about that person. It also gave that person a reputation to live up to. The importance of family responsibility and reputation is a lesson from which we could profit today.

Mordecai had reared his first cousin, Hadassah, after her parents died, so he must have been a good bit older than she. The girl's Hebrew name means myrtle. The name Esther was apparently Persian for star, though some have connected the name to the Babylonian goddess Ishtar. Many Jews have had and continue today to have a Hebrew name as well as a name from the culture, such as Daniel/Belteshazzar and Saul/Paul. Esther's beauty qualified her to be one of the candidates for queen.

Esther 2:9-18—Esther received special treatment during her time of preparation to meet with the king, indicating that the hand of the Lord was with her already. Esther did not reveal her identity as a Jew in accordance with Mordecai's instructions. He understandably feared that a Jewess might not be accepted as queen of Persia. Esther was of foreign ancestry and the descendant of former captives. In addition, anti-Jewish feeling was strong throughout the ancient world. The fact that Esther did not disclose her Jewish ancestry at this point sets the stage for when she does dramatically reveal it later in the story.

When Esther's turn came, she found favor with all who saw her. This was another indication of God's providence. Ahasuerus delighted in Esther more than all the other women. The author uses alliteration when he says that she "found favor and kindness (*chen* and *chesedh*) with him." The king chose Esther to be his new queen.

Esther 2:19-23—Following Esther's selection, an incident took place that advances the plot and foreshadows a coming event. Mordecai learned of an assassination plot against Ahasuerus by two doorkeepers. He told Esther, and Esther informed the king. An investigation confirmed Mordecai's accusations. The conspirators were hanged and a record of Mordecai's service was entered into the book of the chronicles of the king.

Esther 3—King Ahasuerus promoted Haman to the position we would call vizier and ordered all of his servants to pay homage to Haman. Mordecai, however, did not bow before Haman. Although the vizier had all the wealth and power he could ever want, he lacked one thing: subservience from Mordecai; and this infuriated him. Perhaps out of an overpowering desire for revenge, and perhaps because he knew that if one Jew refused to honor him all Jews would do the same, Haman resolved to wipe out the Jewish race in the Persian Empire. We might find his scheme incredible if the world had not witnessed another attempt to destroy the Jews in Nazi Germany.

The date for carrying out Haman's holocaust was set by the casting of lots. The lots were cast in the month of Nisan, the month in which Passover is observed. Passover commemorates God's deliverance of Israel from an earlier threat. The ethnic cleansing was to be accomplished eleven months later. After the decrees were written, translated, and distributed throughout the empire with the king's approval, the king and his cold-blooded vizier sat down calmly to have a drink.

Esther 4—When Mordecai heard of the decree, he went into mourning, as did all the Jews. When Esther learned the reason for Mordecai's grief, her first reaction was to explain why she was powerless to do anything to stop the decree. If she approached the king uninvited, she risked being put to death. The groveling obeisance that the Persian king demanded from all who came before him makes this risk believable. Mordecai reminded her that she was a condemned woman either way, if the king rejected her approach or if she did nothing. She had nothing to lose, so her only hope was to go to the king. Mordecai wanted Esther to do something, but he actually had more faith in God than in Esther's ability to persuade the king.

Scenes from the Book of Esther are pictured on this bowl. The images are based on a Dutch Illustrated Bible published by Nicholaus Piscator that was translated into Russian (Russian, c. 1690).

Help for the Jews would come from somewhere, Mordecai stated, "and who knows whether you have not attained royalty for such a time as this?" (Esther 4:14). God would deliver His people, Mordecai said, and she might be His chosen instrument to bring this about. Esther resolved to go to the king, and she asked the Jews to devote three days to fasting (and presumably prayer) before she went.

Esther 5—Vashti had refused to go before the king when she had been summoned. Esther decided to go before the king even though she had not been summoned. The king's love for Esther led him to receive her and to offer her anything she wanted, up to half the kingdom (compare this with Herod's rash offer to Salome in Mark 6:23). Her first request was for the king and Haman to attend a banquet that day. At the banquet, she requested that they return

for another banquet the next day. She probably took these steps to see how receptive the king was and to snare the egotistical Haman in his own trap.

Haman left the first banquet full of pride; but when Mordecai once more refused to bow to him, his bubble burst. The vizier poured out his frustrations to his wife and friends, who suggested that Haman have Mordecai executed as an example to other Jews and as a way to satisfy Haman's lust for revenge. Haman had custom gallows constructed immediately.

Esther 6—The sleepless king had his official records read to him, either to build up his pride or as a sure way to be put to sleep. Ahasuerus was reminded of Mordecai's intervention to save the king's life; and he learned that nothing had ever been done to honor Mordecai. Just then Haman entered the palace to

Golden Vessels from Persia (c. 5th century BC)

request Mordecai's execution. The king asked him what he thought should be done for the one whom the king wished to honor. Haman, assuming that the person in question was himself, pulled out all stops in describing a lavish ceremony. The king agreed and ordered Haman to honor Mordecai in just this way. Haman was mortified, and the irony was probably not lost on the citizens of Susa.

Esther 7—Haman arrived at the second banquet a discouraged and embittered man. In his mind, he had been at the top but now he could hardly imagine being lower. Finally Esther made her request of the king; it was for her very life and the lives of her people. She said that they had been sold in order to be destroyed (a reference to Haman's offer in Esther 3:9 to pay ten thousand talents to those who carried out the holocaust). If her people had only been sold into slavery, Esther continued, she would not have said anything, even though it would have been a great loss for the king.

Ahasuerus was shocked and demanded to know who would do this. Esther identified the culprit as Haman, the other guest at her table, who had fallen into the trap that he had set for himself by his own pride. Now the king saw the vizier for what he was. Furious, the king stormed out of the banquet.

Haman, meanwhile, knew that he was a dead man and began pleading with Esther to intervene on his behalf. His entreaties were so desperate that he fell across the couch where Esther was reclining for the banquet. At this point the king returned and saw what looked like Haman attempting to assault the queen.

At the word of the king, the courtiers covered Haman's face in preparation for his execution. He was put to death at the very time and place he had hoped to put Mordecai to death.

Esther 8—King Ahasuerus gave Esther the house of Haman, since the property of condemned criminals reverted to the state. Esther in turn appointed Mordecai to be in charge of this property, which apparently was of considerable worth. The effect on Haman's wife is not noted.

The Triumph of Mordecai, *Jacob de Wet (Dutch, c.1670)*

Of even greater significance was the fact that the king gave Mordecai his signet ring, the same one that Haman had used to authorize the edict he had issued against the Jews. This meant that Mordecai was now vizier, with all of the power and prestige that Haman had once enjoyed and abused in that role.

Haman's decree calling for the annihilation of the Jews remained on the books. At their request, the king authorized Esther and Mordecai to write a new decree that helped their people. He told the new vizier to sign it with the king's name and seal it with the royal seal. No more authoritative word of law existed in the empire.

The new edict allowed the Jews to gather together for the purpose of defending themselves. The wording of Mordecai's decree was almost exactly the same as what Haman's edict had called for, except now it applied to the enemies of the Jews (compare 8:11 with 3:13). Now the Jews were on equal footing with their enemies. The day when the Jews could carry this out was the thirteenth of Adar, the same day on which Haman's law had allowed the Jews to be attacked. Copies of the law were distributed in Susa and in all of the provinces, translated into various languages, including the language of the Jews.

The law (or tradition) that said the laws of the Persians and Medes could not be changed was a bad law. It was the result of Persian pride, and it

Esther and Mordecai
Aert de Gelder (Dutch, c. 1685)

created the pretense which said that Persian laws were perfect and ultimate. Any product of man, however, will be flawed in some way. People find a way to work around even ironclad rules. Persian laws actually could be changed, simply by the creation of another law. Haman's edict should have been cancelled, but it is possible that some people might not have gotten the word or simply ignored the cancellation and tried to attack the Jews anyway. The Jews needed to be able to defend themselves, but the unrealistic ideal of Persian law helped bring about extra bloodshed and the potential for civil war.

In what is almost a footnote, the text indicates that many people converted to Judaism. Perhaps some of these were conversions of convenience by people who wanted to be on the winning side, but the implication can be made from the statement in the text that people recognized the power of God through what had taken place and were convinced that God was indeed worthy of being worshiped. The events that had unfolded regarding Haman, Mordecai, and the Jews told the people not that the Jews were merely lucky or that they had somehow manipulated things to gain the upper hand, but that the God of the Jews was truly Lord over all the earth.

Esther 9:1-19—Finally the day arrived, the thirteenth of Adar, when the Jews had been marked out for annihilation. The proposed slaughter became a showdown, and it resulted in one of the greatest

victories in the history of Israel. God's covenant people were triumphant over wicked forces. This came about because one man, Mordecai, refused to believe that God would abandon His people and because one woman, Esther, risked her life to save her people.

Provincial officials used their influence to help the Jews because the officials were struck by fear of Mordecai. They knew how Mordecai had come to power. They knew that the fortunes of Haman and Mordecai had been dramatically reversed. The provincial officials might not have understood the Power behind Mordecai's rise to prominence, but they knew something was there. Mordecai's reputation grew, and he was recognized as a man to be reckoned with.

Even the capital was not exempt from the Jews' power. In the citadel of Susa, the Jews killed five hundred who dared to follow Haman's edict and attack God's chosen people. Ten of the victims are named: the ten sons of Haman. Haman's wife was again forced into mourning because of her husband's sins. In the Hebrew text of Esther, the names of these ten sons of Haman are written perpendicularly, down the page, to call attention to them and to gloat over their death. Though the Jews exacted the ultimate price from their enemies, they did not humiliate them. The Jews did not plunder the possessions of their foes. The action that the Jews took was not about gaining wealth but about securing their lives.

King Ahasuerus was told of the casualties in the citadel of Susa. He then relayed the information to Esther and implied that if this was the toll in the capital, it must have been much greater in the provinces. It was a time of great satisfaction for the royal couple and for the Jews. The king noted that his granting of Esther's request had brought about this victory for her people. Continuing his gracious indulgence of his queen, he wondered what her next request might be.

Esther's desire was to exact more vengeance. She wanted the Jews in Susa to have another day in which they could attack and destroy all who threatened them. The queen also asked that the bodies of the ten sons of Haman be hanged from the gallows, probably the same gallows where their father was executed. The king ordered it done. This sounds cruel, but it was common practice with notorious criminals in ancient times.

After their fierce battles, the Jews in the provinces rested and celebrated on the fourteenth of Adar. In Susa, the Jews defended themselves for two days (the thirteenth and fourteenth), and then rested and celebrated on the fifteenth. What had been intended to be a day of death for the Jews turned out to be a day of triumph for them.

The Jews who lived in the provinces of the Persian Empire celebrated on the basis of their experience. They had successfully defended themselves on the thirteenth of Adar, so they made the fourteenth a day of feasting and gladness and exchanged gifts with one another. In a similar way, the Jews who lived in the citadel of Susa celebrated on the basis of their experience. They had defended themselves for two days, the thirteenth and fourteenth, and so they celebrated on the fifteenth.

Esther 9:20-32—Mordecai issued a decree to settle the question of when to celebrate. He instructed the Jews to observe a two-day festival that commemorated both days of deliverance, the fourteenth and the fifteenth. The festival reminded the Jews of the time when their sorrow turned to joy. They made the feast a time of great rejoicing; and they remembered others as God had remembered them, by exchanging presents and giving gifts to the poor.

The precedent of sharing with others in festivals was set in the Law of Moses (see Deuteronomy 16:11, 14). The feast of Purim occurs about a month before Passover in the last month of the Jewish festival year. It is held in late February or early March on our calendar, depending on how the Jewish lunar calendar coordinates with it.

The Jews called the festival Purim, the Hebrew plural form of *pur* (lot), because the Jews were saved on the day the *pur* indicated they should die. Because of what had happened and because of Mordecai's letter regarding the observance of the feast, the Jews bound themselves and their descendants to keep Purim annually on the fourteenth and fifteenth of Adar. The Jews wanted it to be a universal observance. They did not want later generations to forget the experience that had saved their lives and shown them the hand of God.

Esther sent a letter giving her royal endorsement to Mordecai's proclamation. Mordecai's letter to the provincial leaders, the narrative says, contained "words of peace and truth." This was the typical greeting of oriental letters of the day, and it is a worthy standard for our words today. The vizier's letter confirmed his earlier decree about the observance of Purim and dealt with "their times of fasting and lamenting." This probably had to do with a fast that the Jews held just prior to Purim, remembering the danger they had faced from their enemies. This fast is still observed and is called the Fast of Esther.

Esther 10—This brief chapter mentions one additional fact about Ahasuerus and summarizes Mordecai's tenure as vizier. Mordecai carried out his duties well as one who "sought the good of his people and . . . spoke for the welfare of his whole nation" (Esther 10:3).

Ruins of the Persian Palace of Adapana (c. 500 BC)

Conclusion

Consider the plight of the Jewish people in the Persian Empire. They were strangers in a strange land. They spoke a different language, had different customs, and even used a different calendar from the majority of the people who lived there. The most striking difference about them, however, was that they worshiped a different God.

The wrath of the government was called down upon them because one Jew decided to let his differences be known. When they faced extinction, the courage of one Jewish woman spared them. They had a reason to celebrate and to give thanks that God had not abandoned them in that foreign land.

The feast of Purim is a joyous celebration. The book of Esther is read in a chant. Those assembled cheer and boo at appropriate times, and people often dress in costume to represent characters from the story. They recite blessings, sing hymns of praise, and then enjoy a festive meal. In every way it is a celebratory atmosphere. Later generations were never to forget that the hand of God had saved them.

The book of Esther is a gripping drama, and all the more because it is true. It is a thrilling testimony to God's sovereign and powerful hand working on behalf of His people. As we consider the story, enjoy the narrative, and rejoice in the outcome, we should also rejoice at God's providential mercy that rules our lives and how we have been called to live for Him in such a time as this. May we also never forget.

For if you remain silent at this time,
relief and deliverance will arise for the Jews
from another place and you and your father's house
will perish. And who knows whether you have not
attained royalty for such a time as this?
Esther 4:14

Assignments for Lesson 35

Bible   You have read through the Book of Esther.

Recite or write Daniel 2:20-21 from memory.

Project   Complete your project for the week.

Student Review   Optional: Answer the questions for Lesson 35 and take the quiz for Unit 7.

8

Ancient Asia and Beyond

Summary

In this unit we expand our study outside of the Biblical narrative to give an overview of developments in India, China, Africa, America, and Europe from early times through the early Christian period. The Bible study on the book of Jonah reminds us of the fact that God loves people from all nations.

Lessons

36 - Ancient India

37 - Ancient China

38 - Everyday Life: Chinese Government, Culture, and Science

39 - Ancient Africa, America, and Europe

40 - Bible Study: God's Love for the Nations

Ruins at Jiaohe, Xinjiang Province, China

185

Memory Work

Learn Isaiah 35:4-6 by the end of the unit.

Books Used

The Bible
In Their Words
The Art of War

Project (choose one)

1) Write 300 to 500 words on one of the following topics:

- Many ancient proverbs have been passed down through generations, from the inspired book of Proverbs in the Bible to the proverbs of Confucius. Write down a collection of sayings or proverbs. Include examples which you think are especially insightful and ones that are repeated by your own family. Include proverbs or sayings from at least ten different sources. See Lesson 37.

- Choose one of the developments of the ancient Chinese civilization discussed in Lesson 38. Research the topic in more depth and describe its discovery, development, and use. If applicable, describe how the concept or technology is in use today.

2) Write out your family tree. Go as far as you can this week. Consult with older relatives for information. Where possible, include birth dates and death dates to see how lifespans overlapped. See Lesson 37.

3) Create a painting of hand stencils of your family members. You can also include friends if you wish. Use the photos on page 208 for inspiration.

Literature

The Art of War is not so much a book of military strategy as it is an expression of military psychology. It tells leaders not just how to win battles but how to insure victory before even fighting battles. *The Art of War* has become influential in areas other than military strategy; its principles have been applied to the business world and even to marriage. As a classic piece of Chinese literature, the philosophy expressed in the book continues to be influential in China. It was a major factor in the thinking of Chinese Communist leader Mao Zedong.

Little is known about the author or about the precise circumstances in which the book was written. It is attributed to Sun Tzu, a military commander, strategist, and advisor to Chinese emperors around 500 BC. However, other views suggest that the book is a compilation of the work of many authors, dating as late as 200 BC.

Read the book slowly, a limited amount each day, and try to understand the outlook reflected in the book's statements. With the importance of China in our world today, Americans should understand this foundational element of Chinese thought.

Lesson 36

Ancient India

Wide, straight streets are divided into regular city blocks. Many homes and places of business are built exactly alike with even the same size of bricks. An efficient sewer system serves the residents of the city.

This is not a description of modern America or Europe, but of two great cities of northern India around 2000 BC. About the time of the Egyptian and Sumerian civilizations, another highly advanced group of people lived along the Indus River. Their cities of Harappa and Mohenjo-Daro were discovered in the 1920s and have been excavated since then. Our knowledge of this early civilization is somewhat limited because their writing has not been translated and because archaeological digging is difficult close to the river, but what we do know about them provides more evidence of the amazing abilities which God gave to humans and more proof that the typical view of social evolution is not supported by the facts.

The cities of the Indus people were larger than any Sumerian city-state, and the 950-mile stretch of the Indus River these people inhabited rivaled the size of the older kingdom of Egypt. The Indus people were skilled in surveying and building. They irrigated their crops and were the earliest known producers of cotton. They traded their cloth to Mesopotamia for precious metals and made beautiful jewelry and stone carvings. Apparently they worshiped a mother-goddess and another deity portrayed with three faces. They also worshiped some animals and trees.

The Aryans

The Indus River civilization seems to have flourished until about 1500 BC. After a period of decline (evidenced, for instance, by poorer and less standardized buildings), the area was invaded by tribes known as the Aryans. The Aryans might have come from the area north of the Caucasus Mountains and between the Black and Caspian Seas. Many groups are believed to have migrated out of this region, including the Hittites who settled in Asia Minor and other tribes that moved to Europe. The peoples who are thought to have left this area and settled elsewhere are called Indo-European tribes. The Aryans (their name means noble) pushed the Indus River people further south, where they reorganized and flourished later.

Family and village life was of central importance to the Aryans. Each of the Aryan tribes was led by a rajah or chief. The rajah selected a headman for each village who oversaw life there. An extended

Aryanism and the Swastika

Some 19th-century Europeans developed the theory that white people, especially northern Europeans, were superior to others. Because of their supposed place of origin, this theory referred to northern Europeans as Aryans. Adolf Hitler and Nazi Germany took this idea one step further. They claimed that the Germans were the most superior part of the Aryan race, and they used this belief to justify their hatred of the Jews and their aggression toward other countries.

The swastika was an Aryan Sanskrit symbol of good luck. The Nazis adopted it as a symbol for their political movement. Interestingly, a form of the swastika has been found in many places, including Egypt and Turkey. The photo at left shows a swastika along the Ganges River at Haridwar, India.

family usually lived in the same house. They jointly owned property and cared for the family's sick and elderly. The male head of the family led in religious ceremonies, arranged marriages for his children, and was the family's representative in village decisions. Women were apparently quite active in the earlier stages of Aryan society. Some were warriors and took part in civic affairs. However, after a time the women withdrew from public life and became more devoted to household work. The Aryans developed a written language called Sanskrit. It was used mostly by priests for recording religious literature.

The Aryans maintained sharply defined social classes. The earliest classes were the warriors, the priests, and the commoners. A person could move from one class to another. Later, they recognized four classes: the warriors; the priests (called the Brahmans); the class that included landowners, merchants, and herders (what we might call a middle class); and finally the servants, peasants, and all non-Aryans. As war became less important and religious activity became more important, the Brahmans replaced the warriors as the highest social class.

These classifications hardened into what were called castes. Membership in a caste was the result of simply being born into the caste of one's parents. The jobs to be held by members of each caste were

strictly defined, and one could not marry outside of his or her caste. As though this were not enough, the castes were further divided into a complex system of up to 3,000 subcastes or groups. In addition, the lowest rank was given to those who were outside of any caste. These were the outcastes, and they were considered the untouchables. The caste system came about as the result of the Hindu religion.

Hinduism

The Hindu faith is not based on one person's ideas or teachings. Instead, it is a blend of Aryan beliefs and the ideas of the people they conquered. Hindu teachings are an attempt to express the truth about the meaning of life and the individual's place in the universe.

According to Hindu doctrine, Brahma is the single unifying force that is present in everything and every person. Nothing exists apart from Brahma. The three most important gods that are expressions of this universal spirit are Brahma (the creator god), Vishnu (the preserver god), and Shiva (the destroyer god). Hindus worship many other gods that are different aspects of Brahma. The Aryans were especially interested in gods of nature and in Indra, the warrior god.

In Hindu thought, every individual soul is part of the universal soul or atman. The pursuit of unworthy goals keeps a soul separated from the atman. Worthy goals include a devotion to the truth, respect for life, and detachment from the world. The goal of life is to be free from one's individual life and to be unified with the atman. However, this takes more than one life, so the soul has a series of rebirths.

When the body dies, the soul is reincarnated in another body. The soul can move closer to or farther from the atman depending on how a person lives. If a person lives well, he or she will be reincarnated in a higher caste; if not, the soul will live in someone of a lower caste or in an animal. This is why cows are not slaughtered. They might house the soul of a loved one.

Karma is the sum total of all the actions of a person's life that affects his or her next life. This karma determines into which caste a person is born. Having good karma includes being obedient to one's caste and maintaining proper social behavior. This belief gave a spiritual rationale for strictly maintaining caste lines.

By about 600 BC, the Brahmans, who preserved the religious texts and performed the religious rituals, were believed to be closest to the atman and thus were considered the highest caste. Some objected to the Brahmans being the only pathway to the atman. These dissenters taught that méditation and self-discipline could lead one to a higher spiritual understanding. One result of this belief was the practice of yoga.

Several writings embody Hindu teachings. The *Bhagavad Gita (Song of God)* is an Aryan work. It is an epic in itself, but it is actually part of an even longer epic work that tells of Aryan wars. The Vedas are religious writings that date from 1500 to 1000 BC and provide information about Aryan life. The Upanishads are oral teachings that developed around 800 to 600 BC and offer ideas about the meaning of life and reincarnation.

Buddhism

The Buddhist religion began as an offshoot of Hinduism. It was begun by Siddharta Gautama, a follower of Hinduism, who was born in the foothills of the Himalayas about 563 BC. Gautama was the son of a wealthy warrior and therefore lived a sheltered and privileged life. He married and had one son.

One day, when Gautama was 29 years old, he came in succession upon an old man, a sick man, and a corpse. Seeing these in the way that he did affected him deeply. He left his family and lived as a

This painting from the 1500s depicts a battle scene from the Bhagavad Gita.

This is a Chinese Buddha statue from about 500 AD. Representations of Gautama Buddha generally portray him as slender. The fat and smiling statues called the Laughing Buddha are actually representations of a legendary Chinese Buddhist monk named Budai.

The philosophy of Buddhism adopted some elements of Hinduism, including the belief in karma, the cycle of rebirth, and the view that the world is a place of suffering from which people want to escape. It was different in that Buddha did not believe in the soul or in any gods. He rejected castes and said that priests were not the most important people.

Buddha died in 483 BC, supposedly while visiting a poor blacksmith's family. According to the story, he ate spoiled food rather than embarrass his host family. After his death, Buddha's followers took his ideas throughout India. His sayings were gathered in a collection called *Three Baskets of Wisdom*.

As with almost all religious movements, Buddhism divided into two groups. One continued the way that Buddha had outlined, while the other exalted Buddha to the status of a god and said that other teachers had achieved enlightenment also. In India, Buddhism and Hinduism coexisted.

Later Dynasties

The Aryans weakened their empire from within by inter-tribal wars that occurred after 1000 BC. In 512 BC northwestern India was controlled by Persia. The kingdom of Magadha in northeastern India combined with other groups to push the Persians out. They extended their control further south to the Ganges River. This was the first of several empires in India, but their rule was continually threatened by foreign invaders.

The Maurya dynasty arose in 321 BC and gained control over all of northern India. Its leaders built a luxurious capital on the Ganges. Later rulers established provincial governments and practiced tight administrative control, including sending spies

beggar to try to find the causes of suffering. Gautama did not find the answers in the Hindu writings or in a life of self-denial. After a six-year pursuit, one day while sitting under a tree, Gautama believed that he was enlightened. Buddha means "enlightened one," and this title is how he came to be known. Gautama began teaching his beliefs to others. He organized groups of monks and nuns who were especially dedicated to following his philosophy.

Buddha identified four truths. First, suffering and misery are universal. Second, the cause of suffering is desire. Even the good things that we want bring suffering because they cannot last. Third, the way to end suffering is to overcome desire. The goal of life is release from desire in the state of nirvana, which involves wanting nothing. Fourth, the way to escape pain and suffering is what Buddha called the Middle Way, made up of the Eightfold Path. This path of life involves compassion, knowledge of the good, good intentions, right speech, right conduct, pursuit of a proper livelihood, mindfulness, and meditation. These virtues avoided the extremes of self-denial and of Hindu worldliness.

to check on provincial governors. They might have been influenced by the example of Persia in this (see Lesson 31). The Mauryans used homing pigeons to send messages to their capital. Road building increased and trade with China and Western Asia flourished.

One Mauryan leader, Ashoka, extended his empire across the central plateau of India through war; but when he heard of the death toll from the campaign he repented of warfare, renounced violence, and adopted Buddhism. Ashoka sent out government representatives to teach good works, non-violence, and the way of peace. Buddhism became a strong influence in India because of this change, and Buddhist missionaries took their message to Southeast Asia.

After the reign of Ashoka, India was racked with repeated civil wars and foreign invaders. One invasion was carried out in the second century BC by Bactrian Greeks, the remnants of Alexander the Great's Greek forces who had stayed in northwestern India when Alexander's empire collapsed. Later, the Kushans invaded and guided a culture that flourished for two hundred years. They spread Buddhism throughout India and into other countries and increased trade with China.

From 320 to 535 AD the Gupta dynasty had the upper hand. Chandra Gupta I reunited India and began a Golden Age of peace and advances in the arts and science even as the Roman Empire was collapsing in the West. Advances took place in the fields of medicine (such as the use of herbal medicines and improved surgical techniques) and industry (including the production of steel, textiles, and dyes). The Indians developed the zero as a place holder and a decimal number system that they taught to the Arabs. We call them Arabic numerals because Western peoples learned the system from Arabs when European countries were still using the cumbersome Roman numeral system.

The religious landscape of the region became more diverse. As Hindu belief spread, it absorbed

Buddhist beliefs as well as the beliefs and gods of other peoples. Buddha forbade the worship of idols, but his followers ignored this teaching and created gods and shrines which pictured gods, animals, and scenes from Buddha's life.

During the Maurya and Gupta dynasties, in an attempt to strengthen religious purity, the caste system became stricter and more complex. Women married in their early teens and were in complete subjection to the husband and his family. If she was widowed, she remained with the husband's family. However, a widow was considered unlucky and was often avoided and isolated by the man's family. Rather than endure such isolation, some widows, especially in the upper classes, threw themselves on

Ashoka put up numerous statements on pillars and large and small rocks. These edicts discuss the king's devotion to Buddhism and outline moral and religious guidelines for his empire. This map shows the wide extent of the edicts across the Indian subcontinent.

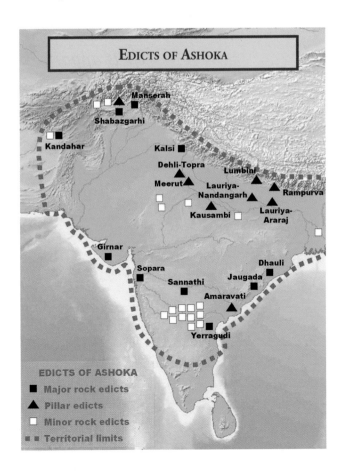

Mauryan coins, 200s BC

their husband's funeral pyre. The belief developed that this was a noble deed that purged the sins of both the husband and the wife and brought them back together. Some members of the upper castes practiced polygamy. Sons were much more highly valued than daughters because they carried on the family name. It was not unusual for female children to be abandoned.

The kingdoms of the southern region of India were never conquered by the empires of the north. The southern people included the proud Tamil, who lived on the southeastern coast. The Tamil

carried on trade with Rome (by means of trading ships that made the round trip to Rome and back) and later with China. Even today, Tamil separatists want to have freedom from the rest of India. The Gupta dynasty ended when Huns from Central Asia invaded. Small independent kingdoms dotted India for about 1000 years.

Conclusion

Hindu and Buddhist teachings did little to bring peace and security to the lives of people on the Indian subcontinent. Instead, they seem to have encouraged the people to accept suffering and misery rather than to try to improve their lot. Since one does not know in what stage of reincarnation he is, one can try his best but never know if he is making progress. This would seem to discourage trying harder. The various tribes and groups of India have been given to wars as much as other peoples. The patterns of the past have definitely contributed to the ways of the present.

[I]t is appointed for men to die once
and after this comes judgment . . . .
Hebrews 9:27

Assignments for Lesson 36

Bible   Read Isaiah 40 and 42. Commentary available in *Student Review*.

In Their Words   Read "The Jackal and the Partridge" and the excerpts from *The Dhammapada* (pages 36-39).

Literature   Begin reading *The Art of War*. Plan to finish it by the end of this unit.

Student Review   Optional: Answer the questions for Lesson 36.

Design on a Bronze Vessel from the Shang Dynasty

Lesson 37

Ancient China

They called themselves *Chung Kuo*, the Middle Kingdom. In their minds, they were the center of the world. They have given rise to significant inventions and developments that have affected the rest of the world. We call this land China.

The Shang Dynasty

The pattern should be familiar by now. Farming villages dot the banks of a mighty river. A few nobles own most of the land and the best houses, and they have the greatest wealth and the most political power. Competing lords vie for power during years of civil strife until one man or one family emerges victorious. This pattern occurred in many countries. In China, it took place along the twisting Yellow River in northern China. It was a river given to alternating droughts and floods. The "River of Sorrows" as it was called often brought destruction to those who depended on it for life.

The Shang Dynasty was the earliest succession of rulers in this region. It held power between about 1600 and 1100 BC. Even at this early date, the Chinese showed their remarkable intellectual capacities. They developed a system of writing using pictograms (agreed-upon symbols illustrating objects

they knew). The next step involved ideograms, symbols that represented concepts. Written Chinese developed some 3,000 symbols, and eventually about 50,000 characters were used. This made the language difficult to use, especially by anyone not wealthy enough to take the time to learn it.

Wine Beaker (c. 12th century BC)

Because they wrote on vertical strips of bamboo and wood, they wrote in vertical columns instead of across a page.

During the Shang Dynasty, the Chinese developed the use of bronze for practical and aesthetic purposes. They created inventions such as the two-wheeled war chariot and an early form of porcelain. Mathematicians in China developed a decimal numbering system. Astronomers created a calendar that consisted of twelve months and 365 1/4 days. Shang artisans developed products of silk, jade, and ivory that became much sought after by traders. Natural barriers of mountains and deserts made contact between the Chinese and other people groups to the west difficult. However, the Chinese established trade with Mesopotamia fairly early on, despite having to deal with invaders from Manchuria and Mongolia.

This silk painting of a man riding a dragon is from the Sichuan province of China (c. 400s BC).

The days of the Shang also saw the spread of a spiritual ritual that continues in some form even today. The Chinese believed that powerful gods controlled life, weather, crops, and all aspects of life. The people tried to influence the gods not only by their own prayers and rituals but by calling on their deceased ancestors to appeal to the gods as well. To impress the ancestors of their sincerity and need, the people began the practice of ancestor worship. People would sometimes want to ask their ancestors a question. A priest would write the question (usually a question that could be answered yes or no) on a piece of bone, make notches in it, and apply a heated rod to the notches. The way the bone cracked would be interpreted by the priest as the ancestor's answer. Thousands of these oracle bones have been found at ancient religious sites. Today many Chinese worship or at least pay their respects to their ancestors in home ceremonies.

The Zhou Dynasty

The Shang Dynasty was overtaken by the Zhou Dynasty around the end of the 12th century BC. The Zhou rulers continued for almost a thousand years, until 256 BC. The Zhou believed in what they called the Mandate of Heaven. They believed that an emperor had a divine right to rule if he ruled well. If he did not, he deserved to fall. They thought the Shang had failed to rule well and so deserved to lose their power. Proclaiming adherence to "the Mandate of Heaven," of course, was a handy rationale for seizing and holding power.

Because the Zhou had to rule such a large area, they developed a feudal system of power. The Zhou emperor allowed nobles to rule their smaller kingdoms as they saw fit and promised protection for them. In return, the nobles promised loyalty, paid tribute, and when called upon gave service to the emperor. The Zhou government encouraged farming, and the period saw the introduction of fertilizer, iron tools, irrigation, and the ox-drawn

The Tomb of Confucius (pictured at right) is part of a large cemetery near Qufu, China, that also includes graves of tens of thousands of his descendants. Genealogical records of the descendants of Confucius have been carefully kept for centuries. The edition published in 2009 contains two million names in eighty volumes.

plow. The feudal system apparently did not work well enough, however. Most of the last half of the Zhou period was marked by wars among the feudal states.

One important development that affected government and society was the growth of a large bureaucracy to oversee the governing of the empire. Government officials eventually became the ruling class because of their power and because they acquired large land holdings. In the Zhou class structure, below the ruling class was the farming class, honored because they worked the fields. Then came the artisans and merchants, who were below farmers because they did not work on the land. At the bottom were the soldiers.

Confucius and Other Philosophers

As Chinese scientists gained insights about the physical world, Chinese philosophers wanted to gain greater insights into human relationships. Although they recognized the spiritual world, they were more concerned about the practical matters of right living in this life. They wanted to determine the way to establish and maintain a stable and orderly society and government. With the frequent instability they saw in their government, their goal is understandable.

Confucius. The best known philosopher in ancient China was born about 551 BC. Confucius became a scholar and was employed as a minor government official. He eventually became a tutor to the sons of wealthy families.

Confucius was deeply troubled by war, and he wanted to learn how to live a life based on high moral ideals. As he thought through the issues that made for a good life and a good society, he tried to teach his philosophy to various government officials. They rejected him, however, so he devoted himself to teaching a small group of disciples who in turn could influence others. He did not write down his insights, but his disciples did and compiled them into what are called the *Analects*.

Confucius tried to identify what practices made for peace among people and between citizens and their government. He believed that the practice of virtues produces harmony in society. These virtues, he said, should be practiced in five relationships: ruler and subject, parent and child, husband and wife, older brother and younger brother, and friend to friend. In each relationship, each party has a duty and the other has a responsibility to fulfill. Family relationships especially, Confucius believed, were the foundation for a happy and stable society.

The disciples of Confucius had greater success in getting their teacher's ideas across to others than Confucius himself did. Confucianism eventually had a great impact on Chinese law, government, and family life. His principles were not always followed, but they were influential. His insights came at a time when the Chinese did not know revealed truth about God and His way, so they were an attempt to fill a void that people, families, and societies always have without such divine teaching. Many of the sayings that Confucius wrote and compiled are good advice; but followers of Jesus know that we will never find true inner peace and salvation merely by trying to live well.

Taoism. Little is known about Laozi, the author of *Tao Te Ching*. Laozi disagreed with Confucius about the value of behavior. He said the way to happiness is by becoming attuned to the *tao,* or the way, the universal force that pervades everything. This is accomplished not by reason but by contemplation. Whereas Confucius encouraged right actions, Laozi encouraged little doing and much contemplation. While Confucius wanted to encourage government to do what is right, Laozi favored a restrained or limited government.

The Taoism (pronounced Dow-ism) that developed in ancient China was a combination of philosophy and mystical religion. Taoist priests had charms and spells to ward off evil spirits. These practices appealed to the common people who believed strongly in such spirits and who believed they had to cope with them every day. Taoism encouraged the simple life and time for personal meditation. It also exalted closeness with nature. By-products of this philosophy included some scientific advances. The Chinese became expert students of astronomy and botany. Gunpowder might have been developed first to use in firecrackers to frighten ghosts. When the compass was developed, it was first used for superstitious purposes, such as the positioning of graves; but sailors eventually recognized its value for navigation.

Legalism. A third philosophy is known as legalism. Its chief advocate was Han Fei Tzu, who died around 233 BC. Han took the opposite approach from Taoism regarding government. He believed that a good society could only be created through a strict, activist government with a ruler who held absolute power. Han saw that people can be swayed by selfishness, fear, and emotional appeals and are not always able to make good decisions. The only way to get people to do right is for the ruler to make laws that are reinforced with attractive rewards and strict punishments.

Later Dynasties

In 221 BC, the feudal state of Qin emerged victorious from another period of civil war and established the Qin dynasty (pronounced *cheen*, from which we get the name China). The new emperor decided to implement legalism and tried to impose unity on the empire. He reorganized the feudal states as administrative units directly responsible to him. The Qin began an extensive program of public works including roads that helped to tie the empire together, but the projects took a heavy toll in workers' lives lost.

One project of the Qin dynasty was the connection of several smaller walls to create a defensive barrier in the north. The Qin did not build

The Changchun Temple is in Beijing, China. This Buddhist temple features a portion of the Tao Te Ching.

This bronze plaque contains an edict from the second Qin emperor (c. 209 BC).

"The Great Wall" as it stands today; future leaders continued the development of this fortification. However, not even their early version of the Wall protected the Qin, for their dynasty collapsed around 206 BC.

The country endured another eight years of civil war before the Han dynasty restored order. The Han adopted Confucianism, expanded the country's borders, and established peace for some

two hundred years. To create a more efficient government, the Han rulers instituted a civil service system. To train people for the difficult civil service exam, an educational system was developed. The exam required knowledge of Confucianism, so the philosophy was taught in the schools.

The Han dynasty oversaw improvements in the written Chinese language, so effective that the language remained largely unchanged until 1949. Paper made from pulpwood and rags came to be produced, which encouraged the use of writing. Books of Chinese history were compiled during this time. Scientific achievements included the recognition that eclipses were regular phenomena and not actions by an angry god, as well as the first known identification of sunspots. The Chinese produced sundials, water clocks, and a calendar that remained in use until 1912. Advances in technology included the wheelbarrow, the water mill, a harness for farm animals, and improved looms for weaving.

This terra-cotta figurine from the Han period represents a female servant (c. first century BC).

Front and Back of a Coin Issued During the Reign of Emperor Wu, Han Dynasty (c. 100 BC)

The Han emperors encouraged foreign trade with western Asia and Europe. So much silk was sent out that the main trade route became known as the Silk Road. Buddhism was introduced into China during this period and gained a wide following among people who identified with the plight of suffering in the world.

The Han dynasty fell in 220 AD, which led to another period of civil war and a decline in foreign trade.

By the works of the Law no flesh will be justified in His sight;
for through the Law comes the knowledge of sin.
Romans 3:20

Assignments for Lesson 37

Bible Read Isaiah 43-44. Commentary available in *Student Review.*

In Their Words Read the excerpt from *The Analects* (pages 40-41).

Literature Continue reading *The Art of War.*

Student Review Optional: Answer the questions for Lesson 37.

Lesson 38 - Everyday Life

Chinese Government, Culture, and Science

The raw materials that produced the ancient Chinese civilization were those God created. People made in His image used the soils, the underground metals, plants, and other products of the land to create a civilization with beautiful art, amazing scientific knowledge, and practical tools for living.

Government

The Zhou Dynasty (c. 1045-256 BC) had a feudal system, with nobles, peasants, and slaves. During the Qin Dynasty the land was divided into administrative districts. Writing, weights, measures, and coinage were standardized. In addition to round coins, Chinese coins were also produced in knife and spade shapes. Roads, canals, irrigation systems, and a precursor to the Great Wall were built.

Government under Emperor Qin Shi Huang (ruled 247-210 BC) was based on the approach called Legalism taught by his main advisor, Li Si. The emperor's palace had 1,000 bedrooms. He changed bedrooms to ward off being assassinated, and he sought to find immortality through potions. Ironically, one of these concoctions might have caused his death.

The Han Dynasty came to power in 206 BC. Each emperor had a bureaucracy of government officials and civil servants. The highest officials were mandarins. The rulers had large land holdings which included palaces and tall pavilions for the emperor and the nobles. During the Han dynasty, bamboo bridges were built over some of the gorges of the Himalayas. In 2 AD a census ordered by the Han emperor determined the population of China to be 59,594,978.

This is a pottery mold from the Zhou Dynasty period for making spade-shaped coins (c. 500s BC).

199

Art

Most Chinese artists and architects worked for the emperor. Rulers required that the arts preserve Chinese traditions. Chinese artists were highly trained and worked in large workshops. Knowledge was passed from generation to generation. Bronze casts were made during the Shang dynasty. During the Zhou dynasty bronze vessels sometimes had inlays of gold or semiprecious stones. Often they were cast to commemorate war victories or land grants. They usually had long inscriptions of what they commemorated. Other art forms of the Zhou period include paintings on silk, wood sculpture, lacquerwork, and glazed ceramics. Written history of the Zhou period indicates that royal homes were adorned with large portraits of emperors and painted murals. During the Zhou dynasty, bronze house decorations were often given as wedding gifts. Bronze mirrors were popular during this period.

Archaeologists have extensively studied art from the Qin dynasty (221-206 BC). When Emperor Qin Shi Huang died, he was buried in a huge burial mound in the Shaanxi province. The burial mound was discovered by Chinese peasants digging a well. First excavated in 1974, the tomb contained some 8,000 terra-cotta figures, representing a real army in battle formation.

The figures include officers, charioteers, archers, and young foot soldiers, all designed to look natural with distinct facial features. The size of the figures reflects their rank, with the commanders being the tallest at 6 feet 5 inches. The shortest figures are 5 feet 8 inches. The soldiers carry weapons and wear uniforms showing their rank. Horses are sculpted in various poses, along with chariots. Originally the terra-cotta army was painted with bright colors.

During the Han dynasty (206 BC - 220 AD), grave architecture included vaults and supporting columns. Graves were furnished with miniature objects that were usually glazed or colorfully painted ceramic. Typical miniatures included a home, a barnyard, pets, servants, and assorted objects from daily life. A model of a rotary winnowing fan found in ancient tombs was made of pottery and had miniature working parts. A beautiful and very realistic bronze horse sculpture was uncovered at a tomb in Wuwei.

Figures from the Terra-Cotta Army

One of the oldest representations of a ship's rudder is on a pottery model found in a first century AD Chinese tomb. The model ship is about twenty-two inches long. It features a slung axial rudder at the stern. This type of rudder can be raised and lowered by rope tackle or chains to navigate in deep or shallow water.

Prince Liu Sheng and his wife Dou Wan died during the Han dynasty. Their grave included lacquers, silks, pottery, and bronze. Some of the bronze was gilded and some was inlaid with gold. Both bodies wore jade suits, each made with more than 2,000 pieces of wafer-thin jade, attached with gold, silver, and bronze thread.

This pottery boat model features an anchor at the front, a steering rudder at the back, roofed compartments, and crew members (c. first century AD).

Farming

Chinese farmers achieved several significant advances in agriculture.

Row Crops. Western farmers began planting in rows in the 18th century AD. The Chinese were planting in rows by the sixth century BC. It is discussed in *Mister Lu's Spring and Autumn Annals*, which says that the crops will not interfere with each other's growth. It recommends straight lines so the wind will pass gently through.

Plows. By the fourth century BC, a sturdy, square-framed, heavy plow was being promoted by the Chinese government. The strut could be adjusted for plowing depth.

Wheelbarrow. Chinese descriptions of the wheelbarrow date from the first century BC. A frieze relief in a tomb-shrine in Szechuan province dates from around 118 AD. Sometimes Chinese wheelbarrows had sails.

Millet. A common food in northern China is millet. It grows well where the weather is cold and dry. The Chinese pictogram for millet is common in Chinese writing. Written together, the pictograms for millet and mouth mean good. The combined pictograms of millet and man mean harvest or year. Kings thought they were descended from a god, the Millet Ruler, and that heaven gave them permission to rule.

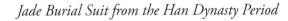

Jade Burial Suit from the Han Dynasty Period

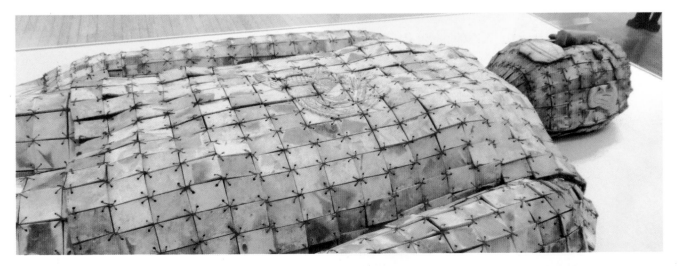

Paper and Writing

Cai Lun was an official in a Chinese court. Though forms of paper already existed in China, he is given credit for developing an improved method of papermaking around 105 AD. His system is still basically what is used today: soaking plant fibers (bark, hemp, cotton, etc.) in water and pressing and drying them in flat sheets. By the mid-100s there were many paper mills producing yellow paper. The Chinese kept the art of papermaking a secret. Muslims began making paper in the Middle East in the 700s. They brought the technology to Spain, and it eventually spread to other European countries in the late Middle Ages.

Hot Air Balloons and Paper Lanterns

The Chinese used eggshells to make miniature hot-air balloons. A book written in the second century BC, *The Ten Thousand Infallible Arts of the Prince of Huai-Nan*, mentions eggshell balloons. To make them, they removed the contents of the egg and then ignited a bit of mugwort tinder inside the hole. Mugwort is a common weed with long, dry stalks, also used to make incense sticks.

Silk from a Han Dynasty Tomb (c. Second Century BC)

During the Han dynasty the military used paper lanterns as signals. Chinese paper lanterns continue to be important in Chinese culture. Chinese New Year celebrations include the paper lantern festival. They have also been used as tiny hot-air balloons.

Clothing

The traditional form of Chinese clothing for both men and women developed during the Shang Dynasty. It included the *yi*, a knee-length tunic, wrapped over the *chang*, a skirt that extended to the ankles. People developed variations that allowed them to show off their wealth and social status. Men also wore different types of hats to show their occupation or position. Silk has been a favorite material for clothes in China since about 1500 BC.

The Abacus

The Chinese developed a modern form of the Suan Pan, or abacus, with beads on rods. This device was mentioned by Xu Yue around 190 AD. The word abacus might have originated from the Semitic word *abq* which means sand and later from the Greek word *abax* or *abakon* (table or tablet). The abacus was used extensively in China well into the 20th century, but its use is no longer commonly taught in schools. However, in speed competitions the proficient abacus user can still beat an electronic calculator user at addition and subtraction.

Medicine

The Chinese medical textbook, *Huangdi Neijing*, was compiled around the second century BC. Most ancient Chinese medicine was based on this book. The Chinese treated wounds, set fractured bones, and had remedies for allergies. They treated anemia with iron. They asked patients about their symptoms, diet, and previous illnesses to help with

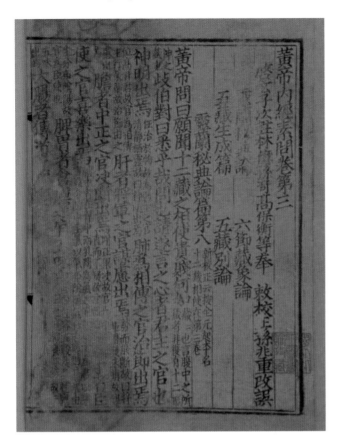

This is a page from the earliest known printed copy of the Huangdi Neijing *(c. 12th century AD).*

diagnosis. Chinese physicians understood the basics of blood circulation and how to check a patient's pulse. Acupuncture treatment improved during the Han dynasty, though it might have begun long before.

Technology

Drilling. The Chinese were extracting natural gas to use as a fuel by the first century BC. They used cast iron for drill bits and bamboo for cables and pipes. They might have been able to drill nearly a mile underground with this equipment.

Parachute. The Chinese historian Sima Qian completed his *Records of the Grand Historian* around 90 BC. He described a parachute legend from centuries before. According to the story, a man jumped from a granary tower which was on fire and used straw hats to slow his fall to earth.

Seismograph. The court astronomer Zhang Heng invented a seismograph during the Han dynasty. It was a richly ornamented copper cauldron six feet in diameter with eight evenly-spaced bronze dragon heads circling its midsection. Each dragon held a ball in its movable mouth. Below the dragon heads were eight toads with open mouths. When an earthquake occurred, a dragon mouth would open and drop its ball into the frog mouth below. The direction of the dragon's head thus affected would indicate in which direction from the capital the earthquake had occurred.

The Han government bought surplus farm products and kept them in warehouses for emergencies like earthquakes. They had canal systems and roads for transporting the supplies. Before the invention of the seismograph, they had to rely on messengers from distant provinces to let the central government know about a quake; but this took too long. With the seismograph, the government could send aid as soon as an earthquake occurred.

A Model Reproduction of Zhang Heng's Seismograph

Let the glory of the Lord endure forever;
let the Lord be glad in His works;
He looks at the earth, and it trembles;
He touches the mountains, and they smoke.
Psalm 104:31-32

Assignments for Lesson 38

Bible   Read Isaiah 52:13-53:12. Commentary available in *Student Review*.

In Their Words   Read the Chinese Poetry (pages 42-43).

Literature   Continue reading *The Art of War*.

Student Review   Optional: Answer the questions for Lesson 38.

Lesson 39

Ancient Africa, America, and Europe

Separating fact from fiction when discussing ancient civilizations is difficult, especially when those cultures did not leave written records. Anthropologists and other scientists often have strong presuppositions that cause them to interpret evidence in certain ways or to announce what they believe to be the truth with little or no evidence at all. Academic speculation gets picked up as scientific conclusions and then repeated as assured facts. Experts sometimes have a hard time admitting that they do not know the answers. The information about ancient cultures in this lesson is based on current proposed theories. Future discoveries might change what is commonly believed today.

Africa

Africa is a huge continent, three times the size of the continental United States. It has a varied geography that includes rain forests, deserts, mountains, grasslands or savannahs, and temperate zones (the latter in its northern and southern extremes). The many rivers in Africa provide water for farming and serve as avenues for transportation.

On its vast landscape live many different tribal groups. Most modern political nations in Africa have multiple tribal groups within them.

Terra-cotta figurines were discovered near Nok, Nigeria, in the 20th century. Most were broken and worn by natural forces. Little is known about their history or use. They might date to around the time of Christ.

Great Zimbabwe developed as a major political center between 1000 and 1400 AD. In this photo, a large circular enclosure is in the background with the ruins of smaller buildings spread around in the foreground. The entire complex covers about 1,800 acres. Glass beads, coins, and porcelain found at the site indicate that the inhabitants had trade routes connecting them with Arabs further north in Africa and beyond to Persia and China.

Some tribes are spread across more than one country. Hundreds of different languages are spoken on the continent.

We have already studied the Egyptian culture in Africa, but many other nations arose on the continent in ancient times as well. The kingdom of Kush, to the south of Egypt, developed early and in 750 BC conquered Egypt. The Kushites later retreated, and the civilization declined by about 200 BC. Axum, to the south of Kush, was strongly influenced by its trade with the Arab world and thus was a mixture of Arab and African cultures. The king of Axum converted to Christianity in the 300s AD.

Kush is mentioned in the Old Testament (spelled Cush; see, for example, 2 Kings 19:9 and Isaiah 20:3-5). The areas of Kush and Axum later came to be known as Ethiopia. It is likely that the presence of Christianity in the region began with the conversion of the Ethiopian eunuch described in Acts 8:26-40. Meanwhile, the abundant resources of salt and gold in West Africa enabled Ghana to become the first major trading state in that part of the continent.

Generally speaking, the nations and tribal groups that we know about were formed during the period between Christ's birth and the Middle Ages. Africa, especially the northern part, was strongly influenced by Muslim conquests beginning in the seventh and eighth centuries AD.

Most African tribes lived in villages overseen by elders. They placed great emphasis on family life and usually lived in extended family arrangements. Men were the accepted leaders of the family and

Oral Tradition

African tribes generally did not keep written records, but their oral traditions are strong. In the early 20th century, Hungarian researcher Emil Torday interviewed the Bushongo (or Kuba) people in West Africa. Their leaders remembered 120 kings, in order; but they had no way to tie their reigns to European years. The Bushongo men mentioned that during the reign of the 98th king, the sun was blotted out one day. Torday knew that this was a solar eclipse. Upon checking, he found that a total solar eclipse visible in that region had occurred in 1680.

Mask from the Kuba Kingdom (19th century)

Work on the Mosque of Uqba, or the Great Mosque of Kairouan (Tunisia), began in 670, making it one of the oldest mosques. The main structure dates primarily from the ninth century. The minaret shown above, completed about 836, is considered the oldest standing minaret in the world.

the village. Women filled different roles in different tribes, but they always played a significant role in the family. Some tribes were matrilineal; that is, they traced their family lines and inherited property through the mother. In a few tribes, wealthier men practiced polygamy. Cultural activities included the arts, music and dancing, and storytelling.

Many African cultures believed in one Great Spirit but also in many lesser spiritual beings. Often the people believed that trees, rocks, and other elements of nature had spirits (this belief is called animism). In coping with everyday life and in trying to please the Great Spirit, the people would seek help from lesser spiritual beings and from their ancestors, who were thought to be closer to the Great Spirit.

The Americas

The traditional understanding of how people first came to the Americas is that they walked from Siberia to Alaska over a land bridge that was later submerged after the ice from an Ice Age melted. However, this is only a guess. A few scholars speculate that the first Americans crossed the ocean by boat. The frank answer is that we do not know.

However they got here, the first Americans found a wide diversity of geography and weather; and tribes spread across two continents to inhabit the land. The Inuit people hunted and fished in the area of Alaska and Canada. During hunting expeditions, they used igloos or ice huts. In what became the southwestern United States, tribes took up farming as well as hunting and used dried mud to build adobe dwellings. The Iroquois and other tribes in what became the northeastern United States built longhouses of wooden frames covered with animal hides or brush. Tribes often moved as a group, but sometimes they divided.

The Codex Fejérváry-Mayer, a religious almanac named after its 19th-century owners, is one of the few Aztec manuscripts that survived the Spanish conquest.

This is a panel from the palace of Maya leader Tajal Chan Ahk in Cancuén (Guatemala, c. 770 AD).

North American tribes generally lived in small villages. The tribes that inhabited Central and South America, by contrast, built great cities and developed complex governmental systems. Archaeologists believe that much of what these peoples built had to do with their religious observances.

The Olmec nation flourished in southern Mexico starting around 1200 BC. They built large pyramids and carved huge stone faces. The Olmec developed a hieroglyphic writing system, a fairly advanced counting system, and an accurate calendar. The Olmecs disappeared around the first century AD for reasons unknown. They might have migrated to another place, been defeated in war, or been wiped out by disease.

Guatemala was the center of the Maya civilization that rose to prominence around 250 AD. They eventually spread into southern Mexico

Hand Stencils

Another fascinating indication that all humans share the same creative capabilities and intelligence are the hand stencils found in caves around the world, including Argentina, Australia, Belize, France, Indonesia, Papua New Guinea, South Africa, and Spain. Until recent centuries, most famous artists were male. Research of the relative hand sizes at some sites suggests that at least some, perhaps a majority, of the hand stencils are female. The photo at left below is from the Cueva de las Manos ("Cave of the Hands") near Perito Moreno, Argentina. The photo at right is from the Gua Tewet cave on the island of Borneo, Indonesia.

and other parts of Central America. The polytheistic Mayans built large cities that included pyramid structures, and many cities had a recreation field where games were played (the nature and purpose of the games are still matters of speculation). Mayan farming was helped by the irrigation systems they built. They followed precise calendars and used a numbering system that included zero. The Mayans declined around 900 AD.

The Aztec civilization arose around 1200 AD in Mexico. Their capital was Tenochtitlan, on the site of present-day Mexico City. The Aztecs were a warlike people that conquered other tribes and demanded payments of tribute. When Spanish explorers landed in the early 1500s, they found allies among the subject tribes who were only too ready to throw off Aztec rule. Aztec religion included human sacrifices made to their sun god.

The Inca people inhabited the mountainous regions of western South America, including what is now Peru. Evidence suggests their presence from around 1200 AD. The Incas were polytheistic but especially worshiped the sun god. They built temples and roads and had advanced medical practices.

European Tribes

The word barbarian was used by the Greeks to describe people who spoke a different language and had different cultural ways (the word expressed what the non-Greek language sounded like to them: *bar-bar*, or jibberish). It did not necessarily mean that the non-Greeks were less intelligent, although that is probably what the Greeks thought. It is generally used in a derogatory sense.

One of the striking early evidences of human society in Europe are the mysterious stone circles. The most famous among the numerous circles that still exist is Stonehenge in southern England.

Golden Celtic Helmet (France, c. 350 BC)

Apparently it was built in stages until about 1550 BC. Experts believe the huge stones were quarried in Wales over 200 miles away, shipped by rafts, and dragged on sleds or over logs to the site. Some stones were set erect with lintels placed across pairs of them.

The motivation for building Stonehenge and its purpose once it was completed have been the subject of much speculation. It could possibly have been arranged to mark the summer solstice. It was definitely not intended as a site for Druid worship, since the Druid cult did not appear until long after Stonehenge was built. The site is near Sarum, an ancient town and fort, and the more modern city of Salisbury.

Four Views of Stonehenge. The earliest known illustration of Stonehenge (top left), depicting a giant helping Merlin construct it, is taken from a Norman history of England (c. 1340). Next is a 1645 illustration from a Dutch atlas published by Joan Blaeu. The third photo shows Canadian troops marching past during World War I (c. 1915). The final image from 2007 shows the results of modern reconstruction efforts.

The nomadic tribes of Europe are thought to have come from the grassy steppes of Eastern Europe and Central Asia. Some tribes migrated south (into Greece, for instance) and southeast (perhaps to India), while others moved west into Europe. Linguists and anthropologists believe that language and other similarities in these widely divergent groups suggest a common origin. As a result, many ancient peoples and their languages are called Indo-European. Some of these peoples include the Celts of western Europe and the Germanic tribes of northern Europe. The contact and interchange between the tribes of western and northern Europe

Arthur might have been a Celtic king of the sixth century AD in southwestern England who fought the Saxon invaders. His reputation became lionized in many legends, and Arthur became the national mythical hero of England. This detail from a tapestry portrays Arthur as one of the heroes of history (French, c. 1385).

and the Mediterranean cultures of Greece and Rome gave rise to what we call Western Civilization.

The Celts (pronounced *kelts*; the origin of the word is Greek) lived in central and western Europe and migrated into Britain by 500 BC. Other Celts settled in France (called Gaul) and Spain. The Celts were fierce and cruel warriors but also produced refined artwork and craftwork. The Druids were a Celtic religious cult.

Julius Caesar led an invasion of Roman forces into Celtic Britain in 55 BC and eventually added much of the island to the Roman Empire. The Romans founded the town of Londinium (later known as London) at a previously-inhabited site on the Thames River. The Romans occupied Britain

The Romans established an extensive mining operation in Britain. These lead ingots from England have Latin inscriptions. The Romans used lead in pewter dishes, coffins, and plumbing. The Latin word plumbum *means "soft metals," and the symbol for lead on the periodic table is Pb.*

The Study of History

The Venerable Bede (673-735 AD) was an English monk who is called the father of English history. He never left the area around his home in northeastern England, but he was one of the most learned men in Europe. Bede knew Hebrew, Greek, and Latin and wrote science, poetry, Bible translation, and Biblical exposition as well as history. The illustration of him at left is from the 1493 Nuremberg Chronicle.

Bede's Ecclesiastical History of the English People, *published about 731, provides many valuable details of the history of England from the Roman invasion to about 600 AD. He wanted to emphasize the arrival and spread of Christianity in England. Bede understood the value of history for those who want to serve the Lord, as reflected in this extract from a message to King Ceolwulf regarding his work:*

And I rejoice greatly at the sincerity and zeal, with which you not only diligently give ear to hear the words of Holy Scripture, but also industriously take care to become acquainted with the actions and sayings of former men of renown, especially of our own nation. For if history relates good things of good men, the attentive hearer is excited to imitate that which is good; or if it recounts evil things of wicked persons, none the less the conscientious and devout hearer or reader, shunning that which is hurtful and wrong, is the more earnestly fired to perform those things which he knows to be good, and worthy of the service of God. And as you have carefully marked this, you are desirous that the said history should be more fully made known to yourself, and to those over whom the Divine Authority has appointed you governor, from your great regard to the common good.

until the threat of barbarian conquest in Italy caused the Romans to abandon the island about 400 AD.

The Saxons were a Germanic tribe that moved across the weakening Roman Empire in northern Europe. They invaded Britain in the fifth century AD after Roman forces left. The Saxons pushed the Celts west and north, so that the Celts came to inhabit what is now Wales, Scotland, Ireland, and the southwestern tip of England called Cornwall. Scots and Picts also lived in what is now Scotland.

Other Germanic tribes, including the Angles and Jutes, also came to the island. By 890 AD the main part of the island of Britain was called Angleland or England. Their language was known as English. As the Saxons and Angles blended together, they originated what are called the Anglo-Saxon people. In the 800s AD Vikings from Norway and Denmark launched repeated invasions of the island and seized control of some areas, especially in the north of England. The last Saxon king, Harold, was killed at the Battle of Hastings in 1066 when Norman invaders (from Normandy in northern France) accomplished the last successful foreign invasion of England.

There is no distinction between Greek and Jew,
circumcised and uncircumcised, barbarian, Scythian,
slave and freeman, but Christ is all, and in all.
Colossians 3:11

Assignments for Lesson 39

Bible   Read Isaiah 55. Commentary available in *Student Review.*

In Their Words   Read the excerpt from *Ecclesiastical History of the English People* (pages 44-45).

Literature   Continue reading *The Art of War.*

Student Review   Optional: Answer the questions for Lesson 39.

Lesson 40 - Bible Study

God's Love for the Nations

The book of Jonah is more than just a big fish story. It is a lesson about how much God loves the nations of the world and how difficult it is for God's people to have that same love for others. Read the book of Jonah as you go through these notes.

Jonah 1:1-16—God commissioned Jonah to preach to the city of Nineveh, capital of the heathen nation of Assyria, because He knew of their sins. A reference to Jonah in 2 Kings 14:25 places his ministry in the first half of the eighth century BC (approximately 790 to 760 BC). The Assyrians were known for their cruelty in war. Within a few decades, they would destroy the Northern Kingdom of Israel and carry many of its people into captivity. Perhaps God wanted to give them a chance to change their ways in order to spare Israel.

However, Jonah did not want to preach to Nineveh. He hated the Assyrians. Rather than head east to Nineveh, Jonah headed west in an attempt to run away from God. He boarded a ship at the port city of Joppa destined for Tarshish (in Asia Minor, later known as Tarsus, home of Paul).

The Lord sent a great storm against the ship, so great that the experienced crew feared for their lives. They learned that Jonah was the reason for their peril. Jonah claimed to fear the Lord, but he certainly did not act like he did. At Jonah's request, they threw him into the ocean, calling on the Lord as they did. When the sea became calm, the men feared the Lord, made a sacrifice, and took vows. The crew evidently were pagans, but they called upon the Lord and sacrificed to Him. Thus the heathens were showing more faith in God than was the Israelite Jonah.

This 16th-century German relief sculpture depicts two separate scenes from the Book of Jonah in one image. On the right, the sailors are throwing Jonah overboard, and the fish is opening its mouth to swallow him. On the left, the fish is spewing Jonah out.

This landscape showing Jonah after being cast on shore is made from pieces of stone (Italian, c. 1620s).

Jonah 1:17-2:10—God appointed a great fish to swallow Jonah. He was inside the fish for three days and three nights. While there, he repented and called upon the Lord. The Lord caused the fish to vomit Jonah onto dry land. Jesus mentioned Jonah's experience inside the fish as a sign similar to his burial. As Jonah called the Ninevites to reprentance, so Jesus calls all people to repentance (Matthew 12:38-41).

Jonah 3:1-10—God renewed His call to Jonah, and this time Jonah obeyed—barely. All the preaching we have of Jonah is one sentence of eight words, and he didn't even go all the way through the city. But it was enough; the pagan people of Nineveh repented, from the king down to the commoners. They believed, fasted, and put on sackcloth (a symbol of mourning and anguish). The king issued a proclamation calling on every Ninevite to call on God in the hope that He would relent from His plan to destroy the city, and God did so.

Jonah 4:1-4—Consider the mercies that God showed. He spoke to Jonah. When Jonah ran away, God allowed him to find a ship. God protected Jonah through the storm and in the belly of the fish. By His merciful warning, the people of Nineveh repented and called on the Lord. Jonah, though, was furious. He had shown insensitivity by refusing to go to Nineveh the first time God told him to, by being asleep on the boat during the storm, by not going through the entire city of Nineveh, and by his minimal sermon to the Ninevites. Now Jonah did not like the fact that the Ninevites were repenting. He hated those heathens and wanted them shown no mercy.

Jonah addressed his frustrations to God. He had not wanted to go to Nineveh because he knew that God was gracious and compassionate. In other words, he couldn't stand the thought of God being merciful towards the pagans of Nineveh; and he had not wanted to be a part of it. In fact, he said that he would rather die than see a city filled with humble, repentant, God-fearing people. God replied by asking a question: "Do you have good reason to be angry?" (Jonah 4:4). In the following scene God showed Jonah that he didn't have a good reason.

Jonah 4:5-11—Once again God showed mercy to Jonah, this time by appointing a plant to provide him with shade. This pleased Jonah, but he became frustrated again when a worm attacked the plant and caused it to wither. Once again, Jonah wanted to die. The Lord asked Jonah again if he had good reason to be angry, this time about the plant; and Jonah said that he did. Then God came to the point of the story. Jonah cared about the plant, for which he had done nothing and which had grown and was gone in two days.

Alabaster relief from Nineveh (c. 695 BC)

Alain Manesson Mallet was a French mapmaker and engineer. His book Description de L'Univers (1683) *featured a variety of ancient and modern maps with information on the culture and government of various countries. At right is his representation of the ancient city of Nineveh with Jonah in the corner sitting under the plant (from the 1719 edition).*

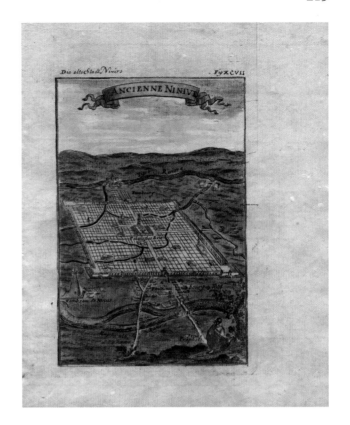

Was it not right, by contrast, for God to care about the tens of thousands of human beings in Nineveh whom he had created in His image and who were so spiritually lost that they did not know their right hand from their left? God even cared about the animals of Nineveh more than Jonah cared about the people of Nineveh.

Lessons from Jonah

In the story of Jonah, God showed that He loved all people and tried to teach Jonah to do the same. Jonah had received blessing upon blessing from God, not least of which was his being born into the nation of Israel, God's chosen people. The prophet was extremely selfish and uncaring about others. He wanted God to love him, but he did not understand that accepting God's love has consequences. We cannot put limits on God's love. God's love extends to people from any and every nation (Acts 10:34-35). Our purpose should not be to try to shrink God's love down to the size of our own hearts, but to grow in our love to become more like God.

The nations of the world were formed by God when He scattered the people from the Tower of Babel. Paul said that God made all the nations from Adam and determined their times and places of habitation (Acts 17:26). Several times in the Old Testament, God says that all the earth belongs to Him (Exodus 9:29, 19:5; Deuteronomy 10:14; Job 41:11). Even the cattle on a thousand hills (held sacred by the people of India) belong to God (Psalm 50:10).

This does not mean that God loves or tolerates the pagan practices of the nations. He wanted the idolatrous nations of Canaan completely driven out so that they would not be a snare to the Israelites when they conquered the Promised Land (Joshua 1:6). God hates idolatry. He ridiculed the idea of a man cutting down a tree, making a fire with part of it, and bowing down to the rest of it as an idol (Isaiah 44:14-17; see also Habakkuk 2:18-20). The Lord also ridiculed pagan fishermen who would worship the net they used to catch fish (Habakkuk 1:15-16).

Three of the Minor Prophets addressed the sins of Gentile nations (Jonah, Nahum, and Obadiah). Jesus came and died because God loves the world (John 3:16). The Lord issued the Great Commission because God wants all men to be saved (Mark 16:15-16, 1 Timothy 2:4). Early church traditions held that the apostles went to various parts of the world preaching the gospel. Thomas, for instance, was said to have gone to Persia and India. Andrew, according to tradition, was crucified in Achaia (the district around Corinth in Greece).

Almost all of the nations of antiquity were pagan. Many of the people in the world today do not know God, but God still loves these people. As we read about religious customs and beliefs that seem strange to us, we should see the religious error for what it is but love the people and want them to know the salvation that comes from the one true God in Jesus Christ. We should not think of ourselves as superior. All that we have has been given to us, and we are not as good stewards of these resources and opportunities as we should be. If we grow in our love for other people and see them as God sees them, we will hurt for them in their lost state and do more to help them know the grace of Jesus.

But I will sacrifice to You with the voice of thanksgiving.
That which I have vowed I will pay. Salvation is from the Lord.
Jonah 2:9

Assignments for Lesson 40

Bible You have already read the Book of Jonah. Read the Book of Nahum about the eventual destruction of Nineveh. Commentary available in *Student Review.*

Recite or write Isaiah 35:4-6 from memory.

Literature Finish reading *The Art of War*. Literary analysis available in *Student Review.*

Project Complete your project for the week.

Student Review Optional: Answer the questions for Lesson 40 and for *The Art of War,* and take the quiz for Unit 8.

9

Greek Civilization

Summary   The Greeks accomplished much and left a rich legacy to later peoples, yet they were far from the ideal civilization. In this unit we will survey Greek history, consider intellectual attainments of the Greeks, focus on the leader Pericles, and look at everyday life in ancient Greece. The Bible study will examine some relevant passages from the New Testament to compare man's concept of wisdom with the wisdom that God has revealed.

Lessons   41 - Survey of Greek History

42 - Key Concept: Philosophy and the Pursuit of Knowledge

43 - Key Event: The Peloponnesian War

44 - Everyday Life: Ancient Athens

45 - Bible Study: God's Wisdom vs. Man's Wisdom

Ruins at Eleusis (Elefsina, Greece)

217

Memory Work Learn 1 Corinthians 1:22-24 by the end of the unit.

Books Used The Bible
In Their Words

Project
(choose one)

1) Write 300 to 500 words on one of the following topics:

   • Discuss the dynamic tension of freedom and control. How is it wrong to take either one to an extreme? How does the New Testament say both are important in the church?

   • Write your Christian philosophy of life and the world. See Lesson 42.

2) Identify 15-20 words in the English language that come from Greek. See Lesson 41. Take an original photograph illustrating each word. Put your photographs together in a slideshow on your computer or as a book. Caption your photos with the English and Greek words.

3) Locate a building in your area that has Greek-inspired architecture. Sketch the building and label the architectural elements inspired by Greek architecture. If you are unable to visit the location, sketch from a photograph.

Lesson 41

Survey of Greek History

Scholars have long viewed Greece as the pinnacle of human achievement in the ancient world. Its story includes intellectual insights which directly influence us today, artistic accomplishments that have been admired for centuries, and military conquests that gave it a far-flung empire and extended the influence of Greek culture into many lands and among many peoples.

Greece does indeed reveal to us amazing accomplishments of human thought and talent. Yet the story is not completely positive. The Greeks suffered from the same sins that have hampered all people. They did not value all human life the same. Greek leaders often acted out of petty motivations such as greed and hatred. Greek morality often revealed the depths to which humans can stoop. Since the Greeks did not recognize the one true God, their worldly accomplishments are of limited value spiritually.

Background

About 2000 BC, a civilization developed on the island of Crete among the people we know as the Minoans. This name comes from Minos, its legendary king. Archaeologists have yet to decipher Minoan writing or to discover much detail about this culture's life.

Other settlements like those of the Minoans were established along the Aegean Sea (the body of water located to the east of Greece). The earliest example of these societies that has been discovered was at Mycenaea in southern Greece; thus these cities are known as Mycenaean settlements. Around 1400 BC, the Minoan civilization collapsed. Some speculate the cause to have been a destructive earthquake, while others suggest a defeat at the hands of the Mycenaeans.

The people of the Greek peninsula were apparently descended from people who had lived earlier along the Danube River in Europe. Their language was of the Indo-European family. Some of these people, called Achaeans, were part of the Minoan and Mycenaean civilizations. A more belligerent group of these people from the north overran Mycenaea, captured Athens around 1150 BC, and began to develop a distinct Greek culture. They called their new land Hellas in honor of Hellen, their legendary ancestor. Around this time, according to tradition (which is backed by some archaeological evidence), a coalition of Greek forces defeated the city of Troy on the northwest coast of Asia Minor, what is now Turkey.

219

Archaeological Discoveries About Troy

Troy was long thought to be a purely mythical city. As a boy, the German Heinrich Schliemann was fascinated by the tales of Homer. He made it his goal to explore the ruins of the Aegean world when he was financially able.

Schliemann made a fortune in petroleum in the mid-1800s and then became an amateur archaeologist. In 1870 he discovered the site of Troy that had several levels of ruins, indicating that several cities had been built there at different times in history. Schliemann also discovered the cities of Mycenae and Tiryns.

This vase from about 670 BC, found on the island of Mykonos, is one of the earliest known depictions of the Trojan Horse, used by the Greeks to sneak into the city of Troy.

The invasion of the Hellenes ushered in what is called the Dark Ages of Greek history. Lasting until around 800 BC, this period is called Dark because little is known about it. What is known indicates a pattern of simple tribal life centered on clan and family relationships. The people of these clan settlements had little interest in forming a unified nation. The Greece that emerged from what we call its Dark Ages had extended its influence throughout the Aegean region and into western Asia Minor.

The story of Greece is an excellent example of how geography helps to shape history. Greece occupies the southern end of the Balkan Peninsula that extends from Europe. Its latitude and location give it a beautiful climate, more temperate than that of Europe to the north and thus attractive to people groups on the move. The peninsula extends into the Mediterranean Sea, which gives it a commanding position for sea trade throughout the region. The rugged coastline offers many good harbors, which also encouraged ship building, fishing, and trade.

Despite the beautiful climate, the soil of Greece is not suitable for large farming pursuits. Early settlers could raise vineyards and olive groves, but they had to obtain wheat and other staples through foreign trade. The peninsula is not rich in other natural resources either. These factors provided an internal push for trade, the planting of colonies as the population grew, and the desire to take control of other lands by military conquest. The many islands off the coast of Greece provided areas for new settlement by people from the mainland.

Greek City-States

The Greek peninsula is covered with mountain ranges separated by valleys. The difficulty of travel across the mountains encouraged the formation of local city-states as the basis for life and government. The geography also fostered a spirit of independence in the minds of the people. Unification of the entire peninsula under a single authority did not happen for many centuries.

The basic unit of Greek society and government during and after its Dark Ages was the city-state. These built on the pattern of family and clan groups. Greek culture had some elements that encouraged unity, such as the common recognition of Hellen as their ancestor. However, most people living in Greece during this period claimed citizenship first of their city and then as Hellenes. The Greek city-states did not have one supreme king until the 300s BC.

Each city had a patron god or goddess to which its citizens gave their allegiance. Every *polis* (Greek for city) had its own government and army. The people of a particular city were usually active participants in civic life. Government was seen not as something imposed from without but as an extension of the people's clan and community identity. The city-states had a wide population range, from a few thousand in some cities to Athens' estimated quarter-million.

City-states encouraged the Greek ideal of freedom and independence. The downside was that city-states frequently fought each other. Each *polis* had its own perceived needs and desires. Cities battled over such issues as real or perceived insults, a precious natural resource that both cities wanted, or a long-standing feud. The two best-known city-states were Athens and Sparta. These cities developed two sharply-contrasting outlooks on life, which was part of the reason they engaged in a series of costly wars.

A Pagan Foundation

The Greeks professed belief in a multitude of divine beings. The gods were similar in many respects to humans except that they were immortal and had greater powers. The Greek gods and goddesses supposedly lived on the summit of Mount Olympus in northern Greece. Greek divinities existed in a hierarchy in which a few were most powerful, namely Zeus of the sky, Poseidon of the sea, and Hades of the underworld.

The gods experienced jealousies, desires, and anger and took these emotions out on one another and sometimes on humans. When the deities had interaction with humans, it was usually to the humans' hurt. Stories developed about the gods and goddesses and their personalities, exploits, and foibles. These are called myths. These stories were told and retold and came to be an accepted part of Greek thought and culture.

The people of Greece offered sacrifices, rituals, and prayers to the gods. Leaders took into account what the gods might think about a proposed action. Temples built to honor the gods were impressive architectural structures. Animals sacrificed to a god were usually eaten in a fellowship meal at the temple.

Some priests and priestesses claimed the power to foretell the future and discern the will of the gods. The most famous of these oracles lived at Delphi and served Apollo, god of the sun and of the arts. Government and military leaders sought the answers that the Delphic oracles could offer before they embarked on new policies or campaigns. The answers supposedly given by Apollo were so ambiguous that they could be interpreted however the seeker wished and could be made to fit whatever happened later. As a result, they were almost always seen as correct!

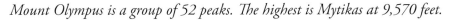

Mount Olympus is a group of 52 peaks. The highest is Mytikas at 9,570 feet.

Those who sought a deeper and more mystical religious experience became involved in what were called mystery cults. The activities of these cults involved only the initiated few and were usually kept secret. Greek religion had little to say about life after death and little hope to offer about a better world.

The way that people thought about the gods did not change their lives the way God wants our relationship with Him to change us. The Greeks accomplished great things in spite of the gods, not because of them. The failings of the Greeks were similar to what they thought were the failings of the gods, since the people had created the gods and the stories about them in the first place.

The Greek pantheon (realm of divine beings) and the stories about it sound very much like ideas that humans would come up with, not divine truth revealed to man. Their gods had superhuman powers—powers that many humans long to have—combined with some noble traits and many shameful behaviors. The Bible says that God created man in His own image, but the Greeks created their gods in their own image.

The philosopher Protagoras (fifth century BC) wrote, "Man is the measure of all things." This belief put man, not God, at the center of their thinking. Man does not make a good object of worship. As talented and remarkable as we are, we are too much given to sin and self-indulgence. If man is the measuring standard, mankind will never measure up to God's standards.

The Rise of Macedonia

In Macedonia, the northern region of the Greek peninsula, Philip came to the throne in 359 BC. He was determined to extend his rule over all of Greece and to mold a Greek alliance against all foreign enemies. Philip exerted diplomatic and military pressure against the city-states to the south. After a decisive military victory at Chaeronea in 338 BC, all Greece lay before him. He placed himself at the head of a league of Greek cities, although he allowed local autonomy except for foreign policy. However, as Philip prepared to seek revenge against the Persians, he was assassinated in 336 BC. His twenty-year-old son, Alexander, who had been taught as a youth by Aristotle, assumed the throne.

Alexander put down attempted rebellions in Greece after his father's death and then turned his sights eastward to build an empire. In the years that followed, Asia Minor, Syria, Palestine, Egypt, Mesopotamia, Persia, and the eastern frontier of India fell before him and his army of about 35,000 men.

The young, determined ruler known as Alexander the Great believed in the superiority of Greek culture. He encouraged its spread throughout the lands his army conquered. Greek became the official language, Greek writings and art were widely distributed, and Greeks and Macedonians were resettled in the newly-controlled territories. Greek civilization became a strong presence, although it did not wipe out the existing cultures. The resulting societies were Hellenistic: Greek to some extent, but still maintaining features of their old ways.

After years on the march, Alexander's army became tired and unhappy. While paused in his conquests, Alexander died of a fever at age 33 in 323 BC and was buried in Babylon, which he had chosen to be the capital of his empire. He

This illustration depicts Alexander's army attacking Athens (Byzantine, 14th century AD).

left no heir, so his leading generals divided up his empire. Seleucus took Persia, Mesopotamia, and Syria; Lysimachus claimed Asia Minor and Thrace; Cassander reigned in Macedonia; and Ptolemy ruled Egypt, Phoenicia, and Palestine. Twenty years later Seleucus defeated and killed Lysimachus in battle and annexed that kingdom to himself. The example of Athenian democracy was lost on these men and their successors. They ruled by absolute power.

The Impact of Alexander the Great

Although Alexander did not live to fulfill his dream, the impact of his exploits was significant. The city-states of Greece gave way to the unified nation-state ruled by a single king. Trade and the exchange of cultures throughout the Middle East increased dramatically. Since Athens was repeatedly overrun by later conquerors, the examples of Greek civilization that Alexander had sent to other places helped to preserve the knowledge of Greek culture that might otherwise have been lost. Rome conquered the Hellenistic kingdoms in later years, but the Romans recognized and preserved the contributions of Greek civilization.

During the first century AD, Greek culture was still influential throughout the Mediterranean world. One contribution of Alexander's day had a major impact on the spread of the gospel. When Alexander organized his army, he brought together men from Macedonia and several city-states of Greece. To communicate with each other, they had to use a common language instead of their local dialects. The form of Greek that developed was called *koine* (Greek for common). It was common not in the sense of gutter talk but in the sense of its being commonly used throughout Alexander's empire.

What We Owe the Greeks

As with any civilization, Greek culture stood on the accomplishments of others. The Greeks borrowed the alphabet of the Phoenicians, the scientific accomplishments and attitudes of inquiry from the Egyptians, and the architectural legacy of the Aegean/Minoan peoples. Greek culture influences our lives even today.

The Greek Language

Koine *(coy-nay) Greek came to be appreciated for its clarity of wording and exact expression of ideas. The language became the standard for international trade and diplomacy. The books of the New Testament were first written in* koine *Greek. Its wide usage and exact expression of ideas made it well suited for spreading the most important ideas in the world. With God's inspiration of the gospel in* koine *Greek, the message of Jesus received the widest possible hearing and readership in the Mediterranean world of the first century AD.*

The papyrus shown at right contains a portion of the Gospel of John (c. 200 AD). Greek was written without punctuation and without spaces between words. It takes careful examination to read Greek manuscripts.

Many English words come from Greek, including democracy, monarchy, philosophy, and geography. We also use terms that are based on Greek life. Spartan, for example, means spare and harsh. An odyssey is a long journey that someone takes in quest of something.

We will see in the next lesson that the Greeks advanced mankind's knowledge of science and mathematics. They made great contributions in sculpture and architecture. Greek literature included epic poetry, plays, and histories. The myths about the gods have become a literature of their own and have influenced our language and literature in countless ways. Methods of Greek education have had an impact on schools and learning for centuries.

The Greeks (specifically the Athenians) valued freedom and the worth of the individual, aspects of life that we esteem today. They help us see the importance of reason and learning and remind us of what human beings can achieve. In a later lesson, we will see how the Lord used aspects of Greek thought to express the truth of Christ so that the people of the first century and later times could grasp the meaning and impact of Christ.

For indeed Jews ask for signs and Greeks search for wisdom;
but we preach Christ crucified, to Jews a stumbling block
and to Gentiles foolishness, but to those who are called,
both Jews and Greeks, Christ the power of God and the wisdom of God.
1 Corinthians 1:22-24

Assignments for Lesson 41

Bible Read 1 Corinthians 1-4. Commentary available in *Student Review.*

In Their Words Read the excerpt from *The Odyssey* (pages 46-50).

Student Review Optional: Answer the questions for Lesson 41.

Detail from The School of Athens *by Raphael (Italian, 1511)*

Lesson 42 - Key Concept

Philosophy and the Pursuit of Knowledge

Greek scholars actively pursued knowledge of the world in which they lived. Many Greek thinkers made contributions to a greater understanding of what is true. Greek artists created works of literary and visual art that were expressions of their ideals of beauty and perfection.

The Greeks valued formal education more than most ancient civilizations. The goal of education in Greece was to produce good citizens who would contribute to the well-being of the state. Teaching was carried out for boys between the ages of six and fourteen by private tutors who were paid by parents. Formal education for girls was rare. Often an older, trusted servant called a pedagogue escorted the boy to and from the tutor's lessons.

Significant as it was, this pursuit of knowledge by the Greeks was not based on spiritual truth. Greek thinkers sought truth within a pagan frame of reference. They believed that the pantheon of Greek deities had little to do with the physical world. Instead, the Greek pursuit of knowledge and understanding began with man and his physical world, although some philosophers understood the reality of absolute truth and man's spiritual nature. Many of Greece's best-known artists, philosophers, and scientists lived in Athens during its Golden Age of the fifth century BC.

Literature

One of the earliest expressions of Greek culture was in the form of songs and epic poetry. An epic poem is a long poetic narration of a great quest by a central hero. An epic often contributes to the identity of the nation from which it comes. Lyric poetry is an expression of more personal emotions. The term lyric comes from the fact that these poems were often recited to the accompaniment of the lyre.

The fables and legends of earlier days were told and retold by minstrels and storytellers. The best-known Greek poet, Homer, is something of a legend himself. He supposedly lived in the 700s BC and was blind. His two great works are the epic poems *The Iliad* (which tells of the battle of Troy) and *The Odyssey* (the saga of Odysseus, a Greek warrior returning to his home after the fall of Troy).

Greek drama grew out of the annual festival honoring Dionysius, during which a chorus would chant some well-known story or moral tale. Music and dancing were part of the performance. At some point in the development of these plays, the format changed and a single performer stepped out and spoke lines as a soliloquy. Then later another actor or two were given separate lines. These dramas dealt with universal themes as opposed to stories

Statue of a Greek Actor (second century BC)

rendering the story in poetry. The Greek word for history means investigation. Herodotus (484-425 BC) wrote a history of the Persian War based on his investigation of what really happened. Thucydides, a general who lived a generation later and who fought in the Peloponnesian War, is credited with an even more precise, scientific treatment of history in his account of that conflict.

Art

Artistic endeavors provided an even greater expression of Greek culture than literature. Early Greek sculpture apparently was influenced by the stiff Egyptian style. It then progressed to idealized forms, as seen in sculptures of athletes and gods. Still later, Greek sculpture entered a realistic period in which the figures more accurately reflected the way people look.

In addition to sculpture and pottery, the Greeks found expression for their love of order and balance in architecture. This is seen most easily in the beautiful temples and other public buildings built by the Greeks, most notably the Parthenon and other structures on the Acropolis in Athens.

about specific individuals. The actors wore masks to represent ideas or emotions and to hide their individual identities. Plays were performed in open-air amphitheaters that had remarkable acoustics.

Some of the best-known Greek playwrights were Aeschylus (525-456 BC), who is said to have written some eighty plays (not all of which have survived until today); Sophocles (496-406 BC), whose surviving plays are considered better than those of Aeschylus; and Euripides (480-406 BC), known for works that display skeptical or cynical themes. Aristophanes (c. 448-c. 380 BC) wrote satirical plays. Greek literature and drama contain much inappropriate content, which is not surprising considering their pagan philosophical base.

Some Greek writers took up the study of past events to record what actually happened instead of

The Theater of Dionysus in Athens was built in the fourth century BC. Remodeled over the centuries, it could hold 17,000 spectators. Performances at Greek theaters included the use of background scenery, trap doors, and cranes that allowed actors to fly.

Acropolis and Areopagus in Athens
Leo von Klenze (German, 1846)

Science and Mathematics

The basic nature of the physical world was a topic many Greek scholars actively investigated. Again, most looked for purely physical and not spiritual causes. Some scholars believed in a god; but they were convinced, for instance, that lightning had some natural explanation and that it was not an angry reaction by Zeus.

Thales (c. 624-c. 546 BC) surmised that the basic element was water, but Democritus (c. 460-c. 370 BC) came up with the idea of atoms: tiny, indivisible, and all alike. The differences that exist among material things, Democritus said, were the result of the different ways that atoms combine. As science later showed, his theory was not exactly correct but it did reveal a great insight into the physical world.

Euclid (c. 323-285 BC) wrote the first compilation of principles of geometry, although others had pursued the field long before him. Thales found that the diameter always bisects a circle and that the angles at the base of an isosceles triangle are equal. The school of Pythagoras developed significant number theories, such as even-odd and prime-composite numbers. Pythagoras himself (c. 570-c. 495 BC) identified the theorem that bears his name: the square of the hypotenuse of a right triangle equals the sum of the squares of the other two sides.

Eratosthenes (c. 276-c. 195 BC) calculated the circumference of the earth with amazing accuracy, developed a system of latitude and longitude, and created a map of the world. Aristarchus (c. 310-c. 230 BC) proposed that the sun, not the earth was at the center of the solar system.

A manuscript fragment from Elements *by Euclid that features one of his diagrams (c. 100 AD).*

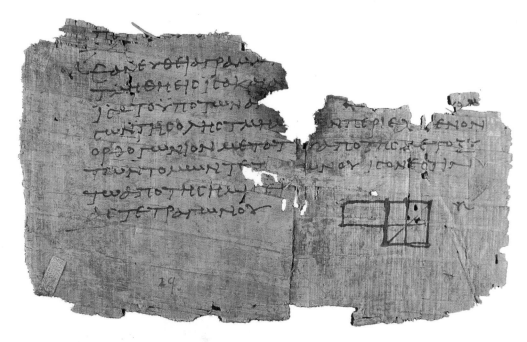

Medicine

The study of the human body advanced with the Greeks also. Empedocles (c. 490-c. 430 BC) established that blood flows to and from the heart. He also identified the optic nerve and showed that the brain is the center of the nervous system.

The best-known Greek practitioner of medicine was Hippocrates (c. 460-c. 377 BC). He believed that diseases have natural (as opposed to spiritual or superstitious) causes, improved the practice of surgery, and made use of drugs to treat illness. On the negative side, Hippocrates believed that health was maintained by keeping in balance four humors in the body: blood, phlegm, yellow bile, and black bile. This erroneous idea encouraged for centuries the practice of bleeding patients, which often caused the patient to become even weaker and sometimes to die.

Philosophy

What is the basic nature of truth? How can we know truth? What is good? What is best? The answers to these and other questions were pursued by philosophers. The word philosopher means lover of wisdom. Modern scholars, philosophers, theologians, and others still debate the positions that Greek philosophers developed over two thousand years ago.

One of the earliest groups of thinkers was called the Sophists (from *sophos*, wisdom). The main proponent of Sophist ideas was Protagoras (c. 490-420 BC), who said that man is the measure of all things. Sophists held that absolute truth does not exist. The meaning of goodness, truth, and other such qualities is only relative to the needs of man at any given time. As a result, man should not trouble himself trying to find absolute truth. Instead, he should pursue pleasure (*hedone*, from which we get hedonism) in this life.

Many thinkers arose in opposition to the Sophists. These opponents feared that the Sophists'

According to legend, Hippocrates taught his students under a tree on the island of Kos. The tree above is about 500 years old and is known as the Tree of Hippocrates. Though not old enough to be the original tree, it might be a descendant. Seedlings from this tree have been planted at medical schools in Australia, Scotland, and the United States.

beliefs would result in anarchy, and so they tried to think through and determine absolute truth and permanent standards for mankind. The best-known of these scholars were a series of three teachers: Socrates, Plato, and Aristotle.

Socrates, Plato, Aristotle

Socrates (c. 469-399 BC) was born in Athens. He gathered groups of students and followers around him as he pursued truth. Socrates believed that absolute truth existed and that it can be known. His method for finding this truth was to ask questions that exposed fallacious thinking and that defined as much as possible what was true. This way of determining truth by asking questions is called the Socratic method. As Socrates put it, "The unexamined life is not worth living." His constant questioning of people and ideas irritated many in

Athens, who were reeling from the aftermath of the disastrous Peloponnesian War.

Socrates was condemned to death for corrupting the youth and introducing false beliefs. He could have gone into exile, but instead he chose to take his life by drinking hemlock, a poison.

Socrates left no written material. What we know about him comes from one of his students, Plato (c. 427-347 BC). Plato was also born in Athens and taught in the grove of Academus; thus his school is called the Academy. Plato's Academy continued to function for hundreds of years after his death. Plato was a prolific writer; and many of his works are known today, including *The Republic*, *Phaedrus*, and *The Laws*. Much of his writing is in the form of dialogues in which Socrates is cast as one of the speakers. Plato might have been honoring Socrates' beliefs, or he might have been putting his own ideas into Socrates' mouth.

The Death of Socrates
Jacques-Louis David (French, 1787)

Plato believed that something exists besides the physical world. This is the world of ideas. For instance, color does not just exist in the physical world; we can know the idea of color. We can know not only beauty but the idea of beauty. The ultimate idea is the Idea of the Good. This idea of goodness guides the universe and is where we can find perfection. The universe has intelligence and purpose, he said, and the soul of man is both pre-existing before a person's physical life and exists eternally after life.

Society, Plato wrote, should be built on reason and good. One's physical life and physical desires should be subordinated to reason. In *The Republic*, Plato attempted to outline the ideal society. Human institutions, he said, should aim to produce social justice and order. Human life and work should be organized by the natural abilities of people. He believed that children should be taken from their parents and reared in a community nursery and that unfit babies should be left to die. Obviously, some of what Plato held to be good is not. This is what happens when man's reason is considered the ultimate standard instead of God's Word.

Aristotle (384-322 BC) was a student of Plato, and he wrote even more than Plato did. Aristotle had a great interest in the physical world and its

Aristotle, *Francesco Hayez (Italian, 1811)*

operation. He gained great insights in the field of biology, for instance. Aristotle believed in God but only as an intelligent First Cause of the world.

To Aristotle, God had no ethical meaning or purpose. Aristotle said that the highest good of man is self-realization, the full exercise of human nature. Government and society, he believed, should encourage this individual self-fulfillment.

Various other schools of thought emerged in the Greeks' pursuit of truth. The Cynics, for instance, held that the highest human good was to have a complete absence of need. Without needs, a person can be self-sufficient. Today, a cynic is someone who doubts the sincerity or goodness of others and who believes that everyone is motivated by self-interest.

Schools of Philosophy

Around 300 BC, following the death of Alexander the Great and with the mixing of Greek thought with Middle Eastern and oriental influences, other schools of philosophy emerged. These were more concerned with the individual as opposed to society and had a materialistic, not spiritual, focus.

Stoicism was best expressed by the philosopher Zeno (c. 334-c. 262 BC). He held that the cosmos is completely ordered and fixed. Man, he said, is simply one cog in the big machine. We can either accept our lot or fight it, but we cannot change it. The greatest happiness comes from accepting one's situation, and bitterness about it is pointless. The way to live, the Stoics said, is to focus on duty and self-discipline. They promoted tolerance, acceptance, and forgiveness toward others and condemned slavery and war as attempted cures that were worse than the ills they sought to remedy. Today a stoic is someone who claims not to have passions or feelings.

By contrast Epicurus (341-270 BC) held that the world is not an auto-machine. Man has free will to choose his lot. The highest good is pleasure, but not pleasure taken to excess. He encouraged moderate mental and physical pleasures in order to derive inner, spiritual peace. We should do good

to increase our happiness, he said; and laws should be followed because doing so brings happiness, not because they are based on absolute truth. The term epicurean is used today for someone who is devoted to sensual pleasures, especially with regard to food and drink.

The Skeptics believed that human knowledge is limited and results only from sense perception. As a result, we can only say that things appear to be true and should not claim that things are absolutely true. Skeptics said that giving up the pursuit of absolutes such as truth, knowledge, and good and evil is how one can gain peace of mind. Today a skeptic is one who always doubts that something is true or final, especially with regard to religious matters.

Conclusion

The Greeks contributed to our understanding of ourselves and of the world around us, but the answers they gave to life's questions were not complete. The physical world and our physical

Arab scholars of the Middle Ages preserved and commented on the ideas of Greek philosophers. This illustration shows Socrates teaching his students (Turkish, 13th century).

selves are truly amazing and worthy of study, but the material realm is not the whole story. Seeking knowledge of our world without a reason for knowing it is ultimately an empty pursuit.

The various philosophers and their schools of thought gave perspectives on truth, but one perspective does not provide the full picture. We see many times throughout history that focusing on one idea magnifies that idea out of proportion to the whole and ignores other important factors.

The pursuit of truth by philosophers is one of the legacies of Greek culture we know best. The Greeks attributed very human and often silly behavior to their gods. Many Greek philosophers thought that this was an inadequate understanding of reality, and they took up the search for ultimate truth. Even though the Greek philosophers had valuable insights, we understand that without God's revelation, their pursuit fell short of the complete grasp of the truth that God's Word provides.

Where is the wise man? Where is the scribe?
Where is the debater of this age?
Has not God made foolish the wisdom of the world?
1 Corinthians 1:20

Assignments for Lesson 42

Bible   Read 1 Corinthians 5-8. Commentary available in *Student Review.*

In Their Words   Read the ancient and modern Hippocratic Oaths and the excerpt from *The Republic* (pages 51-54).

Student Review   Optional: Answer the questions for Lesson 42.

Greek Soldiers in Battle

Lesson 43 - Key Event

The Peloponnesian War

onflict between city-states was common during Greek history, but the Peloponnesian War represented a major turning point. In this war, two major alliances faced each other: the Delian League led by Athens and the Peloponnesian League led by Sparta.

This conflict is sometimes called the Second Peloponnesian War because Athens and Sparta and their respective allies engaged in an earlier conflict from about 460 to 446 BC. The second war was much more decisive and critical in its effects.

Sparta: Military Control

Sparta was located on the Peloponnesus, the large peninsula that forms the southern end of Greece. The conquering invaders who established Sparta took control of the land and the resident people, even though the residents outnumbered the invaders ten to one. The fierce Spartan warriors subjugated the natives to be their workers and then lived in constant fear that they might revolt. As a result, Spartans became highly regimented and militarized in order to maintain control.

Dual kings from two prominent families led the Spartan military. Government was in the hands of a council of thirty elders, chosen for life from among the nobility, and five executive officers, chosen every year. The people of the city had almost no direct voice in lawmaking. The popular assembly of all free adult males could not debate proposals but could only give voice approval or disapproval to proposed laws. The *polis* of Sparta was largely sealed off from outsiders and from new ideas because its leaders feared subversive influences.

The government claimed authority over all Spartan children. Children who were considered physically weak were abandoned to die. At age seven boys began physical and military training. Girls also received physical training to be able to bear children and to support the city's army. All Spartan males were required to be soldiers. They lived in army barracks with other soldiers until they were thirty. A man was allowed to marry after he turned twenty (he was encouraged to marry to produce more soldiers for the cause), but he still had to eat the main meal of every day with the other soldiers. The conquered people, called *helots*, operated the farms. Spartan women had few domestic duties. The fierce attitude of Spartan women was expressed by one mother who supposedly told her son to return from battle either carrying his shield (in victory) or being carried on it (as a martyr for Sparta).

Athens: Personal Freedom

The city of Athens, by contrast, developed a tradition of intellectual openness and personal freedom. Athens was about one hundred miles northeast of Sparta, four miles from the coast (with a coastal suburb that handled its sea trade). After periods of rule by kings, then by councils, and occasionally by tyrants who took power in the name of the people, around 500 BC Athens developed into a democracy.

The Assembly of the city included all adult male citizens. It met about once per week. Usually less than 5,000 men attended a given meeting. It debated proposals put forth by the Council of Five Hundred, which was chosen each year by lot. Assembly debates were lively and encouraged the development of public speaking skills. Voting was done by a show of hands, and measures passed by a simple majority.

The executive officers, who led the army and navy as well as city government, were called the Ten Generals, selected each year by the male citizens. Civic officials of Athens, who numbered about one thousand and who were selected annually by lot,

Greek and Persian Soldiers (fifth century BC)

carried out governmental business. Since they were paid for their work, men of all classes could serve. Courts consisted of about five hundred men, who served as judge and jury. Parties in a case argued their own side; they had no lawyers, which gave them another reason for developing persuasive speaking abilities!

Athens led a coalition of Greeks in the defeat of Persian forces in the first half of the fifth century BC. Darius I of Persia wanted to defeat the Greeks because they had encouraged a rebellion again him. The Persians lost their first battle against the Athenians at Marathon in 490 BC. According to legend, a messenger ran about 25 miles to Athens to carry the news, warning the citizens of a possible revenge attack. The runner announced his message and then fell dead. (This running feat became the inspiration for the modern marathon, first run at the 1896 Olympics in Athens. The distance of 26.2 miles was established at the 1908 Olympics.)

In 480 BC the Athenian navy defeated the Persian fleet in the Battle of Salamis Bay. Spartan forces helped with the defeat of the Persians, but Athens had paid the dearer price for its victory. On two occasions, the Persians burned the city of Athens. Through great sacrifice, the Athenian forces defeated the much more numerous Persian army and navy. The Delian League developed around this time, and fighting against the Persians continued, generally away from the Greek mainland.

Victory gave Athens great civic pride. They believed in the superiority of their culture and lived with great self-confidence. The life of Athens during this Golden Age (the 400s BC) is what most people have in mind when they think of Greek civilization.

The Peloponnesian War

The Golden Age of Greece crumbled because of the war between Sparta and Athens that consumed most of the last third of the fifth century BC (431-404 BC).

Model of a Greek Trireme

Athens had claimed the role of leading city-state after the defeat of the Persians. The Athenian government wanted the assistance that had been given by other city-states during the war with Persia to continue in the form of tribute. Many cities refused, and Sparta led the opposition. Athenians called the resulting conflict the Peloponnesian War since Sparta was located on the Peloponnesus peninsula.

Sparta fielded a highly-trained infantry force, while Athens had built a powerful navy. Neither side could gain a decisive advantage during the first few years of the war, so Sparta attempted to lure away the allies of Athens, and Athens tried to disrupt the work of the *helots* who supported the Spartan economy.

A terrible plague that struck Athens in 430 BC and a failed campaign to the island of Sicily depleted Athenian manpower. Persia began to support the Peloponnesian League financially, which helped to tip the balance in favor of Sparta.

Athens surrendered in 404 BC, removed its defenses, and accepted a forced alliance with Sparta, its bitterest rival. The Peloponnesian War was over, but Greek culture never recovered. The city-states continued to quarrel and fight among themselves, and the proud and once-independent people of the southern part of the Greek peninsula eventually became subservient to the rule of others.

Pericles

The most important leader of Athens during its period of greatest power and influence was the soldier, statesman, orator, politician, and patron of the arts Pericles. He was born around 495 BC into a family of wealth and prestige. His father was a renowned military commander.

Following the victory of the Greeks over Persia, Pericles used his position and abilities in the Athenian democracy to encourage Athens to rebuild and to exert itself in Greece and the world. Pericles was seen as cold and aloof. He was not deeply loved, but he was widely respected. He encouraged broader participation in government by all citizens. Pericles was elected to the group of Ten Generals and to the chairmanship of that body for sixteen years.

As civic leader, Pericles oversaw the building of the Parthenon and other structures on the Acropolis and throughout Athens. He encouraged the development of arts and education. Pericles was a friend to the dramatist Sophocles, the historian Herodotus, and the philosopher Protagoras.

Under his leadership in foreign policy, Athens became the leading city-state in Greece. He oversaw the building of a navy and drew many other city-states into an alliance with Athens. Unfortunately, the power of Athens (and the tribute that other city-states paid to her) built resentment among her allies. This resentment led to the Peloponnesian War with Sparta.

Pericles was far from perfect. He divorced his first wife and maintained a mistress. He managed to offend both friends and enemies of Athens by his

These Roman busts of Pericles and his mistress Aspasia were copied from Greek originals. The couple had a son, Pericles the Younger. The son became a military commander also and helped to win a victory against the Spartan navy near the end of the Peloponnesian War. A storm prevented the rescue of some Athenian sailors, and Pericles the Younger and five other officers were charged with dereliction of duty. Socrates happened to be serving as president of the assembly on the day they were found guilty. He opposed the verdict, but the six were nonetheless executed.

strong pro-Athens beliefs. However, his influence was so great that the Golden Age of Greece in the 400s BC is sometimes called the Age of Pericles.

Following one of the early battles of the Peloponnesian War, Pericles was asked to give the eulogy for Athenian soldiers who had died in the conflict. He used the occasion to remind Athenians what they valued and what they were fighting for. The essence of the speech was preserved by the historian Thucydides. Pericles was somewhat optimistic in his portrayal of Athens. The city was not universally admired. Its enemies hated its pride and aggressiveness.

The plague that struck Athens in 430 BC provoked the citizens to express their grief and frustration by removing Pericles from office and fining him. A year later, he was reinstated, but the unknown disease continued to take its toll. Pericles' two sons by his first wife died, followed by Pericles himself. The loss of Pericles so early in the Peloponnesian War was a contributing factor in Athens' eventual defeat.

Your beauty, O Israel, is slain on your high places!
How have the mighty fallen!
2 Samuel 1:19

Assignments for Lesson 43

Bible Read 1 Corinthians 9-12. Commentary available in *Student Review.*

In Their Words Read the excerpt from *The History of the Peloponnesian War* (pages 55-60).

Student Review Optional: Answer the questions for Lesson 43.

Porch of the Caryatides in Athens (late fifth century BC)

Lesson 44 - Everyday Life

Ancient Athens

The center of activity in ancient Athens was the agora or market. Rows of stalls offered the products of potters, weavers, and metalworkers. Some craftsmen specialized in silver, lead, or marble. Merchants offered wines, olive oil, and manufactured goods. Farmers offered fresh foods daily, which was necessary since people had no means of refrigeration or food preservation. Products that were made in Greece were sold abroad for grain, fruit, textiles, and lumber. Athens imported up to 1.5 million bushels of grain each year. Discussions on issues of the day or on philosophical topics took place on street corners and in the gymnasiums, where young men trained for athletic contests. Few women were seen in public, although women from poor families might help in a stall in the agora.

After the time of Pericles, the visual highlight of the city was the Acropolis. Acropolis means high city. Athens had been founded on the hill because it was more easily defended. As the city grew, it expanded around the base of the hill. The brilliant white temples on the elevated site served as a beacon for incoming ships and were a source of pride for almost all Athenians. The Parthenon was dedicated to Athena, the city's patron goddess.

The Parthenon was built by order of Pericles in the fifth century BC. It is considered the best example of Greek architecture. The white marble structure was 237 feet long, 110 feet wide, and 60 feet high. Statues and carvings from history and mythology decorated the building. A huge, gold-and-jewel-studded statue of Athena dominated the interior. Architects used several construction tricks to create what appeared to be visual perfection. The columns, for example, bulge slightly in the middle and lean slightly inward but appear to be straight. At different times in history, the building was used as a church and a mosque. The remains of the Parthenon, ravaged by thieves, war, and time, still stand.

Early Athenian coins featured the head of Athena on one side and an owl on the other (c. fifth century BC).

The American Parthenon

Nashville, Tennessee, is called the Athens of the South because of the many universities located there. In 1897, a full-size replica of the Parthenon was constructed out of wood and plaster as the centerpiece of the celebration marking Tennessee's centennial of statehood. The structure was intended to be temporary, but Nashvillians wanted it left standing. The years took their toll on the wood and plaster, so in the 1920s the original replica was replaced with a permanent concrete structure. It is the only full-sized replica in the world of the Parthenon of Athens. The interior of the Parthenon in Nashville even has a huge statue of Athena.

Dwellings in the city were small, made of sun-dried brick, and built close together. Craftsmen often lived above or behind their shops. Most people had one main meal a day, usually consisting of grain, fruit, vegetables, and fish. Meat was a special treat reserved for holidays. Athens had no garbage disposal or sewer systems, so waste was dumped into the street. This led to a foul smell in the littered streets and to the greater likelihood of disease. A bath consisted of pouring olive oil on the body, scraping it and the dirt off, and then rinsing with water.

Most men in Greece were farmers who supported their families and raised what extra crops they could to trade in the agora for other things the family needed. In the city, most men were artisans or merchants.

The people of Athens were divided into three classes. Citizens were the offspring of two citizens of Athens and had the most rights. The metics were resident aliens from other city-states or from other countries. They had few legal and political rights but were permitted to engage in business. The third and lowest class were the slaves.

Perhaps the aspect of Athenian life that would most impress an observer from today was its simplicity. The city had its share of the poor; but few were extremely wealthy, and most of the wealthy contributed financially to civic projects. The driving ambition for most Athenians was not the acquisition of wealth but instead having time for leisure: exercise, conversation, and contemplation of their world. Clothing for almost everyone consisted of a simple wraparound garment and a pair of sandals.

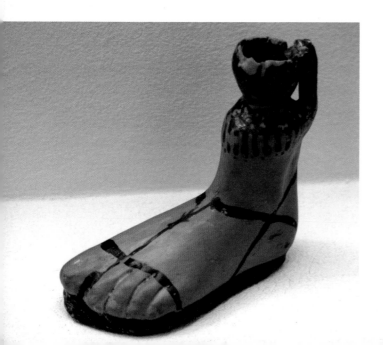

Some Greek vases were made in the shape of animals or of a human head or foot (c. 500 BC).

The Other Side of Athenian Life

As noble and inspiring as these facts about ancient Athens are, the picture was not completely good. Greek men were often sexually immoral. Greek attitudes about unwanted children were discussed in an earlier lesson. The Greeks practiced slavery, as did most of the ancient world. Slaves were usually captives from war. The Greeks justified slavery by saying that since slaves performed the heavy, mundane tasks, the "superior" Greeks were free to pursue more intellectual and culturally uplifting pursuits. Slaves were the property of their owners. Many were treated well, and some were given significant household responsibilities in keeping with their training and abilities; but they were not free.

Women in Athens were considered inherently inferior to men and had few legal rights. Poor women sometimes worked outside the home as a wet-nurse or midwife, or in the market. Wealthier women seldom left their homes, spending their time managing their slaves.

As refined as the Athenians were, they still saw the military defeat and subjugation of foreign enemies as a worthy goal. The rationalizations they used for this were diverse. Sometimes they wanted to take revenge on a rival. At other times they justified aggression by citing the need for more land or more natural resources.

Olive oil was used extensively around the Mediterranean in the preparation of food, as a lubricant, as a body ointment, and as fuel for lamps (Matthew 25:3-4). It was taken as an antidote for gastric disorders and as a laxative. Olive oil was applied to wounds to soften the skin and to aid healing (Luke 10:34). Oil is obtained from olives by large presses. The Mount of Olives outside of Jerusalem is the location of the Garden of Gethsemane (Gethsemane means oil press). Today, extra virgin olive oil refers to oil that was extracted using a cold press method and that contains less than one percent acidity. Pictured below are olive trees in Kardamyli, Greece.

What Else Was Happening? (500-200 BC)

① Nomads known as the Tehuelche ("fierce people") lived in the southern part of what is now Argentina and Chile. They apparently hunted guanacos (similar to the camel) and rheas (similar to the ostrich). They are thought to have stenciled the handprints at the Cueva de las Manos.

② The Punic Wars between Carthage and Rome continued off and on for over a century. In 218 BC, the Carthaginian general Hannibal led an army from Spain into Italy, crossing the Alps (pictured in the 1866 illustration at right). For fifteen years he harassed the Romans and won many battles, but his army was not able to capture the city of Rome.

③ Kapisa (modern Bagram, Afghanistan) was known for its wine, called Kapisayana. Glass flasks, jars, and drinking cups have been found there. The town had been destroyed by Cyrus the Great in the 500s, and it was captured by the armies of Alexander the Great about 329 BC.

④ Sri Lanka was likely settled by immigrants from India. About 300 BC, residents began to develop an extensive irrigation system that eventually included underground canals and artificial reservoirs. Buddhism, introduced to Sri Lanka in the 200s BC, had a major influence on the culture. At right is a 1535 reproduction of a first-century AD map.

⑤ Crossbows were in use in China by the fifth century BC. A bronze trigger mechanism (shown at right) fired bronze crossbow bolts. Improved models that could rapidly fire multiple bolts were soon developed. Some poorly-equipped Chinese soldiers were still using essentially the same technology as late as the 1890s while fighting the Japanese.

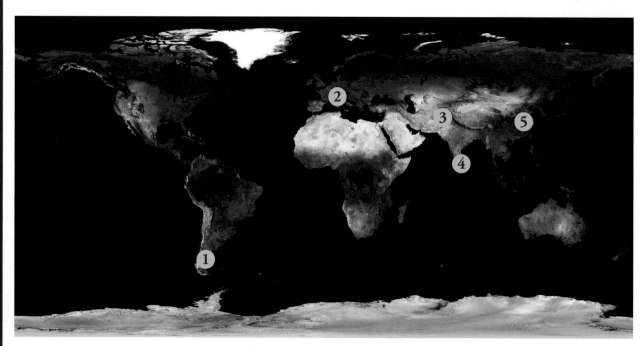

The idea that a civilization is a success if it can conquer other lands and people has been a standard used from ancient times to today. In more recent times we have seen it in Communism, Nazism, and at least some contemporary expressions of Islam.

This perspective defines greatness as being able to rule the world under whatever guise might be used. It is what Satan offered Jesus in the wilderness. It is also what the Bible says is a vain pursuit that will not last.

---

*Now all the Athenians and the strangers visiting there
used to spend their time in nothing other
than telling or hearing something new.
Acts 17:21*

Assignments for Lesson 44

Bible Read 1 Corinthians 13-16. Commentary available in *Student Review.*

In Their Words Read the selected Fables of Aesop (pages 61-63).

Student Review Optional: Answer the questions for Lesson 44.

View of the Acropolis from the Areopagus, Athens

God's Wisdom vs. Man's Wisdom

The New Testament describes several encounters between the good news of Jesus and the Greek culture. Knowing what we do about Greek thought, we can see that the Bible provides an accurate account of this clash of philosophies. We can also see how God's inspired messengers used concepts familiar to the Greek mindset to build a bridge between Greek pagans and the message of the Savior.

As we study these passages, we need to remember that the time of the early church was several centuries after the last period we discussed in this unit. Greek civilization had continued, but it was not the Golden Age described previously.

Paul's Sermon in Athens

After preaching in Macedonia in response to a vision (Acts 16:9), Paul traveled to Athens (Acts 17:10-34). The apostle was provoked by the multitude of pagan idols in the city. He taught in the synagogue and in the agora every day. Some Epicurean and Stoic philosophers debated with him (Lesson 42 described these philosophies). Others who were listening generally dismissed Paul as a (literally) "ragpicker" philosopher, someone who gathered snippets of ideas here and there and then regurgitated them, trying to sound intelligent. In the minds of his pagan listeners, Paul was proclaiming two new deities: Jesus and Resurrection (the Greek word is *anastasis* in Acts 17:18).

His Athenian audience took Paul before the Council of the Areopagus, which usually met in the agora in the first century AD. At one time the Council met on the small hill called the Areopagus near the Acropolis. Areopagus means "hill of Ares," the Greek god of war which corresponded to the Roman god Mars. This is why the King James Version says that Paul spoke on Mars Hill.

The Council, one of the oldest institutions in Athens, heard cases involving homicides but it also served as something like a grand jury in matters of morals and religion. Paul's audience wanted the council to pass judgment on the apostle's strange new teaching. The Athenians liked to bounce new ideas around, but that didn't mean they were willing to take them to heart.

Paul began his defense by acknowledging the religiosity of the Athenians, a trait recognized by even secular writers of the day. The apostle noted an altar inscribed "To an Unknown God" (in fact, probably several such altars existed in Athens). As worshipers of many gods, the Athenians wanted to cover themselves in case they missed a deity that they should have worshiped. Paul used this altar to teach about God. The Athenians intended the altar to honor just another deity, but Paul told them that the God they did not know was in fact the one and only true God whom they needed to know.

The apostle described God as the maker of the universe. God is thus not bound by human temples and worship practices. He made all of mankind from one person and guided their lives on earth. God's intention was that man seek Him because He is not distant and unknowable. Even Greek thinkers recognized God. Paul does not quote from the Bible in this sermon because the Council would not recognize its authority. Instead, in verse 28 Paul quotes from two Greek poets. "In Him we live and move and have our being" is a line from Epimenides of Crete. "For we also are His offspring" is a line from Aratus. Paul probably hoped that these connections to Greek literature would help the Athenians more readily accept his message. If we are His offspring, Paul reasoned, we should not think that God is like an idol.

Paul said that God had waited patiently while mankind wandered in ignorance of Him. Now in Christ ("a Man whom He has appointed"), however, God was commanding that all people should repent because a day of reckoning is coming for all. The credibility of Jesus as Judge was proven by God raising

Him from the dead. Most of those listening to Paul, having little interest in life after death, dismissed Paul's reference to the resurrection of Christ. A few said that they might like to hear Paul again on this matter. A handful of people were moved to believe, including one member of the Council.

The apostle found little fertile soil for the seed of the gospel in Athens. The gospel generated more of a response in the city-state of Corinth, where Paul went next. He preached there for eighteen months, apparently a much longer time than he had been in Athens. Still, Jewish opposition contributed to his being taken before the local authorities. The charge against him was dismissed, but Paul left soon afterward (Acts 18:1-18).

1 Corinthians: The Display of God's Wisdom

While on his third missionary journey, Paul wrote the letter of 1 Corinthians to the Christians in Corinth who had become splintered and who were plagued with many questions (they might have written to Paul about some of the issues they had; see 1 Corinthians 7:1, 8:1, and 12:1). Before he could effectively address their questions, however, Paul had to unify their hearts in submission to the cross of Christ. His approach in the first few chapters of 1 Corinthians is an eloquent reply to the influence of worldly Greek thinking among the Christians at Corinth.

Paul did not claim wisdom or eloquence of speech, which would have impressed Greek minds. Instead, the power of his message was in the story of the cross (1 Corinthians 1:17). Greeks honored beauty and order, but the cross of Jesus was anything but beautiful. Yet in the cross was the hope of salvation. It accomplished what others only talked about. The wise man (literally, *sophos*) and debater could not stand before the power of the cross (1 Corinthians 1:20). Greeks searched for wisdom, but God provided the effective answer to sin in the cross.

St. Paul Preaching in Athens, *Raphael (Italian, 1515)*

This was foolishness to the typical Greek mind, but it demonstrated God's wisdom in providing the real solution to sin (1 Corinthians 1:22-25).

Paul did not claim worldly wisdom for his message. Instead, it was filled with God's wisdom that no thinker from the world could touch (1 Corinthians 2:6-8). The gospel did not reflect worldly wisdom, and Paul knew it. It revealed heavenly wisdom, combining spiritual truths with spiritual words (1 Corinthians 2:13-14). The wisdom of the world is foolishness to God (1 Corinthians 3:19). All of the centuries of speculation, debate, and philosophizing by the Greeks had not led them to a knowledge of God or to salvation in Christ, which is what they needed. What seemed foolish to them (as it had appeared to most of the Areopagus and to most Athenians and Corinthians) was in fact God's wise mystery of salvation, that the innocent Son of God would become man and die on behalf of the sins of all men.

Paul wrote to them as God's humble servant. The Corinthian Christians prided themselves on their wealth of understanding and worldly wisdom. Paul was just a poor servant of Christ, but the irony is that this is what they needed to become also. They needed to see the emptiness of the world's wisdom and to accept the true wisdom of God (1 Corinthians 4:7-13). They thought that their human reasoning and worldly knowledge would give them the answers they needed. What they really needed was a commitment to Christ first and then to dealing with each other in love. Knowledge alone makes one arrogant, but a heart of love builds up others (1 Corinthians 8:1).

One of the main characteristics of Greek culture, the pursuit of knowledge and wisdom, was ineffective in bringing spiritual wholeness to people. As a goal in itself, the pursuit of knowledge and wisdom in a worldly way actually hinders a person from being submitted to Christ, who is the revelation of God's other-worldly wisdom. Christians in Corinth needed to understand that they still had to seek wisdom, but it needed to be God's wisdom and not the world's. As Paul addressed the Corinthians' issues, he taught

Ruins of the Temple of Apollo at Corinth (c. 540 BC)

Ancient roadway in Corinth

them God's meaning of such concepts as being a temple (1 Corinthians 3:16, 6:19) and how to handle freedom in Christ (1 Corinthians 9:1-19). He used the illustration of competing in the games to urge the Christians in Corinth to seek to win God's imperishable wreath of glory (1 Corinthians 9:24-27).

Logos in Greek

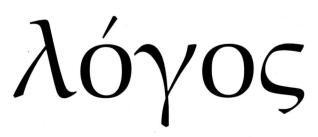

Jesus as God's Logos

One concept that developed in Greek thinking was the idea of the logos. The basic meaning of logos is word or message. It came to be used as a technical term in philosophy and the sciences to mean a discourse or teaching. Logos was then extended to refer to the central meaning of a topic or (sometimes) of the world in general. (We today sometimes get close to this meaning when we say in slang, "What's the word about _____?"). The Hellenistic Jew Philo, who lived in Alexandria, Egypt, just before and during the life of Christ, used logos to refer to the true content and orderly operation of the world. Sometimes the word referred to wisdom or insight into a subject.

John applied the concept of logos to Christ in the opening verses of his gospel account. The true Logos, John says, was co-existent with God and in fact was God (John 1:1). Then, in a crucial insight, John says that God's Logos—His essential wisdom, the message He wanted to reveal to man—became a person and lived among us (John 1:14). Jesus as the Logos of God connected with the Greek understanding of the word but carried its meaning further. All of the nibbling about the idea of logos that had gone on in Greek philosophy for centuries had come to completion in Jesus.

For the Greeks, logos was wisdom that man derived from a study of the physical world. God's Logos was the revelation that He gave to man, the saving message He wanted all men to know.

As some Greeks saw it, logos was subject to man's reason; in other words, it was what man could rationally conclude from his observation of the world. God's Logos is not unreasonable, but it is above reason. It is not subject to the mind of man but instead stands over it.

The Greek concept of logos involved the balance and order of the physical world. God's Logos brought spiritual harmony between God and man by bringing reconciliation to sinful man.

The Greek logos was a concept or thought process that could not be dated or quantified. God's Logos, by contrast, was also timeless and eternal; but He lived among us at a given time and place.

As with Athenian speculation and the Greek pursuit of knowledge and wisdom, God brought the concept of the logos to completion in Christ. The Greeks were right in pursuing an understanding of the world. The answer that they needed and that all mankind needs is found in Jesus, who is God's wisdom, God's self-revelation to a world that does not know Him, and God's Logos or ultimate Word.

And the Word became flesh and dwelt among us,
and we saw His glory, glory as of the only begotten
from the Father, full of grace and truth.
John 1:14

Assignments for Lesson 45

Bible Read 2 Corinthians 1-5. Commentary available in *Student Review*.

Recite or write 1 Corinthians 1:22-24 from memory.

In Their Words Read the excerpt from *Ethics* by Aristotle (pages 64-65).

Project Complete your project for the week.

Student Review Optional: Answer the questions for Lesson 45 and take the quiz for Unit 9.

10

Roman Civilization

Summary   The story of Rome has fascinated professional historians and amateur students of history for over two thousand years. In this unit we will survey the different phases of Roman history, take an especially close look at Augustus Caesar, consider Roman contributions to law, and have a look at everyday life in Rome. The Bible study considers the kingdom of God, especially as it contrasted with the Roman Empire.

Lessons   46 - The Rise of Rome
47 - Key Person: Augustus Caesar
48 - Key Concept: Roman Law
49 - Everyday Life: The Roman Empire
50 - Bible Study: The Kingdom of God

Roman Aqueduct, Pont-du-Gard, France (First Century AD)

Memory Work	Learn Romans 5:6-8 by the end of the unit.
Books Used	The Bible *In Their Words* *Julius Caesar*

**Project
(choose one)**
	1) Write 300 to 500 words on one of the following topics:
	    • Why do you think Rome achieved the success it did as a civilization? What were its key strengths?
	    • Write a news article that tells about the assassination of Julius Caesar: what happened, when and where, who was involved, why it happened, and what is expected to happen as a result of it. Write it for a newspaper or a radio news broadcast. See Lesson 46.
	2) Write a short play that takes place in ancient Rome. Make the actors, dialogue, and action realistic. Let the point you are trying to make be obvious from what happens in the play instead of having someone say it as a line.
	3) Create a model of a real structure built by Romans. Locate one or more photos of the structure. Make your model as close to scale as you can and from the material of your choosing (wood, cardboard, clay, STYROFOAM™, LEGO® bricks, etc.).

Literature	William Shakespeare (1564-1616) was born in the English country town of Stratford-upon-Avon and moved to London to become an actor and playwright. His plays were being performed by the early 1590s, and his popularity grew immensely over the next twenty years. Shakespeare retired to Stratford a few years before his death. Shakespeare is generally regarded as the greatest writer in English literature, and *Julius Caesar* is one of his best works. Shakespeare's plays are categorized as either comedies, tragedies, or histories. *Julius Caesar* is a hybrid of history and tragedy, but it is usually classified as a tragedy. The play is a study of power and political motivation. Though Caesar himself is a relatively minor character in the play, everything in the drama revolves around him. Was Caesar a tyrant who would destroy Rome or a savior who would rescue Rome? Was his assassination a blow for liberty from oppression or an act of treason against the best interests of the people? Like any major figure, Caesar had supporters and critics. In the play, Cassius opposes Caesar and is suspicious of his motives. Brutus wants to do what is good and is at war within himself over what course to take regarding Caesar. Cassius recruits Brutus to join the assassination plot. The result of Caesar's assassination is civil war. Octavian (or Octavius, later known as Augustus), supported by Mark Antony (Marcus Antonius), emerges as the winner. Read the play in an annotated edition that has notes explaining vocabulary and other elements of the dialogue that might be obscure to the modern reader. You might also consider listening to a complete audio edition or watching a video presentation while following along with the printed text. Shakespeare relied on Plutarch, other ancient writers, and more contemporary sources for his information about Caesar and his times. Shakespeare sometimes plays fast and loose with historical facts, and the dialogue includes some anachronisms; but concentrate on the beauty of the language and the insight into human nature that Shakespeare reveals.

Lesson 46

The Rise of Rome

Romulus and Remus were abandoned twins who were rescued and nursed by a she-wolf. A shepherd's family reared them. As young men, the twins decided to build a city at the place along the Tiber River where they were rescued. They disagreed on the location, however; and Romulus killed Remus. Romulus founded a city on seven hills in 753 BC and named it Rome in his own honor.

That is one myth about how Rome began. If that story doesn't appeal to you, you can find others. The poet Virgil offers a different legend in the *Aeneid*, which dates from the first century BC, when the Empire was reaching the height of its power. Virgil mentions Romulus and Remus but focuses on Aeneas, an intrepid soldier in the Trojan War who encountered many adventures and tribulations on his way to founding the city of Rome. Virgil clearly borrowed from Homer's *Odyssey* to tell this story.

Neither story, of course, is true. Our best indications are that Italy was invaded by tribes from Central Europe around the 12th century BC, much as Greece was. Those who settled in central Italy became the shepherding and farming Latin people and founded Rome as a city-state around 750 BC. The area was then invaded by the Etruscans around 600 BC. We know relatively little about the Etruscans. They are thought to have come from Asia Minor. The Etruscans used an alphabet based on the Greek alphabet, employed the arch in building, and practiced gladiatorial combat.

Around 509 BC, the Latins on the seven hills reasserted themselves, threw off Etruscan rule, and became the most powerful people of the area known as Latium. Here begins the distinct history of the people of Rome. Being done with Etruscan kings, the Romans established a form of government called a republic, which means "the affairs of the people." The Roman Republic lasted for almost 500 years.

The Republic

During the early part of the Republic, Roman life and government were controlled by wealthy landowners called patricians. The ruling body of government, the Senate, was composed of three hundred representatives of patrician families who were elected for life. Every year the Senate elected two consuls to be chief executives and military leaders. The consuls had equal power, and each had veto power over the actions of the other (*veto* is Latin for "I forbid").

Cincinnatus Leaves the Plow for the Roman Dictatorship, *Juan Antonio Ribera (Spanish, 1806)*

After his term, a consul became a member of the Senate. In a time of crisis, the Senate could name a dictator; but he could serve no longer than six months.

In the other main social class were the plebeians. These were farmers, artisans, small merchants, traders, and other such working people. The plebeians were citizens, but they could not be elected to the Senate or to the consulship. A plebeian by law could not marry someone from a patrician family. The Assembly, made up of representatives elected by the plebeians, had little practical power. A third group in Roman society were the slaves. These were usually prisoners of war; and although some were well-educated and highly talented, they had no legal rights.

The service that Cincinnatus rendered in 458 BC embodied some of the highest ideals of the Roman Republic: duty, efficiency, sacrifice, and country above all. Imagine a Roman army surrounded by enemy forces. Five soldiers escape to carry word back to Rome. The Senate decides to appoint a dictator, who can rule with absolute power for six months. A delegation goes to the home of Cincinnatus, a wealthy landowner who is plowing his field. Cincinnatus leaves his plow, hurries to Rome, and calls for every eligible man to enlist for service. The commander defeats the enemy and returns to Rome victorious. Then, sixteen days after being appointed, Cincinnatus hands back the reins of power and

picks up once again the reins of his farm animal to continue plowing.

The government of the Republic fought a series of wars over several centuries, mostly for two reasons: perceived need, and greed. The growing Roman population needed new areas in which to settle. Roman merchants also wanted to expand their economic activity, which could be accomplished by trade but also by the conquest of other lands. Roman armies were usually successful in these wars. They were well-trained and dedicated to their cause. They were also well-organized. A Roman legion of about 6,000 men was divided into smaller units that could be dispatched and moved quickly.

Military success led to greater wealth for Rome, both through the tribute paid by the defeated armies and by the increased trade brought to the city. However, the warfare also had a domestic impact. The army was all-patrician at first; but with the greater need for fighting men, plebeians were pressed into service. As a result, the plebeians began to demand a greater voice in the government they were called upon to defend.

The Republic, which was based on the older patrician-plebeian social system, was forced to consider changes when society changed. An Assembly of Centuries was formed to represent the army. This Assembly began to choose the consuls. The Assembly of Tribes became the plebeian body. It chose ten tribunes each year as the spokesmen for the average people. One of the most important developments urged by the Assembly of Tribes was the formulation and publication of a code of laws in 451 BC. The Twelve Tables of Law were posted in the Forum (the central marketplace, equivalent to the Greek agora). These laws were no great advancement for plebeians, but at least they could now insist that judges apply the law fairly and without partiality toward the patrician class.

Plebeians continued to work for a greater role in government. Tribunes were granted the veto power, and the Assembly of Tribes gained the right to pass laws without Senate approval. In 367 BC a plebeian was elected consul. Eventually the plebeians were allowed to marry patricians. Some were elected to the Senate.

Another change in Roman society that threatened the old structure was the rise of a middle class, composed mainly of plebeians who had married into patrician families and who had become wealthy through trade and government contracts. These people did not fit the standard definition of patricians or plebeians, but they wanted a role in government and exercised their influence to get it.

International Expansion

The Romans subjugated the other tribes on the Italian peninsula by 264 BC and began to look for new lands to conquer. Rome's chief rival was the kingdom of Carthage on the north African coast. Carthage had been founded as a colony by the Phoenicians around the same time that Rome was founded. The colony became a power in its own right, primarily because of a strong naval fleet. Trading vessels from Carthage plied the Mediterranean and the Atlantic coast of Europe.

Carthage established colonies on the island of Sicily, just off of the Italian coast; and therein lay her downfall. Rome felt threatened as well as stymied in its expansionist desires. Over 120 years, Rome fought three costly wars against Carthage. These are known as the Punic Wars, from the Latin word Punicus, which means Phoenicia. The first war lasted twenty-three years and centered on control of Sicily. Rome defeated Carthage and pushed the conquered nation off of the island.

The second Punic War came as a result of Carthaginian expansion in Spain, which again threatened Rome. In this war the great military leader of Carthage, Hannibal, executed an invasion of Italy from the north over the Alps that involved the use of elephants for carrying equipment and for striking terror in his opponents' hearts. All but one of the elephants died, but Hannibal was still able to win battle after battle in Italy. Rome won the war,

however, by invading Carthage itself, which forced Hannibal to return home to defend his city. There he was defeated and fled to Asia Minor. After sixteen years of fighting, Carthage surrendered in 201 BC, paid a heavy tribute, and promised not to start another war without Rome's consent. With these events Rome became the unquestioned major power in the western Mediterranean.

In 150 BC Carthage fought a nearby kingdom without getting Rome's permission. The Roman government was outraged and embarked upon the Third Punic War. Roman forces invaded and burned Carthage. The city's population was killed or sold into slavery. Rome took over the region and added it to its expanding list of overseas colonies. Roman armies brutally subjugated Corinth in Greece about the same time Carthage was destroyed (146 BC). Rome could then boast of control over Spain, Greece, Egypt, Asia Minor, and much of the eastern Mediterranean.

This expansion was again a mixed blessing for Rome. The Romans developed an effective and flexible system for governing a growing empire. Governors appointed by the Senate oversaw the collection of taxes and other aspects of Rome's interests, but local peoples were allowed a significant degree of control over domestic matters. Roman coffers were greatly enriched through tribute paid by subject nations and by increased trade. However, provincial governors were sometimes corrupt.

Grain shipments flowing into Rome, often as tribute, lowered food prices and caused many small farmers to lose their land. A small group of wealthy landowners built huge estates called *latifundia*,

Ruins at Carthage (Tunisia)

worked by slaves. Many farmers, unable to compete with low prices and slave labor, moved to Rome to find work. When most of them didn't, they became a restless mob that increased economic and political pressures in the city.

From Republic to Empire

For about a century before Julius Caesar rose to power, the Republic of Rome was shaken by bitter disputes between powerful individuals and political factions as well as by dramatic social upheavals. As wealth increased, many senators became more concerned about protecting their possessions than about doing what was best for the Republic. Meanwhile, the number of the poor increased, as did their plight; and some politicians took up their cause and demanded reforms.

Tiberius Gracchus was elected consul in 133 BC. He was from a wealthy and distinguished family, but he championed the cause of the poor. Tiberius wanted to limit the amount of land one person could own and to give excess land to the poor. Members of the Senate, however, were unwilling to part with

their holdings. A group of noblemen murdered Tiberius and about 300 of his followers. A few years later, his younger brother Gaius Gracchus took up his fallen brother's cause and proposed new reforms; but he met a similar fate. Gaius and some 3,000 of his followers were killed.

In 88 BC a civil war broke out between two ambitious and powerful generals and their followers. Sulla was victorious. In 82 BC he was declared dictator, whereupon he abolished the six-month limit on a dictator's rule. For the next several decades, Rome was ruled by a series of generals. One of them, Gnaeus Pompey, won great military victories but was opposed by the Senate. Pompey found an ally in Julius Caesar, who himself had extended Roman rule in Spain. Pompey and Caesar approached another general, Crassus, and formed the First Triumvirate to rule Rome. Crassus died in war, while Pompey and Caesar came to distrust each other. Pompey aligned himself with the Senate, and Caesar was declared an enemy of the state.

In 49 BC the Senate ordered Caesar, then in Gaul, to dismiss his army and return to Rome. Caesar refused to do so. He crossed the Rubicon River, the boundary between Gaul and Italy, heading for Rome with his army. He defeated the forces loyal to Pompey, but he then continued to engage in warfare in various parts of the empire. In 44 BC the Senate appointed Caesar dictator for life. A brilliant, crafty, and power-hungry politician, Caesar gave land to the poor, extended citizenship to people who lived in provinces outside of Italy, and undertook extensive public building projects. However, Caesar was strongly opposed by Senators who feared (or who were jealous of) his popularity and who saw him as a tyrant. On March 15, 44 BC, Caesar was stabbed

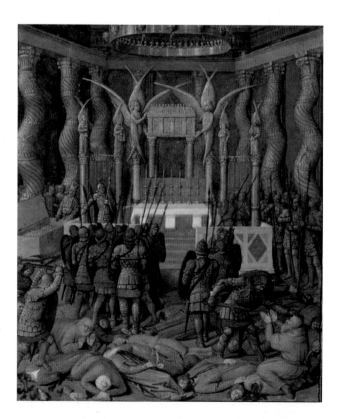

Pompey led forces that participated in a war between opposing Jewish armies in the 60s BC. According to Josephus, after Pompey's side captured Jerusalem, he entered the temple. This illustration of the event is from a 15th-century manuscript of Josephus by French artist Jean Fouquet.

Cleopatra VII Philopator was part of the Ptolemaic dynasty that ruled Egypt after the death of Alexander the Great. As the last Pharaoh of Egypt before it became a Roman province, she was a shrewd politician. She bore a son to Julius Caesar, and after his death bore three children to Mark Antony. Helen Gardner (shown at right) portrayed Cleopatra in a 1912 silent film.

to death as he entered the Senate. Conspirators led by Gaius Cassius and Marcus Brutus fomented the assassination plot.

Caesar had adopted his eighteen-year-old grand-nephew Octavian as son and heir shortly before he was assassinated. Octavian enlisted the allegiance of Mark Antony and Marcus Lepidus, two of Caesar's military commanders, to form the Second Triumvirate and reclaim Caesar's power for themselves. Antony and Octavian, however, fell into a quarrel. Antony allied himself with Queen Cleopatra of Egypt, and Octavian declared war against them. The forces of Octavian defeated Antony and Cleopatra at Actium in 31 BC. Octavian offered to rule with limited powers, but in actuality he was already dictator. The Senate declared him to be Augustus, "Exalted One" (a divine title), in 27 BC. We will examine the reign of Augustus in the next lesson.

The power of the Roman dictator had been growing for some time at the expense of the Senate and the populace. With Augustus, the transition was complete. The Senate named him imperator, or emperor, and the Roman Empire began. After centuries of almost continuous warfare against other nations, the period from 27 BC to 180 AD was relatively peaceful. The Empire enjoyed increasing prosperity under this *Pax Romana* (Roman Peace).

Roman emperors never devised an orderly process of succession, which meant that the character and abilities of later emperors varied greatly and the country was victimized by repeated internal clashes among competing claimants to the title. The most common approach to succession was adoption and designation. The emperor adopted a relative or close associate to be his son and successor. The choice might be made for a variety of reasons, not necessarily character and competency. Tiberius, Claudius, Trajan, Hadrian, and Marcus Aurelius

Caesar was the family name of Julius Caesar. In his honor, later emperors were given the title of Caesar. Many centuries later, the titles of the German kaiser and the Russian czar were also derived from the name.

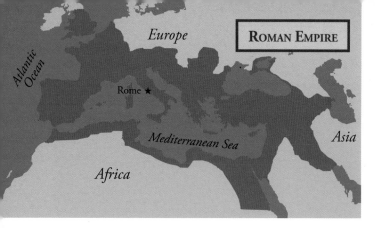

Around 117 AD under Trajan, the Roman Empire reached its greatest size and strength. The green areas on the map show the territory controlled by Rome in Europe, Africa, and Asia.

were able leaders; Caligula and Nero, on the other hand, were evil and probably insane.

When people refer to Rome, they might be referring to one of many different periods and forms of government: the city of Rome, the Republic, the Empire in its days of power, the Empire in its slow decline, pagan Rome, or Christian Rome. Each period and form of government had its distinctive features, triumphs, and struggles. In this unit we focus on Roman history through the reign of Augustus. In future lessons we will discuss later developments.

And as the toes of the feet were partly of iron and partly of pottery, so some of the kingdom will be strong and part of it will be brittle.
Daniel 2:42

Assignments for Lesson 46

Bible   Read Romans 1-3. Commentary available in *Student Review.*

In Their Words   Read the excerpt from *The Histories* by Polybius (pages 66-67).

Literature   Begin reading the play *Julius Caesar* by William Shakespeare. Plan to finish it by the end of this unit.

Student Review   Optional: Answer the questions for Lesson 46.

Lesson 47 - Key Person

Augustus Caesar

The Roman Republic ended after decades of instability. Politicians did not just criticize each other; they had each other assassinated. Generals competing for political power each had their own armed force of loyal troops. The rise to power of Julius Caesar and his resultant assassination were not exceptional. They were instead merely the culmination of a long-developing trend.

Julius Caesar was killed in 44 BC. His grand-nephew, adopted son, and chosen heir, Octavian, was only eighteen at the time. Seventeen years later, after more bloody conflict, Rome finally had peace and a new emperor: Octavian, now titled Augustus. Before his death in 14 AD, he oversaw the golden age of Roman culture and established the foundation for peace and progress that lasted many decades. His talents and accomplishments have led some to call Augustus the greatest person in Roman history.

Rise to Power

Octavian was born in 63 BC. After he turned fifteen, Octavian accompanied his great-uncle Julius Caesar on military campaigns. It was clear that Caesar was grooming him to be his successor. When Caesar died, Octavian was in Illyricum on the Balkan peninsula. Octavian hurried to southern Italy, but only as a private citizen. There he learned that Caesar had named him as heir in his will. Octavian took command of a large army near Brundisium. His family feared for his life, thinking that those who had killed Caesar would come after him also.

Octavian, however, waded into the dangerous political waters without hesitation. Being Caesar's heir did not mean that Octavian automatically inherited Caesar's power, but he could use his position to his advantage in the competition for power in the Roman government that followed. The conspirators who killed Caesar found that the people of Rome loved Caesar and hated what they had done. Octavian took the name Caesar to capitalize on Julius Caesar's popularity.

After overcoming all rivals and opposition in sometimes ruthless fashion, Octavian achieved the pinnacle of power by winning the Battle of Actium in 31 BC. Octavian maintained and increased his power by appearing not to want power. In 27 BC he expressed a desire to retire from public life, but the Senate pleaded with him to remain; so naturally he did. The Senators saw in him a refreshing change toward stability and strength of character that had been sadly lacking over the previous century.

Augustus said that he would rule only the major provinces while leaving the oversight of Rome and Italy in the hands of the Senate. He was generous and respectful toward the Senate, although he controlled the real power as emperor. Augustus was given many titles and positions, including consul, imperator, pontifex maximus (chief priest, a position given him in 12 BC), and "Father of His Country" (given in 2 BC with the suggestion that Roman history started over with him). However, Augustus most preferred the title of princeps, or first citizen. His rule is sometimes called the Principate for this reason. As first citizen, he led a simple life, in the fashion of a Roman patrician without the regal splendor that Julius Caesar had come to use.

Reforms Under Augustus

Augustus reformed the military and had the armies under his personal command, but he did not maintain power by resorting to the threat of military force against his fellow citizens. When he came to power, the standing army consisted of about 300,000 professional volunteers in sixty legions. Augustus cut the size of the army by half, guaranteed regular pay for the troops, and provided pensions for those who were discharged. He encouraged retired soldiers to live throughout the provinces to help in the defense of the empire should such help be needed. Every soldier swore allegiance to Augustus personally (not to the state or the empire), and the soldiers looked to him as being personally responsible for their pay.

The new emperor did not see warfare as a way of life. Instead, he wanted peace as a way of life throughout the Empire with the army positioned to defend against invaders and to preserve peace should internal uprisings occur. Augustus defined and accepted the extant territorial limits of the empire and did not seek to expand them. The area under Roman control stretched 3,000 miles east to west, 2,000 north to south, and included an estimated 50 million people. To strengthen the empire, he extended Roman citizenship to many in the provinces, cleared pirates from the seas, built a network of roads, and improved the postal service in use at the time.

Augustus also reformed government. He placed the day-to-day work of government in the hands of professional civil servants, not political appointees. Augustus appointed able, trustworthy men to be provincial governors, unlike the corrupt political hacks that had previously held these positions.

Construction on the Temple of Kalabsha in Nubia started about 30 BC. This image depicts Augustus in Egyptian style. The entire temple was relocated for preservation when the Aswan High Dam was built.

Roman Literature

Three prominent Roman poets lived during the reign of Augustus. Virgil is best known as the author of the epic Aeneid. *Horace and Ovid published collections that included a variety of shorter poems. This was also the period when the historian Livy wrote a history of Rome, known not so much for its historical accuracy as for its encouragement of traditional Roman ideals by telling stories (and myths) from Rome's past.*

Virgil Reading the Aeneid to Augustus, Octavia, and Livia, *Jean-Baptiste Wicar (French, 1793)*

These men were now paid salaries, which meant (1) they were answerable to Augustus and (2) they did not have to be wealthy to serve. Augustus also called for a census of the empire so that taxes might be levied and collected more fairly. This was the census that led Joseph and Mary to go to Bethlehem to be registered.

In addition, Augustus undertook a major program of construction. He ordered the building of major public facilities to keep people working and to renew pride in Rome. Augustus said that he found Rome a city of brick and left it a city of marble.

Trade and industry increased during his tenure. Augustus also tried to rebuild Roman character. He oversaw the passage of laws that encouraged marriage and morality and that discouraged adultery and divorce (although Augustus himself was not always faithful to his wife).

Legacy of Augustus

The title of Augustus ("Exalted One") suggests how he was viewed by the political leaders of his day. He appeared to them to be a gift of the gods, bringing order and stability to the city and the empire. Some, especially in the provinces, came to worship him as divine. Augustus accepted and even encouraged this practice. Whatever he might have believed about himself, he knew that such emperor-worship would increase loyalty to the empire in the sometimes troublesome outlying areas.

Later emperors sometimes were given and sometimes demanded worship as divinity (it became routine for emperors to be voted into divine status by the Senate upon their death). This emperor-worship became something of an official civil religion, and as time went on those who refused to take part (such as Christians) were seen as suspect by governing authorities.

Coin from the reign of Augustus (c. 14 AD)

Cicero

Cicero (106-43 BC) is regarded as one of the greatest thinkers, writers, and orators that Rome produced. He served as a consul of Rome and was a long-time member of the Senate. In the turmoil that followed the assassination of Julius Caesar, Cicero made a series of speeches in the Senate against Mark Antony and in favor of the Senate supporting Octavian (who became Augustus later). Although Cicero had nothing to do with Julius Caesar's assassination, Antony marked him and his family for death. They saw him as a supporter of the status quo and thus an enemy of their purposes. Supporters of Antony killed Cicero, his brother, and his nephew. Cicero's son, Marcus, was not in Italy at the time and thus escaped execution. Marcus later served as consul after Octavian's triumph over his opponents in 30 BC.

Cicero Denounces Catiline
Cesare Maccari (Italian, 1889)

Augustus was like any human, a mixture of good and bad. He was a pagan, but he did genuinely try to maintain peace and improve the lives of people in the empire. Roman political leaders and the population in general wanted rule by able persons and not continued conspiracy and civil strife. Augustus provided this leadership and enabled the Pax Romana, during which time Jesus lived, died, and arose again and the gospel of true peace in Him began to be proclaimed.

*Now in those days a decree went out from Caesar Augustus,
that a census be taken of all the inhabited earth.
Luke 2:1*

Assignments for Lesson 47

Bible Read Romans 4-6. Commentary available in *Student Review*.

Literature Continue reading *Julius Caesar*.

Student Review Optional: Answer the questions for Lesson 47.

Lesson 48 - Key Concept

Roman Law

We are indebted to the Romans for much that is in our world today. The Latin language, for example, was the basis for many European languages spoken today and also played an important role in the development of English. This lesson focuses on Roman law as a key illustration of Roman accomplishments.

The Roman practice of law provided at least two basic principles of jurisprudence that have greatly influenced the administration of justice in the Western world: standard legal procedure and the principle of natural law. (Jurisprudence, by the way, is from the Latin *jurisprudentes*, which means skilled in the law).

Roman Legal Practices

The Twelve Tables of Law codified legal practices in the fifth century BC. From 366 BC a praetor, appointed by the Senate, oversaw the law courts of the Republic. The courts applied the law; but the praetor interpreted the law, and his interpretations became the standard for the application of the law thenceforth. This practice came to be called common law, which is important in the British and American legal systems. The Romans practiced a double standard for many centuries, applying one set of laws to citizens and another to the rest of the empire's people; but the two standards were gradually brought into alignment by 212 AD.

A complete codification of Roman laws, legal principles, and commentaries took place in the 500s AD with the *Corpus Juris Civilis* ("Body of Civil Law"). Its compilation was overseen by the Emperor Justinian. The result is often called the Justinian Code. Specific legal procedures that we inherited from Rome include the accused being considered innocent until proven guilty, a verdict based on evidence (not social status or wealth), and the following of due process in all legal proceedings.

The Romans believed that the laws of the state should reflect that which is right and just according to universal reason—that is, what seems reasonable to all people. They recognized a standard of right and wrong that is separate from and prior to the state and any particular leader or form of government. This natural law is what they wanted their code of laws to reflect. The source for this natural law in their thinking was not God but the natural order of the world. This concept of natural law was an important influence on Enlightenment thinking in the 1600s and 1700s. This directly influenced the American Declaration of Independence, which proclaimed, "We hold these truths to be self-evident . . . ."

What Else Was Happening? (200-1 BC)

1. Chinese astronomers had been keeping records of eclipses and comets for centuries. In the first century BC they began keeping detailed records of sunspots, darker patches visible on the surface of the sun. They noted that more sunspots led to warmer weather.

2. The Badakhshan area (modern Afghanistan) has long been the world's major source of high quality lapis lazuli, a gemstone with a deep blue color (example at right). Increased activity along the Silk Road helped to distribute lapis lazuli from Africa to China.

3. After the conquests of Alexander, many Jews in Palestine began to adopt Greek customs. The Hasmonean family (also known as the Maccabees) established an independent Jewish nation from 164 to 63 BC, when Palestine was taken over by Rome.

4. Juba II was a prince of Numidia in North Africa. After the Romans made Numidia a province, Juba went to Rome, learned Latin and Greek, and was adopted by the Caesars. Augustus arranged his marriage to Cleopatra Selene II, a daughter of Cleopatra and Mark Antony, and appointed him king of Mauretania (modern Morocco and western Algeria). The tomb of Juba and his wife is shown at right.

5. Cuicuilco is one of the oldest known cities in the Valley of Mexico. By the first century BC, it had grown to prominence in the area. It was destroyed about 50 BC by the eruption of the volcano Xitle, and the nearby city of Teotihuacan assumed greater importance.

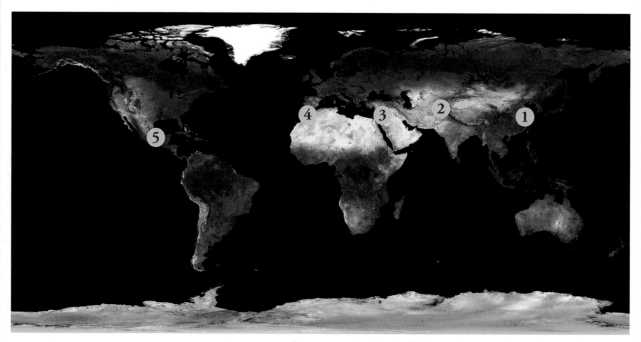

Law in the New Testament

The New Testament contains examples of the impact of Roman law as well as the use of natural law. For instance, in the Empire, subject peoples did not have the right to carry out capital punishment. This is why the Jewish authorities had to get the approval of the Roman governor Pontius Pilate before Jesus could be crucified. Additionally, Paul appealed to his rights as a Roman citizen to avoid being beaten (Acts 22:25-29) and when he wanted his case heard by Caesar (Acts 25:11). The apostle made use of God's natural law in his argument that sinful man was without excuse for not following the way of God since His attributes were obvious from the created world (Romans 1:19-20). In his discussion of the head covering issue in 1 Corinthians 11, Paul asked, "Does not even nature itself teach you . . . ?" (1 Corinthians 11:14).

As with many accomplishments by the Romans (and by mankind in general), the recognition of a higher or natural law had both good and bad elements. It was good that they recognized a foundation of truth that was not the creation of one particular ruler or culture. It is unfortunate, however, that they did not know God and recognize Him as the source of ultimate truth. In addition, the Roman concept of natural law is limited because it makes man's reason the final arbiter of truth, and man's reason is flawed and influenced by culture and tradition. Not everything that seemed natural, reasonable, and just to the Romans would seem that way to us. In our own day, the loss of a consensus about what is right and just has shown up in debates over such topics as homosexual marriage. As good and helpful as reason and tradition are, they cannot replace God's truth as the one true, lasting standard for all places and times.

Conclusion

Unfortunately, the Roman culture did not honor God. This fact has two consequences. First, their accomplishments honor man's abilities but not God's. We should seek to use our talents to serve the Creator. When we do, God can truly act through us in a way that is "far more abundantly beyond all that we ask or think" (Ephesians 3:20). Second, in the Roman legacy we see the depth to which sinful humans can stoop when they do not acknowledge and serve the Creator.

The personification of Justice as a woman holding scales and a sword dates from Roman time. This 1940 carving by Abolhassan Sadighi is on the courthouse in Tehran, Iran.

Tens of thousands of people watched as people and animals killed other people for entertainment. Slaves were an integral part of Roman life and economy and were generally treated as mere property. Immorality, homosexuality, and divorce became commonplace. Solutions to political conflicts were often sought not by ballots and debates but at the ends of swords and daggers. We must remember these facts as we appraise the glory that was Rome.

The contributions that Rome made to our world are a good reminder of why we need to understand history. We can appreciate what is good, be inspired by what is remarkable, understand the factors that have influenced world cultures even until today, and be warned of the evils into which man so easily and so often falls. Those people who wore togas, spoke what is now called a dead language, and knew nothing of modern inventions are not so distant from us after all.

The commander came and said to him [Paul], "Tell me, are you a Roman?" And he said, "Yes." The commander answered, "I acquired this citizenship with a large sum of money." And Paul said, "But I was actually born a citizen."
Acts 22:27-28

Assignments for Lesson 48

Bible   Read Romans 7-8. Commentary available in *Student Review.*

In Their Words   Read the excerpts from the Twelve Tables of Law (pages 68-69).

Literature   Continue reading *Julius Caesar.*

Student Review   Optional: Answer the questions for Lesson 48.

Wheel Ruts in a Street at Pompeii

Lesson 49 - Everyday Life

The Roman Empire

Since the republic and empire of Rome survived over one thousand years, Roman life and culture went through several phases. Think about how life in America today is quite different from how things were a short two hundred years ago. Nevertheless, we can identify some basic characteristics of Roman culture.

Life in Imperial Rome

During the *Pax Romana*, the city of Rome had a population of about one million people. As has always been the case, the lifestyle of the poor was quite different from that of the rich. Many poor lived in multi-story tenement buildings. Some were as tall as seven stories. Besides being crammed together in small apartments, residents always faced the risk of fire because the tenements were built of wood. Many wealthy families, by contrast, had large, beautiful villas with many rooms, a courtyard, and other amenities. Dinner parties lasting several hours were common.

In the Roman family, the father had absolute control. He could decide whether a newborn baby would be kept or abandoned. Deformed infants and unwanted girls were often "exposed" (left to die or to be picked up by slave-traders). Wealthier families provided for the education of their children by hiring a tutor or sending their children to a private school. Girls as well as boys received a formal education, although girls usually ended theirs at a younger age. Fathers arranged the marriages for their children, and girls would often be married by the age of fourteen. A boy became a citizen at the age of sixteen with a ceremony in the Forum. Women had more rights than in Greek society. They could own property and would sometimes go to public events.

Rome was a teeming, busy city. One dominant reality in the city was the presence of hundreds of thousands of slaves. Slaves were usually captives of war and often filled responsible positions for their masters. Another dominant presence were the many poor people. The Roman government eventually began making welfare payments to those who were not able to find work. To entertain the masses, the government sponsored gladiatorial combat in the Colosseum and races at the Circus Maximus.

Architecture

Romans built public buildings on a grand scale. They used bricks, large blocks of stone, and concrete. Rather than building entire structures with marble, they often used less expensive building materials and

263

Much of what we know about life in the Roman Empire is from archaeological work at the city of Pompeii, which was buried by a volcanic eruption of Mount Vesuvius in 79 AD. The eruption caught the city unprepared. People, houses, and businesses were covered and preserved by the ash. The site was forgotten for centuries. It was discovered in the late 16th century during work on an underground water line. Archaeological work began in the mid-1700s and continues today. Beautiful paintings have been found in many of the buildings. Shown clockwise from top left are a still life with a bowl of fruit, a husband and wife holding symbols of literacy, a banquet, and a market.

Roman Road on the Spanish Island of Minorca

covered the exterior with marble. This made their buildings beautiful as well as durable.

The building abilities of Romans are seen in many ways. They crisscrossed the empire with roads primarily to enable more rapid movement of armies and officials, but trade and travel benefited also. The Romans built over 50,000 miles of roads, some of which are still in use today. A typical road was fifteen feet wide and five feet deep. The base of gravel was topped with large, smooth stones. Roman civil engineers learned how to cut through mountains to build their roads.

A key element of Roman construction was the arch, which they learned from previous civilizations. They found that an arch of stones could hold greater weight than a single lintel across an opening. The Romans employed a series of arches to make barrel vaults and tunnels, and they used intersecting barrel vaults to allow more light and to enable larger areas to be enclosed.

A series of arches built side to side made possible the construction of long structures such as walls and aqueducts. To move water from mountains or springs, the Romans built a system of pipes and ditches and—to bridge valleys—aqueducts.

Aqueducts were raised channels that used gravity to carry water. Some also had pathways for pedestrians and chariots. Some aqueducts are still standing and a few are still in use. One such structure in southern France (see photo on page 247) stands 160 feet high, runs a length of 900 feet, and is made of stone block with no mortar. It is estimated that Roman aqueducts carried 200 million gallons of water per day.

The Pantheon temple in Rome stands as a testament to Roman architecture and Roman efficiency. After all, why not build one temple to honor all the gods? The original Pantheon was built during the time of Augustus, but after fire destroyed it, construction on another began around 120 AD. Sixteen granite columns support the porch, and the doors weigh fifteen tons; but the main feature is its massive concrete dome. It reaches a height of 142 feet, which is the same as its diameter. A thirty-foot hole in the middle allows light to enter. The dome was built using a wooden mold to hold the concrete, and the walls of the building are twenty feet thick to support the huge dome. The building was eventually used as a place of Christian worship many centuries after it was built. It has been the

The Roman propensity to build is evidenced by the remnants of their structures that stand on three continents. Concrete—gravel and sand mixed with mortar—was not used for several centuries after Rome fell because the secret of its composition was lost. Its rediscovery enabled a revitalization of building in Europe.

Roman construction took several forms. Public bathhouses, some quite elaborate, were constructed across the Empire as places for men to meet and relax. An example from Beirut, Lebanon, is shown below at left. Hadrian's Wall in northern England (below at right) was built in the second century AD to keep the troublesome Scots out of Roman-controlled territory. In Rome emperors built monuments and arches, often with sculptures and reliefs, in their own honor. The Arch of Titus is shown at the bottom of the page.

inspiration for other famous domes, such as St. Paul's Cathedral in London and the U.S. Capitol Building in Washington, D.C.

Many cities throughout the empire had a structure for public games. The Colosseum in Rome was begun in 69 AD and finished eleven years later. It rose almost fifty feet high and covered about six acres. The top supported beams that held a covering which protected spectators from the sun. The Colosseum floor (280 feet by 175 feet) was made of heavy wooden planks, usually covered with dirt or sand.

Beneath the Colosseum floor was a network of corridors and rooms where animals and people waited to perform—or to go to their deaths. The floor could be removed and the entire area flooded to stage a mock sea battle. The seating capacity of the Colosseum has been estimated at 50,000 to 60,000. The structure has been damaged by earthquakes; and much of the original material was used to build other structures, including part of St. Peter's Basilica in Rome.

Religion

Most Romans believed in a spirit world that influenced this world. This spirit world included gods but also lesser spirits and even the deification of such virtues as victory, hope, health, and success. The main purpose of religious activity was to appeal for blessings. Rome did have temples and priests (who were government functionaries), but the center of Roman spiritual life was the home. The father led a daily worship exercise that kept spiritual realities (as they saw them) ever-present in the people's minds.

The Romans tended to adopt the gods of other peoples if they thought those gods would be helpful. Many Greek gods, for instance, came to be seen as the same as the gods the Romans worshiped. Rome's chief god, Jupiter, for instance, was identified with the Greeks' Zeus. Venus was parallel to the Greeks' Aphrodite, Mars to Ares, and so forth. However, Romans did not see the gods as glorified, out-of-control humans the way the Greeks did. This would have gone against the Romans' guiding principles of duty and order. We have mentioned earlier the adoption of certain Greek philosophies and the practice of emperor worship that were part of the religious landscape of Rome.

The multiplicity of divine beings, which included the often very ungodly emperors, suggests the shallowness of Roman belief. Thinking that human beings might be gods suggests a low view of the spiritual realm rather than a high view of people. Roman religion was an attempt at finding ultimate truth, but it failed to do so.

Marcus Aurelius

The Greek philosophies of Epicureanism and Stoicism became popular among many upper class Romans. Stoicism had an appeal because of the time-honored Roman values of duty, discipline, and civic obligation. For those looking for something to believe in, Stoicism became something of a religious faith. Perhaps the most famous Roman Stoic was Marcus Aurelius, a general who became emperor in the second half of the second century AD. His book Meditations *is a statement of his Stoic philosophy. Unfortunately, as emperor Aurelius approved a persecution of Christians in response to a plague which many believed the Christians had caused by their refusal to worship the Roman gods.*

Roman Virtues?

Roman culture honored what it called virtue. The Latin word *virtus* originally meant manliness or bravery in battle but came to be applied more broadly to any traits which were considered good. Rome exalted duty, courage, and sacrifice, but above all it honored Rome itself (meaning the empire) as worthy of all devotion.

However, many Romans were far from what we would call virtuous. Immorality, adultery, and homosexuality were common and accepted. Divorce was rampant. Events at the Colosseum displayed a penchant for cruelty. As time went on, people became more interested in pleasing themselves than in doing what was best for the country. Many virtues were based on the strength of the family and the country. When these failed, so did the virtues.

The Romans had a belief system that was not revealed to them by God. Instead, they made it up themselves. The result was that some virtues were honored and others were not. The Christian emphasis on personal morality was a striking contrast to the Roman worldview. Christian evangelists found quite a challenge presenting to the Romans the gospel of a crucified and resurrected Jew, who wanted them to abandon belief in all other gods and live a life of purity and self-sacrifice.

Finally, brethren, whatever is true, whatever is honorable, whatever is right, whatever is pure, whatever is lovely, whatever is of good repute, if there is any excellence and if anything worthy of praise, dwell on these things.
Philippians 4:8

Assignments for Lesson 49

Bible   Read Romans 9-12. Commentary available in *Student Review*.

In Their Words   Read the excerpt from *The Training of Children* (page 70).

Literature   Continue reading *Julius Caesar*.

Student Review   Optional: Answer the questions for Lesson 49.

Detail from The Pearl of Great Price, *Domenico Fetti (Italian, c. 1615)*

The Kingdom of God

An observer in the Roman Forum remarked that the "merchandise of the whole world" could be found in that one spot. A second century AD visitor to Rome spoke of the "endless flow of goods" that came into the city. Supporting this world-wide trade was the best-trained and best-equipped army the world had ever known. The Roman emperor ruled a huge area that extended around the Mediterranean Sea and into Europe and the Middle East. He had a network of governors and other representatives in all of the major provinces. Rome had been growing and expanding for centuries and appeared to be invincible.

The Nature of the Kingdom of God

As this greatest of all empires held sway over tens of millions of people, another kind of kingdom emerged from an out-of-the-way place on the eastern Mediterranean coast. It was a kingdom based on a different kind of power. This kingdom had a different kind of beginning and existed for a different purpose.

The story of the New Testament is in great measure the story of these two kingdoms: one large, and one like a mustard seed; one based on military might, and one based on self-giving love; one that

seemed unconquerable, and one that seemed weak and fragile. One was the kingdom of Rome, the other was the kingdom of God. In this lesson we will examine the nature of God's kingdom and see its true and lasting power.

The kingdom of God is where God is King. It is not a geographical realm like Great Britain or the Roman Empire; it is a spiritual kingdom. One person can be in the kingdom of God and the person next to him not be in it. When Jesus stood before Pilate, the Roman governor thought in geographical and political terms when he asked, "Are you the King of the Jews" (John 18:33). Jesus said, "My kingdom is not of this world" (John 18:36). He admitted to being a King, but His realm was not any kingdom that Pilate could understand. Jesus' kingdom does not operate the way that worldly kingdoms do.

The kingdom of heaven is like a mustard seed. A mustard seed is the smallest of all seeds, yet the bush it produces is far out of proportion to the size of its beginning (Matthew 13:31-32). In the same way, the kingdom of God started out small, but its reach and impact have been dramatic and global. The kingdom of heaven is like leaven in a lump of dough (Matthew 13:33). Its influence might not be obvious and direct, but it is real nonetheless.

269

The kingdom of God does not arrive with an army and royal regalia. It cannot be located on a map. The kingdom of God is within you (Luke 17:21). If you want to find the kingdom of God, you have to look in the hearts and lives of people.

You cannot purchase or earn your way into this kingdom. Instead, you must accept it as a little child, or you will not enter it at all (Luke 18:16-17). Membership in the kingdom of God is on God's terms, not ours. We are not in charge; we must accept God's rule with a trusting and willing heart the way a child trusts his parents. Our citizenship in the kingdom of God is not something we earn. It is accomplished for us by the One who transfers us from the kingdom of darkness to the kingdom of the Son (Colossians 1:13). A person can be born into an earthly kingdom, but citizenship in God's kingdom requires being born again (John 3:3-5).

The Lord's Prayer

In the Model or Lord's Prayer, Jesus stated "Your kingdom come. Your will be done, on earth as it is in heaven" (Matthew 6:10). These two phrases should be understood as saying the same thing. The prayer is for God's kingdom to come; in other words, for God's will to be done on earth the way that it is done in heaven. God's kingdom has come into this world, but people still need to let God's kingship come into their hearts. We show that God is our King when we do God's will.

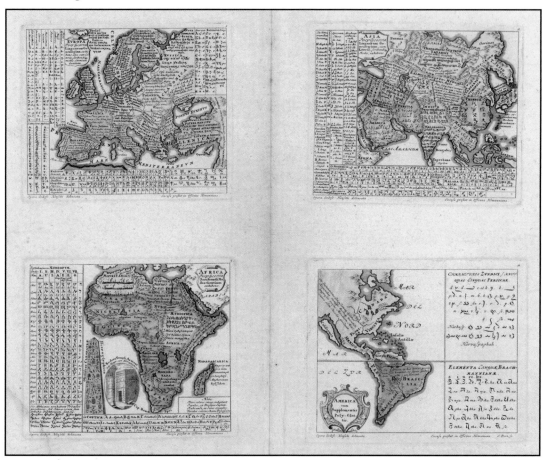

This set of illustrations is from the 1741 book Synopsis Universae Philologiae *by Gottfried Hensel. It shows his understanding of the distribution of languages across Europe, Africa, Asia, and the Americas. The first phrase from the Lord's Prayer is printed in many of the languages.*

The kingdom of God is not a political realm, but it does have ambassadors (2 Corinthians 5:20). Every Christian is to be a personal representative of his King. When we live as His representative, we are likely to be persecuted the way our King was; but when this happens, we will know most assuredly that we belong to His kingdom (Matthew 5:10).

Now and Not Yet

At times the New Testament refers to the kingdom of God as a present or immediate reality. Jesus said, "If I cast out demons by the finger of God, then the kingdom of God has come upon you" (Luke 11:20). He told His disciples that some who were with Him would see the kingdom of God come with power (Mark 9:1). Other passages in the New Testament, however, speak of the kingdom as a future reality. Paul encouraged some persecuted disciples by saying, "Through many tribulations we must enter the kingdom of God" (Acts 14:22). James said that Christians are heirs of the kingdom, suggesting that the kingdom is an inheritance which Christians have not yet received (James 2:5).

The kingdom of God is a real presence now, but it will be an even greater and more glorious reality in the future. God is working now. He is King in the hearts of some people now. However, His reign will be unquestioned and overwhelmingly glorious with the coming of Christ in the future.

The Kingdom of God and The Kingdom of Rome

The New Testament teaches that, in some ways, no conflict existed between the kingdom of God and the kingdom of Rome. When someone asked Jesus if the Jews should pay taxes to Caesar, Jesus replied by saying, "Render to Caesar the things that are Caesar's" (Matthew 22:21). The coins were Roman coins and had Caesar's image on them, so paying taxes with them was no big deal.

The more important matter to Jesus was giving to God what has His image, namely ourselves (Matthew 22:21). Paul, despite being jailed and beaten by government officials several times, said that Christians were to be in subjection to the governing authorities (Romans 13:1-7). In general, a Christian should have no conflict about obeying the government.

However, in the bigger picture God's kingdom and Rome's kingdom were locked in mortal conflict because of their absolutely opposite natures. Rome was pagan and of the world, while the Way of Jesus was from God. When Pilate had the sign posted on Jesus' cross that said, "This is Jesus, the King of the Jews" (Matthew 27:37), Pilate was giving one final, hateful kick to Jesus. The sign was saying, in effect, "This is what happens to the King of the Jews when Rome is in charge." In the book of Revelation, Rome is the great enemy. It is described as the beast and the mother of harlots (Revelation 17:1-18).

The contrast between Caesar and Christ was a choice between two lordships. The Roman emperor eventually was considered to be divine and was called *dominus* (Latin for lord). The claim of the gospel is that Jesus is *kyrios* (Greek for lord). The people of the first century had to choose: was Caesar lord, or was Jesus Lord?

Dozens of catacombs have been discovered in Rome. They were neither built by nor used exclusively by Christians, but many of them are illustrated with paintings such as this one of a woman praying (c. fourth century AD).

In the first century, Rome appeared to be invincible. The city was called "Eternal Rome." The Empire appeared to have all that it needed to survive indefinitely. The church, by contrast, was tiny and struggling. When Christianity came to be seen as a religion separate from Judaism and not just a Jewish sect, it was perceived to be a threat to the security of the empire and its members were persecuted.

Today, Rome is a memory of history while the kingdom of God is an active force that has spread around the world. Jesus has been Lord for millions more people than ever confessed Caesar as lord. The Kingdom of God has indeed come with power—the power of the Spirit—just as Jesus said, while the grandeur that was Rome lies in empty ruins. The mustard seed won.

The kingdom of the world has become
the kingdom of our Lord and of His Christ;
and He will reign forever and ever.
Revelation 11:15

Assignments for Lesson 50

Bible   Read Romans 13-16. Commentary available in *Student Review*.

Recite or write Romans 5:6-8 from memory.

In Their Words   Read the excerpt from *The Martyrdom of Ignatius* (pages 71-73).

Literature   Finish reading *Julius Caesar*. Literary analysis available in *Student Review*.

Project   Complete your project for the unit.

Student Review   Optional: Answer the questions for Lesson 50 and for *Julius Caesar*; take the quiz for Unit 10; and take the second history, English, and Bible exams.

11

The Central Event in History

Summary This unit examines the most important event in the history of the world, the coming of Jesus Christ. We approach it through an in-depth study of the Gospel of Luke. We will look at the narrative that Luke provides of Jesus' life and ministry, and we will also examine themes that are emphasized in Luke's account. As you study the Gospel of Luke as a literary unit in its historical context, you will have a good combination of the three parts of this curriculum: history, literature, and faith.

Lessons 51 - Introduction to the Gospel of Luke
52 - The Revolution Jesus Brought
53 - Unlikely Heroes
54 - Major Themes in Luke
55 - Bible Study: Jerusalem

Sea of Galilee, Israel

273

Memory Work

Learn Luke 11:9-10 by the end of the unit.

Books Used

The Bible
In Their Words

**Project
(choose one)**

1) Write 300 to 500 words on one of the following topics:

- Study an incident, a teaching, or an idea in Luke and develop a paper that expresses the meaning of it for your life.

- Write a first-person account of an incident in Luke, as though you were personally involved or observing it.

2) Using authoritative sources as a guide, draw a map of Jerusalem in Jesus' day. Label at least ten significant sites from the life of Jesus.

3) Follow Jesus' example of service by volunteering to serve someone in need either on your own or with an organization.

St. Luke the Apostle (Church in Macedonia)

Lesson 51

Introduction to the Gospel of Luke

Everything that came before it led up to it. Everything that has happened since has been impacted by it. It is the single life, the single event, around which all of history revolves. It is the event that has influenced history the most and without which history would be most changed. More books have been written about it and more lives have been devoted to it than to any other life, event, or topic.

People have changed their lives radically because of it. Some have taken great journeys and made huge personal sacrifices for it. Inestimable good has been accomplished because of it. Many have been willing to die for it. Your life and the lives of your family and your nation have been profoundly affected by it.

History's Most Important Event

This single most important event in all of history is the life, death, and resurrection of Jesus Christ, the Son of God. His importance in world history is even more remarkable when we realize that He was not a military, political, or business leader. Except for a hurried trip to Egypt when He was a baby, He never traveled more than one hundred miles from the obscure village where He was born or the other obscure village where He grew up.

Large crowds listened to Him, but He was opposed by the religious and political power structures of His day. He engendered so much fear and hatred in His opponents that they had Him arrested, run through a mock trial on trumped-up charges, and publicly executed. Nevertheless, within a few weeks His small band of loyal followers bravely began proclaiming the story about Him. Thousands were converted to faith in Jesus as Savior. Opposition to this growing movement continued, but that opposition only fed the flames of this growing fire upon the earth.

Why It Is Central

The impact of Jesus goes beyond psychological, sociological, economic, and even theological analysis, although experts in all of these fields and others have studied Him and His followers. His impact stems first from the fact that He is the Son of God and that He came to reveal divine truth to man. He is the answer to mankind's quest for God. Millions of people have recognized this and believed in Him.

A second reason for His impact is that Jesus told us the truth about ourselves. He addressed the reality of sin but offered salvation and forgiveness

275

for our sin. He gave us hope when all that mankind had was despair. Jesus is the Savior of the world, the One who is able to save us from ourselves and the just consequences of our wasted lives. Individuals, families, and societies have been made better by His teaching and influence.

Third, Jesus changed the world because of the facts of His life. He revealed the power of God throughout His years on earth. His birth was a miracle. He demonstrated supernatural power and knowledge throughout His life. He faced death with trust in God and forgiveness toward His accusers and executioners. Three days after He died, God raised Him from the dead never to die again. He appeared to many witnesses who were convinced that He was alive. These witnesses had been frightened, bewildered, and despairing as a result of His death; they were not expecting to see Him alive again. Jesus was able to overcome the power of sin and death and to change individual lives and the world by what the book of Hebrews calls "the power of an indestructible life" (Hebrews 7:16).

Fourth, Jesus has changed the world by working spiritually through His devoted followers. He recognized spiritual reality and knew the spiritual nature of each person. He promised to be with His followers and to empower them to tell others about Him so that the world would have an opportunity to know God and to overcome sin and death. Despite all of its human failings, the church is an amazing body

of people. The church consists of ordinary humans from all ethnic groups and languages, empowered by the extraordinary power of God to be servants, teachers, evangelists, health care professionals, and moms and dads, and to fill other roles in society. The unseen God uses them to make an impact in this world on behalf of the crucified and risen Savior to whom they have dedicated their lives.

How Jesus Was Unique

Jesus was a great teacher, but the world has seen many great teachers. Jesus was noble, but many people have been noble. Jesus had personal integrity, but many people have lived virtuous lives. Jesus endured hardship and opposition, but many heroes have done that. People have died for Him, but many causes and leaders have inspired martyrs.

Several factors set Jesus apart as unique. He lived this life perfectly, without sin. He showed us the truth about God and about ourselves in a way that no one else ever has. He lived and died as the one and only Son of God, the one person who could bear our sins and offer us eternal forgiveness. God confirmed all that He did and all that He is by raising Him from the dead and seating Him on the throne in heaven. Before Him every person will stand in judgment on the last day.

Because of who Jesus is and what He has done and continues to do, the life of everyone in the world has been profoundly affected now and will be affected into eternity.

The Gospel

The story of Jesus and what it means for every person is called the gospel. The Greek word is *euanggelion*, good message. Our current English word is based on the older English compound word *godspell*, meaning good spiel or good message. There is one gospel, but in the New Testament God inspired four men to write it down in slightly different ways. The best titles in Biblical manuscripts for the first four books of the New Testament are "According to Matthew," "According to Mark," and so forth. They all give the one gospel, inspired by God, as presented in written form by each of these men.

A gospel account is a unique literary work. It is not a biography, since it focuses on relatively few events and teachings in Jesus' life. It is not a history of the period. It is not a memoir of the author, since the author himself has little or no part in the story. A gospel is a presentation of the life and ministry of Jesus, focusing on the crucifixion and resurrection, with a distinct literary purpose.

Matthew's account shows the strong connection between the Old Testament and the ministry of Jesus. It has about fifty quotations or allusions to the Old Testament and talks the most of the four about the Jewish background of Jesus.

Mark tells what it means to be a disciple of Jesus. It is presented in a rapid-fire, almost breathless pace. In the first part of Mark, the author repeatedly says, "And immediately Jesus . . ." Almost a third of Mark is devoted to the last week of Jesus' life.

John is the gospel of faith. He tells us in John 20:30-31 that he presented what he did "so that you may believe that Jesus is the Christ, the son of God; and that believing you may have life in His name." In John, Jesus speaks often about who He is. John records seven miracles plus the resurrection to demonstrate who Jesus is. Many people in John make a confession of faith about who they believe Jesus is. Jesus' words and actions, coupled with eyewitness testimony about Him, lead to the reader being challenged to put his faith in Jesus as well.

In this curriculum we will study the Gospel of Luke for a number of reasons. First, Luke sets the story of Jesus in its historical context. He also emphasizes the worldwide spiritual revolution that Jesus ushered in. Luke is a good account of the life and ministry of Jesus for those studying world history. Second, Luke is excellent literature. He has woven several themes throughout his account as many good writers do. In addition, some of the most memorable stories about Jesus and stories that Jesus told are found in Luke. Third, Luke helps us to have faith in Jesus, as do the other gospel accounts. We see who He is, as demonstrated by His power, His teachings, and His character; and we have to decide whether we are going to put our trust in Him.

Greek Manuscript with a Portion of Luke 22 (c. 300 AD)

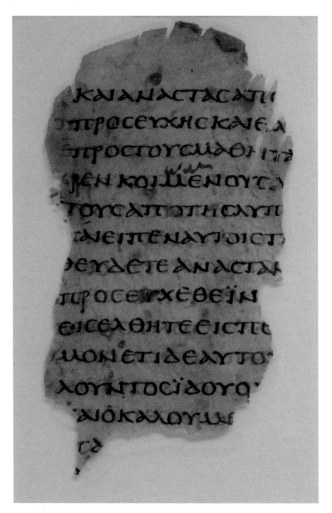

Author and Audience

None of the four gospel writers names himself in his own book, but the name of each writer has been associated with each respective book from the early years of the church in a strong and probably accurate tradition. Paul mentions "Luke, the beloved physician" in Colossians 4:14 as someone known well to himself and to the first-century church. He is described as a fellow worker of Paul in Philemon verse 24 (a letter that was also sent to Colossae). Acts 13:1 mentions one Lucius from Cyrene. This Lucius might be the same person we know as Luke.

We understand that Luke also wrote the book of Acts. Both Luke and Acts begin with addresses to

Painting of St. Luke, St. Mary's Church, Åhus, Sweden (17th-century)

Theophilus, and Acts 1:1 speaks of the first account that related what Jesus began to do and teach. From the way Paul groups people in Colossians 4, it appears that Luke was a Gentile and not a Jew. Thus, a Gentile is credited with being the writer of a large portion of the New Testament.

The Book of Luke is addressed to "most excellent Theophilus" (Luke 1:3). This was a common way of starting a book in the ancient world, especially in honor of the person who was the author's patron or financial supporter. Luke, of course, was actually writing for a wider audience than just one person. We all get to read over the shoulder of Theophilus and see what Luke had to say. The name Theophilus means "lover of God" or "loved by God." In a sense, we are all Theophilus because the meaning of his name is true for all of us.

Luke says that many people had written accounts of the life of Jesus. These were based on the accounts of eyewitnesses and "servants of the word" (Luke 1:2, probably a reference to inspired evangelists). Since Luke had researched the story, it seemed fitting to him to write down an orderly account so that Theophilus might have a firm grasp of what he had been taught (Luke 1:1-4).

Luke's introduction confirms several important details. First, this is one of several accounts of Jesus' life and ministry. We know this to be true. Second, Luke did research in the writing of his gospel. We trust that God inspired his research and his writing. Third, Theophilus had already been taught about the Lord and was probably already a Christian. Evidently all of the books of the New Testament were addressed to believers. Even the four gospels were intended to teach Christians.

Time and Place

Luke gives us specific historical notations in 1:5, 2:1, and 3:1-2. His story is not a once-upon-a-time fairy tale. Instead, it happened in history in a time and place that could be checked. Luke also tells us that Jesus was about thirty when He began His public ministry (Luke 3:23). We use the references to the Passover feasts in John to determine that Jesus' ministry lasted about three years (John 2:13 when He begins; then John 5:1, understanding this to mean the feast of Passover; John 6:4; and finally John 13:1).

A sixth-century monk, Dionysius Exiguus, worked out a time line in which he determined that Jesus was born in 1 AD. His system of counting years was eventually adopted in western countries, though later research indicated that he was off by a few years.

The Jewish historian Josephus mentions that Herod the Great died in the year of an eclipse. Astronomers tell us of a partial lunar eclipse in 4 BC. This date seems to work out best with other historical information we have. Since Jesus was born before Herod died (Matthew 2:19), the best date for Jesus' birth is about 4 BC. Determining the year of Jesus' birth, as calculated by a sixth-century monk, does not involve a matter of salvation or of believing the accuracy of the Bible.

Nearly all of the story of Jesus' life takes place in the nation of Israel on the eastern edge of the Mediterranean Sea. The Gospels include a few references to His trips outside Israel, including His trip to Egypt as a child with Mary and Joseph and His brief visits to Gentile areas during His ministry.

The Historical Setting

Paul says that Jesus was born when "the fullness of the time came" (Galatians 4:4). In other words, when God determined the best time for it, He sent Jesus to earth. A study of the historical setting show this to be true.

The Greek culture, especially its spread under Alexander the Great and those who came after him, gave the Mediterranean world a common language. The *koine* or common Greek that was spoken and written in the first century AD was widely known throughout that part of the world. Romans, Jews,

The ministry of Jesus took place during the reign of Tiberius Caesar (14-37 AD). The coin that Jesus used when talking about paying taxes to Caesar might have been one of these coins, called the "tribute penny" by coin collectors.

the people of Asia Minor, and many others were conversant with Greek.

The New Testament was written in Greek, even though Jesus Himself apparently spoke Aramaic (as indicated by the quotations of Jesus given in Mark 5:41, 7:34, and 15:34). Thus the message about the Savior of the world was written down in a language that was widely known in the world.

The Roman Empire gave the Mediterranean world a unified government and a relatively peaceful setting. The Romans were known for encouraging advances in transportation, such as the building of roads. The Jews did not like being under the domination of the Romans, but the good that came from this situation was that evangelists could travel throughout the empire with relatively few restrictions.

The Jews gave the world an understanding of the one true God. Most cultures of the world at the time believed in many gods. Many people worshiped a local god but believed in other deities as well. The Jews were a living testimony to the concept of one God over all the earth. They believed that God would one day send His Messiah to redeem His people from oppression.

So the stage was set for the most important event in the history of the world to take place.

*. . . so that you may know the exact truth
about the things you have been taught.*
Luke 1:4

Assignments for Lesson 51

Bible   Read Luke 1-5 while referring to the notes on this page and the next.

Student Review   Optional: Answer the questions for Lesson 51.

Herod directed the construction of palaces and fortifications at Masada near the Dead Sea in the decades before the birth of Christ.

Notes on Luke 1-5

Chapters 1-2—Luke shows how God's power and plan surrounded the birth of Jesus. Not one but two miraculous births were involved.

1:5—Herod the Great ruled the area of Israel from 39 BC to 4 BC. He allied himself with the Romans when they took control of the area in 64 BC, and they helped him secure his position of power. Herod oversaw the building of great structures during his reign. He financed a remodeling and restoration of the temple to try to win the favor of the Jews.

One reason this was necessary was that Herod was from Idumea. This was the region formerly known as Edom. The Edomites were descendents of Esau, Jacob's brother. Edom and Israel, like Esau and Jacob, did not get along well. To have the pagan Romans in control of God's Promised Land was bad enough, but to be under the immediate thumb of an Idumean was especially galling to the Jews.

In his old age, Herod was increasingly paranoid and violent. He had three of his sons killed when he feared that they wanted to take his throne. It is entirely within his character to order the death of babies in Bethlehem when he heard of a potential rival to his throne (Matthew 2:16-18).

1:11-17—The angel predicts the birth of John the Baptist, who will be a forerunner of the Christ. He quotes the last verse of the Old Testament, Malachi 4:6, to indicate the revolution of the heart that John would begin to usher in and that Jesus would complete.

1:46-55—Mary's song is similar to that of Hannah in 1 Samuel 2:1-10 when she brought her son Samuel to the tabernacle. Notice the theme of radical change: rulers will be brought down and the humble will be exalted; the hungry are filled and the rich go away empty-handed.

1:67-79—The beautiful prophecy of Zachariah (or Zacharias) develops the idea of Jesus as the Savior of His people.

The Nativity of St. John the Baptist
(Russian, c. 15th century)

2:1-2—After a period of civil war and sharing authority with others, Augustus Caesar (also written as Caesar Augustus) ruled from 27 BC to 14 AD. God's providence oversaw a decree from a pagan ruler that led Mary and Joseph to Bethlehem. This enabled the fulfillment of the prophecy that the Christ would be born in Bethlehem (Micah 5:2).

2:25-38—The prophecies of Simeon and Anna point toward Jesus as the Christ.

3:1-2—Luke places the beginning of John's ministry and Jesus' ministry in a clear historical setting.

3:23-38—Compare the genealogy in Luke to that in Matthew (Matthew 1:1-16). Matthew's goes back to Abraham, while Luke's goes back to Adam. Matthew emphasizes Jesus' connection with Israel, and Luke demonstrates Jesus' connection with all mankind. Luke's is longer, suggesting that Matthew might have listed only some of the generations. The two lists are not exactly the same, but with all of the intermarrying among families in Israel and the many sons of David this is not surprising.

4:16-30—This dramatic scene in Jesus' hometown comes at the beginning of His public ministry. He quotes a passage that everyone knew described the Messiah and then says, in effect, "Here I am!" He is met with questions, not faith. His illustrations shame the Jews and compliment Gentiles. This is why they want to run Him out of town.

5:17-26—Conflict begins with the Jewish leaders, who question His ability to forgive sins. It is easier to say "Your sins have been forgiven you," because one cannot prove it one way or the other. It is harder to say "Get up and walk" because the proof must be forthcoming. The man does get up and walk, which proves that Jesus has the authority to forgive sins as well. The conflict with Jewish leaders continues for several scenes.

Detail from Christ Blessing the Children, *Lucas Cranach the Elder (German, 1537)*

The Revolution Jesus Brought

Ever since the Jews were carried off into captivity by the Babylonians around 600 BC, the people of Israel nursed a burning desire to regain control of the land that God had given them. For centuries, this was not to be. First the Babylonians, then the Persians, then other foreign, pagan nations ruled what we call Palestine.

The Seleucid dynasty, begun by the successors to Alexander the Great, introduced Greek culture and religion into the areas of the Middle East that the Seleucids controlled in the late 300s and 200s BC. One move that was a sacrilege to faithful Jews was the Seleucids' use of the temple in Jerusalem for pagan worship. When pagan sacrifices were ordered in an outlying town in 168 BC, Jews rose up in what is called the Maccabean Revolt. The Maccabees defeated the Seleucid forces in Israel, and for about a century Jews were able to rule their own land with a degree of independence.

Then the Maccabees lost power because of their poor leadership. Meanwhile, the might of Rome was growing; and in 64 BC Rome took Judea as part of its empire. Once again the Jews were under the heel of foreign pagans, and the desire for freedom grew.

The Messianic Hope

The Jews circulated writings that expressed and fed a longing for a leader whom God would raise up to liberate His people. They read the Old Testament prophecies about the Mighty One whom God would send one day and interpreted them to mean that God's Messiah would be a military leader who would come onto the scene, gather an army of dedicated Jews, run the Romans into the

In 165 BC Jews restored the temple to the worship of God. This event is still remembered every year in December by the Festival of Lights or Hanukkah. The menorah is used to commemorate the traditional story of one flask of oil lasting for eight days at the temple rededication. This 1951 photo shows U.S. President Harry Truman (left) receiving a menorah as a gift from David Ben-Gurion, Prime Minister of the new modern country of Israel (center), and Abba Eban, Israeli Ambassador to the United States.

Mediterranean Sea, and re-establish the glory days of David and Solomon in Israel.

Those who most fervently devoted themselves to the cause of Jewish liberation were called Zealots. One of Jesus' disciples was Simon the Zealot (Luke 6:15). This must have made for some interesting discussions around the campfire, especially with Matthew having been recently in the employ of the Roman government as a tax collector. Barabbas, the prisoner who was freed when Jesus was condemned, might have been a Zealot. He had taken part in an attempted uprising (Luke 23:18-19).

The rule of Rome and Herod and the burning desire for independence were the main political realities for Jews in the first century AD. The Sadducees were a small but influential group of wealthy political leaders who had allied themselves with Rome and Herod. Because of their interest in material things, they came to deny the existence of angels and the possibility of resurrection and life after this world. The Pharisees were another relatively small group who took upon themselves the job of being strict interpreters of the Law of Moses and watchdogs for everyone else's spiritual lives. To them, faithfulness meant proper outward obedience to the Law as they saw it and interpreted it. They were aided by scribes, who because they copied the Law came to be seen as experts in it, and other teachers of the Law (sometimes called lawyers, but they did not function the way attorneys do today).

A Surprising Messiah

Jesus as the Messiah indeed brought a revolution to Israel. However, it was not the political and military revolution that many Jews wanted and expected. It was a revolution of the heart, a revolution in the way people lived, and a revolution in the relationship between God and man. Luke picks up some words and ideas related to this Messianic zeal and shows how Jesus fulfilled their true meaning. What is more, Jesus was the Savior not just of Israel, but of the whole world.

When the angel spoke to Zachariah in the temple, he quoted Malachi 4:6. The forerunner of the Coming One would turn the hearts of fathers back to their children and the hearts of children back to their fathers, "to make ready a people prepared for the Lord" (Luke 1:17). The Messiah was coming! The Zealots understood Malachi 4:6 to be talking about being ready for the Lord and His political upheaval. Luke shows us, however, that the prophecy was just what it said. Through the ministries of John and Jesus, the hearts of family members would be turned back to each other; and all hearts would be turned back to God.

This painting of Simon the Zealot is from a chapel in Austria. Simon is often depicted in art with a saw, by which he was put to death according to tradition.

Simeon the Righteous
Alexei Egorovich Egorov (Russian, c. 1840)

Gabriel predicted to Mary that God would give her Son the throne of David and that "His kingdom will have no end" (Luke 1:32-33). Mary predicted that through the mighty deeds of Jesus, God would topple rulers and exalt the humble in fulfillment of His promises to Abraham (Luke 1:51-55). This is Messiah talk! However, Zachariah says that the Lord would give His people "the knowledge of salvation by the forgiveness of their sins" (Luke 1:77). This was the real revolution that Jesus brought.

When Mary and Joseph took the infant Jesus to the temple to make the sacrifices of purification, they met two elderly servants of God. Simeon was looking for "the consolation [or comfort] of Israel" (Luke 2:25). Anna spoke of Jesus to all "who were looking for the redemption [or setting free] of Jerusalem" (Luke 2:38). This, the people must have thought, could be nothing else but a reference to the Coming One they had been waiting for. He was that One, but not in the way they expected.

At a critical moment in Jesus' life, as He was beginning His public ministry, Jesus spoke in his hometown synagogue. He quoted a clearly Messianic passage in Isaiah 61 and claimed that He fulfilled this text. He came, He said, to set the prisoners and the downtrodden free and to announce the year of God's favor (Luke 4:16-21). Jesus had them in the palm of His hand, but then He put a twist on their preconceptions. He started complimenting Gentiles and pointing out the failures of Israelites in the Old Testament. When the people heard this, their smiles quickly turned to frowns and their praise to angry shouts. They wanted nothing more to do with this Messiah who did not fulfill their expectations (Luke 4:24-29).

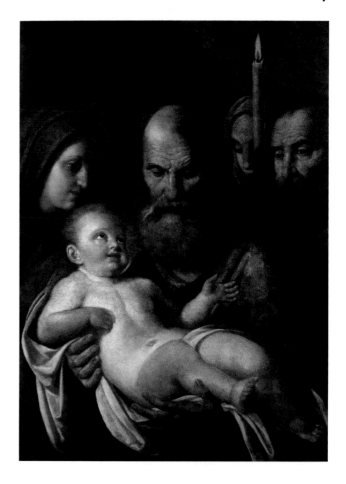

Often during His ministry, Jesus refused to let the demons speak. He also told people whom He healed not to talk about it to others (Luke 4:41, 5:13-14, 8:56). This seems odd for someone who came to teach and who eventually wanted His followers to tell the whole world about Him. However, Jesus wanted to reveal the truth about Himself and not allow speculation to feed the common (and erroneous) perception of the Messiah. The demons knew who He was because they knew something of the spiritual battle going on. They would love nothing more than to wreck Jesus' ministry by causing people to believe the wrong thing about Jesus. If Jesus' miracles were not properly understood, word of His power would get out and people would be grabbing their swords to follow Him as their leader. This is what happened at the feeding of the 5,000, when the people saw what Jesus did and wanted to make Him their king by force (John 6:14-15).

"Who Do You Say I Am?"

After Jesus had taught and healed the masses and had been with His disciples for some time, He asked the Twelve what people were saying about Him. They told Him the speculation they had heard, all of which was wrong. He then asked them the much more important question, "Who do you say I am?" Peter replied, "You are Messiah! You are the one all of Israel has been waiting for."

Peter thought that Jesus' being the Messiah meant that Jesus would be a bold and courageous military leader, a charismatic figure who obviously had the power of God. Peter thought that, for Peter himself, Jesus as the Messiah meant glorious battle, a crushing defeat of the Romans, the exhilaration of victory, and God's pleasure in a renewed kingdom like that of David.

Jesus then told the disciples what being the Messiah really meant: He was going to suffer, be rejected by the religious leaders, and be crucified; then He would rise on the third day (Luke 9:22). This was definitely not the Messianic script that all of Israel had been rehearsing and thought they knew by heart. Peter thought that Jesus had it all wrong and perhaps had a lack of confidence in His followers. This is why Peter rebuked Jesus just after he confessed Jesus' identity as the Christ (Matthew 16:22).

Jesus told the Twelve what it meant to them that He was the Messiah: not taking up a sword, but taking up a cross; not glorious military victory but giving up their lives; not changing governments but changing their hearts (Luke 9:23-24). Luke does not record Peter's rebuke of Jesus, but the rest of Luke 9 shows how the disciples revealed their lack of understanding over and over in the days that followed. Luke 9:57-62 is a powerful summary of the cost of discipleship. Jesus was indeed bringing a revolution.

To All the Nations

Jesus brought a revolution not just to Israel but to the entire world. It had little to do with politics beyond rendering to Caesar what belonged to him already (Luke 20:19-26). The revolution of Jesus involved personal repentance. Through Jesus' sacrifice, people received the forgiveness of sins (Luke 24:47). Instead of attempting to change society as a whole, Jesus empowered individuals to experience an inner revolution. These personal revolutions changed the world drastically and permanently. Jesus changed the relationships people have with God, other people, and the material things of this life. The resurrection of Jesus from the dead is the ultimate revolution in human life because death is no longer a threat.

The Ascension of Christ *(Bulgarian, 16th Century)*

The end of Luke leads perfectly into the story of Acts, where we see Jesus guiding the church through His Spirit to carry the gospel to the ends of the earth (Acts 1:8). From the humble beginning of an itinerant teacher with twelve followers who didn't quite get it, the church grew to include millions of people from every tribe and tongue.

The revolution of Jesus brought freedom, but not freedom from the Romans. It brought the greater and more important freedom from sin. The real Messianic revolution of Jesus was of world-changing proportions, more than any first-century Jewish zealot could see but not more than our eternal and powerful God could do.

And He was saying to them all,
"If anyone wishes to come after Me, let him deny himself,
and take up his cross daily and follow Me."
Luke 9:23

Assignments for Lesson 52

Bible   Read Luke 6-9 while referring to the notes below and on pages 287-288.

Student Review   Optional: Answer the questions for Lesson 52.

Notes on Luke 6-9

6:12-16—The importance Jesus placed on choosing the twelve is shown by His praying all night before He does so.

6:17-48—This is Luke's presentation of what is called the Sermon on the Mount in Matthew 5-7. This passage is different in some ways from Matthew's account, and it is possible that Luke recorded a similar sermon on another occasion.

7:18-23—John, who was languishing in prison (Luke 3:18-20), had some questions about Jesus. People being healed while he was stuck in prison was not his idea of what the Messiah was supposed to be about. So he sent some of his disciples to ask Jesus point blank, "Are you the One, or do we

keep looking?" Jesus answered by not answering—verbally, anyway. Instead, He did the work of the Messiah that had been described in Luke 4:18-19. Then He sent this reply to John: the answer is in what I am doing. In other words, Jesus was the Messiah; and the proof was in what He did. Jesus then has some highly complimentary things to say about John.

8:4-21—The parable of the sower prompts people to determine what kind of soil they are: resistant, flighty, busy, or productive. Jesus wants us to listen well and to put His words into practice. His illustration of a lamp on a stand says that our learning about Him is not to be kept in but is to be shown forth through our lives. The family of Jesus is more than biological relation; he wants those who hear and obey the word of God.

Saint John the Baptist in Prison Visited by Two Disciples, *Giovanni di Paolo (Italian, c. 1455)*

8:22-9:6—The quality needed to live this way is faith, something we all lack to some degree. The disciples had fear and not faith on the boat in the storm. The people who lived near the Gerasene demoniac feared the change that Jesus wrought in the man's life. They did not have faith in Jesus but instead asked Him to leave. Jairus struggled with his faith when he asked Jesus to heal his daughter. The woman with the long-standing hemorrhage was an example of faith in action when she reached out and touched Jesus' garment. Jesus called on the Twelve to have faith as they went out on a limited preaching and healing mission.

9:7-27—Jesus' questions about His identity took place immediately after the feeding of the five thousand. Especially in John's account of the miracle, we see that Jesus was faced with the temptation of letting the people decide what His Messiahship meant and abandoning the mission God had for Him.

9:28-36—God reinforces Jesus' call to discipleship that denies self with the scene of transfiguration and His command to Peter, James, and John to "listen to Him." Moses and Elijah, two leading figures of the Old Testament representing the Law and the Prophets, talk with Jesus about His "departure," which was about to take place at Jerusalem. The word in the Greek is literally "exodus." Since Jesus had His own exodus to undergo, Moses was a good person with whom He could discuss it.

9:37-56—This is a series of scenes in which the disciples show that they do not understand what following Jesus means. They fail to heal the boy with the unclean spirit, then they immediately argue among themselves over which one was the greatest (perhaps to determine who got the blame for failing to heal the boy). John shows an exclusive spirit when he wants to stop someone from healing in Jesus' name because he is not part of their little group. Then James and John want to destroy a Samaritan village because they do not welcome Jesus and the disciples as they pass through.

Luke says that Jesus set His face to go to Jerusalem. This begins what some Bible scholars call the great travel narrative, which continues to Luke 19:28, when He approaches and enters Jerusalem. In this section are several passages found nowhere but in Luke. Luke says that Jesus did this when the time was approaching for Jesus' (literally) "taking up," focusing on His ascension as the triumph of the cross.

9:57-62—The last three encounters in this chapter illustrate excuses people make for not submitting to Jesus. The first person gleefully wants to follow Jesus but has not counted the cost. The second responds to Jesus' call with a request for a delay. Jesus is not heartlessly telling the man to ignore his father. Perhaps his father was not even dead yet, and the man was saying that he would follow Jesus after his other responsibilities were cared for. Those who are spiritually alive will not let other things get in the way of serving Jesus. The third man offers to follow Jesus with a condition: first he wants to say good-bye to his family. Jesus knows that many of those who say "But first . . ." never get around to following Him.

Plowing in Israel (c. 1943)

Annunciation to the Shepherds, Sand Sculpture in the Canary Islands
Iryna Kalyuzhna (Ukranian, 2008)

Unlikely Heroes

Celebrities in our culture are often movie stars, musicians, athletes, or successful business leaders. People tend to idolize those who are powerful and sensational, not those who are humble and modest.

To the Jews of first-century Israel, Jesus was no celebrity. He didn't fit the mold or sound like what they expected. Instead, He was a surprising Messiah who ushered in a surprising revolution. It shouldn't have been surprising, since Jesus' ministry and the changes He brought were in keeping with God's will. The surprise occurred because the way Jesus taught was not expected by people who had come to think in the world's terms and who accepted the religious traditions of the day.

The surprising revolution of Jesus called for people's thinking to change. One of the most important changes involved how people see others. We tend to put people in categories (old, young, rich, poor, good, bad, foreign, different, etc.) and then judge individuals through the preconceptions we have of those groups. This is not, however, God's way of evaluating people. "Man looks at the outward appearance, but the Lord looks at the heart" (1 Samuel 16:7).

The Gospel of Luke shows how Jesus shattered the stereotypes that people usually hold. God honors people using a different standard from that which most people—even Christians—use. Jesus did indeed bring a revolution that has changed the world, and a big part of that is in the way Christians are to view others. We need to recognize God's unlikely heroes. This will help us to see who is worthy of honor in world history and in the world today. It should also encourage you to believe that, even though the world may never know about you, you can be a hero in God's eyes.

An Unlikely Beginning

The surprises start quickly in Luke. We wouldn't expect a childless older couple or an unmarried virgin to be the people God would honor as parents with special missions, but these are the people God chose to fulfill His will. Zachariah and Elizabeth were the unlikely parents of John the Baptist, and Mary was chosen as the handmaiden of God to give birth to the Savior.

The news of Jesus' birth was spread in an unlikely way. Matthew tells of wise men, learned astronomers and philosophers of the East, who came

Lazarus, *Soichi Watanabe (Japanese, 2005)*

the way of Jesus. Those to be congratulated, He says, are the poor, the hungry, those who weep, and those who are persecuted. These are the ones who will find their comfort in God. On the other hand, those to be lamented include the rich, the well-fed, those who laugh, and those widely praised by men. Such people might be successful in this world, but they can expect no comfort from God if they are content with worldly pleasures (Luke 6:20-26).

The world's standard of success is challenged most pointedly by what Jesus teaches in Luke about blessedness and wealth. The parable of the rich fool warns against making possessions the focus of one's life (Luke 12:13-21). To warn against the example of the Pharisees, who loved money, Jesus taught the story of the rich man and Lazarus. The rich man had everything and Lazarus had nothing in this life, but when they died their fortunes were reversed. The rich man wound up in torment while Lazarus rested in the bosom of Abraham (Luke 16:14-31). Wealth is not a factor in blessedness except that it can keep one from closeness to God.

The rich young ruler was a surprising failure. He seemed to have it all. He was a synagogue ruler who had faithfully adhered to God's Law from his youth. In addition, he had been financially successful. Jesus said that he lacked this one thing: his heart was not devoted to God above everything else he had acquired and accomplished. As a result, the rich young ruler was a failure. After the man walked away, dejected at the price tag of following Jesus, the shocked disciples asked Jesus, "Then who can be saved?" In other words, if he can't be saved, who can? Jesus replied by reminding them that God saves, not man. Nothing that a person might do will ever earn his salvation before God. Salvation requires trust (Luke 18:18-30).

a long distance to give honor to Jesus. In Luke, by contrast, angels tell of Jesus' birth to nobodies: lowly shepherds just outside of town. Shepherding was not an honored profession in Jesus' day. Although the Lord is portrayed as our shepherd in Psalm 23, a shepherd was usually seen as someone who did unattractive work and who smelled like the sheep he cared for. Yet these were Jesus' first visitors, unlikely witnesses who praised God for the amazing and world-changing things they had seen (Luke 2:8-20).

Who is Blessed?

In Jesus' Beatitudes, the word usually translated "Blessed" can also be translated "Congratulations!" These statements of blessedness reveal the irony of

Vivid Contrasts

In several passages, Luke portrays a sharp contrast between those who come to Jesus in humble repentance and faith and those who stand aloof from Jesus in prideful self-righteousness and judgment of others. Once again, those who come to Jesus are the unlikely ones. The religious leaders that Jesus met were often entrenched in their religious tradition. They became defensive about any suggested changes to their religious system and comfort zone. By contrast, those who had been social outcasts were often eager to follow Jesus. They demonstrated a vibrant, meaningful faith that showed gratitude for what Jesus did for them.

Pharisees and Sadducees came to John at the Jordan River to be baptized, but John called them snakes (Matthew 3:7). Unexpected seekers such as tax-collectors and soldiers, by contrast, came to John and asked what they should do to show their repentance (Luke 3:12-14).

After Jesus called Levi to follow Him, the former tax-collector gave a banquet in Jesus' honor. He invited, of course, his tax-gatherer friends and other "unsavory characters" who were willing to listen to Jesus. The scribes and Pharisees, on the other hand, stood apart and threw questions like darts at Jesus (Luke 5:29-6:11).

A dramatic confrontation came when a Pharisee invited Jesus to dinner. The Jewish leader probably wanted to find something wrong with Jesus. He didn't have to wait long. A woman of the city, known as a sinner (one who did not keep the ritual law faithfully) barged into the dinner and wiped Jesus' feet, first with her tears and then with expensive perfume. Simon the Pharisee was shocked, but Jesus knew that the woman understood something about forgiveness that Simon did not.

Apparently Jesus had met the woman before. At that time Jesus had taught her about the love of God. The woman was convinced and now wanted to show her gratitude to the Lord. Jesus taught Simon that those who have been forgiven much love much, but those who think they have little to forgive feel little need to love (Luke 7:36-50).

One of Jesus' most famous parables presents the contrast between seekers and skeptics in unforgettable terms. As tax-gatherers and sinners were coming to Jesus and Pharisees and scribes were condemning Him for eating with such, Jesus told the story of the prodigal (or wasteful) son.

After the younger of two brothers left home and wasted his share of the family wealth, he returned in humble, sincere repentance. The father welcomed him with open arms. The older brother, on the other hand, had never left home; but his self-righteousness and his condemnation of his brother prevented him from appreciating the joy of his father's loving nature (Luke 15:1-32).

The Return of the Prodigal Son
Pompeo Batoni (Italian, 1773)

Jesus' Surprising Celebrities

Repeatedly in Luke, Jesus honors those whom the Jews would be least likely to recognize as having any spiritual interest and any hope for a relationship with God.

Samaritans. The people of Samaria were an ethnic group descended from remnants of the idolatrous Northern Kingdom of Israel and Assyrians who moved into the area when thousands of people in the Northern Kingdom were carried into captivity in 721 BC. Samaritans who worshiped God did so on Mount Gerizim, not in Jerusalem; and they accepted only the first five books of the Old Testament as Scripture. Thus the Samaritans were ethnic and religious half-breeds in the eyes of the Jews, who had as little to do with them as possible (John 4:9).

However, the hero in Jesus' parable that showed how to practice love for one's neighbor was a Samaritan—a Samaritan, moreover, who was far away from home and who showed compassion when the proper Jewish priest and Levite did not (Luke 10:25-37). Later, when Jesus healed ten lepers, the only one who stopped long enough to praise God and give thanks to Jesus was a Samaritan (Luke 17:11-19).

Tax-gatherers. Jewish tax-collectors were seen as traitors by other Jews. Tax-gatherers, or publicans, were Jews who cooperated with the Romans. The Roman Empire contracted out the collection of taxes to local people, who set the tax rate at whatever they

could get by with. They sent to Rome the required amount and pocketed the rest as profit. To loyal Jews, therefore, tax-collectors were not only traitors but crooked traitors as well.

As described in Luke, however, tax-gatherers came to John the Baptist in humble repentance (Luke 3:12-13). They came to Levi's banquet in honor of Jesus (Luke 5:29). The hero of Jesus' parable about prayer was the repentant tax-gatherer, not the prideful Pharisee (Luke 18:9-14). The repentance of the tax-collector Zacchaeus symbolized what Jesus' ministry was all about: seeking and saving the lost (Luke 19:1-10).

Women and Children. In Jesus' day, women had few legal and social rights. Their testimony was not accepted in court. A woman was not to appear in public unless she was accompanied by her father or husband. The traditional daily prayer offered by a Jewish man expressed thanks to God that he was not a Gentile, a slave, or a woman.

Yet women were vital to the ministry of Jesus and were honored as examples of faith. Women supported His ministry financially (Luke 8:1-3). When the synagogue ruler Jairus was struggling with his faith, the woman with the issue of blood exemplified faith when she touched Jesus' garment and thereby received healing (Luke 8:43-48).

Widows were the true have-nots in Jewish society. A woman was dependent on her father until she married, then on her husband until he died, and then on her children until she died. Jesus, however, took notice of widows. The widow in Nain was in

During the early centuries after Christ, there were perhaps one million Samaritans in Israel, but their population has declined to less than 1,000 today. They adhere to strict observance of their rituals, some taken from the laws given to Moses and some modified over the centuries. This photo shows a Passover ceremony on Mount Gerizim. In recent years, in an effort to increase their population and avoid genetic diseases, they have allowed Jewish women and women from the Ukraine to convert and marry Samaritan men.

Light-and-Heavy Parables

The parable of the persistent widow (Luke 18:1-8) is an example of what is called light-and-heavy teaching. This style of instruction says that if something is true in a less important case, surely it is true in a more important case. If a poor widow with no legal standing can get the attention of a heartless judge, surely God's people will have the ear of their loving Father. The illustration of the parable at left was designed to help people in Mozambique understand it in their culture. It is wrong to see the judge in this parable as an illustration of God. Luke includes other examples of light-and-heavy teachings (see Luke 12:28 and 16:1-13).

a particularly difficult situation, since her only son had died. Jesus raised her son (Luke 7:11-17). When Jesus told a parable to illustrate persistent prayer, His hero was a widow, a woman who had no legal standing but got what she wanted from a reluctant judge (Luke 18:1-8). The gift to the temple treasury that Jesus noted was not a large donation by someone who would never miss it, but the two coins of a widow who gave all she had to live on (Luke 21:1-4).

If women had few legal rights, children had even fewer. On two occasions, however, Jesus used children to illustrate the attitudes of humility and trust that He wanted in His followers (Luke 9:46-48, 18:15-17). These examples showed the true nature of Jesus' kingdom as opposed to the common conception of the kingdom in people's minds.

Gentiles. The typical Jew saw Gentiles as little better than dogs. In Jewish understanding, they were God's chosen people and the Gentiles were not. That settled the question of the worth of Gentiles in most Jewish minds. Jesus was not limited by such prejudice, however; He saw faith in some Gentiles that put Jewish attitudes to shame.

Jesus condemned the people in his hometown synagogue by saying that they fell into the typical pattern of rejecting a hometown boy, even though He was a prophet. In His sermon, Jesus pointed

out that the Gentile widow of Zarephath and the Gentile army officer Naaman showed faith (Luke 4:24-27). The unfavorable comparison filled His listeners with rage.

As commanders over about one hundred men, centurions were trusted veterans in the Roman army. Centurions were not known as being tender, spiritually-minded men. Yet consistently in the Gospel of Luke and in Acts, centurions are praised for their faith. When a centurion's slave was dying, the officer sent word to Jesus asking for help. The Roman recognized the authority of Jesus and appealed to it. Jesus complimented him by saying that this Gentile's faith was far above any faith He had seen among the Jews (Luke 7:2-10). When Jesus died on the cross, after being jeered and condemned by Jewish religious leaders and others who should have known better, a Gentile centurion was the one who praised God and declared his belief that Jesus was innocent (Luke 23:47).

The One Whom Jesus Accepts

Luke tells about no more surprising hero than the criminal on the cross. Here was a man staring death in the face for what he had done wrong. He had no hope whatsoever, but he called out to Jesus for mercy. Jesus promised him that, because of his faith, the thief would be with Him in Paradise (Luke 23:39-43). If a condemned and dying criminal can come to Jesus, surely any person, regardless of his or her background, can come to the Savior.

You might be part of a religious family and attend church regularly. Never lose sight of the fact that religious people were the most ardent opponents of Jesus. Be sure that your faith is not in a religious system or certain religious traditions, but in Jesus.

You might face uncommon difficulties. You might be part of a group that many people look down on. Your family might not have wealth or prestige. None of that stands in the way of being welcomed as a follower of Jesus.

God preserved stories of Jesus' heroes to let us know whom He honors. The world will be different when people decide that they can be different because God sees them differently from the way the world does.

In the same way, I tell you, there is joy in the presence of the angels of God over one sinner who repents.
Luke 15:10

Assignments for Lesson 53

Bible Read Luke 10-14 while referring to the notes below and on pages 295-296.

Student Review Optional: Answer the questions for Lesson 53.

Notes on Luke 10-14

10:1-24—Jesus sends seventy disciples (some manuscripts say seventy-two) on a limited commission. They are to travel on faith. Jesus utters woes on Jewish cities because their citizens had not responded to Jesus' ministry. If He had done the same thing in Gentile cities, they would have repented. When the seventy return, they are excited about the power they had wielded (i.e., what they could do). Jesus is pleased also, but admonishes them that they should take more joy over their names being recorded in heaven (i.e., what was done for them).

10:25-37—This passage gives us one of several beautiful stories included in Luke's account. An expert in the Law wanted to test Jesus and wound up being tested himself. The key to eternal life is to love God with all your being and to love your neighbor as though he were you. The lawyer wanted to define and limit how he had to show love by asking, "Who is my neighbor?" In other words, whom do I have to help?

Jesus told the story of the Good Samaritan, who went to great lengths to help someone who was in obvious need. Jesus turns the question around. He does not answer, "Whom do I have to help?" Instead, He asks, "Who helped someone?" Who

was a neighbor to another person? A neighbor is not someone you have to love. You are a neighbor; therefore you are to love others.

10:38-42—This is another well-known event in Jesus' life. The scene at the home of Mary and Martha teaches us to be most concerned about the most important things.

11:14-28—These are teachings about God's strength and about our being strong in the face of Satan's attacks. It ends with Jesus reply to a woman's emotional outburst praising Jesus' mother. Jesus said that true blessedness comes by obeying God's word.

11:37-54—The Pharisee who invited Jesus to lunch probably never had another guest who took him to task as Jesus did. The Lord condemned his concern with outward show and his neglect of inner, spiritual cleanliness. When a lawyer complained, Jesus issued woes on the experts in the law. They should have known better because of their knowledge of Scripture. Jesus mentions the first and last innocent victims of murder in the Old Testament (in the Hebrew arrangement of the Old Testament, Genesis is first and 2 Chronicles [see 24:20-22] is last). Rather than taking His rebukes to heart, the Jewish leaders stiffen their resistance and plot to catch Jesus in something He says.

12:1-12—In the context of the Pharisees' conspiracy against Him, Jesus warns the crowd of the influence of the Pharisees' thinking, which amounted to hypocrisy. People did not need to fear them; the people needed to fear God instead.

12:13-48—A man's desire for Jesus to use His influence to help him get his share of the family estate leads to a series of teachings about materialism, including the well-known parable of the rich fool. Instead of being bogged down with the stuff of this world, we need to travel light and be ready to meet the Lord. When Peter asks to whom the teaching applies (perhaps trying to get off the hook), Jesus says that it applies to anyone who has responsibility for how he lives, namely everyone.

12:49-59—A day of reckoning is coming, but people seem not to notice or not to care.

13:10-17—Jesus' healing of a woman in the synagogue on the Sabbath causes the ruler of the synagogue to rebuke Jesus and say, "There won't be any Sabbath healings in this synagogue; come some other day!" This puts the synagogue official in the ridiculous but sad position of trying to tell God when He can and can't heal people.

Woman, You Are Freed . . .
Hanna Varghese (Malaysian, 2007)

This tenth-century wall painting illustrates Christ healing the man with dropsy. It is located in St. George's Church on Reichenau Island in Lake Constance, southern Germany.

13:31-35—Herod here is Herod Antipas, the son of Herod the Great. Antipas ruled Galilee and Perea and had John the Baptist executed. Jesus says that His destiny cannot be thwarted by man.

14:1-6—It is amazing that the Pharisees still had anything to do with Jesus. They must have really wanted to trap him. Dropsy is the accumulation of fluid in body cavities. It often indicates heart disease. The Jewish leaders' refusal to approve of healing on the Sabbath shows that they were the ones with diseased hearts.

14:7-24—Jesus uses the setting of a banquet to teach proper attitudes. It is better to humble yourself and be exalted by another than to exalt yourself and be humbled by another. Our acts of generosity should be done for those who cannot

repay us instead of for those from whom we want to get favors in return. The latter way is not generosity at all but is a focus on self. When someone calls out to say how blessed it will be to sit at the banquet table in the kingdom of God, Jesus tells a parable to teach the shocking truth that some people reject the invitation to the banquet.

14:25-35—Large crowds were following Jesus, but He warns them that a person must reject self and carry his cross to follow Him. Being a disciple of Jesus involves a cost, and a potential follower must weigh that cost and pay it. His obedience must be undiluted. When salt becomes contaminated with other materials, it loses its effectiveness and is worthless. So it is with someone who is not willing to put everything else aside to follow Jesus.

Stained-Glass Depiction of Christ as King
Annunciation Melkite Catholic Cathedral, Boston

Major Themes in Luke

One way to determine if a topic is important to a writer is to see how often he mentions it. Charles Dickens, for example, wrote frequently about the plight of the working poor in London. Mark Twain found a great deal of meaning in his frequent descriptions of the Mississippi River.

As a good writer who was inspired by God, Luke develops several themes in his gospel account which we should note. All of the facets of the jewel of Jesus are important for us to consider, but here we will study some of the topics that Luke emphasizes in his presentation of the life of Jesus.

The Kingdom of God

Jesus used the word church only twice as recorded in the gospels (Matthew 16:18, 18:17), but the word kingdom is used over one hundred times (some references are parallels of the same teaching). Obviously, the kingdom of God was an important topic to Jesus. The Jews of Jesus' day were looking for the restoration of the political and geographic kingdom of Israel, but Jesus taught what the kingdom of God really meant. He wanted people to let God truly rule their lives.

The Coming of the Kingdom. The angel Gabriel predicted to Mary that her Son would receive the throne of David and that His kingdom would never end (Luke 1:32-33). This set the tone in Luke of Jesus as King. Jesus Himself predicted that the kingdom would come within the lifetime of some who were with Him (Luke 9:27). He taught His disciples to pray for the kingdom to come (Luke 11:2).

As Jesus preached, He proclaimed the kingdom of God (Luke 8:1, 9:11). He sent his disciples out to proclaim the kingdom (Luke 9:2, 10:9). He told another potential follower to proclaim the kingdom of God (Luke 9:60).

Yet the kingdom was not going to come immediately. When He was about to enter Jerusalem for the last time, Jesus taught a parable to correct the idea that the kingdom was coming right away (Luke 19:11-27).

The Nature of the Kingdom. The kingdom of God belongs to some surprising people. The poor are to be congratulated because the kingdom of God belongs to them (Luke 6:20). Those who are willing to be like children have the kingdom (Luke 18:16-17). Half-hearted followers are not fit for the kingdom (Luke 9:62).

God's kingdom has some surprising qualities. It is like a mustard seed: its reach and influence far exceed its small beginnings. It is like leaven:

its presence might not be noticed but its influence is unmistakable (Luke 13:18-21).

We are to seek the kingdom (Luke 12:31), but we have to be alert spiritually to find it. It will not be obvious by external indicators because the kingdom of God is within (Luke 17:20-21). The kingdom operates by God's power, not by man's (Luke 11:20).

Membership in the kingdom is on God's terms, though some have tried to force their way in by defining it in their own terms (Luke 16:16). It is hard for a rich person to enter the kingdom; we must give up all we have (Luke 18:24-30).

The Surprising King. As Jesus was dying on the cross, He did not look like a conquering King. The soldiers mocked the claim that He was King of the Jews. The sign that the Romans put on the cross was intended to be an insult. It was saying that this is what happens to somebody who claims to be King of the Jews (Luke 23:37-38).

Yet the criminal on the cross put his trust in Jesus as King when he said, "Remember me when You come in Your kingdom" (Luke 23:42). The religious Jews missed it and the mighty Romans missed it, but the criminal understood it and believed in the kingdom.

The coming of the kingdom to which Jesus referred was the Day of Pentecost, when the church began with the power of the Holy Spirit, as described in Acts 2. When people responded to the gospel, God became King of their hearts through Jesus.

The Holy Spirit

The presence and work of the Holy Spirit is another major theme in Luke. Luke is the Bible author who gives us the phrase "filled with the Holy Spirit." John the Baptist was to be filled with the Holy Spirit while still in the womb (Luke 1:15). Elizabeth and Zechariah are said to be filled with the Holy Spirit (Luke 1:41, 67). The aged Simeon had the Holy Spirit upon him (Luke 2:25, 27). Mary would become the mother of Jesus even while a virgin because the Holy Spirit was to come upon her (Luke 1:35).

Luke emphasizes the role of the Holy Spirit in Jesus' ministry. John said that Jesus would baptize in the Holy Spirit (Luke 3:16). The Spirit descended upon Jesus at His baptism (Luke 3:22). When Jesus went into the desert for forty days, He was full of the Spirit and was led by the Spirit (Luke 4:1). Jesus preached in the power of the Spirit (Luke 4:14). The Messianic passage in Isaiah that Jesus claimed when He spoke in the Nazareth synagogue said that the Spirit of the Lord was upon Him (Luke 4:18). When the Seventy returned from their preaching tour, Jesus was full of joy through the Holy Spirit (Luke 10:21).

Jesus taught about the Holy Spirit as well. In His teaching on prayer, Jesus said that God will give the Holy Spirit to those who ask (Luke 11:13). Blasphemy against the Holy Spirit cannot be forgiven (Luke 12:10), apparently because the person

This Chinese porcelain plate (c. 1730) depicts the baptism of Christ, with the Holy Spirit shown in the form of a dove.

Continuing Themes in Acts

Themes from Luke's gospel continue as he tells the story of the early church in the book of Acts. The kingdom is a major theme, as it is mentioned frequently from the beginning to the end of the book. Prayer is an important theme in Acts also. Of the twenty-eight chapters in Acts, twenty have a reference to prayer. The New Testament church was a praying church.

The Virgin Mary in Prayer
Albrecht Dürer (German, 1518)

holding such a position denies who Jesus is and thus denies the source of salvation. Such a person can change his beliefs, but as long as he doesn't he cannot be forgiven. Jesus assured His disciples that the Holy Spirit would teach them what to say when they were brought before accusers (Luke 12:11-12). Finally, Jesus told the Eleven that they would be "clothed with power from on high" (Luke 24:49), a reference to the coming of the Spirit in Acts 2.

Joy

Luke makes special use of the idea of joy. The angel told Zechariah that he would have joy and gladness at the birth of John (Luke 1:14). The unborn child John leaped for joy in Elizabeth's womb when Mary came to Elizabeth's home (Luke 1:44). Mary expressed joy in God at the news of God's choosing her to be the mother of Jesus (Luke 1:47). The angel brought to the shepherds good news of great joy (Luke 2:10).

The Seventy returned from their mission with joy (Luke 10:17). Jesus rejoiced in the Holy Spirit (Luke 10:21). The crowds rejoiced at what Jesus did (Luke 13:17). After Jesus ascended to heaven, the Eleven "returned to Jerusalem with great joy" (Luke 24:52).

Prayer

Prayer also receives special notice in Luke's account. When the angel appeared to Zachariah in the temple, the people outside were in prayer (Luke 1:10). The angel told Zachariah that God had heard his prayer and was going to enable Zachariah and Elizabeth to bear a son (Luke 1:13).

When the Spirit descended upon Jesus at His baptism, Luke notes that it was while Jesus was praying (Luke 3:21). Jesus often withdrew to the wilderness to pray (Luke 5:16). John's disciples (and the disciples of the Pharisees) often fasted and prayed (Luke 5:33).

Before He named the Twelve, Jesus spent the entire night in prayer (Luke 6:12). Before he fed the five thousand, Jesus blessed the food (Luke 9:16). When He asked the disciples who the people were saying that He was, He had been praying (Luke 9:18). The Transfiguration took place when Jesus went up to the mountain to pray (Luke 9:28). Luke 10:21 records a prayer of praise and thankfulness by Jesus.

In the Garden before He was arrested, Jesus prayed and urged His followers to pray (Luke 22:40-46). In addition, Jesus often taught about prayer (Luke 6:28, 11:1-13, 18:1-14).

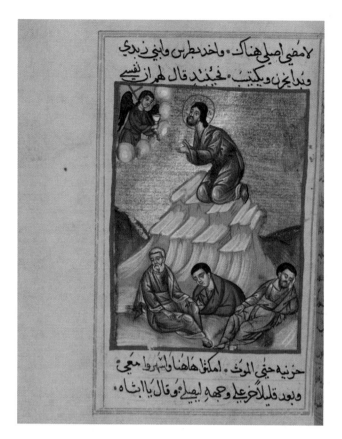

This illustration of Jesus praying in Gethsemane is from a 17th-century Egyptian manuscript of the gospels.

Repentance

Luke emphasizes the importance of repentance. John's ministry was to turn the hearts of people back to the ways of God (Luke 1:16-17). John preached a baptism of repentance for the forgiveness of sins (Luke 3:3). He told his hearers to bear the fruit of repentance in their lives (Luke 3:8). Jesus said that He had come to call sinners to repentance (Luke 5:32). The Lord warned the crowds that unless they repented, they faced grave consequences (Luke 13:1-5). Jesus taught that heaven rejoices over one sinner who repents (Luke 15:7, 10).

The sinful woman who came to Simon's house had obviously repented of her sins (Luke 7:36-50). The turning point in the parable of the prodigal son

Parable of the Great Banquet
Anonymous (Dutch, c. 1525)

comes when the young man comes to himself and returns in repentance to his father (Luke 15:17-21). The Lord's commission to the Eleven after His resurrection stated that it was God's will that repentance for forgiveness of sins be proclaimed to all the nations (Luke 24:46-47).

The Messianic Banquet

The revolution of the Messiah is presented powerfully by Luke's use of the banquet idea. A banquet is a time of celebration, often honoring victory and accomplishment. Isaiah 25:6 speaks of a banquet to describe the time of the Messiah. Jesus employed this image to portray the celebration of heaven.

The Lord urged people to be ready so that they would be called to recline at the banquet in the kingdom of God (Luke 13:29). One person's idea of blessedness was to eat bread in the kingdom of God (Luke 14:15). When Jesus shared the meal with His disciples on the night He was betrayed, He predicted that He would not eat it again until the coming of the kingdom (Luke 22:15-18). He promised that the disciples would share a meal at His table in His kingdom (Luke 22:29-30).

Jesus used meals to teach important truths. He was willing to sit down and eat with people whom others called sinners (Luke 5:29-39, 19:5-7). In keeping with His woes on the well-fed, Jesus said that if one selfishly indulges in large meals now,

he might miss reclining on Abraham's bosom (Luke 6:25, 16:25). He used a meal to teach whom to invite and how to respond when invited (Luke 14:1-24). The feast in the parable of the prodigal son was a time of great rejoicing (Luke 15:22-32).

To overfed Americans, a banquet might not be exciting; but to the poor of Jesus' day—and to the poor of the world today—the prospect of a banquet has great appeal. The banquet idea is an effective portrayal of what the bliss of the redeemed will be.

And they will come from east and west,
and from north and south, and will recline
at the table in the kingdom of God.
Luke 13:29

Assignments for Lesson 54

Bible   Read Luke 15-20 while referring to the notes below and on pages 302-303.

Student Review   Optional: Answer the questions for Lesson 54.

Notes on Luke 15-20

15—The parables in this chapter are told when tax-gatherers and sinners are coming to Jesus and scribes and Pharisees are complaining about it. All three parables teach that it is only natural to rejoice when something that has been lost is found, whether it be a sheep, a coin, or a person. The attitude of the scribes and Pharisees, then, is unnatural and sinful. Heaven rejoices more over one sinner who repents than over many people who think that they do not need to repent.

The parable of the prodigal son is a wonderful example of storytelling. The younger son (who represents sinners) was completely alienated from his father by his own attitude. He would be just as happy if his father were dead, since people usually receive an inheritance when someone dies. The kind father gave him his share (probably one-third, since the elder son usually got a double portion), and the younger son promptly blew it. He could not have fallen any lower in Jewish eyes: feeding pigs in a foreign land. Finally, in the depths, he came to himself. He was willing to go humbly to his father and accept the position of a hired man, far below the level of a son and even lower than a slave. The father rejoiced when his son returned, and he spared no expense in celebrating his son's homecoming.

The older son (who represents the Pharisees) was angry at the father's acceptance of his younger son. The older son had always worked hard in his father's house, not realizing the blessings that were there. His eyes were on himself, not his father or his brother. The older brother is not even willing to call the younger son his brother: "this son of yours," he says (Luke 15:30). The father refers to the prodigal as what he is: "this brother of yours" (verse 32). The older brother needed to accept the love of his father and the repentance of his younger brother to free himself from a bondage of his own making and to see God's marvelous grace.

16:1-13—The parable of the unrighteous steward has mystified many students of the Bible. Jesus seems to be praising a scoundrel for monkeying with the books. It is, however, another example of light-and-heavy teaching: if an unjust steward can realize what to do with money to give himself a softer landing once he has been dismissed, how much more should sons of the kingdom of God use the things of this world to prepare for eternity, since we know that one day we will be dismissed from this life? We are not to serve wealth; we are to use the wealth we have to serve God.

Complaining Pharisee
Matthias Grünewald (German, c. 1511)

16:14-31—The Pharisees tried to amass wealth and serve the Lord, but they had redefined service to make it fit what they wanted to do. They needed to listen to God's Word to learn His real expectations for them. The story of the rich man and Lazarus has been the subject of much debate. Some see it as merely a parable, while others see it as a glimpse into the afterlife. It is effective just as a parable, but it does appear to convey something of what happens after death. The punch line of the story is the last verse: if people are not willing to listen to Scripture, they will not be convinced even by a resurrection. The Pharisees' failing was not that God did not give them enough evidence; it was that they refused to listen to what God had put before them.

17:1-10—We should not do things that cause us to be stumbling blocks to others. Instead, we should help people come back to God when they have sinned. To do this requires greater faith, which the apostles recognized. Jesus says that faith does accomplish great things. Being a servant of God requires great faith. It shows faith to work hard for the Lord and then to say (and believe), "I am an unworthy slave; I have only done my duty"; but that is the attitude we should have. .

17:20-21—This brief encounter teaches the surprising nature of the kingdom. It does not come with fanfare or with obvious external signs. Instead, the kingdom of God is within you (or perhaps "in your midst," within a small circle of relationships). The kingdom of God is not a geographic territory with Jesus sitting upon a literal throne. The kingdom of God is where God is King, and that has to happen in the hearts of individuals.

18:1-8—God's justice and action are not in question. The only question is whether we will have faith to live for Him.

18:31-34—Jesus predicted His suffering and death several times to His disciples, but they did not understand what he was saying. His words were so different from what they expected that His predictions did not fit their preconceived ideas.

We should not try to fit Jesus' words into our preconceptions, but instead we should adjust our thinking to fit the truth of Jesus.

18:35-43—The incident that showed a blind beggar's faith must have made a big impression on the followers of Jesus, since it is told in Matthew and Mark also.

19:1-10—Zacchaeus was a Jew who had left his roots. The coming of Jesus convicted him of his wrongs and led him to change his ways. Jesus said that this embodied what His coming was all about.

19:11-27—A day of reckoning is coming for all, whether they accept or reject Jesus' authority. Verse 14 parallels an actual historic event. When Herod's son Archelaus received a portion of his father's kingdom, he had to go to Rome to be endorsed. A delegation of Jews followed him there to ask that he not be given power because they disliked him so.

19:29-48—Jesus' entry into Jerusalem begins the dramatic days leading up to His crucifixion.

20:1-8—The chief priests and scribes were not willing to admit that John's authority was from God, so they would not agree that Jesus' authority was from God.

20:9-18—God would reject the people whom He had left in charge of His vineyard (Israel) because they rejected His Son. That Son, the stone they rejected, would become the cornerstone and would crush those who opposed Him.

20:19-26—Paying taxes to Rome was a hot issue in that day. Some said paying taxes to Caesar showed disloyalty to God. Roman coins, with their image of Caesar, seemed to some to violate the commandment against graven images. Apparently a denarius was readily available, so Roman coins were in use. The coins bore the image of Caesar, so they belonged to him. People bear the image of God, so we belong to Him.

Zacchaeus, *Niels Larsen Stevns (Danish, 1913)*

20:27-38—The Sadducees did not believe in life after death. They tried to trap Jesus with a ridiculous example to show that life after death was an absurd idea. Jesus explained that life after death was not like this life (the Pharisees thought that it generally was). The quotation from God in the burning bush said, "I am (present tense) the God of Abraham, Isaac, and Jacob." God was still their God long after they had died physically. Using the exact wording of Scripture, Jesus showed that the resurrection is real.

20:41-44—Everyone assumed that the Christ (the Messiah) would be a descendant of David. This would appear to make Him inferior to His physical ancestor. However, in Psalm 110, which was recognized as a prophecy of the Messiah, David called the Messiah his Lord. How could a descendant, someone physically inferior, be David's superior as Lord? The only possible answer was that the Christ was alive as the Son of God before David lived. Jesus, the pre-existent Christ come to earth as the son (descendant) of David, was the only person who could fulfill this prophecy and this role.

View of Jerusalem from the Mount of Olives

Lesson 55 - Bible Study

Jerusalem

At various times in history, certain places have had a powerful hold on the minds and hearts of people. Just mentioning the name of a place to a certain group has often been able to arouse deep emotions.

When Rome was locked in a bitter struggle for power with Carthage, Roman political leader Cato often ended his speeches with the phrase, "Carthage must be destroyed!" The city of Mecca is dear to the hearts of Muslims. The site of the Battle of the Boyne in Ireland, where English Protestants defeated Irish Catholics in 1690, is remembered there over three hundred years later.

Few places have held as strong a hold on as many people for as long as has the city of Jerusalem. For thousands of years it has been revered and fought over. It stands as a symbol for millions of people. Although the symbolic meaning is different for different people, the feelings are deep for all of them.

Of the four gospel accounts, Luke conveys this meaning of Jerusalem in the ministry of Jesus most clearly. Luke has thirty-one references to Jerusalem, either by name or by clear indication. It is the only gospel that begins and ends in Jerusalem (in fact, the narrative begins and ends in the temple: Luke 1:8-9 and 24:52-53). In the story of Jesus as presented by Luke, Jerusalem holds great meaning.

Historical Background

Jerusalem sits on an elevated site. It is a good location for a capital and a military stronghold. Archaeological evidence indicates that the place was inhabited long before the Israelites came. David's first capital was Hebron, but after he captured Jerusalem from the Jebusites, it became his capital (2 Samuel 5:6-12). Because of the mercy that God showed to David, it was the location where the great temple was built (2 Chronicles 3:1). Isaiah 52:1 refers to it as the holy city. Its name means city of peace (the *salem* ending is related to the Hebrew word for peace, *shalom*).

However, this city on a hill became the leading symbol for Israel's rebellion against God and its dependence on idols, which were usually worshiped on high places. As the prophet Micah expressed it:

What is the rebellion of Jacob?
Is it not Samaria?
What is the high place of Judah?
Is it not Jerusalem? (Micah 1:5)

Because of its sin, Jerusalem was invaded and conquered by the Babylonians in 586 BC. For about seventy years the city sat devastated. Then the returning Jews rebuilt the wall and the temple, and the city once more became the capital of God's people. However, it was still officially under foreign domination. It continued to be under the thumb of whatever foreign power happened to hold sway in the region (except for the brief period of the Maccabees; see Lesson 51). In Jesus' day, it was part of the Roman Empire. Jerusalem remained captive. It was not free, and the Jews longed for it to be so.

The Redemption of Jerusalem

When Joseph and Mary came to Jerusalem to complete the ritual of purification, the devout old man Simeon was "looking for the consolation of Israel" (Luke 2:25); that is, the person who would console and comfort Israel and bring peace. On that same occasion, Anna is said to have talked about Jesus "to all those who were looking for the redemption of Jerusalem" (Luke 2:38).

If Jerusalem were redeemed or set free, then all Israel would be set free. Jerusalem held the key to what happened to God's people. Jerusalem did need to be redeemed, but not from the Romans. It needed to be set free from sin and to be the light of God's redemption from sin for the whole world.

This is why Jesus had to be there. Only Luke records the scene when Jesus was twelve and became separated from Joseph and Mary. When they found

This 1581 stylized map by Heinrich Bünting places Jerusalem at the center of the world.

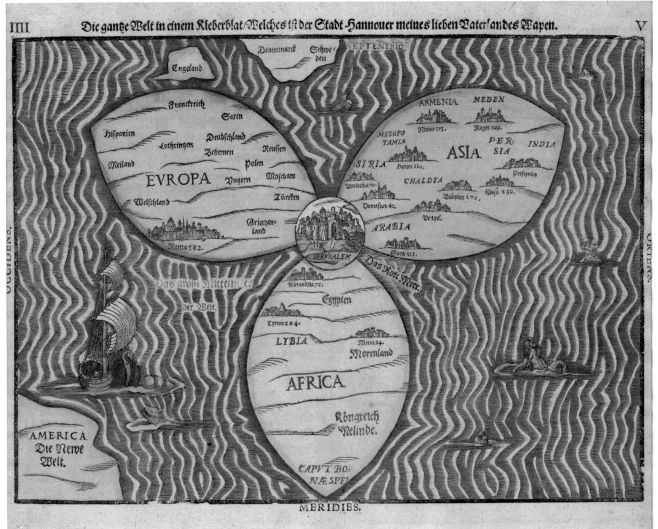

He Wept Over It *(Based on Luke 19:41-44), Enrique Simonet (Spanish, 1892)*

him, Jesus said, "Did you not know that I had to be in the things of My Father?" (Luke 2:49, literal translation). This has been translated "in My Father's house" or "about My Father's business." Either way we understand the wording, Jesus knew that he had to be devoted to God's mission for Him.

God's mission for Jesus involved difficulty, however. In Matthew, the temptations of Jesus in the wilderness are listed in the order of bread, temple, and kingdoms. In Luke, the last two are switched (Luke 4:1-12). Jesus' ultimate temptation took place in Jerusalem; there He faced His greatest test.

Heading for Jerusalem

Jesus' destiny in Jerusalem cast a long shadow over His later ministry. On the Mount of Transfiguration, Jesus discussed with Moses and Elijah His coming departure (or exodus), "which He was about to accomplish at Jerusalem" (Luke 9:31). A short time later, Jesus "was determined to go to Jerusalem" (Luke 9:51). The Samaritans who lived in the village that he and His disciples passed through did not receive them "because He was traveling toward Jerusalem" (Luke 9:53). The simple meaning of this rejection was that Jesus and His disciples were Jewish; but the more profound reason might have been that Jesus was committed to following God even at the cost of His own life. The Samaritans were not willing to recognize that level of commitment.

Despite threats against Him, Jesus was determined to continue His journey to the holy city because "it cannot be that a prophet would perish outside of Jerusalem" (Luke 13:33). In other words, over and over again Jerusalem was the site of the showdown between God's way and the world's way. Yet Jesus' love for Jerusalem was still great. His touching lament expresses His longing that the people of the city would come to Him in faith despite their rejection of Him (Luke 13:34-35).

Luke 19:28 says that Jesus was going ahead, "going up to Jerusalem." Since Jerusalem is situated on a hill, one always ascends when going there. In a symbolic sense, Jesus was ascending to fulfill His destiny on this journey. After His resurrection, Jesus would ascend to heaven from near Jerusalem.

In the City

Jesus knew how the Jews honored the city of Jerusalem and the temple in it, but He had to predict its coming destruction (Luke 21:5-6). In His explanation that followed, Jesus said that Jerusalem would be "surrounded by armies" (Luke 21:20). This must have been a shocking and unnerving prediction to hear. His listeners would not have expected to hear the Messiah predict the destruction of Jerusalem. The physical Jerusalem would be destroyed, but Jesus would nevertheless accomplish its redemption.

The story of Jesus' ministry culminated dramatically in Jerusalem. Observing the Passover in the city was a goal for many Jews. The population of the city would swell several times its normal size each year at the time of the feast. This year, adding to the constant tension of the desire among many Jews to see a revolt against the Romans was Jesus' triumphant entry into the city as the crowds cheered. What would the amazing Teacher do in this setting?

The confrontation was not just Jesus versus the Jewish leaders or even the Messiah versus the Romans. It was nothing less than the Son of God

These broken stones, excavated in Jerusalem, are believed to be remnants of the destroyed temple.

versus Satan. After the devil confronted Jesus in the wilderness at the beginning of His ministry, Luke told us that the devil "left Him until an opportune time" (Luke 4:13). Now, Luke tells us that Satan "entered into Judas," who was one of the twelve (Luke 22:3), with the result that Judas agreed to turn Jesus over to the authorities.

Following the Passover meal with His disciples, Jesus went to the Garden of Gethsemane on the

As Jesus predicted, Jerusalem was destroyed by the Romans in 70 AD after an attempted Jewish rebellion against Roman authority. The Western Wall is considered to be a remnant of the wall around the courtyard of the temple in Jerusalem. Known in Arabic as el-Mabka (Place of Weeping), it has become known in English as the Wailing Wall. Hundreds of thousands of people visit the wall each year to pray.

Mount of Olives and engaged in anguished prayer. There Judas betrayed Him to the soldiers, who led Him away to the house of the high priest. While Peter watched from the courtyard, he denied three times that he knew Jesus, just as Jesus had predicted that he would do and just as Peter had vehemently denied that he would ever do. Luke tells us that, after Peter denied Jesus for the third time, Jesus looked directly at him. Peter then went out and wept bitterly (Luke 23:54-62).

During the hearings that took place through the night and into the daylight hours, Jesus was subjected to unbelievable physical abuse and terrible injustice. The crowds that had cheered his entrance into Jerusalem just a few days earlier now turned on Him and demanded his execution. Pilate condemned Jesus to death by crucifixion.

An innocent man, Simon of Cyrene, was forced to carry the cross for Jesus, in a miniature portrait of the innocent Jesus carrying the cross for the sake of the world. The daughters of Jerusalem wept and mourned for Jesus as He made His way to the cross. Jesus tenderly admonished them to weep not for Him but for themselves as they faced their own tragedy in the years ahead (Luke 23:27-31).

Jerusalem Is Redeemed!

Then came the cross. Only Luke tells us of Jesus' amazing prayer for God to forgive those who were putting Him to death. Only Luke tells us of the gripping interchange between the thieves being crucified on either side of Jesus, the desperate plea by one of them for Jesus to remember him, and Jesus' compassionate promise that the convicted man would be with Him that day in Paradise (Luke 23:33-43).

When Jesus died on the cross, He carried the burden and penalty of the sins of the world—the sins of His executioners, the sins of Judas, the sins of the Jews, the sins of the Romans, the sins of you and me, and the sins of all mankind. Justice was done as God used the injustice of the cross to offer redemption to all mankind.

The Messiah did not change the political condition of Jerusalem. However, He dramatically changed the spiritual prospects for the people of Jerusalem and of the world. Jerusalem was indeed redeemed, not from the Romans but from sin. Its inhabitants were set free not by the Zealots' military victory but by Jesus' death.

God confirmed who Jesus was and all that He had claimed to be by raising Him from the dead. Jesus appeared to His followers in several settings. Then the Lord gave to His apostles their new marching orders. The good news of Jesus, calling for repentance and forgiveness in His name, was to be proclaimed to all nations "beginning from Jerusalem" (Luke 24:47). It was too small a matter for only Jerusalem to be redeemed; Jesus' death and resurrection made eternal redemption available to the entire world. The symbol of spiritual rebellion had become the starting point for the story of spiritual victory. Following Jesus' ascension, His followers joyfully returned to the city, praised God in the temple, and waited for "power from on high" to clothe them (Luke 24:49). The book of Acts will tell us the thrilling story of how this message of redemption would be taken to the world, beginning from Jerusalem.

But the Jerusalem above is free;
she is our mother.
Galatians 4:26

The Last Supper, *Hanna Varghese (Malaysian, 2007)*

Assignments for Lesson 55

Bible   Read Luke 21-24 while referring to the notes on the next page.

Recite or write Luke 11:9-10 from memory.

In Their Words   Read "The Watchman" by Lucy Maud Montgomery (pages 74-75).

Project   Complete your project for the unit.

Student Review   Optional: Answer the questions for Lesson 55 and take the quiz for Unit 11.

Notes on Luke 21-24

21—Jesus here predicts the coming persecution of believers, the fall of Jerusalem in 70 AD (see 21:20-24), and (at some undetermined point in the future), the coming of the Son of Man. The fall of Jerusalem would take place within the lifetime of some who heard Jesus, which it did (verse 32). His point was to be prepared for whatever might happen (verses 34-36).

22:1-22—The Jewish Passover meal had come to include several elements in a prescribed order, including several times when the cup was shared. This is why Luke mentions two cups. Jesus redefines the bread and the second cup mentioned into the Lord's Supper. Moving beyond the Passover meal that remembered Israel's deliverance from slavery in Egypt through the death of a lamb, Jesus gives His followers a simple meal to remember our deliverance from slavery to sin through the death of the Lamb.

22:23-30—Jesus' prediction that one would betray Him led to an argument among the Twelve as to who would do it and who was the greatest and would never do it. Jesus taught them that they were not to be defensive but servants instead.

22:31-34—Jesus says that Satan had demanded to sift them all (plural you, verse 31), but He had prayed especially for Simon Peter (singular you, verse 32) that he would strengthen his brethren after he recovered from his failing. Peter declared that he would never fail Jesus, but Jesus knew the truth.

22:35-38—Jesus had tried to show them that they could always trust Him, but their faith was still not what it should have been. Jesus says here that if they still want to acquire swords and stand for Jesus as a political Messiah, now was the time to do it. Even with all of their noisy talk about a political revolution, they only had two swords. Jesus said that would be all they would need.

22:47-53—In the dark of night, without a clear knowledge of Jesus' appearance, the arresting soldiers would need some indication of who Jesus was. Judas provided this identification with a kiss, the customary

This limestone block, called the Pilate Stone, was discovered in 1961 in Caesarea. The fragmentary inscription on it refers to Pontius Pilate as prefect of Judea. This confirms the Biblical account of his position and authority over the trial of Jesus.

greeting of love. This shows the perversity of his betrayal. Peter struck a blow to defend the Lord, but Jesus called a halt to the political revolution in His name after one sword thrust.

23:26—It could be that the convicted person only carried the cross-piece and not the upright part of the cross.

23:44—The Jews reckoned twelve hours of daylight in every day (John 11:9). In some seasons of the year, the hours were longer than in other seasons. The sixth hour would correspond to our noon, the ninth hour to our 3:00 p.m.

24:13-35—Only Luke records the story involving the two whom Jesus met on the road to Emmaus.

24:36-43—The disciples were startled by Jesus' appearance among them. Jesus asked for something to eat to prove that He was not a ghost because, as everyone knows, ghosts don't eat.

24:44-47—Jesus tied to Scripture His life, death, and resurrection and the proclamation of the good news to the world.

12

The Church Age

Summary

This unit looks at how Jesus continued to change the world through the church, as recorded in the book of Acts. We will examine how the church began, the significance of the conversion of Cornelius, the life of the great apostle Paul, and what Acts tells us about everyday life in the first century Mediterranean world. The Bible study is an exercise in how to study a New Testament letter.

Lessons

56 - The Church Begins
57 - Key Event: The Conversion of Cornelius
58 - Key Person: Paul
59 - Everyday Life: The First Century Mediterranean World
60 - Bible Study: How to Study a New Testament Letter

Manuscript Illustration of The Seven Churches of Asia Minor (English, c. 1260)

Memory Work

Learn Acts 2:42-44 by the end of the unit.

Books Used

The Bible
In Their Words

Project (choose one)

1) Write 300 to 500 words on one of the following topics:

- Write about one of the paintings that appears in this unit. What is the painter's style? How did his time period and nationality influence the way he painted? What is the painter trying to say in this work?

- Write about the life of a famous Christian preacher from history.

2) Perform an act of service for your church. Discuss with your parents and church staff what an appropriate job would be. Perhaps you could clean and organize the church library, refresh a flower bed, or paint a Sunday School classroom.

3) Write a poem or song of at least sixteen lines that expresses one or more of the truths that Paul communicates in his letters.

Home in Dura-Europos, Syria, Converted for Use as a Church Meeting Place (c. 250 AD)

Lesson 56

The Church Begins

"These that have turned the world upside down are come hither also." (Acts 17:6b, KJV)

The remark was not meant as a compliment. The Jews of Thessalonica were complaining to city officials about Paul and his traveling companions because of the commotion they had caused after preaching the gospel there. Although it was a complaint, the statement was ironically true. The first generation of believers literally did turn the world upside down with the gospel of Jesus.

Never before had people gone out in such numbers to try to convert others to their religious beliefs. Conquerors had imposed their religion on the vanquished, and many philosophers had promoted their ideas; but the message of the church was something new. These who called themselves followers of the Way were committed to living a new kind of life because One had died and had risen again on their behalf. They believed that they had learned an important truth about the One Almighty God, truth that they felt compelled to tell others. The disciples believed that God had provided the answer to man's universal need: salvation from the consequences of their sins and a firm expectation of blessing after this life ends. This conviction led them to turn the world upside down.

Empowered Witnesses

Before Jesus ascended into heaven following the resurrection, He told His disciples that they would be empowered by the Holy Spirit to be His witnesses in Jerusalem, Judea, Samaria, and the remotest part of the earth (Acts 1:8). This verse gives an outline of how the gospel spreads in the book of Acts. The gospel was first proclaimed in Jerusalem, and by the end of the book some thirty years later the message had been told to citizens of three continents and was being preached in the capital of the Roman Empire.

The coming of the Holy Spirit and the beginning of the church on the Day of Pentecost was an event of international significance. Jews living in Jerusalem had come "from every nation under heaven" (Acts 2:5). Luke lists many of the nations to show the vast reach of the gospel even on the first day it was proclaimed (Acts 2:9-11). Through the miracle of the Holy Spirit, these men of many nations heard the gospel preached in their own languages (Acts 2:8, 11). Pentecost was thus a reversal of the Tower of Babel. At Babel, men's languages were confused; and people who were saying different things drifted apart across the globe because of sin. On Pentecost,

313

people were brought together by the one message of salvation that was spoken in many languages.

Peter proclaimed the resurrected Christ and the way of salvation in Him for the first time that day. Three thousand responded. They were baptized for the forgiveness of their sins and received the gift of the Holy Spirit (Acts 2:14-41). These new disciples sensed that a radical change had come over their lives and that they were part of a movement from God. They devoted themselves to further teaching by the apostles, to the fellowship of believers that gave them great encouragement, to the breaking of bread together (probably a reference to meals, a part of which was the Lord's Supper), and to being a people dedicated to prayer (Acts 2:42).

Persecution and Praise

As the band of disciples continued to grow, the healing of a lame man at the temple attracted the

attention of the Jewish authorities. They arrested Peter and John and demanded an explanation. A few weeks earlier Peter had denied even knowing Jesus, but on this occasion he boldly proclaimed his faith in the risen Lord (Acts 4:8-12). The Jewish leaders realized that these were some of the men who had been with Jesus. They ordered the apostles not to teach in His name, but the followers of Christ would not be stopped (Acts 4:13-31).

The congregation of disciples assembled at the temple from time to time, probably to hear the apostles' teaching and to see what might happen next. They also gathered in small groups in homes for fellowship and meals as well as additional teaching (Acts 2:46). Purpose-built structures for their assemblies (i.e., church buildings) were not thought of, desired, or even possible. The life of the fellowship was not tied to buildings. Instead, it permeated their daily lives in a natural way.

The church developed a life with two main aspects. First, within the fellowship, the believers were "of one heart and soul" (Acts 4:32). They shared what they had with other believers who were in need. This was a remarkable result of their faith in Jesus. It was different from the pagan world's separation of religion and lifestyle, and it was a much more vibrant faith than was practiced by the Jews. The believers received encouragement and

This 12th-century icon from the country of Georgia depicts the coming of the Holy Spirit on Pentecost. Pentecost was the Greek name for the Jewish Feast of Weeks. It came fifty days after Passover and celebrated the end of the wheat harvest (Leviticus 23:15-16). At least some of those who were present for the day's miraculous events might have come for Passover and remained through Pentecost. All of the people present for the event were Jews, even though they had come from many nations. They were part of the Dispersion of the Jews throughout the world, and many of them probably took the gospel back to their homelands. The visitors from Rome, for instance (Acts 2:10), might have started the church in that important city.

practical assistance from this arrangement and were greatly blessed.

The second aspect of their lives in Christ was their relationship with the world. Here they often encountered opposition, sometimes violent. The Jewish leaders felt threatened by the disciples' newfound faith. Rather than investigating the validity of the Christians' claims, the Jewish leaders sought to intimidate the believers into silence. The church found strength to endure the persecution as they remembered the words of Jesus. They rejoiced to be able to suffer for Him (Acts 4:27-31, 5:41-42).

As with any endeavor that involves humans, the church had problems. Difficulties developed when people inside the fellowship started acting like those who were outside the fellowship. Ananias and Sapphira wanted to appear more generous than they really were, and they paid the supreme price for lying to the Holy Spirit (Acts 5:1-11). Hellenistic Jewish Christians (those from outside of Palestine) complained about the Jewish Christians from Judea because widows in the former group were being overlooked when food was given out daily by those in the latter group. The problem might have been a result of the Judeans' insensitivity toward those not like them. The apostles solved the problem by having the fellowship name seven godly, responsible men to oversee the distribution of food (Acts 6:1-6).

Building Bridges to Other Groups

God brought about the next major change in the life of the church by bringing good out of bad, as He often does. Members of a synagogue composed of former slaves from other countries (synagogues were often organized by some special interest) falsely accused Stephen of blasphemy, which led to his being taken before the Sanhedrin for a hearing. In his defense, Stephen accused the Jews of being hardhearted against the will of God, as Israelites had been many times in the past.

The Death of Ananaias, *Raphael (Italian, 1515)*

In response, the Jews stoned him to death in a mob execution witnessed and approved of by the young Saul of Tarsus (Acts 7:1-8:1). This event opened the door for the Jews to begin a broader persecution of the disciples. All Christians except the apostles scattered throughout Judea and Samaria. As the believers went, they told others about the Savior (Acts 8:1-4).

Philip bridged a great cultural gap when he shared the good news with Samaritans, who had long been outcasts in the minds of most Jews. When the apostles in Jerusalem heard of this development, they sent Peter and John to confirm what had happened and to enable the Samaritan believers to receive the Holy Spirit (Acts 8:4-17). The gospel was beginning to spread to other groups besides Jews. The persecution that arose following the death of Stephen was God's nudge to the church to take the gospel to other places besides Jerusalem.

Another ethnic wall was hurdled when Philip taught and baptized an Ethiopian court official who was returning home from worshiping in Jerusalem. The official was Jewish, but he might have been a proselyte (a Gentile who had converted to Judaism). In any event, now a man from outside of Palestine had become a disciple of Jesus (Acts 8:26-40).

The conversion of Saul (also called Paul) prepared the way for the great expansion of the gospel into the Gentile world. God said that Paul was His "chosen instrument" to take the message of Jesus to the Gentiles (Acts 9:15). However, Peter made the first proclamation of the gospel to Gentiles, when he spoke to Cornelius and his household (Acts 10). This event was so significant that it merited over a full chapter in the narrative of Acts.

The conversion of Cornelius closed another huge cultural gap, since prejudice between Jews and Gentiles was strong in both directions. Jews were prejudiced against Gentiles because the Jews saw themselves as God's special and favored people and the Gentiles as unclean, rejected sinners. Gentiles were prejudiced against Jews because the Jews were exclusive and kept to themselves and did not go along with much that Gentiles did, including the worship of just about any god they heard about.

The great missionary expansion of the church originated not in Jerusalem but in Antioch of Syria, where many Gentiles had been converted to Christ. The fellowship in Jerusalem sent the encourager Barnabas to Antioch to see what had happened. Barnabas knew that Saul would be a good man to work in Antioch, so the encourager brought Saul to Antioch, where the Lord worked powerfully through both of them. In Antioch the disciples were first called Christians (Acts 11:20-26). Being

---

The Herods

Four generations of the Herod family are mentioned in the New Testament. Herod the Great was ruling when Jesus was born. His son, Herod Antipas, had John the Baptist beheaded and interviewed Jesus during His trials (Luke 23:7-12). Herod Agrippa I, a grandson of Herod the Great and nephew of Antipas, had James

killed (Acts 12:2). His son, Herod Agrippa II, heard Paul's defense in Acts 26. All of the Herods ruled in the region of Palestine but only with the permission of Rome.

Coin Issued by Herod Agrippa I

---

called a Christ-person was probably not meant as a compliment by those who first used it, but the tag stuck (as often happens when such labels are applied to people). The term Christian is only used three times in the Bible (see also Acts 26:28 and 1 Peter 4:16), but it has become the most common term used to describe those who follow Jesus.

The Pattern of Church Life

Typically, a congregation of believers was established in a city by the preaching of the gospel. Those who became Christians met regularly to give praise to God, receive encouragement from the fellowship, and listen to the teaching of an apostle or an evangelist such as Timothy or Titus. Elders were appointed as pastors over the local flock (Acts 14:23, 20:17; Titus 1:5). Since the groups met in houses, elders might have overseen several house fellowships in the same city. The Christians probably met several times during the week, but on the first day of the week they came together to break bread, that is, to share a fellowship meal including an observance of the Lord's Supper as they worshiped and studied together (Acts 20:7).

Early on, the church established a pattern for helping others. The sharing of goods in Jerusalem was noted earlier. Christians in Antioch sent a contribution to believers in Judea to help them through a time of famine (Acts 11:27-30). Paul took up a collection for poor saints in Jerusalem on his third missionary journey (1 Corinthians 16:1-3, Romans 15:25-27). These collections helped connect Gentile Christians and Jewish Christians.

Christians were aware of their potential influence on people of the world. Jesus wanted His followers to live in such a way that others would glorify God because of them (Matthew 5:16). He also said that people would be able to identify His disciples by their love for one another and by the fruit they bore in their lives (John 13:35, 15:8). In the New Testament, "saint" does not mean someone who is unusally righteous or who performs miracles.

The catacombs on the Greek island of Milos might predate the catacombs of Rome. They were initially used as a burial site for Christians and later for worship and refuge.

It refers to any believer, any Christian. The word literally means "holy one," indicating a person whom God declared to be holy through His grace.

Paul urged Christians to live wisely among outsiders and to "redeem the time" by doing what was right. Their speech was to be "seasoned with salt," filled with good and not given to evil (Colossians 4:5-6). Peter urged his readers to have a ready defense for their actions for anyone who asked them, but to do so with gentleness (1 Peter 3:15).

Not everyone was expected to be an evangelist. An evangelist was a role given by God to particular people for the proclamation of the gospel (Ephesians 4:11). An evangelist also had a teaching role within the church (Ephesians 4:12, 2 Timothy 4:5). All Christians were, however, to be aware of their influence and to live and speak in such a way that would draw people to the Savior. Any Christian could have a teaching role (Acts 18:26, Hebrews 5:12).

From the Gaza Road in old Philistine territory to Damascus and Antioch in Syria, in cities all across Asia Minor including the small town of Colossae and the major urban center of Ephesus, throughout the peninsula of Greece to Illyricum (near present-day Bosnia), and even in the capital city of the mighty Roman Empire, good news was proclaimed about a crucified Jew who rose from the dead and was the unique Son of God. Not only Jewish leaders in Jerusalem but also some officials of the Roman Empire felt threatened by this grassroots religious movement. Some people believed the message and their lives were changed. Even those who rejected the message were impacted by it. The message of the gospel, intended to have international significance from its first proclamation, has continued to change the world two thousand years later as no other idea, philosophy, or force has ever done.

*God was in Christ reconciling the world to Himself,
not counting their trespasses against them,
and He has committed to us the word of reconciliation.
2 Corinthians 5:19*

Assignments for Lesson 56

Bible Read Acts 1-8 while referring to the notes on the next page.

Student Review Optional: Answer the questions for Lesson 56.

Notes on Acts 1-8

1:1-3—This introduction, with its reference to Theophilus and "the first account," connects Acts to the same author as the one who wrote the Gospel of Luke. The first book told "about all that Jesus began to do and teach" (verse 1) while He was on earth. This book tells about what Jesus continued to do in the church through the presence of the Spirit.

The Ascension of Jesus
Andrei Rublev (Russian, 1408)

1:4-11—The disciples still do not quite understand about the kingdom. They were expecting some kind of earthly, political restoration of Israel's power and status.

1:12-14—The early church was devoted to prayer.

1:15-26— Matthias fills the place of Judas among the Twelve. When James is killed later (Acts 12:2), his place is not filled. Acts does not teach the practice of apostolic succession.

2—Peter says that what Joel described was being fulfilled on that occasion.

4:12—The apostles make an exclusive claim for the gospel. It is never presented as only one of many ways to heaven.

7—Peter's sermons as well as this one given by Stephen tie the story of Old Testament Israel to what was happening among them at that time. The church saw itself as the fulfillment of God's plan for Israel and claimed to be the Israel of God (Galatians 6:16).

8:32-39—The official was reading from Isaiah 53 about the Suffering Servant of God. Philip takes that text and teaches Jesus. The official's response of faith is to want to be baptized. The pattern in the book of Acts was for those who came to faith to be baptized (the literal meaning of the Greek word means immersion).

Ruins at Caesarea

The Conversion of Cornelius

Peter was a dedicated Jew. During the ministry of Jesus he stood up for what he believed to be the way of the Messiah. When Peter became a follower of Jesus, he devoted himself to being a dedicated disciple. He risked ridicule, beatings, imprisonment, and even death to stand up for the Savior who had called him. However dedicated a person might be, though, God can still nudge him to a greater understanding and a higher level of service. This is what happened to Peter in the encounter he had with a Gentile named Cornelius. What God taught Peter in this incident had a profound effect on the nature and growth of the church.

When Jesus told the apostles to go preach to every nation, they probably thought He meant for them to go preach to Jews in every nation. They could not imagine God accepting Gentiles, whom they considered unclean sinners. God had a different idea, however; and He opened the eyes and hearts of Jewish Christians through the faith of a Roman military man.

The God-Fearing Centurion

Caesarea was on the Mediterranean coast about thirty-five miles north of Joppa. It was a Roman city, built to strengthen the army's position in Palestine. Cornelius was stationed there as a centurion. Centurions were the backbone of the Roman army. The rank had the function of a captain. The one hundred men under his command were expected to move quickly to any point of danger. The skill and flexibility of these troops was one reason that the Roman army was as effective as it was.

Cornelius was a God-fearer. This meant that he believed in YHWH as the one true God, but he had not submitted to circumcision and become a full Jewish proselyte. He was devout, prayerful, and generous to the Jewish people. Because of his

Vision of Cornelius the Centurion
Gerbrand van den Eeckhout (Dutch, 1664)

faith, an angel appeared to Cornelius in a vision and told him to summon Peter from the town of Joppa, which he did (Acts 10:1-8).

The next day, Peter was praying when he fell into a trance. He saw a large sheet lowered toward the earth that was full of animals which were unclean in terms of the Law. Peter heard a voice say, "Get up, Peter, kill and eat"; but he could not imagine doing such a thing. Peter was devoted to God and would never eat anything that God had declared unclean. The voice from heaven replied with foreshadowing significance, "What God has cleansed, no longer consider unholy." This vision appeared three times to Peter (Acts 10:9-16).

Just then, the messengers from Cornelius the Gentile arrived where Peter was staying. The Holy Spirit prompted Peter to receive them and to hear their request. The next day, Peter returned with them to Caesarea. When he entered Cornelius's home, the centurion fell at his feet and worshiped him. Cornelius believed in God, but he also believed in the possibility of divine visitors in the form of humans. Peter protested this treatment and said he was only a man (Acts 10:17-27). The apostle noted that in terms of Jewish practice he should not be there. Jews considered it wrong to enter the home of a Gentile. But Peter knew that God was teaching him something, so he had come without protest. Cornelius explained what had happened to him and said that they were all waiting to hear what Peter had to say (Acts 10:28-33).

Peter was beginning to see the point that God was making. God does not play favorites, he realized. Any person in any nation who fears God is welcome to come to Him. The message of Jesus was a message of peace, not of hostility among differing groups. Peter summarized the story of the gospel and then told how God had called him and the other apostles to tell people about Jesus, who is the Judge of all and who is the Savior of all who believe in Him (Acts 10:34-43). Then God nudged Peter and the other Jewish Christians who were present. God poured the Holy Spirit upon Cornelius and the other listeners

Woodcut illustration of Peter's vision
Julius Schnorr von Carolsfeld (German, c. 1853)

even as Peter was speaking. Having seen this proof of God's acceptance of them, Peter knew that no one could refuse to have these Gentiles baptized into Christ (Acts 10:44-48). Without God's nudge of the Holy Spirit being poured out, Peter might have wondered if he should baptize the Gentiles.

Opposition in Jerusalem

When Peter returned to Jerusalem a few days later, he met stiff opposition from Jewish Christians. "You went to uncircumcised men and ate with them!" they charged. Peter recounted what had happened, making it clear that it was God's decision, not his. They withdrew their opposition, saying, "Well then, God has granted to the Gentiles also the repentance that leads to life" (Acts 11:1-18). It was clear that God had put the welcome mat in front of the doorway to the kingdom for all people, not just for Jews.

The eyes of Jewish Christians had been opened, but they still did not completely understand God's plan. When disciples were scattered from Jerusalem after the death of Stephen, Hellenistic Jewish Christians from the island of Cyprus and from Cyrene (the area of Libya in northern Africa) caught the vision more readily than Jewish Christians from Judea. They preached the gospel to Gentiles—not just Jews—in Antioch (Acts 11:19-21).

Jewish Christians from Jerusalem were not satisfied. They went to Antioch and said that men had to be circumcised in order to become Christians (Acts 15:1). In other words, they believed that people had to become Jews first in order to become Christians. These Jewish disciples had always obeyed the Law as the word of God and they saw no reason to quit doing so now. In their minds, Jesus simply completed what God had previously done through the Law, so obeying the Law should still be a requirement for everyone who wanted to please God.

The Christians in Antioch decided to send Barnabas, Paul, and others to Jerusalem to talk the matter over with the apostles and elders in the church there. At the meeting, Peter, Barnabas, and Paul reported what God had been doing through them in reaching out to Gentiles. To them it was not a matter for men to decide since God had already made His decision. Under the leadership of James, the Lord's brother, the leaders of the church in Jerusalem decided to send a letter to the Christians in Antioch, Syria, and Cilicia encouraging them and saying that "it seemed good to the Holy Spirit and to us" for them to avoid certain sinful practices that were closely associated with pagan idolatry.

The Significance of the Decision

The decision to accept uncircumcised Gentiles into the fellowship recognized what God was saying about Gentiles. In addition, it prevented the church from becoming merely a Jewish sect whose members followed their rabbi Jesus while other sects followed other teachers and rabbis. It also meant that the church was not to be segregated into Jewish congregations and Gentile congregations. This would not have presented a positive message to the world, where separation by ethnicity was—and still is—a common practice.

Herod the Great established the city of Caesarea before the time of Christ. He authorized the construction of a harbor and the theater pictured below.

Relations between Jewish Christians and Gentile Christians was one of the major issues in the early church. The decision reached in Jerusalem in Acts 15 did not prevent conflict from arising repeatedly. Paul's letters to the Romans and to the Ephesians deal with it directly, and the influence of Judaizing teachers was an issue in Galatia and Colossae as well. Even Spirit-renewed people can have a hard time giving up old prejudices, but God had clearly revealed His will and His goal for the fellowship He had created. The more that Christians followed His will in this matter, the stronger the fellowship was and the stronger the church's testimony to the world was that the way of Jesus was indeed revolutionary.

For He Himself is our peace, who made both groups into one and broke down the barrier of the dividing wall.
Ephesians 2:14

Assignments for Lesson 57

Bible Read Acts 9-15 while referring to the notes on this page and the next.

Student Review Optional: Answer the questions for Lesson 57.

Notes on Acts 9-15

Acts 9:1-30—As Saul is going to Damascus to arrest Christians, he is arrested by the Lord. His conversion is complete, and he immediately begins proclaiming the faith that he had been attacking. Also immediately he begins to face opposition, something that would be a regular part of his life. Barnabas the encourager again takes up his cause and helps him to be accepted among the disciples in Jerusalem.

Acts 9:31-41—Peter performs miracles that were similar to what Jesus had done. Paul also later heals people and even raises someone from the dead (Acts 20:9-10)

Acts 12—The positive response that Herod received from the Jews concerning his execution of James emboldens him to have Peter arrested. Perhaps Herod wants to win the favor of the Jews, and he thought that Christians were expendable. Peter enjoys a miraculous escape from prison which even surprises the disciples who were praying for him! Luke relates how God later punished Herod for his arrogance.

Acts 13:1-13—God calls Barnabas and Saul to their work as missionaries. Their journey takes them first to Cyprus (Barnabas' home territory) and then to south-central Asia Minor, not far from Paul's home of Tarsus. Verse 9 makes the transition of referring to Saul by his Roman name of Paul.

Acts 13:14-52—Paul's sermon in the synagogue of Antioch in Pisidia illustrates the custom of synagogues giving visitors a chance to speak. The message recorded here is probably an example

The Liberation of St. Peter
Hendrik van Steenwijck II (Dutch, 1619)

had come to earth. Paul clarifies their identity and preaches a short sermon in which he does not use many Old Testament references but instead speaks of God in a way that relates to Gentile minds.

Acts 14:19-28—The missionary journey ends with Paul and Barnabas revisiting the churches they had begun and appointing elders from place to place. This first journey probably took two or three years.

Acts 15:36-41—Paul and Barnabas discuss revisiting the Christians in the cities they had visited on their first journey. However, they have a sharp disagreement over whether or not they should take John Mark with them. John Mark left them during the first journey and went home to Jerusalem (Acts 13:13), so Paul does not want to take him along again. Barnabas the encourager believes in John Mark's potential and wants to give him another chance.

Paul and Barnabas part ways here, an unfortunate end to what had been a good working relationship. Much later in his life, Paul recognized that John Mark had proved himself to be useful (2 Timothy 4:11). Paul almost always had other men with him, not only to help him but also so they could learn ministry on the job, in much the same way that Jesus had taught the Twelve.

of what Paul usually said when he preached an evangelistic sermon in a synagogue. He uses many references to the Old Testament and ties God's work and revelation to Jesus. Because of the opposition of some Jews, Paul and Barnabas begin teaching Gentiles. This chapter also begins referring to the team as "Paul and Barnabas," instead of the other way around, because Paul begins to take the leading role in the work.

Acts 14:8-18—After healing a man at Lystra, Paul and Barnabas are worshiped as Greek gods who

Lesson 58 - Key Person

Paul

Tarsus was a large inland city in southeastern Asia Minor involved in agriculture and trade. It became the chief city of Cilicia, a Roman province, and featured a major university. Here, perhaps five to ten years after the birth of Christ, was born a Roman citizen named Saul.

He was circumcised on the eighth day, the first step on his journey as a strict Pharisee. He had at least one sister, and circumstantial evidence suggests that his family had some prominence. He grew up in Jerusalem, learning at the feet of Gamaliel, one of the wisest and most respected teachers of the law. There as a young man Saul had contact with the new movement called The Way.

A Persecutor

As a well-trained Jew, Saul was confident in his faith. He was zealous and blameless before the Law. His conscience motivated him to oppose the church, which he considered to be a threat. He gave hearty approval to the stoning of Stephen, which initiated Saul's persecution of the church.

Saul ravaged the church, entering house after house, and dragging men and women to prison. He realized later that he was a blasphemer and a persecutor and a violent man (1 Timothy 1:13),

but at the time he believed that his murderous threats against the disciples were justified. He obtained letters from the high priest to continue his persecutions in Damascus.

He was nearing Damascus with his companions when a light from heaven flashed around him. He fell to the ground and heard a voice saying, "Saul, Saul, why are you persecuting Me?" It was the voice of Jesus, who instructed him to enter the city and learn what he must do. Saul arose unable to see, and those with him led him by the hand into Damascus. He arrived at the house of Judas on the street called Straight.

After three days of blindness and fasting, the Lord sent the disciple Ananias to Saul. Ananias knew what Saul had done in Jerusalem and what he had planned to do in Damascus, so he was fearful at first. The Lord assured him that He had chosen Saul to be His instrument.

After Ananias laid his hands on Saul, something like scales fell from his eyes. Saul regained his physical sight and also gained a new spiritual view as he was baptized. Immediately he began proclaiming in the synagogues that Jesus was the Son of God. After many days, some Jews decided to get rid of him. He escaped in a basket through the city wall and began his new life as an itinerant preacher.

325

Conversion on the Way to Damascus
Caravaggio (Italian, c. 1601)

A Preacher

Saul's first task was to overcome his reputation. The disciples in Jerusalem were afraid to associate with him. Barnabas proved himself to be an encourager once again by speaking up for Saul's sincere change of heart. Saul drew the ire of the opposing Jews, and the believers sent him back to his home town of Tarsus. There he spent a few years, perhaps, until Barnabas found him and brought him to Antioch. Together they ministered in that city, where the disciples were first called Christians. The church in Antioch took up a collection for the needy brethren in Judea, and they entrusted it to Barnabas and Saul.

Saul was evidently in Jerusalem when Herod killed James and imprisoned Peter. Saul well knew the dangers that faced followers of The Way. However, opposition could not stop the spread of the gospel, and Saul (henceforth Paul) became one of its strongest advocates.

Paul took a series of missionary journeys around the Mediterranean. He spoke in synagogues, where some Jews accepted his message, while others frequently opposed him. He spoke to government officials, to the high-brow men of Athens, to a group of women by the river, and to a jailer's household.

Truly this messenger learned how much he had to suffer for the sake of the Lord's name as he faced imprisonment, torture, and death. From the Jews he received a whipping of thirty-nine lashes five times. He was beaten three times with rods, stoned once, shipwrecked three times, and spent a day and a night in the deep. In his many journeys he faced perils crossing rivers, perils from robbers, perils from Jews and Gentiles, perils in the city and country, perils at sea, and perils from false brothers. Added to all this, he had his constant concern for the churches (2 Corinthians 11:24-28).

The Holy Spirit used Paul to write a large portion of the New Testament. He wrote letters to individuals and to congregations, giving instruction, chastisement, or encouragement as needed. He spoke of "some things hard to understand, which the untaught and unstable distort, as they do also the rest of the Scriptures" (2 Peter 3:16), but his overall message was clear: "It is a trustworthy statement, deserving full acceptance, that Christ Jesus came into the world to save sinners, among whom I am foremost of all" (1 Timothy 1:15).

His Final Years

Paul went to Jerusalem prepared not only to be bound but even to die for his Lord. Jews from Asia Minor stirred up the crowd to lay hands on him. They accused him of preaching against the Law and the temple and of bringing Gentiles into the temple.

The Roman commander rushed to Paul's assistance. Paul spoke to the crowd, but they began to cry out against him again. Paul spoke to the Sanhedrin, but they broke into great contention. Paul spoke before the Roman governors Felix and Festus and before King Agrippa and his wife Bernice. As a Roman citizen, Paul appealed his case to Caesar; and he was sent to Rome according to the Lord's plan (Acts 23:11).

Paul spent two years under house arrest in Rome but he saw his imprisonment as a blessing. His situation encouraged others to preach more boldly. The whole praetorian guard knew about his situation, and even members of Caesar's household came to faith through Paul or through other believers in Rome (Philippians 1:13, 4:22). Paul might have been released after this imprisonment, as is suggested by his letter to the Philippians (1:21-26, 2:24).

However, he knew what was coming to him eventually: "For I am already being poured out as a drink offering, and the time of my departure has come. I have fought the good fight, I have finished the course, I have kept the faith; in the future there is laid up for me the crown of righteousness, which the Lord, the righteous Judge, will award to me on that day; and not only to me, but also to all who have loved his appearing" (2 Timothy 4:6-8).

Saint Paul Writing His Epistles *(French, c. 1620). The artist is likely Valentin de Boulogne.*

"But may it never be that I would boast, except in the cross
of our Lord Jesus Christ, through which the world
has been crucified to me, and I to the world."
Galatians 6:14

Assignments for Lesson 58

Bible   Read Acts 16-21 while referring to the notes below and on pages 329-330.

Student Review   Optional: Answer the questions for Lesson 58.

Notes on Acts 16-21

Acts 16:1-5—Paul meets Timothy and adds him to his entourage. Paul has Timothy circumcised to avoid conflict with Jews in the region, who would object to Paul traveling with an uncircumcised man. Paul does not believe that circumcision is necessary for salvation, but he wants to eliminate any potential sources of conflict for the spreading of the gospel.

Acts 16:6-10—How the Holy Spirit forbids them from going to Bithynia is not stated. Paul receives a vision of a Macedonian calling to him. In response, he leaves Asia Minor and goes to the peninsula of Greece.

Acts 16:11-40—The regular participation of ten men was necessary to have a Jewish synagogue. Since this number was not present at Philippi, Paul goes to a place where the Jews who were there might gather for prayer. There he meets a God-fearing Gentile businesswoman, Lydia, herself away from home. Lydia and her household obey the gospel.

The masters of a slave girl possessed by a spirit of divination profited from her prophesying. The girl follows Paul and his party, announcing (accurately) their mission; but her doing so annoys Paul, who casts the spirit out of her. The girl's masters realize

Timothy and His Grandmother
Rembrandt (Dutch, 1648)

their lost source of revenue and stir up the crowd and the chief magistrates. Paul and Silas are beaten and thrown into jail.

While they are singing hymns at midnight to their captive audience, an earthquake opens the jail doors and loosens the chains from the prisoners. The jailer thinks that suicide is more honorable than facing the charge of losing all of his prisoners. He is about to take his own life when Paul stops him. None of the prisoners escape. The jailer is overcome with gratitude and, sensing that Paul has something he does not, begs the apostle to know what he has to do to be saved. Paul teaches and baptizes him and his household, and the jailer becomes Paul's host.

The next day, the chief magistrates order Paul to be released. However, Paul knows that his rights as a Roman citizen have been violated by the beating he received the day before. The chief magistrates are afraid that news of their mistake might get back to Rome, so they beg Paul and his party to leave town.

In his narrative, Luke uses the pronoun "we" up to this point, but at 17:1 he says "they." Many speculate that Luke stayed behind in Philippi until the "we" narrative picks up again at Acts 20:5, when Paul passes back through Philippi.

Acts 17:1-15—Though some Jews in Thessalonica believe Paul's message, most of the Jews reject it with violence. The Jews in Berea, by contrast, are more noble, since they are willing to study the Scriptures to determine the truth of Paul's message. Paul leaves Berea and goes to Athens, that city of learning and philosophy. His message before the Areopagus is intended to speak to the Greeks where they are spiritually and intellectually about the reality of God and His Son, Jesus Christ. The response is less than overwhelming, so Paul leaves Athens and goes to Corinth.

Acts 18:1-17—In Corinth, Paul meets Aquila and Priscilla, Jewish Christians who had been expelled from Rome when Claudius ordered all Jews to leave the city (see Lesson 62 for a more complete explanation). Paul works as a tentmaker to support himself until Silas and Timothy join him from

Apostle St. Paul, *El Greco (Spanish, c. 1612)*

Macedonia, probably with a gift of support from the Christians in that region. Then Paul is able to work full-time preaching the gospel. The response to Paul's preaching in Corinth is much more positive than it had been in Athens. The Lord encourages Paul with a vision, assuring him that many people will come to faith in Corinth; so Paul stays there for eighteen months. His stay is brought to an end when the Jews rise up against Paul and bring him before the proconsul. Gallio is not interested in what he sees as nitpicking religious differences, so he dismisses the case.

Paul then travels to Jerusalem and Antioch, ending his second missionary journey. Meanwhile, back in Ephesus, Apollos begins preaching about Jesus accurately. However, since he only knows about John's baptism, Priscilla and Aquila take him aside and privately teach him the more complete truth. The disciples encourage Apollos to go to Corinth because he teaches the gospel effectively and powerfully.

Acts 19:1-41—Beginning his third missionary journey, Paul spends considerable time in Ephesus. His visit there starts with an encounter with twelve men who were similar to Apollos. They are disciples, but they only know about John's baptism. Paul teaches them more completely and baptizes them in the name of Jesus so they can receive the Holy Spirit.

Paul teaches in the synagogue for three months; but when he meets with opposition, he moves to the school of Tyrannus. He teaches there for two years, probably in the afternoons after Tyrannus finished his teaching. God accomplishes amazing things through Paul while he is in Ephesus. Verse 19 mentions magicians burning their valuable books. These were probably copies of a collection of chants and incantations that were well-known at the time. Paul purposes in his heart to see Rome, but little did he know how he would get there.

The Temple of Artemis at Ephesus is considered one of the Seven Wonders of the Ancient World. Goths destroyed it in 268 AD. Many of the ruins were used for other building projects, including columns that were used in the Hagia Sophia Church in Constantinople in the sixth century. The site of the temple near modern Selçuk, Turkey, was rediscovered in 1869. A single column was reassembled from fragments found there.

While Paul is in Ephesus, a great disturbance arises when Demetrius the silversmith sees the response Paul is getting. Demetrius fears that Paul's preaching will cut into his business of selling little statues of Artemis, patron goddess of Ephesus. Demetrius incites the other silversmiths to stage a protest against Paul, which escalates into a riot in the theater, an arena that could seat up to 25,000 people. The "image which fell down from heaven" (verse 35) was either a meteorite fragment considered to be sacred, or a refrerence to a myth about the image of Artemis. The town clerk dismisses the assembly as bordering on illegal.

Acts 20:1-16—At Troas, the Christians gather on the first day of the week to break bread (probably a meal with the Lord's Supper, which was their custom). Paul gives a long sermon, and Eutychus falls out of the third story window. Paul raises him back to life, and the assembly continued.

Since Paul is hurrying to Jerusalem for Pentecost, he invites the elders in Ephesus to meet him at Miletus. He reviews his work there and warns them of dangers to come within the fellowship. Ephesus was a major city in the Roman Empire, and many passages in the New Testament refer to it.

Acts 21:1-26—Paul arrives in Jerusalem to find that Jewish Christians there are strongly opposed to Paul's ministry because they misunderstand what he is teaching. James and the elders encourage Paul to demonstrate his faithfulness to the Law by paying the vows of some other Jewish believers. At the temple, however, Jews from Asia Minor stir up the crowd against Paul, thinking he had brought an uncircumcised man into the temple. The Roman cohort takes Paul into custody, rescuing him from the beating the Jews were giving him. The Roman commander allows Paul to address the crowd.

Lesson 59 - Everyday Life

The First Century Mediterranean World

Acts tells how faith in Jesus spread from Jerusalem throughout the Roman Empire. The story of Acts involves many cultures, including Jewish, Roman, Greek, Asian, and African. This reflects the active interchange of ideas and cultures that characterized the Mediterranean world at the time. Because it is an accurate account, and because Christianity impacted people in real life, the Biblical narrative tells us a great deal about everyday life in the places described. Rome had conquered most of the regions mentioned in Acts, so Roman customs and government permeate the book. However, since Rome allowed the peoples it conquered to keep their customs, religions, and governing authorities, these practices are evident throughout the book as well.

Jewish Practices

The Temple in Jerusalem was a cornerstone of Jewish life. The first converts to the way of Christ continued going to the temple on a daily basis, as they had been accustomed to doing (Acts 2:46; all Scripture references in this lesson are from Acts). Peter and John went up to the temple at the ninth hour (3:00 p.m.), which was an hour of prayer (3:1; the designated hours of prayer were early morning, the time of the morning sacrifice, afternoon, the time of the evening sacrifice, and sunset). Peter gave his second recorded sermon in the area of the temple complex known as the portico of Solomon, which ran along the east side of the outer court of the temple (3:11-26; see also 5:12).

The Book of Acts mentions several Jewish feasts. The Holy Spirit came upon the apostles on the Day of Pentecost (2:1-4). Herod had Peter arrested during the Days of Unleavened Bread and wanted to present him before the people after Passover (12:3-4). Officially Passover was one day and the Feast of Unleavened Bread was the week immediately following; but often the entire period was simply called Passover, as it is here. Peter's arrest must have reminded him of the Passover when Jesus was arrested. During the third missionary journey, Paul and Luke sailed from Philippi after the days of Unleavened Bread (20:6). Paul hurried because he wanted if possible to be in Jerusalem on the Day of Pentecost (20:16).

For centuries Jews had been meeting in synagogues on the Sabbath. Perhaps as many as one hundred synagogues met in Jerusalem in the first century. The early missionaries took advantage of opportunities to speak in the synagogues. Luke mentions synagogues in Israel (6:9-12), Syria (9:19-

22), Cyprus (13:5), Turkey (13:14-15, 18:19-21), and Greece (17:1-18:8). One of the striking features of the early church was the change that Sabbath-observing Jewish Christians made when they started meeting on the first day of the week (20:7).

The Jewish practice of circumcising males was a major issue in the early church. A controversy arose regarding whether the practice would be mandatory for new Christians, and a meeting in Jerusalem discussed the matter (chapter 15). Paul circumcised Timothy because of the Jews in the area around Lystra (16:3). James and the elders in Jerusalem told Paul about the thousands of believing Jews who had heard that Paul was telling the Jews among the Gentiles not to circumcise their children (21:17-21).

It was a common Jewish practice to have a Hebrew name and a Greek name, perhaps to be able to get along in both cultures. Joseph was called Barsabbas and also called Justus (1:23). Peter raised from the dead a woman named Tabitha, which is Dorcas in Greek (9:36-42). Simon was called Peter (10:5). The name of the Jewish false prophet Bar-Jesus is translated Elymas (13:6-8). Saul was also known as Paul (13:9). Judas was called Barsabbas (15:22).

Though Jerusalem was under Roman rule, the Romans allowed Jewish leaders to handle issues related to their religion. But the Jews were divided among themselves. The Sadducees and the Pharisees were the two main groups. The Sadducees didn't believe in resurrection, angels, or spirits while the Pharisees did. The Pharisees were known as the strictest sect in the Jewish religion. The stoning of Stephen (chapter 7) was technically illegal, since the Jews had to have permission from the Romans to execute someone.

Roman Authorities

Luke always used the appropriate titles of officials in the places he is describing, which is another evidence of his accuracy and inspiration. Paul was a Roman citizen by birth, which provided him valuable legal protections when he encountered various officials. Citizenship could be purchased (22:28); but Paul had been born a citizen, which meant that his father had been a citizen.

Like modern armies, the Roman army had various ranks. Cornelius (10:1) and Julius (27:1) were centurions (*hekantarchos*), in command of about one hundred men, while Claudias Lysias, who came to Paul's aid in Jerusalem (21:32, 23:26), was a chiliarch (*chiliarchos*), over about 1,000 men.

Cities and regions had various levels of officials also. Sergius Paulus was a proconsul (*anthupatos*) on the island of Cyprus (13:7), and Gallio was a proconsul in Achaia (18:12). In Philippi, the chief magistrates (*stratagos*) had Paul and Silas beaten with rods and thrown into prison. They were under the watch of the jailer (*desmophulax*). The city also had policemen or constables (*rhabdouchos*).

Paul had friends in Ephesus among the chiefs of Asia (*asiarches*), a group of prominent citizens who oversaw public festivals (19:31). The town clerk (*grammateus*) of the city helped to disperse the rioters. Felix and Festus held the position of governor (*hegemon*, 23:26 and 26:30), while Agrippa was a king (*basileus*, 25:13) under the Romans.

The ruins of this synagogue in Kfar Bar'am, Israel, date from the 200s AD.

The Roman Army and Chariot Experience (RACE) is based in the ancient Roman city of Gerasa (modern Jerash, Jordan). Daily performances reenact Roman military tactics (shown above), gladiator fights, and chariot races.

Language

Greek was the language that unified the Roman Empire. As the international language of commerce and diplomacy, it helped spread the message of Jesus. Many people in the time of Acts were able to speak in more than one language. People knew their local or ethnic language and often knew Greek as well. Latin was the official language of the Roman Empire, so it was also widely known.

When Paul spoke to the commander of the Roman cohort in Jerusalem, the commander asked if Paul knew Greek. Paul spoke to the crowd in the Hebrew dialect (probably Aramaic, 21:37-40). When Paul spoke to King Agrippa, he said that

when he saw the great light, Jesus had spoken to him in the Hebrew dialect (26:14).

Pagan Worship

Throughout Paul's missionary journeys, he found people who were religious. However, they worshiped in error. Paul did not have to convince people of the reality of the spiritual world. Instead, he had to teach people the truth about the spiritual world.

In Lystra, when the crowds saw that a man lame from his mother's womb had been healed, they began to say that the gods had become like men and come down to them. They said that Barnabas was

Zeus, and Paul was Hermes because Paul was the main speaker. The priest of Zeus brought oxen and garlands to the gates of the city and wanted to offer sacrifice. Barnabas and Paul stopped them, saying that they were men, too. The evangelists said the people should turn from those vain things to the living God, whom they then described. Still, they had a hard time keeping the crowds from offering sacrifice to them.

After being shipwrecked on the way to Rome, Paul, the other passengers, and the crew swam or floated to the island of Malta. It was cold, so Paul gathered a bundle of sticks for the fire. A viper came out and fastened to his hand. The natives thought he would swell up or die. When he didn't, they said he was a god (28:1-6).

The story of Paul's mission work in Acts begins and ends with him being taken for a god. What Paul wanted to do, of course, was convince people of the reality of the one true God.

Sorcery and Magic

The practice of sorcery was another false approach to spirituality that was common in the first century world. A magician named Simon lived in

St. Paul Before the Proconsul
Raphael (Italian, 1515)

Paul and Barnabas at Lystra
Nicolaes Pieterszoon Berchem (Dutch, 1650)

Samaria and so impressed the people that they called him the "Great Power of God." Simon believed and was baptized after hearing the preaching of Philip. He wanted to buy the ability to give the Holy Spirit to people. Peter reprimanded Simon and told him to repent and pray for forgiveness (8:9-24).

In Paphos on the island of Cyprus, Saul and Barnabas found a magician, a Jewish false prophet named Bar-Jesus. He opposed Saul and Barnabas and tried to turn the proconsul away from believing. Saul called the magician a son of the devil and an enemy of all righteousness. The Lord made him blind for a time. The proconsul believed, being amazed at the teaching of the Lord (13:1-12).

A slave girl in Philippi had a spirit of divination and did fortune-telling for her masters (16:16-40). Many of the converts in Ephesus burned their books of magic after they became Christians (19:18-19).

Travel in Acts

Traveling from one place to another is a major theme in Acts. Paul's evangelistic strategy focused on preaching in the larger cities of the empire. These included Rome, Athens, Corinth, Ephesus, Philippi, and Thessalonica. He also preached in leading provincial cities, such as Antioch and Iconium in Pisidia (in modern Turkey).

The extensive Roman road system enabled relatively easy movement by foot (20:13) and on horseback (23:24). The Mediterranean Sea provided rapid access to all of the major ports in southern Europe, western Asia, and northern Africa. Paul and his companions spent a good deal of time on ships.

Luke provides extensive detail about Paul's last journey recorded in Acts. Roman soldiers accompanied Paul and other prisoners by ship. They encountered a tremendous storm, and Luke describes efforts by the crew to preserve the ship and its passengers using cables, anchors, sounding devices, and rudders. The ship finally wrecked on the island of Malta. After three months on the island, they were able to board another ship bound for Italy. Luke observes that ship had the Twin Brothers (Castor and Pollux) for a figurehead.

St. Paul's Bay, Malta, is the traditional location of the shipwreck described in Acts.

Conclusion

The Book of Acts confirms that Jesus came at the right time and place. The cultural and political environment of the first century Mediterranean region provided fertile ground for the church to take root and begin to spread across the world. God works through big and small events and famous and not-so-famous people to accomplish his purposes.

*And the disciples were continually filled
with joy and with the Holy Spirit.
Acts 13:52*

Assignments for Lesson 59

Bible Read Acts 22-28 while referring to the notes on the next two pages.

In Their Words Read the excerpt from "A Death in the Desert" (pages 76-77).

Student Review Optional: Answer the questions for Lesson 59.

Notes on Acts 22-28

Acts 22:1-30—Paul recounts the story of his conversion, explaining that he was a faithful Jew whom God called to tell the Gentiles about the Messiah. The crowd is not convinced, however, and the Roman commander is confused. The commander orders Paul to be beaten to extract some sort of explanation. His plan is stopped when Paul tells him that he is a Roman citizen. Citizens were exempt from such treatment. Still looking for an explanation, the commander orders the Sanhedrin to meet the next day to hear Paul.

Acts 23:1-11—Paul begins his defense before the Sanhedrin by proclaiming his innocence. After this remark the high priest orders him struck on the mouth. This is in violation of the law, which Paul notes with words of condemnation. Paul might not have known who wanted him struck because of bad eyesight.

Paul then tries to divide the opposition by speaking about the resurrection. At this the Sadducees and Pharisees begin arguing among themselves over the doctrine of the resurrection. The Roman commander fears for Paul's life and withdraws him to the Roman barracks. The Lord speaks to Paul in the night, assuring him that he will preach in Rome.

The Apostle Paul Explains the Faith
Vasily Surikov (Russian, 1875)

Acts 23:12-35—Some Jews take an oath not to eat until they kill Paul. This plot against his life is reported to the Romans by Paul's nephew. The commander makes arrangements for Paul to be taken to Caesarea under heavy guard and for his Jewish accusers to lodge their charges there before the governor. The Roman governor usually resided in Caesarea. Pontius Pilate had been in Jerusalem only because of the special event of the Passover at the time of Jesus' crucifixion.

Acts 24:1-27—The Jewish leaders make their case before Felix the governor. The address of Tertullus the attorney is in the form used by anyone speaking before the governor. Paul proclaims his innocence and states that he had gone to Jerusalem in peace and for good purposes but had been falsely accused by Jews from Asia Minor (the Romans called the province Asia). Felix keeps Paul in loose custody. Once when Paul was speaking to him, Felix became frightened (probably convicted but not willing to change). Felix also hopes that Paul will pay him a bribe to be released. Paul remains in jail in Caesarea for two years. Felix is replaced by Festus, and Paul's imprisonment continues.

Acts 25:1-12—The new governor Festus, while visiting Jerusalem, hears the charges against Paul. The Jewish leaders want Paul brought to Jerusalem because they hope to kill him in ambush along the way. Festus responds by ordering the Jews to bring their charges in Caesarea. Festus asks Paul if he would be willing to go to Jerusalem to face the charges. Paul replies by appealing to Caesar, a legal maneuver which any citizen could use. Festus has no choice but to remand him to Caesar in Rome.

Lesson 59 - Everyday Life: The First Century Mediterranean World

The Appian Way was an ancient Roman road connecting Rome with southeastern Italy. The portion pictured is in the town of Minturno. Paul probably walked along this stretch of road on his journey to Rome.

Acts 25:13-27—King Agrippa makes a courtesy visit to Festus. Festus explains the situation to him, and Agrippa says that he would like to hear Paul speak on the matter.

Acts 26:1-32—In Paul's defense before Agrippa, the apostle again tells the story of his conversion. When Paul starts talking about the Lord and his resurrection, Festus cries out that Paul is going mad. Paul defends his sanity and appeals to Agrippa. The king replies that Paul must be hoping to convert him. Later, Agrippa and Festus agree that Paul has done nothing worthy of any legal punishment. Agrippa comments that Paul might have been able to go free if he had not appealed to Caesar.

Acts 27:1-28:15—Regular passenger ships did not sail the Mediterranean, so the Roman officials must find a ship going in the right direction. This is another "we" passage, indicating Luke is with Paul.

The description of the journey has been confirmed by Bible scholars and navigators as accurate in every detail. How comforting it must have been to meet brethren at Puteoli when the harrowing journey was over (Acts 28:14)!

Acts 28:16-31—Paul asks to meet with Jews in the city (Claudius had died by this time, and his edict banishing Jews from the city had thus expired). The Jews have not heard about Paul, but they have heard of the movement of Christ-followers. Paul later makes a presentation to a large group of Jews.

Some believe, while others do not. Paul tells them that they are doing just what Isaiah had prophesied. Since they reject Paul's message, he will take the gospel to the Gentiles. The book ends with Paul under a form of house arrest, awaiting trial, and able to receive visitors and preach freely about the kingdom of God.

The Ministry of the Apostles
Fyodor Zubov (Russian, 1660)

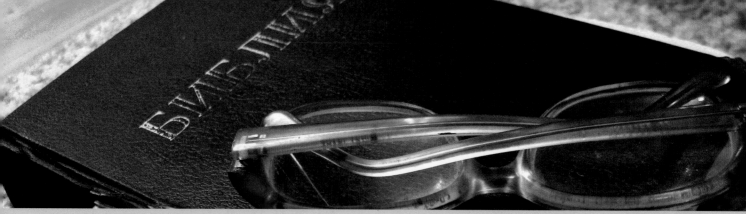

Russian Bible

How to Study a New Testament Letter

People have used many different methods of studying the Bible. They range from the pious devotional approach ("How does this verse speak to you, brother?") to picking and choosing phrases as proof texts for what a person wants to do. Many people have looked at the Bible as a treasury of single verses (perhaps because of the way the King James Version is printed) without paying much attention to the context.

The best way to read the Bible might sound surprising: read it the way it was written! The Bible was written in books, with each book to be considered as a whole unit. The books were written to specific people as the primary audience and secondarily to us. When we read the Bible this way, its vitality and meaning are even more powerful.

In order to read and understand a book of the Bible the way it was written, we need to keep a few things in mind:

1. We have to consider the context of an entire book and the verses in the book. We need to know when, by whom, and to whom a book was written. We need to understand the overall message of a book to grasp the significance of an individual verse.

2. We need to understand the author's original, inspired intent and how the book's first audience would have understood his meaning. A passage cannot mean now what it could not have meant when it was written.

3. Scripture is the best interpreter of Scripture. We can gain understanding of a difficult passage by seeing what related passages have to say. We should let passages that are relatively clearer help us understand passages that are relatively more obscure.

4. We must remember that our interpreting Scripture is not the first step. The first step is that the Bible interprets us. It challenges and convicts us and reveals much about ourselves and God. If we take it as God's Word, we should assume that it has meaning for us unless there is clear evidence in the text that it has only a limited application to others.

Reading a New Testament Letter

Greek letters had a typical form and function in the first century, just as letters today have a typical structure. The typical letter in Paul's day had a formal greeting, an introductory section that raised the matter at hand, the body of the letter that discussed the matter, a summary, then the closing greetings and a farewell. When we look at Paul's letters in this light, we can see this structure (somewhat adapted in a few cases) and thus can identify Paul's main point in the letter. What Paul mentions at the first and the last of a letter is often what he is writing about.

Two key elements in understanding Paul's message are: (1) considering what specific issues he addresses and then what general ideas he writes, and (2) identifying repeated themes, words, or ideas. Paul did not write in a vacuum, nor did he decide to write a treatise on a subject just because he had been thinking about it. Paul's letters addressed real situations in churches, usually involving a problem that needed to be confronted. Someone has said that if the early churches didn't have any problems we wouldn't have any of Paul's letters (or any of the other letters in the New Testament for that matter).

After we have studied a letter carefully and drawn some conclusions about what it is saying, then we can go to the commentaries to get some other ideas. Commentaries are helpful and have been written by people who have studied the Bible carefully; but commentaries sometimes use previously written commentaries, and commentators can develop traditions that are passed on from one book and one generation to another. Don't let someone else do your thinking and Bible study for you! You will gain new insights and the Word will be powerful for your life if you dig out its meaning as best you can for yourself first.

An Overview of Philippians

For this lesson we will study Paul's letter to the Philippians as an example of how to study a Pauline letter. Read through the book now. Make notes on specific issues that Paul addresses and look for repeated themes and ideas.

Paul addresses the letter to the saints in Christ Jesus at Philippi and specifically mentions the elders and deacons (1:1). Apparently his message was something he wanted the elders and deacons to note especially. The apostle expresses great love and thanks for the Christians in Philippi. He cares about them very much. Paul prays for the Philippians in 1:9-11. If we note Paul's opening prayer in a letter, we get another clue about his main point. He prays that they be filled with knowledge and discernment (1:9) and that their lives be filled with the fruit of righteousness (1:11).

These plates of metal type were used to print the Bible in the Maori language in New Zealand in the 1800s.

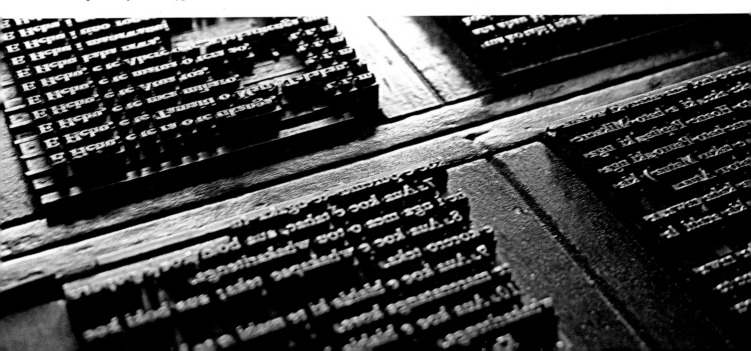

Reading the Bible in Lalibela, Ethiopia

The apostle mentions that he is in prison (1:13) and describes how good has come from this difficult situation. He is confident about the future as well (1:19-26). Paul's first instruction to the Philippians is that they live worthy of the gospel, so that they will be unified and will be able to withstand persecution (1:27-30).

Chapter two begins with an appeal for unity of mind and heart by looking out for what is best for others. He then uses the example of Jesus, who had this selfless attitude himself (2:1-11). Paul urges them to work out their salvation and to do everything without grumbling or disputing (2:12-18). He hopes to send Timothy and has sent Epaphroditus (probably the carrier of this letter). These men are good examples of selfless concern and service to others (2:19-30).

In chapter three, Paul urges them to rejoice in the Lord, as he has done before (3:1). They do need to be aware of the "dogs" (dangerous people), whom he calls the false circumcision (probably teachers who were insisting that Christians had to be circumcised and obey the Law of Moses; 3:2). Paul had reason to put great confidence in the flesh, but he had given up all of his material and worldly status for Christ (3:3-15). He wants all who are mature to have this same attitude (3:15-16) and urges them to follow his example of faithfulness to Christ (3:17-4:1).

At the first of chapter four, he urges Euodia and Syntyche to "live in harmony in the Lord" (4:2). He asks a comrade to help these women get along since they had done so much for the Lord (4:3). He again urges them to rejoice and turn everything over to God in prayer. If they do so, they will know God's peace of mind (4:4-7). He wants them to think about good and positive things (4:8-9).

Philippians 4:10-19 is a thank-you note for a gift they had sent to him by means of Epaphroditus. He is gracious in his thanks, but he conveys his trust in the Lord to accomplish everything. The apostle closes with greetings and final blessings (4:20-23).

Paul talks about thinking, regarding, knowing, having a particular attitude, and being united in their thinking about thirty times in this short letter. In the original Greek, he uses the noun joy or the verb rejoice a total of fourteen times. You get the idea that Paul is aiming for their heads! He wants them to develop the self-denying attitude of Christ so they can be unified.

Taiwanese Bibles

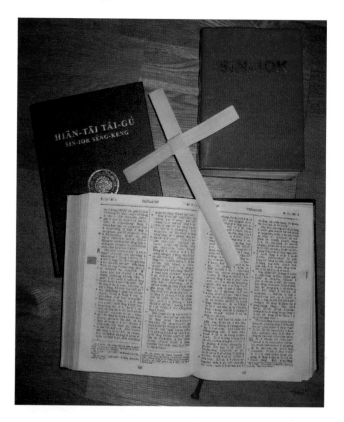

The most specific problem he mentions is the conflict between two women in the congregation who needed to be of one mind. Perhaps their disagreement, coupled with the persecution the church was facing, was causing dissension among the members. Timothy and Epaphroditus, as well as Paul himself, were good examples of the self-denying attitude they needed to have.

We also need to consider any information about Philippi elsewhere in the Bible or from other sources. We discover that Philippi was a major city in the district of Macedonia, in what is now northern Greece. Paul established the church there on his second missionary journey, as described in Acts 16:13-40. Lydia and her household responded to the gospel, but the owners of a slave girl who had a spirit of divination had Paul put in prison when he cast the spirit out of the girl and ruined their business. The Philippian jailer and his household were baptized, and then Paul left the city. As best we can tell, Paul wrote this letter about twelve years later while in a Roman prison.

Conclusions About the Letter

Paul dearly loved the Christians at Philippi. They had sent him a gift while he was in prison, and he had heard about some problems they were having. Two sisters in the Lord were not getting along. They were facing persecution and the danger of false teachers. Some grumbling and dissension were being heard in the congregation. The threat of the world was growing stronger.

The apostle urged his precious brothers and sisters in Philippi to get a good attitude. They needed to rejoice in the Lord and have the positive outlook that Paul did—and he was in prison! They needed to learn from Jesus Himself about the attitude that would cause them to give up everything for others. Paul reminded them that he had given up everything for the Lord. It's hard to keep arguing when you have nothing to defend.

The Christians at Philippi needed to be aware of the threats from the outside. Being joyful and confident about where their lives were headed would lessen the influence of outsiders. Their generosity toward Paul was the kind of selfless giving they needed to practice toward each other. When Euodia and Syntyche started to get along, the rest of the fellowship would be happier also.

So we see that the individual ideas Paul expressed in the letter have an overall context that gives them even more meaning. Paul's description of the mind of Christ, for instance, was the core of his message to them. We have to have the mind of Christ not just in church assemblies on Sunday but in dealing with others all week.

If we can detach ourselves from the things of the world as Paul did, we will find more reason for joy and less reason for argument. The love of Christ and our love for each other, not worldliness and conflict, ought to define us as God's people.

As you study other New Testament letters the way they were written, perhaps this exercise will help you have a deeper appreciation for the powerful lessons waiting for you in God's Word.

U.S. Marine Lance Cpl. Lesley Raulerson reads the Bible during his tour of duty in Iraq.

Have this attitude in yourselves
which was also in Christ Jesus . . . .
Philippians 2:5

Assignments for Lesson 60

Bible   You have already read Philippians.

Recite or write Acts 2:42-44 from memory.

Project   Complete your project for the week.

Student Review   Optional: Answer the questions for Lesson 60 and take the quiz for Unit 12.

13

Changes in Rome and in the Church

Summary

As the Roman Empire declined in power, the influence of the church grew. However, the church that developed changed from the simple fellowship that we read about in the New Testament. As Rome became more Christian, the church became more like a worldly empire. As we look at these changes, we also examine the life of the pivotal figure Constantine. For the Bible study, we look at the power of God's Word.

Lessons

61 - The Decline of Rome

62 - The Way of Christ: Attacked, Then Accepted

63 - Changes in Church Practice

64 - Key Person: Constantine

65 - Bible Study: The Inspiration and Authority of Scripture

The Colosseum of Rome at Night

343

Memory Work	Learn 1 John 2:15-17 by the end of the unit.
Books Used	The Bible *In Their Words* *The Imitation of Christ*

**Project
(choose one)**
	1) Write 300 to 500 words on one of the following topics:
	   • Tell in what ways you think the worldly power of the church was a good thing and how it was a bad thing. What was lost from the nature of the church as recorded in the New Testament?
	   • Write about the life of an early Christian leader, such as Justin Martyr, Origen, Tertullian, Jerome, or Augustine.
	2) Visit services at two churches of denominations other than your own. Discuss with your parents what you noticed about similarities and differences compared to your own church. What did you learn? Was there anything said or done that you found inspiring or troubling? Why?
	3) Make a sculpture in the medium or media of your choice representing one of the longtime symbols of Christianity—the fish, the anchor, or the cross. See Lesson 63.

Literature	

Thomas Hammercken was born around 1380 in the small German town of Kempen (hence his identity of "à Kempis," meaning from Kempen). His father was a blacksmith and his mother ran a small school for young children. When Thomas was twelve, he enrolled in a monastery school. A few years later he became a monk at the monastery in the Netherlands where his older brother served. Thomas spent the rest of his life (except for three years) at that monastery copying manuscripts, preaching, counseling others, and writing books. He died in 1471.

The best-known work by Thomas à Kempis is *The Imitation of Christ*, a collection of devotional meditations which he wrote in Latin about 1427. The book first appeared in an English translation in 1460. Thomas encouraged his readers to devote themselves wholly to God and to find peace by doing so. The book was intended to be read by other monks, but it reflects a deep spiritual understanding that can bless anyone in any walk of life. *The Imitation of Christ* has inspired, comforted, and challenged readers in every generation from the time of its appearing.

The voice of the book is different at different places. Sometimes Thomas speaks to the reader. Sometimes he speaks to the Lord. At other times, he takes the voice of Christ speaking to the reader. The book has a strong Scriptural basis. A few passages reflect specific Catholic doctrines, especially in the last section that deals with partaking of communion. Overall, the book can help you grow in devotion to Christ.

Older translations of *The Imitation of Christ* convey the flavor of the King James Bible, while modern translations render the thoughts in contemporary language. Both have advantages. Read a limited amount each day, and give yourself time to think deeply about its significance for your own life. Meditating on godliness, holiness, and righteousness will help you grow as God's person.

Roman Ruins at Umm Qays, Jordan

The Decline of Rome

Within a century of the Pax Romana and the tenure of one of the last able emperors, Roman government, power, and society began to decline rapidly. In this lesson we will discuss what happened and then analyze how and why it happened.

The Unraveling of Government

One major factor contributing to the decline of Rome was the lack of an orderly process of succession for emperors. Typically, an emperor would declare his son or adopted son to be his chosen successor and the Senate would endorse his choice. This was the precedent that Julius Caesar had set in choosing Octavian (Augustus) to follow him. However, when Marcus Aurelius chose Commodus in 180 AD, the tenuous system broke down. This became the pattern: rival generals competing for the throne with frequent civil wars and assassinations. Between 234 and 284 AD, some twenty-six emperors ruled. Some were in power for only a few months, and all but one were assassinated. Government corruption was widespread, and many citizens lost respect for governmental authority.

In 284 AD, Diocletian was named emperor by his armies. The son of a freed slave, Diocletian was from Illyricum in the Balkans. He instituted reforms to renew the strength of the imperial government, but his autocratic ruling style weakened his reform efforts. The city of Rome was becoming increasingly corrupt while the eastern part of the empire offered greater trade revenue and loyalty to the emperor. Diocletian divided the empire east and west. He established a new capital at Nicomedia, near the Bosporus in northwestern Asia Minor, where he himself ruled as augustus. To govern the west, he named another augustus who answered to him. Each augustus was assisted by a caesar.

Diocletian also reformed the army and instituted a civil service system for government. In an attempt to help the Empire's economic woes, Diocletian imposed wage and price controls. He also issued a decree forbidding people from changing jobs. Neither they nor their children or grandchildren could enter a new profession. This was an attempt to stabilize the economy, but it served to frustrate and discourage the populace.

In his personal life, Diocletian indulged himself in grand and elaborate style. He built a 2,000-room palace, and for official functions he sat on a huge throne beneath an emblem of the sun. The emperor

Foreign Invasions

wore elaborate royal regalia, gold fingernails, and a crown of pearls. Anyone who received an audience with the emperor (a rare occurrence) had to lie flat on the floor. Diocletian tried to create the image of a sacred emperorship. He accepted the title *dominus* (lord), a far cry from Augustus' title of *princeps* (first citizen). Diocletian ordered what became the most intense persecution of Christians in the Empire.

When Diocletian retired because of ill health in 305 AD, another period of instability followed. Constantine emerged victorious in 312 AD. Twelve years later he reunited the empire under his single leadership and built another new capital in the east at Byzantium on the Bosporus. The new city came to be called Constantinople. Constantine built upon the policies of Diocletian, but one major policy shift came in 313 AD when he declared toleration for Christianity in the Edict of Milan. However, the empire was plunged into turmoil once again at Constantine's death.

To the north of Italy lived several tribes of herders and farmers. One group was the Germani, and people in Rome called all of the tribes by this name. Each tribe was led by an elected king, who was assisted by a council of chiefs. The chiefs were chosen because of their bravery in battle, and each chief led a band of warriors.

In the third century, some of these Germanic tribes began to move. Some desired more land for their growing population, while others wanted to take advantage of Rome's wealth and southern Europe's warmer climate. As the tribes began moving into the outer fringes of the Roman Empire, a few confrontations resulted in warfare; other encounters were peaceful.

About 370 AD the dynamics changed. One key factor was the invasion of the Huns from Central Asia. Scholars are not sure what prompted the movement of the Huns into Europe. The reasons might have included population shifts and other issues in China. The Huns defeated the Ostrogoth tribe that lived north of the Black Sea. The Visigoth tribe feared the same fate and appealed to Rome to let it move within its boundaries. Rome agreed but then treated the Visigoths badly.

The Visigoths turned on their hosts and began raiding the empire. In 378 AD they defeated a Roman army and killed the emperor who was on the battlefield. The Visigoths continued to grow in power. They invaded Italy in the early fifth century, while the Vandals (another European tribe) moved through Gaul and then to Spain ahead of the advancing Huns. The tribe of the Franks moved into and settled in Gaul (and thus the area is now called France).

The Cathedral of St. Domnius in Split, Croatia, was built around the preserved mausoleum of Emperor Diocletian, the octagonal structure shown at left. His body was removed when the cathedral was established.

Freezy Boi

The Feast of Attila, *Mór Than (Hungarian, 1870)*

The presence of Germanic tribes affected the politics of the empire. The tribes used their power to extract concessions from the emperor, sometimes in the form of land and tribute. At times they dictated who became emperor. The western emperor began wearing the tunic and pants of the Germans instead of the classic Roman toga. The German tribes respected Roman culture and did not completely annihilate it.

Large Roman landowners generally maintained their considerable wealth, although the Germans demanded large land grants from them. The Germanic attacks usually had a pretext. For instance, in response to what they perceived to be mistreatment by Romans, the Visigoths raided Rome itself in 410. The weakened Roman government could do little to stop the advance of the Germanic forces.

The threat of the Huns increased with the rise to leadership of Attila, called the "Scourge of God" for his fierce practices in war. He led the Huns across the Rhine River into Gaul, but a coalition of Roman and Germanic armies stopped his advance in 451. Attila withdrew and died shortly thereafter. The Huns began to dissipate, some returning to Asia while others merged into the European population. For three-quarters of a century, however, they terrorized Europe and helped bring Rome to its knees.

The Vandals moved from Spain into northern Africa. From the site of Rome's old nemesis Carthage, the Vandals invaded Italy and sacked Rome in 455.

Then in 476, the Germanic chief Odoacer captured Rome. Odoacer declared himself to be king after forcing the puppet emperor, Romulus Augustulus, to resign.

Reasons for the Fall of Rome

Scholars have been fascinated with the rise and fall of Rome for centuries. Several strengths contributed to its rise. The Romans were great builders, as seen in their impressive buildings and roads. The Romans were practical. They were willing to learn and implement technology from other cultures.

The Vandals have a reputation for malicious destruction of property, though they probably did not wreak more havoc than the average army of ancient times. A French bishop coined the term "vandalisme" to describe destruction of art during the French Revolution.

Sack of Rome by the Vandals
Heinrich Leutemann (German, c. 1870)

The flexible republican form of government worked well for a long time, and the structure of the empire maintained peace and control over a wide area and among diverse populations. The Romans believed in themselves and in what they could accomplish. They honored duty and discipline and failed in few of the goals that they set. Geography also contributed to their success. Italy occupies a prominent position in the Mediterranean, and Rome stands at the center of the peninsula.

Many factors contributed to the decline of the Roman Empire, not a few of which had to do with realities of the empire itself. The maintenance of an army large enough to control the vast empire was costly. Any reduction in force left the empire vulnerable. In the later empire, citizens avoided military service, so more mercenaries were hired who had little loyalty to Rome. The later empire saw a swollen urban population in Rome, an increased dependence on slavery, and political corruption.

The empire suffered many economic woes. The Roman economy became dependent on imported luxuries and developed a negative balance of trade. When no new lands were being conquered and taxes on the empire's holdings were lowered, the government suffered a loss of revenue. This, coupled with an ever-increasing desire for state welfare programs, put the government's treasury in a constantly tighter squeeze. Late in the empire, Roman currency was devalued in an attempt to put more money into circulation; but this only meant that merchants charged more for goods in order to have the same income. The currency eventually became worthless, and trade largely took place on the basis of bartering.

The Circus Maximus in Rome was used for chariot races and other forms of entertainment. The remaining outline of the stadium is pictured below.

Roman government was one of its own worst enemies. The in-fighting of political and military leaders cost the government the support of the people. The weaker western empire was vulnerable to attack, and the eastern government was of no mind to help. Landlords in the west became heads of huge estates that operated as their own little kingdoms with serfs working the land, and these landlords had no interest in taking any risks for the central government. Class strife became common. Townspeople despaired. Internal weakness invited attacks from outside of the empire. Within this context, natural disasters such as the plagues that swept over Italy in the second and third centuries took an emotional as well as physical toll.

Without a doubt, human weaknesses contributed to the decline. As with everything in this world, empires eventually pass away. No human arrangement will last forever because at some point other humans will exploit a weakness. Many Romans pursued a wanton and immoral lifestyle. They sought immediate pleasure while ignoring long-term consequences of government policies and social practices. The qualities that made Rome strong gave way to selfish characteristics that made her weak. The proud patricians and plebeians were replaced by selfish leaders and by masses who demanded bread and circuses.

One key factor was a low view of human worth. From early in Roman history, patricians believed they were worth more than plebeians; and both groups believed they were worth more than slaves. A desire for power justified the cruel execution of enemies. Rome became dependent on the labor of slaves, whose numbers rose steadily. By 150 BC about one-third of the population of Italy were slaves; and the percentage continued to rise after that. The occasional slave uprisings were crushed mercilessly. In the revolt led by Spartacus in 73 BC, some 6,000 slaves were crucified. The use

This first century mosaic from Libya depicts various forms of entertainment. Musicians are shown at top with scenes of humans and animals fighting in the lower panels.

of crucifixion for those considered enemies of the state shows the depth of cruelty to which the Romans stooped. Moreover, any culture that watches the killing of human life for entertainment is deeply flawed within; and Romans did just this in the Colosseum and Circus Maximus.

The fall of Rome did not take place overnight. Its power declined gradually but decisively for almost three centuries. Probably many Romans of the late empire could not believe that the glory of Rome was fading; however, its external accomplishments could not hide its internal weaknesses. We can learn much good as we study the story of Rome, but we must also admit the presence of many evils.

And a strong angel took up a stone like a great millstone
and threw it into the sea, saying, "So will Babylon,
the great city, be thrown down with violence,
and will not be found any longer."
Revelation 18:21

Assignments for Lesson 61

Bible   The readings for this week relate to Lesson 65 on the inspiration and authority of Scripture. Read Deuteronomy 4:2 and Revelation 22:18-19. Commentary available in *Student Review*.

In Their Words   Read the Letters Between Pliny the Younger and Emperor Trajan and the excerpt from the Letter to Diognetus (pages 78-80).

Literature   Begin reading *The Imitation of Christ*. Plan to finish it by the end of Unit 14.

Student Review   Optional: Answer the questions for Lesson 61.

Detail from Nero's Torches *Henryk Siemiradzki (Polish, 1882)*

Lesson 62

The Way of Christ: Attacked, Then Accepted

As the Roman Empire was fading, the church was growing. As the empire was weakening, the church was growing stronger. As the empire became more Christian, the church became more worldly.

In the centuries after Christ and the apostles, paganism and mystery religions were still the predominant forms of religious activity in the Roman Empire. The cult of emperor worship was growing and became the official religion of the state. The peculiar ways of Judaism were tolerated by the Roman government; but as Christianity grew, government officials had to decide how to deal with this new religious movement.

Over the four centuries that followed the first century AD, Christianity underwent many changes. It went from being an illegal cult to the official religion of the Roman Empire. It changed from the simple, grassroots movement described in the New Testament to a powerful, highly organized institution. Christianity became a complex movement in which its members sought to serve the Lord Jesus Christ in differing ways. We will examine these changes in this lesson and the next.

Persecution of the "Pests"

The Roman historian Suetonius tells us that the emperor Claudius ordered all Jews to leave the city of Rome in 51-52 AD because of a disturbance in the Jewish section of the city over one called "Chrestus." This is the edict mentioned in Acts 18:2 which brought Aquila and Priscilla to Corinth. Chrestus is quite possibly a misunderstanding of the name Christus or Christ. Perhaps when the gospel of Jesus was being preached in Rome, some Jews reacted by causing a disturbance similar to what Paul experienced in many cities. Jews who had become Christians were still forced to leave the city. This is the first official government policy that affected Christians other than the actions of the Jewish leaders in Jerusalem and the occasional rulings by local authorities mentioned in Acts.

In 64 AD a fire destroyed a major part of the city of Rome. Many Romans blamed emperor Nero for being irresponsible. Looking for a scapegoat, Nero blamed the strange, new cult called Christians. According to historians, Nero had Christians crucified, wrapped in animal skins and attacked by

The Destruction of Jerusalem

The Jewish independence movement in Palestine that had been smoldering for over a century burst into flame in 66 AD with a full-scale revolt. It took the Romans four years to put down the rebellion, but the climax came in 70 AD when Roman forces took Jerusalem and destroyed the temple, which has never been rebuilt. The last holdouts of the Jewish resistance took their own lives rather than surrender to the Romans in the hilltop fortress of Masada near the southern end of the Dead Sea in 74 AD.

Titus was the Roman general who oversaw the destruction of Jerusalem. He served briefly as emperor after his victory. His brother Domitian succeeded him as emperor and authorized construction of the Arch of Titus in Rome about 82 AD. The panel pictured below shows Roman soldiers carrying treasures away from the temple.

dogs, and bound to stakes and set on fire to light his garden during parties. According to tradition, Peter and Paul were put to death during this persecution.

The persecution of Christians was generally treated as a local issue for about two hundred years. Sporadic persecutions arose during the reign of emperor Domitian in the 90s AD. Pliny the Younger (or Plinius Secundus) was governor of the province of Bithynia in Asia Minor in the early second century. He wrote letters to the emperor Trajan about almost every administrative matter imaginable. One of these letters, written about 112 AD, deals with the interrogation and prosecution of Christians.

As the Christian movement grew, Roman officials tried to determine the exact nature of the sect. Rome had to decide whether Christianity was merely a Jewish sect or if it was an illegal new religion. When emperor worship became a requirement, the issue was brought to a head because Christians worshiped God and refused to worship the emperor. To the Romans, it was a question of loyalty: Christ or Caesar.

A general principle of life is that if what you are doing is having an impact, you will probably be criticized for it. As the movement of Christ grew, it generated increasing criticism from skeptics and opponents who did not or would not grasp what it was about. Lucian of Samosata ridiculed the Christians' dislike of material things. A critic in France in the late second century charged that Christians practiced incestuous marriages (he had heard something about brothers marrying sisters in the church) and ate flesh and drank blood (apparently he had heard enough about the Lord's Supper to be confused).

Celsus in 180 AD questioned a God who would choose a disciple that would betray Him. Celsus also expressed serious doubt that any respectable God would work in Palestine through a child of questionable background (rumors persisted that twisted the Lord's virgin birth into a story of illegitimacy). Some called the Way the third race, meaning they were neither pagans nor Jews, and thus they did not know what to think of them. A few observers, however, did express respect for the Christians' moral code, character, and bravery in the face of martyrdom.

Attacks on Christians escalated to more than verbal criticism. Some gave their lives and thus became martyrs (the term comes from the Greek word which means witness or testimony; a martyr gives the ultimate testimony to what he believes in). Ignatius, for example, was bishop of the church in Syrian Antioch. During a period of persecution there, he was condemned to be put before wild beasts in Rome. Ignatius was taken overland to Rome. Along the way he was allowed to visit some churches and write letters to others. He was martyred in 116 AD.

Polycarp, bishop of Smyrna, was a student of the apostle John. About 156 AD he was arrested and sentenced to die. When he was in the arena, the proconsul tried to get Polycarp to recant. He said to Polycarp, "Swear by the fortune of Caesar; change your mind; say, 'Away with the atheists!'" (Christians were called atheists because they did not believe in the gods of Rome.)

Polycarp looked at the crowd and then up to heaven and said, "Away with the atheists!" (meaning the Roman pagans who did not believe in God). The proconsul tried again. "Take the oath and I shall release you. Curse Christ." Polycarp replied, "Eighty-six years I have served Him, and He never did me any wrong. How can I blaspheme my King who saved me?" After repeated refusals to deny Christ, Polycarp was put to death.

In response to these increasing attacks, some Christians spoke out or took up their pens to write defenses of the Christian faith. These men were called apologists. The word apology comes from the Greek and means to speak to or defend a subject. Christian apologists defended the faith as true, reasonable, and posing no threat to Rome or anyone else. Justin and Irenaeus were two apologists in the mid- to late second century.

Official Roman policy changed repeatedly depending on the whims of the emperor. In 250 AD, Decius saw a need to return to Rome's traditional paganism as a way to preserve the empire he saw crumbling around him. As a result, he ordered the execution of Christians who would not worship the pagan gods. Many Christians were martyred, but also many renounced the faith in order to save their lives. However, the emperor Gallienus issued a decree that ended the round of persecution.

The Christian Martyrs' Last Prayer
Jean-Léon Gérôme (French, 1883)

The Maison Carrée in Nimes, France, was built as a Roman temple in the first century. During the fourth century, it was converted into a Christian church. While many temples were destroyed after Christianity became the favored religion of the Empire, this structure has remained as one of the best preserved Roman temples anywhere. Over the centuries it has served as a government building, a residence, a stable for horses during the French Revolution, and a museum.

By the end of the third century, many people once again saw a need for a common religion to unify the empire. Those who refused to go along with the worship of the emperor (primarily Jews and Christians) were considered enemies of the state. In 303 AD the emperor Diocletian ordered church buildings confiscated, church officials condemned, and Christians given the choice of either repenting or being put to death.

The example of faith set by the martyrs led to a greater respect for the way of Christ, and the church grew as a result. As the Christian writer Tertullian expressed it around 200 AD, "The blood of the martyrs is the seed of the church."

Christianity Becomes Accepted

In the early 300s AD, the actions of Emperor Constantine changed the status of Christianity in the Empire. He did not make it the official religion, but he prohibited the persecution of believers. It became safe to be a Christian. This caused some people to profess Christianity, not because of genuine conversion, but in order to gain or maintain the emperor's favor. In addition, because he was the emperor, Constantine began to influence church practices and policy. With the blessing of safety came the danger of compromise with the world.

Julian became emperor in 361 AD. He was a pagan who did not care for some aspects of the practice of Christianity, including the veneration of Mary and the supposed remains of apostles and others. He tried to revive paganism, but his efforts failed. The tide had turned, and a growing number of people in the empire wanted to follow Christianity.

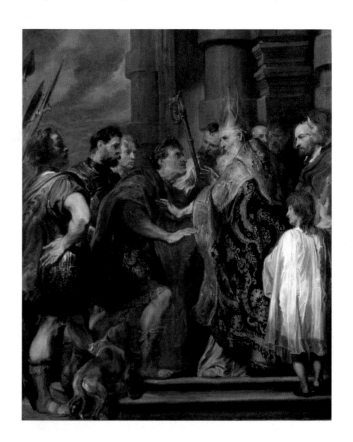

Ambrose, bishop of Milan, had a strong influence over Emperor Theodosius I. Ambrose believed that Jews and pagans should be persecuted, and he encouraged the emperor to promote such actions. This painting by Flemish painter Anthony van Dyck depicts Theodosius and Ambrose (c. 1619).

The Jubail Church in Saudi Arabia, dating from the fourth century, is one of the oldest church ruins.

In 381 AD Emperor Theodosius I at the Council of Constantinople declared Rome to be a Christian state. Pagan rituals were banished, and paganism and any heretical teachings were forbidden. Church facilities became the property of the state. In the early church, some wondered whether Christians could conscientiously serve in the army. Now, only Christians could serve in the army since pagans were not allowed. Pagans began to be persecuted. In 438 the Roman government declared death as the punishment for all who did not profess faith in Christ.

Beloved, do not be surprised at the fiery ordeal among you,
which comes upon you for your testing,
as though some strange thing were happening to you;
but to the degree that you share the sufferings of Christ,
keep on rejoicing, so that also at the revelation of His glory
you may rejoice with exultation.
1 Peter 4:12-13

Assignments for Lesson 62

Bible Read 2 Kings 22:1-23:3. Commentary available in *Student Review*.

In Their Words Read the excerpt from *The Annals* and "Shepherd of Tender Youth" (pages 81-85).

Literature Continue reading *The Imitation of Christ*.

Student Review Optional: Answer the questions for Lesson 62.

Painting of the First Council of Nicea, Church of Stavropoleos, Bucharest, Romania

Lesson 63

Changes in Church Practice

The practice of Christianity underwent significant changes after the days of the apostles. As we consider these changes, we need to keep in mind the situation that the church faced. A wide variety of doctrines had developed as people were influenced by non-Christian beliefs and philosophies. The New Testament was not yet readily available to every congregation and believer to serve as a standard and guide. Church leaders felt a need to protect the flock from false doctrines and to encourage the faithfulness of the members.

Church Leadership

In the New Testament, local congregations were overseen by elders, who were also called shepherds or overseers (see Acts 20:28 and 1 Peter 5:1-2 for examples of these three terms being used for the same role). The word for overseer is *episkopos*, which is also translated bishop. The New Testament always refers to elders in the plural, which suggests that each city or congregation had more than one.

Early evidence is sketchy, but apparently by around 100 AD some congregations recognized a chief elder or bishop who presided at services and who was considered the leading man in the congregation. By the late second century, the pattern was to have one bishop over a city, with individual congregations led by elders. Bishops then claimed authority over larger areas.

As this pattern was established, the Roman Catholic Church copied in great measure the political divisions of the Roman Empire. In 303 AD Diocletian divided the 120 provinces into twelve dioceses, or administrative divisions. The Empire had local officials, provincial governors, and diocesan administrators.

In the name of efficient oversight, the Church developed a similar leadership hierarchy (the word means sacred rule). First, a division arose between the ordinary people in the Church, often called the laity (from the Greek word for people, *laos*), and those considered qualified to lead the Church, called the clergy (from the Greek word for priest, *cleros*). Then a hierarchy developed among the clergy. A priest was

> *From this point in the curriculum, we use the word* church *when referring to the early church or to the church in a general sense. We use the word* Church *(with a capital C) when referring to a specific group, such as the Roman Catholic Church, the Orthodox Church, or the Church of England.*

356

declared to be qualified to carry out the rites and rituals of a parish or local district of the Church. A bishop oversaw a diocese of several parishes. An archbishop was over several dioceses.

The bishop of Rome claimed the authority to oversee all churches just as the emperor oversaw the empire. As the head of the church in the capital city, the bishop of Rome came to have great influence over other churches. The bishop of Rome eventually buttressed his position by saying that Peter was the first bishop of Rome. The bishop of Rome further claimed that since he was the successor to Peter's position, Jesus' statement in Matthew 16:19 giving Peter the keys of the kingdom applied to him as well.

Jesus' reference to the keys of the kingdom in Matthew 16:19 referred to Peter being the one who first proclaimed the gospel message that told people how they could enter the kingdom. It had nothing to do with the power of the bishop of Rome to guide the church.

Christ Giving the Keys to St. Peter
Giovanni Battista Castello (Italian, c. 1598)

This claim, which was not made until 354 AD, was opposed by bishops in the east; but as the bishop in Rome claimed this authority and others deferred to it, the pattern was established. In 455 Emperor Valentinian III decreed that all western bishops must submit to the pope. His decree was ignored to some degree in the West and almost completely in the East, but the decree reflected the movement toward viewing the bishop of Rome as the head of what became the Roman Catholic Church.

The doctrine of apostolic succession from Peter is the basis for the pope making decisions for the Roman Catholic Church. Official Roman Catholic doctrine states that the pope is infallible when speaking in his official capacity on Church doctrine. The historical evidence does not support the idea that Peter was the bishop of Rome, and Peter never claimed to be infallible.

By the fifth century, the bishop of Rome was called *papa* or pope, the ultimate father figure of the Church. This is the origin of the word papacy that refers to the position. Another indication of the influence of the Roman Empire is that the pope is also called Pontifex Maximus or highest priest. This was one of the titles held by Roman emperors.

Councils and Creeds

The Church faced threats from false religions without and false teaching within. For instance, the philosophy of gnosticism, with its emphasis on inner knowledge and a skepticism about the material world, grew in the second century and began influencing the view of Christ that some people held. Some gnostics denied that Jesus really came in the flesh, since to them anything that partook of the flesh was inherently evil. Mystery religions were also growing and influencing the thinking of Christians.

The emperor called a council whenever he wanted the bishops to decide a matter of controversy that had arisen in the Church. The councils were significant for a number of reasons. First, they demonstrated and confirmed the power and influence of the bishops in the Church. Second, they established the process of formulating Church doctrine by council. Third, the creeds (from the Latin *credo*, which means "I believe") developed by the councils defined orthodoxy and thus identified who would be considered faithful. Finally, the councils demonstrated the role of the emperor as de facto leader of the Church; that is, the Church did what the emperor said.

Monasticism

Even before Christ came, some people wanted to escape the defilements of the world and move closer to God through contemplation and separated living. The Jewish sect of the Essenes, for instance, lived separated from the rest of Israel near the Dead Sea. Some Christians desired to get away from the influences of the world to live a more holy life for Jesus. Some also wanted to overcome personal failures or the desires of the flesh.

In 285 AD Antony went to live by himself in the Egyptian desert. By the fourth century, thousands of believers were living in the Egyptian desert, some in solitary huts and some in small communities. The first monasteries were established in the mid-fourth century. Pachomius built a compound for monks on the Nile River. (Monastery and monk are from the Greek *mono,* which means one or alone.)

Hermit monks lived austere lives, including once-a-week meals, self-inflicted beatings to drive away the lusts of the flesh, and occasionally some even more unusual practices. Simon Stylites of Syria lived atop a pillar for thirty years. His food was raised to him in a basket, and he occasionally preached from his perch. As monastic communities matured, orders or daily rituals were developed to regulate group life. Benedict established monastic orders (groups of monks living by specific guidelines) in Italy in the early 500s. These Rules of Saint Benedict have been influential among monks and nuns ever since.

To overcome sexual temptations, monks committed themselves to a life of celibacy. They believed that the sexual relationship in marriage was not wrong, but abstaining from marriage and marital intimacy was better. Sometimes monks

The Apostles' Creed

The Apostles' Creed is widely used among Christians today in the West. Tradition says that it was handed down from the apostles, but the evidence is unclear. An early form was circulating in the second century, but modified versions appeared into the eighth century. The word catholic as used in the last section means universal. The image at right shows the Apostles' Creed painted on the wall of a church building in Wales.

I believe in God the Father Almighty, Maker of heaven and earth.

And in Jesus Christ his only Son our Lord; who was conceived by the Holy Ghost, born of the Virgin Mary, suffered under Pontius Pilate, was crucified, dead, and buried; he descended into hell; the third day he rose again from the dead; he ascended into heaven, and sitteth on the right hand of God the Father Almighty; from thence he shall come to judge the quick and the dead.

I believe in the Holy Ghost; the holy catholic Church; the communion of saints; the forgiveness of sins; the resurrection of the body; and the life everlasting. Amen.

This 16th-century Polish icon depicts the monk Simon Stylites sitting on the top of his pillar.

were chosen to serve as priests and bishops. When they re-entered the world, they remained celibate. The expectation developed that Church leaders needed to be unmarried and celibate.

Monasteries played a role in evangelism as the dedication of the monks attracted the attention of outsiders who were moved to investigate the claims of Christ. In many communities, the monks provided education and health care. Many monasteries were devoted to copying the Scriptures and classic literature. In this way they helped preserve ancient works for future generations.

One monk, Jerome, studied Hebrew as a way to overcome sexual temptation. He used his knowledge of Biblical languages to translate the Bible into Latin about 400 AD. It was not the first Latin translation, but it was the best. It is called the Vulgate because Latin was the common language (the Latin word *vulgus* means common people). Jerome's Vulgate became the standard, authoritative translation used in the Roman Catholic Church until translations into other languages were permitted over one thousand years later.

Other Church Issues

Membership. In the New Testament, a person became a Christian by confessing his faith and being baptized into Christ immediately after hearing and believing the gospel message (see, for instance, Acts 8:26-40 and 16:14-34). Over time, the Church developed a training period for potential converts, during which they learned and memorized the catechism, a series of questions and answers that taught essential Church doctrines. Some studies took up to three years.

The only examples of baptism in the New Testament are the immersion in water of adults. By the late second century, pouring water was accepted for someone who was too ill to be immersed. Later, sprinkling developed as an easier method that still retained a connection with water. Infant baptism apparently arose first out of the desire of parents for a dying baby to be saved. It later became a way for parents to commit themselves to rearing a child in the Church's teachings.

Mary

In seeking to make humble requests before God, the practice developed in the Church of praying to Mary and other deceased Christians to intercede for them. Mary was eventually declared to be the Mother of God and given a special place in Roman Catholic teaching. Traditions grew up around her, such as the Immaculate Conception (the belief that Mary was not born in sin) and her Perpetual Virginity (the idea that Mary was always a virgin and that Jesus' brothers and sisters mentioned in Mark 6:3 were either children of Joseph by another marriage or cousins of Jesus). Mary was certainly a special person whom God chose to be the mother of Jesus; but other than appreciating her in this way, no adoration or exaltation of her is supported in Scripture.

The icon at right of Mary and the infant Jesus is from St. Catherine's Monastery on the Sinai peninsula (c. 600).

The Fish Symbol

The fish was used as a symbol of Christianity perhaps as early as the first century. The letters of the Greek word for fish, ΙΧΘΥΣ (pronounced ick-thoos), are the first letters in the phrase "Jesus Christ, God's Son, Savior" (Iesus Christos Theou Uios Soter). The fish symbol was used to designate meeting places or as a secret code for Christians to identify each other. The cross was not used much as a symbol before the fourth century. It was too obvious a reference to Christ and was not something greatly admired by people in general. Some Christian paintings used anchors, which include the shape of the cross. Pictured at right is a memorial stone for a Christian named Licinia Amias from the third century.

Some who had become Christians and then denied the faith later wanted back into the Church. A debate arose over whether this should be permitted. The Church eventually allowed such sinners to return after a period of penance during which they performed acts of contrition.

Communion. The practice of the Lord's Supper changed from a remembrance of Christ's sacrifice to a more mystical event in which Christ was supposedly sacrificed all over again. The bread and wine were said to became the body and blood of Jesus (the doctrine of transubstantiation). At some point only priests began drinking the wine of communion instead of allowing all members of the Church to share in it. Communion came to be seen as a sacrament, a means whereby God's grace was dispensed. Church leaders could excommunicate someone, which meant denying that person the right to participate in communion.

Church Practices. The Church sometimes adapted pagan rituals by giving them a Christian meaning. For instance, evidence suggests that the celebration of Jesus' birth on December 25 was a replacement for the celebration of the birth of the sun. The Church added many feast days throughout the year.

The earliest church buildings date from the late third century. The first baptisteries were used in church buildings in the third century. Music in the early church was apparently the reciting of psalms or the singing of new compositions in chanting form. Musical instruments were introduced in the Middle Ages.

The Role of Christians in Society. Believers struggled with what it meant to be a Christian in a pagan world. Should a Christian eat meat that had been sacrificed to a pagan idol? This was commonly done in civic gatherings or at weddings that involved pagans. Could a Christian artist sculpt or paint pagan scenes or act in pagan plays? Should a Christian marry (or continue to be married to) an unbeliever? These and other questions confronted the early believers. How they answered them reflected how much they adapted their faith to the world and how much they were willing to be different from the world.

The world is passing away, and also its lusts;
but the one who does the will of God lives forever.
1 John 2:17

Assignments for Lesson 63

Bible   Read John 10:35-36 and 14:10 and Matthew 26:51-56. Commentary available in *Student Review*.

In Their Words   Read the excerpts from *The Didache* (pages 86-88).

Literature   Continue reading *The Imitation of Christ*.

Student Review   Optional: Answer the questions for Lesson 63.

The Brescia Casket is an ivory box, probably dating from the late 4th century. It may have once held the bones of a martyr, but its original intended use is uncertain. The carvings on the lid and all four sides illustrate various Biblical individuals and scenes.

Detail from The Battle of Milvian Bridge
Giulio Romano (Italian, c. 1524)

Constantine

About 274 AD Flavius Valerius Constantinus (Constantine) was born in the town of Niš in modern-day Serbia. His father, Constantius Chlorus, was a soldier. His mother, Helena, was a camp follower or perhaps an innkeeper.

The ambitious Constantius rose in the ranks of the Roman army. Diocletian became emperor in 284 and created a power-sharing arrangement with his subordinates. One person with the title of augustus led the western part of the Empire, and another augustus led the eastern part. Each augustus had a caesar under him. In 293 AD Constantius was appointed caesar under Maximian, who was the augustus in the west.

About this time, for political purposes, Constantius divorced Helena and married Theodora, the daughter of Maximian. Constantius and Theodora had six children together.

Constantine did not spend much time with his father as a child. He was sent to the court of Emperor Diocletian. To ensure the loyalty of Constantius, Diocletian held Constantine almost like a hostage. Constantine served in the military under Galerius, who was Caesar in the eastern part of the empire.

When Diocletian instigated a severe persecution of Christians in the early 300s AD, Constantius

was reluctant to follow these instructions, perhaps because he wanted the Christians to support his political ambitions. When Diocletian and Maximian resigned in 305 AD, Constantius was recognized as Augustus in the west. Galerius was Augustus of the east. Constantine joined his father for a military campaign in Britain.

Constantius' rule was short. He died the next year, 306 AD, in Britain. His soldiers acclaimed Constantine as Augustus in the West. For the next several years, Constantine used a combination of political maneuvers and military power to establish himself as supreme ruler.

Maxentius, who had some support in Italy, was an adversary of Constantine. Constantine led his army across the Alps toward Rome. According to the traditional story, Constantine had a vision in which Christ told him to put "chi" and "rho" (the first two letters of Christ in Greek) on the shields of his soldiers. Another story says that Constantine saw a cross over the sun and the words "*In hoc signo vinces*" (meaning "In this sign conquer").

The Battle of Milvian Bridge near Rome took place in 312 AD. Constantine's army was significantly smaller, but his troops had more experience than those of Maxentius. Constantine won the battle, in which Maxentius died.

The Roman Senate commissioned the Arch of Constantine after the Battle of Milvian Bridge. Completed in 315 AD, it is decorated with scenes from Roman history. The main inscription says that Constantine was "inspired by the divine". Since the monument has no overtly Christian imagery, this generic phrase might have been chosen to avoid offending both pagans and Christians.

Faith and Politics

Constantine credited the God of the Christians for his victory. He announced that Christians would no longer be persecuted for their faith. Constantine also abolished the practice of crucifixion and made the first day of the week (called the Sun's Day or Sunday) a holiday. In 313 AD Constantine issued the statement known as the Edict of Milan with the approval of his co-emperor Licinius Augustus, who ruled in the east. It offered toleration for all religions but focused on Christianity, and it ordered the restoration of confiscated property to the disciples.

Licinius did not accept Christianity as did Constantine, and he eventually renewed persecution against believers. Constantine and Licinius vied for ultimate control of the empire, with Constantine gaining the upper hand in 324 AD.

A council helped Constantine administer the government. He reorganized the army, divided civil and military authority, and issued gold coins that were a standard currency until the 1400s. Constantine also involved himself in Church affairs, enacting rules and making contributions in support of the Church.

Arius, an elder in Alexandria, Egypt, began teaching that Christ was created, meaning that there was a time when Christ did not yet exist. In response, Athanasius said that Christ's relationship with God was always the same. Many bishops believed the Church needed to declare which was orthodox doctrine. In 325 AD Constantine called a council of all bishops at Nicea in Asia Minor to discuss the Arian controversy. The three hundred bishops who were present decided that the Father and the Son were consubstantial, meaning they were of the same substance (thus refuting Arius). To make Church orthodoxy clear, a statement was formulated to which all faithful Christians were expected to adhere. This statement was called the Nicene Creed.

This and other councils contributed to a blending of civil and ecclesiastical power. For instance, Constantine banished from the Empire those who refused to go along with the decision at Nicea. The power of the Christian state was thus turned against other Christians to enforce conformity.

Conformity, however, was a shifting position. Arius was eventually reinstated, and one of his followers baptized Constantine near the emperor's death. Constantine did not understand the Bible's teaching that baptism is a birth, a beginning, and that repentance and confession enable a Christian to continue walking in the light (see 1 John 1:9). As the tide of belief shifted toward the Arian position, those who agreed with the decision at Nicea were viewed with suspicion.

Family Life

A woman named Minervina bore Constantine a son named Crispus about 305 AD. Whether or not Constantine married her is uncertain, but he married another woman, Fausta, in 307. She bore him three

The Nicene Creed

The original form of the Nicene creed, developed in 325 AD, contains a strongly-worded rebuke of those who accepted the Arian position. The image below is a stylized representation showing members of the council holding a scroll with the text of the creed in Greek.

We believe in one God, the Father Almighty, Maker of all things visible and invisible.

And in one Lord Jesus Christ, the Son of God, begotten of the Father the only-begotten; that is, of the essence of the Father, God of God, Light of Light, very God of very God, begotten, not made, being of one substance with the Father; by whom all things were made both in heaven and on earth; who for us men, and for our salvation, came down and was incarnate and was made man; he suffered, and the third day he rose again, ascended into heaven; from thence he shall come to judge the quick and the dead.

And in the Holy Ghost.

But those who say: 'There was a time when he was not;' and 'He was not before he was made;' and 'He was made out of nothing,' or 'He is of another substance' or 'essence,' or 'The Son of God is created,' or 'changeable,' or 'alterable'—they are condemned by the holy catholic and apostolic Church.

An alternate and expanded version, perhaps introduced at the Council of Constantinople in 381 AD, dropped the condemnation of Arianism.

We believe in one God the Father Almighty, Maker of heaven and earth, and of all things visible and invisible.

And in one Lord Jesus Christ, the only-begotten Son of God, begotten of the Father before all worlds, God of God, Light of Light, Very God of Very God, begotten, not made, being of one substance with the Father by whom all things were made; who for us men, and for our salvation, came down from heaven, and was incarnate by the Holy Spirit of the Virgin Mary, and was made man, and was crucified also for us under Pontius Pilate. He suffered and was buried, and the third day he rose again according to the Scriptures, and ascended into heaven, and sitteth on the right hand of the Father. And he shall come again with glory to judge both the quick and the dead, whose kingdom shall have no end.

And we believe in the Holy Spirit, the Lord and Giver of Life, who proceedeth from the Father and the Son, who with the Father and the Son together is worshiped and glorified, who spoke by the prophets. And we believe in one holy catholic and apostolic Church. We acknowledge one baptism for the remission of sins. And we look for the resurrection of the dead, and the life of the world to come. Amen.

Constantine's mother Helena made a visit to Palestine in the 320s AD. She established the Church of the Nativity in Bethlehem and the Chapel of the Ascension in Jerusalem. According to legend, she discovered the true cross of Christ, as depicted in the Italian manuscript above from about 825.

of the Eastern Roman Empire, which survived for nearly a thousand years after the fall of the city of Rome in the 400s. He oversaw the construction of elaborate churches, and Constantinople was the site for several Church councils, including one in 381 AD that affirmed the decisions of Nicea.

His Legacy

Constantine died in 337 AD. Some have titled him "the Great," and he did accomplish "great" things as one of the powerful men of his time. He exercised strong leadership in a weakened Roman Empire. His religious convictions were evidently sincere; but he, like all of us to varying degrees, did not always live them out in practice.

Constantine contributed to the foundation of medieval church and state politics as the winds of change swept across Europe. He believed in absolute power for himself as the ruler. Such absolute power tends to corrupt, as history has shown numerous times.

This coin, issued by Constantine in 313 AD, shows him with the sun god Sol Invictus ("Unconquered Sun").

sons, Constantine II, Constantius II, and Constans; and two daughters, Constantina and Helena.

In 326 AD Constantine ordered the execution of Crispus and Fausta. Some have accused them of having an affair, but the evidence is unclear. The three remaining sons served as Caesars during their father's reign. They became Augusti after his death when they killed potential rivals and divided the empire among themselves.

Constantine built a city for himself on the Bosporus, the site of the ancient city of Byzantium. He called it Constantinople and modeled it on Rome. It became his capital in 330 AD and was capital

What Else Was Happening? (200-500 AD)

1. The Zapotec civilization in the Valley of Oaxaca (modern Mexico) built the city of Monte Alban. It featured elaborate buildings, tombs, and ball courts (example shown at right). Their system of writing is one of the earliest known in Central America.

2. Ephrem the Syrian (c. 306-373 AD) was a Church leader in Nisibis (modern Turkey). He composed many hymns and poems and wrote sermons in both verse and prose. He taught at the Church of St. Jacob (ruins pictured at right). Ephrem died while ministering to victims of a plague.

3. Settlers from Borneo (modern Indonesia) likely came in waves to Madagascar. They cleared the rainforests to make room for agriculture and, on the isolated island, encountered unusually large animals such as giant lemurs and Malagasy hippopotami.

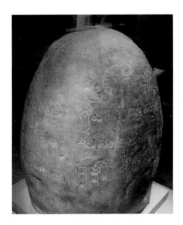

4. Purnawarman (ruled c. 395-434) was a distinguished leader of the Taruma kingdom on the island of Java. He had stones inscribed with declarations of his power and prestige (example at right). This people had diplomatic relations with India and China.

5. The kingdom of Goguryeo became a powerful empire on the Korean peninsula in the centuries after the coming of Christ. Buddhism became the official religion in the fourth century, and Gwanggaeto (c. 374-413) was one of its prominent rulers.

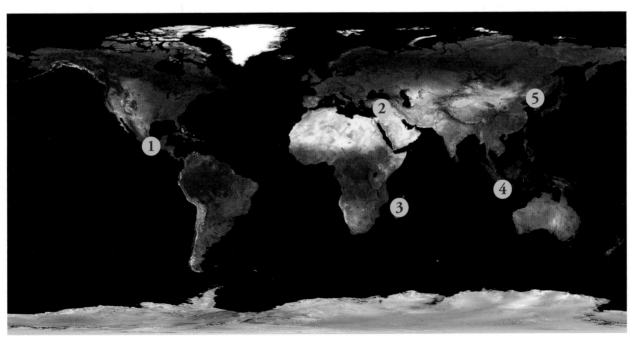

Augustine

Augustine was born in 354 AD, the son of a Christian mother and pagan father. As a young man, he lived an immoral life and investigated several philosophies to find the best way to live. His mother, Monica, continually influenced him to become a Christian; he was finally converted in 387 after her death. He became a monk and later bishop of Hippo in northern Africa. Augustine was impressed with the moral depravity of man, which he believed to be inborn, influenced no doubt by his own experiences. He also believed that the elect were predestined by God to obtain salvation.

Augustine's life story is told in his compelling book Confessions. *Written as a prayer to God, it includes this statement: "You have made us for Yourself, and our hearts are restless, until they rest in You." Another of Augustine's major works is* The City of God. *The destruction of Rome by the Visigoths in 410 disheartened many Christians since it happened so soon after Christianity became the official religion of the empire. Augustine explained that Rome fell because of its sin, just as all material things have an end, even though Rome did help in the spread of the gospel. The only eternal city is the City of God in heaven. Augustine is one of the most influential writers in Christian history.*

Saints Augustine and Monica, *Ary Scheffer (Dutch, 1846)*

There is one body and one Spirit, just as also you were called in one hope of your calling; one Lord, one faith, one baptism, one God and Father of all who is over all and through all and in all.
Ephesians 4:4-6

Assignments for Lesson 64

Bible   Read 1 Corinthians 2:12-13, 2 Timothy 3:16-17, and 2 Peter 1:16-21. Commentary available in *Student Review*.

In Their Words   Read the Edict of Milan and "The Dawn Is Sprinkling in the East" (pages 89-90).

Literature   Continue reading *The Imitation of Christ*.

Student Review   Optional: Answer the questions for Lesson 64.

Lesson 65 - Bible Study

The Inspiration and Authority of Scripture

God has always provided guidance for how He wants people to live. In the commandments He gave Adam and Eve in the Garden of Eden, in his call to Abraham, in the Law of Moses, in the words of the prophets, and in the documents of the New Testament, God has never left His people guessing as to what He expected of them.

Since the time of Moses, the religion of God's people has been based on an authoritative word from God. Jesus, in fact, is described as God's ultimate Message, the Word that became flesh (John 1:14, Hebrews 1:1-2).

Scripture in the Early Church

The Bible of the early church was the Jewish Scriptures, what we know as the Old Testament. Jesus often quoted from the Scriptures, as in Matthew 4:1-10. He knew that His life and ministry were the fulfillment of the Scriptures (see Luke 24:44). The apostles saw what happened in the early church as continuing to fulfill the Scriptures, as Peter did in Acts 2:16-21.

The teaching of the apostles was authoritative for the first Christians (Acts 2:42). Apostles, including Matthew, John, and Paul, or people closely associated with apostles such as Mark and Luke, wrote letters and other documents at different times and places in the first century. Bible scholars today generally believe that Mark was the first gospel account written down, followed at some point by Matthew and Luke. John was written later in the first century. Luke wrote Acts at some point after writing the gospel account that bears his name. Paul wrote his letters during his years of ministry in the mid-first century AD. The specific dates in the first century for the other letters of the New Testament are less clear. Revelation is often dated in the mid-90s. These documents were copied and circulated individually for some time.

Other writings appeared also. Some were legitimate, such as the Epistle of Clement of Rome to the church at Corinth (c. 96 AD). Others were quickly recognized as false, such as accounts of the childhood of Jesus and letters that claimed to be by apostles but that taught heretical doctrines.

The process of identifying the canon or authoritative list of New Testament Scriptures was not an arbitrary decision by a council or a single person that some books were acceptable and others unacceptable. Although some people in the church of the second and third centuries had questions about some of the books that were circulating, believers

Multiple artists have depicted Matthew writing his gospel with an angel speaking to him or assisting him. This example is Landscape with St. Matthew and the Angel *by Nicolas Poussin (French, c. 1645).*

identified and accepted as inspired those books that had an apostolic connection and agreed with the apostolic message. The twenty-seven books we have in the New Testament were clearly recognized as authoritative and belonging in the canon before the mid-300s AD.

The books of the New Testament are arranged in the order they are for good reason. The gospel is about Jesus, so naturally the accounts of His ministry, death, and resurrection come first. Matthew is the first of these because of the strong connection it has with the Old Testament. It contains about fifty quotations from or allusions to the Old Testament. The other gospel accounts follow. Acts describes the beginning of the church that took place after the ministry of Jesus. Paul's letters to churches are

Christian writers from the early centuries of the church are called the Church Fathers. Some were apologists while others taught and encouraged the faithful. Those who wrote before the Council of Nicea in 325 AD are called the Ante-Nicean Fathers, while those who came later are the Post-Nicean Fathers. Tertullian (c. 160-220, depicted at right) was a prominent church father from Carthage in northern Africa.

arranged from longest to shortest, then come his letters to individuals. The other letters are next, and the New Testament concludes with Revelation, the last book written and the one that looks the most toward the future.

God's Inspired Word

"All Scripture is inspired by God" (literally "God-breathed," 2 Timothy 3:16). We need to let Scripture itself define what inspiration means. In the Bible, different writers had different styles and different emphases. Luke did research as part of his writing work (Luke 1:3). Moreover, the writers of the gospels have some variation in the details of their accounts (see, for instance, the accounts of Jairus' daughter in Matthew 9:18 and in Mark 5:21-24, 35). Different writing styles, research, and variation in detail are all acceptable in the Biblical definition of inspiration.

Some claim that the ideas of Scripture are inspired but not the exact words. This is a difficult proposition to maintain. Jesus said the words

He spoke—not just the ideas—came from God (John 14:10). A person needs the right words to communicate the right ideas (1 Corinthians 2:12-13). Just as Jesus is both the sinless Son of God and lived on earth as a man, the Bible uses both God's words and man's style to be God's inspired, infallible, and authoritative message.

God's Word is reliable because God is reliable. God cannot lie (Titus 1:2). In Him is no variation or shifting shadow (James 1:17). Thus Scripture cannot be broken (John 10:35). God is true and His word is infallible; it will not lead you astray. Such would go against God's very nature. God's Word is as reliable as God is.

Scripture presents itself as authoritative and inspired (2 Timothy 3:16-17, 2 Peter 1:20-21). The Bible commands people not to add to or take from its message (Deuteronomy 4:2, Revelation 22:18-19). We understand the Bible to be the Word of God; therefore, it is authoritative for our lives.

The Power No Other Book Has

People have spent their lives translating and copying the Bible so that others could have the chance to read it. Some have literally given their lives making the Bible accessible to others. Not only do people work to share the Bible with others, but people work hard to have a Bible for themselves.

When the Iron Curtain of Communism fell in Russia and Eastern Europe, citizens of the newly-free countries often stood in long lines to get a copy of the Bibles being made available by missionaries. One immigrant from Russia to the United States showed a friend his copy of Scripture. It was hand-written, painstakingly copied from the few printed editions that had been available there.

The Bible also generates strong negative emotions. One of the most hated books in history has been the Bible. Governments have worked hard to eliminate copies of the Bible from within their borders. Christians and Communist border guards in the former Soviet Union and in China

A Father in the Netherlands Reads the Bible to His Family at Christmas, 1949

have played cat and mouse, the Christians trying to smuggle Bibles into the country and the guards trying to keep them out. Communist leaders know what the Bible means to people. These leaders have tried to keep it away from their citizens so those citizens would not have divided loyalties.

This Book has a strong hold on people because it is God's holy Word—precious, inspired, authoritative, challenging, hope-giving, and absolutely vital. The inspiration and authority of the Bible is one of the key doctrines of Christianity. Since the Bible is what it says it is, we have a responsibility to believe the Bible as God's Word and to follow it completely.

One practical, convincing proof of the authority of the Word is the effect it has had on people's lives for literally thousands of years. The author of Psalm 119 could not praise the commandments of God enough. When Josiah heard the words of the book of the law, he tore his clothes and was convicted of the need to obey it (2 Kings 22:8-13). Many in the first century were convicted when they heard the preaching of the apostolic message. Augustine, a well-educated man, said that he had never read words that affected him as did the words of Jesus, "Come to Me, all who are weary and heavy-laden, and I will give you rest" (Matthew 11:28).

No other book has brought such hope, joy, uplift, and rebuke. No other book has had the transforming effect in the lives of individuals and on the world. This effect is not just because of the words and ideas in the Book, but it is because of the Spirit of the living God that empowers those words and introduces people to the mighty God and the loving Savior.

But know this first of all, that no prophecy of Scripture is a matter of one's own interpretation, for no prophecy was ever made by an act of human will, but men moved by the Holy Spirit spoke from God.
2 Peter 1:20-21

Assignments for Lesson 65

Bible　Recite or write 1 John 2:15-17 from memory.

In Their Words　Read The Letter of Paula and Eustochium to Marcella and "Lord Jesus, Think On Me" (pages 91-94).

Literature　Continue reading *The Imitation of Christ.*

Project　Complete your project for the unit.

Student Review　Optional: Answer the questions for Lesson 65 and take the quiz for Unit 13.

14

The Early Middle Ages

Summary   Europe underwent tremendous changes in the 500 years after the fall of Rome. The single ruler in Rome gave way to local kings and lords. The recognition of Charlemagne as Emperor of the Franks was an attempt to bring back a single ruler over a large area. The power of the Roman Catholic Church increased and the new religion of Islam arose in the Middle East. We will also look at one king in early medieval England, at life among the marauding Vikings, and at what the Bible says about evangelism.

Lessons   66 - Europe After the Fall of Rome
67 - Key Event: The Rise of Islam
68 - Key Person: Alfred the Great
69 - Everyday Life: The Vikings
70 - Bible Study: Methods and Motives in Evangelism

Hagia Sophia in Istanbul, Turkey (Sixth Century)

373

Memory Work

Learn Acts 4:11-12 by the end of the unit.

Books Used

The Bible
In Their Words
The Imitation of Christ

**Project
(choose one)**

1) Write 300 to 500 words on one of the following topics:

• What are the attributes of a great leader? See Lesson 68.

• Describe a missionary that you know. See Lesson 70. Where does he work and how does he minister? What character traits stand out about him or her? What have you learned from this missionary?

2) Build a model of a Viking ship. See Lesson 69. Look at photographs or drawings of Vikings ships and choose one to copy. Make your model as close to scale as you can and from the material of your choosing (wood, cardboard, clay, STYROFOAM™, LEGO® bricks, etc.).

3) Make a short video documentary about evangelism. See Lesson 70. Your video should be at least five minutes long.

Lesson 66

Europe After the Fall of Rome

A 17th-century Dutch writer divided history into three periods. One was ancient, one was modern, and the one-thousand-year epoch between them he called the middle era, or medieval times. The millennium between the fall of Rome in the fifth century and the beginning of the Italian Renaissance in the fifteenth has sometimes been called the Dark Ages. Like many labels, the term is not accurate. Western Civilization was not stagnant. Learning and change did take place. Europe in 1500 was not the same as Europe in 500, although the changes were gradual and progress was made at different rates in different places. In addition, significant intellectual development occurred in some areas.

Religion was the primary influence dominating life in the Middle Ages. The Roman Catholic Church took on a central role in politics and government with the decline of the Roman Empire. The Church was in a sense the only international superpower at the time. Meanwhile, the Byzantine Empire, the eastern remnant of the Roman Empire, was also strongly influenced by the expression of Christian faith that predominated within it. In addition, the new religion of Islam burst onto the scene and had a profound effect not only in the Middle East but also in Europe. Islamic influence touched culture, architecture, and science.

A second main influence in European life was the social arrangement called feudalism. This highly structured system determined what just about everyone, from the kings and nobles to the village peasants, did on a day to day basis. Feudalism influenced economics, politics, war, religion, and social relationships.

A third factor was the almost continual warfare in Europe. The entire continent was not embroiled in conflict during the entire period; but some group was almost always fighting some other group, upsetting the lives of the peasants, causing shifts in political alignments, and contributing to the already-fragile life that most people lived.

The Rise of the Franks

The Germanic tribes that controlled Europe and brought down the western Roman Empire did not have one single king. Instead, each tribe had its own king supported by his warrior chiefs. Government was simpler among the tribes than it had been in Rome. They had few government officials, no taxation, and laws that were based on customary decisions rather than a detailed legal code.

Frankish Clothing in the Early Middle Ages

As a result of inter-tribal warfare, the Franks established dominance in central Europe under the rule of Clovis in 481. He professed conversion to Christianity, but some have wondered if this was a political move to gain the support of the Church. When he died, Clovis willed that his kingdom be divided among his sons, a move which left each son with a smaller and weaker kingdom. The descendants of Clovis were not effective leaders, even though his family ruled the kingdoms of the Franks until 751. The Frankish kings during this era were more interested in making war and indulging in personal excesses than in governing, so they generally handed real power over to the mayor of the palace, who was something like a prime minister.

A man named Charles, who came from a politically-powerful family, became mayor of the palace in 714 and used his position to increase his influence in the Frankish kingdom. He stopped an Islamic invasion that threatened all of Europe. Muslim armies had spread out from Arabia and taken control of northern Africa, Spain, Sicily, and the Balkans. From Spain, they began heading into western Europe. In 732 an army led by Charles defeated an invading Muslim force at Tours, south of Paris. Charles was hailed as the savior of Europe and given the nickname Martel (the Hammer).

Charles had done all of this while still mayor of the palace. His son Pepin (nicknamed the Short) was elected king by the Frankish nobles in 751, and a new dynasty replaced the family of Clovis (which had been known as the Merovingians for Meroveus, the family patriarch). The pope in Rome endorsed Pepin's reign, perhaps to give the Church's seal of approval and perhaps so that the pope could call on Pepin for help, since Rome was being threatened by the Lombard tribe that was gaining power in Italy.

The pope appealed to Pepin for assistance in 756. Pepin defeated the Lombards and granted to the pope a strip of land across central Italy. This became the States of the Church or Papal States, a sovereign country under the political jurisdiction of the pope, which existed until Italy was unified in 1870. More importantly, the Frankish dynasty and the papacy, the two most powerful forces in Europe, became allies.

Charlemagne

Pepin's son and successor, Charles, was one of the leading figures of medieval Europe. He is best known by the title given in his memory many years later: Charlemagne, or Charles the Great.

During his forty-six year reign (768-814), Charlemagne expanded the Frankish kingdom to include almost all of present-day France and Germany, much of southeastern Europe to the Balkans, and the northern half of Italy. He strengthened the Franks' ties with the pope and sought to further the spread of Christianity in Europe, where the presence of paganism was still significant. Some of Charlemagne's bloodiest battles were fought in the effort to extend Christianity to other tribes.

The line between church and state was further blurred as Charlemagne appointed bishops and used Church leaders as agents of his government. Royal inspectors (usually a pair, a nobleman and a clergyman) traveled throughout the kingdom to check on local administrators. Charlemagne, by the way, abolished the position of mayor of the palace. He wanted no question about who held the real power in the kingdom.

The king encouraged the work of Christian missionaries as well as artists and artisans. The beautiful palace he ordered built at Aachen in what is now Germany was the first significant stone building to be constructed north of the Alps following the fall of Rome.

Dismayed at the low level of learning among priests (some of whom did not understand the Latin masses they said), he required better education of the clergy. Charlemagne organized a palace school at Aachen where copies were made of ancient Latin literature. Previously, Latin and Greek had been written in all capital letters. Alcuin was an English scholar who served in Charlemagne's court. Under Alcuin's leadership, copyists began to use capital and lower case letters to create a handwriting that was easier to read. This was the beginning of the writing style that we use today. Charlemagne himself could read but could not write. (Historians have conflicting opinions about whether he eventually learned to write.) Besides training clergy, some monasteries provided schools for the children of nobles; however, formal education for the general public was non-existent.

In 799 the people of Rome became convinced that Pope Leo III was a scoundrel. He was severely beaten and run out of town. Leo went north and enlisted the help of Charlemagne, who used his power to restore the pope to his position. On Christmas Day 800, Charlemagne was attending mass at St. Peter's Basilica in Rome. In what was apparently a surprise to the king, the grateful pope placed a crown on Charlemagne's head and declared him to be "Charles Augustus, Emperor of the Romans." The pope thus attempted to restore the Roman Empire under the leadership of a Frankish king.

The coronation of Charlemagne as emperor was significant for many reasons. First, it was an attempt by the pope to create a unified rule over all Europe. Second, the pope claimed the power to bestow the throne as a gift from God, which put him above the king. Charlemagne exercised authority in local Church affairs, but matters had reversed since Emperor Constantine called Church councils and set Church policy. Third, the move strengthened the alliance between the Frankish king and the papacy. Fourth, it was a slap in the face of the emperor in Byzantium, who still claimed to rule the western lands of the empire. The ruler in Byzantium at the time was the empress Irene, whom the pope did not recognize.

The Throne of Charlemagne, located at the Aachen Cathedral in Germany, is made of marble slabs from Jerusalem.

The new (or restored) Roman Empire was, however, only a shadow of its former self. It was not nearly as large or as powerful as the empire based in Rome had been. It had no unified government and bestowed no citizenship. Few large cities existed in the lands claimed by Charlemagne, and no road system tied the domain together. The only thing Roman about it was that it included the city of Rome and was declared by the bishop of Rome; otherwise, it was really a Frankish kingdom based in central Europe.

The Decline of Charlemagne's Empire

Charlemagne's empire was short-lived. His son, Louis, tried to pass it on to his oldest son, Lothar; but Lothar's younger brothers staked claims to shares of the kingdom based on the precedent Clovis had set many years earlier in dividing his kingdom among his sons. The Treaty of Verdun in 843 divided the Frankish kingdom three ways: Lothar received Italy and the territory north of the Alps, Louis received the region east of the Rhine, and Charles got the lands west of the Rhine. Lothar's portion was merged into the other kingdoms through continued family feuds. The areas of the other two brothers were the beginnings of what became France and Germany many centuries later.

In the midst of this weakened domestic situation, numerous foreign invaders besieged Europe. Muslim raiders took control of southern Italy and even Rome itself for a time. The Magyars or Hungarians moved in from Asia, established control in eastern Europe, and at times attacked as far as the Netherlands and southern France. The most dangerous attacks, however, were launched by men of the north, or Norsemen (also known as Vikings), from Scandinavia. Fierce pagan warriors looking for more land for their growing population, the Vikings gained control in northern Europe, the British Isles, and the Baltic and Black Sea regions. They threatened most of the rest of Europe at various times. Other Viking invaders entered Russia, Greenland, and Iceland. In 911 the king of the Franks gave the Norsemen the region of northern France that came to be named after them: Normandy. Another Norse explorer, Leif Erikson, apparently sailed as far west as Newfoundland in North America about 1000.

Faced with these threats of invasion, Europeans turned to whatever source of defense they could find, which was usually not the weak king in their area. Instead, the people promised to serve wealthy local nobles, who in turn promised to use his resources to defend them. Peasants agreed to work the noble's land in exchange for a place to live in relative safety. Warriors who owned relatively less land vowed to fight for a lord of greater stature. Kings depended on the nobles to collect taxes and to provide defense for the realm. Thus the most powerful people in Europe around the year 1000 were not kings but

The Slavs were the first known inhabitants of the region north of the Black Sea we now know as Russia. Viking invaders descended on the area in the eighth and ninth centuries, and some settled there. The Viking Rurik began to rule in the Slavic town of Novgorod in 862, thus creating the first dynasty in Russia. The monument at left was dedicated in Novgorod in 1862, when this photograph was taken. It is called the Millennium of Russia, and commemorates Rurik's arrival.

landowning nobles or lords. This was the beginning of the system of feudalism, which remained in place in Europe to varying degrees until modern times. We will discuss feudalism in more detail in lesson 72 of the next unit.

The Role of the Roman Catholic Church

During the early Middle Ages, the Roman Catholic Church played a central role in European life. We have seen the influence of the pope in the naming of kings. In the first century, Paul taught Christians to be subject to the governing authorities. In the early Middle Ages, the Church had grown in power to such an extent that governing authorities were subject to the Church.

The Church greatly influenced daily life as well. Charlemagne developed the system of local parishes, each with its own priest, that brought the Church hierarchy down to the local level. Church buildings became the center of village and town life. Priests and bishops gave their blessings to armies going off to war, to marriages, and to every other significant event in village life. Often the priest was the only person in town or on the manor who had any kind of formal schooling.

A tax or tithe was collected by the Church from the people. Some of the money stayed in the parish, some went to the pope, and the rest was directed to the treasury of the king. We must remember that the separation of church and state was not a common concept at the time. The government was seen as ruling by the blessing and permission of God and as protecting the Church from harm. In return, the Church blessed the government and gave it spiritual guidance.

The Roman Catholic Church was a large umbrella that included many different activities. The pope and the bishops were involved with politics and power, both in the Church and in government. The local priest was the face of the Church that common people saw on a weekly basis. Monks were

Mont Saint-Michel is a tidal island off the northwestern coast of France. A monastery was established there in the 700s. Over the centuries, a small town developed on the island around the abbey.

withdrawn from everyday life in one sense, but in another sense the monasteries were a major presence in local communities. The Church was other-worldly and this-worldly at the same time. It claimed to be the route to heaven; but its hierarchy, political influence, and accumulation of property were all very much involved with this life. The Church taught about Jesus' way of life, but many Church leaders did not live that way.

Byzantium

The eastern remnant of the Roman Empire was still a key player in world events during this period. Byzantium is the Greek name for the site of Constantinople. Byzantine culture was a mix of European, Greek, Hellenistic, and Oriental influences. Its power did not lie in the size of its territory, which by this time only included Syria and Palestine, Asia Minor, Greece and Egypt, and southeastern Europe. The Byzantine Empire served as a bridge between Western and Oriental cultures and provided European culture with significant gifts. Practically speaking, the Byzantine Empire protected the West from attack from the East until Byzantium fell in 1453. It also helped spread the Christian faith into areas such as the Balkan Peninsula and Russia.

Byzantine scholars copied the literature of ancient Greece to keep it available to future generations. Its craftsmen worked wonders in gold, silver, enamel, and other mediums. The outstanding accomplishment of Justinian's building program was the Church of Hagia Sophia (Holy Wisdom). This complex structure, built in only six years, features domes and half domes and is highlighted by the main dome, which is 100 feet across, 180 feet high, and supported by four huge arches.

Byzantium and the Greek Orthodox Church had important interaction with the Slavic peoples of Eastern Europe. In the sixth and seventh centuries, the Slavs moved out of Western Asia and seized control of southeastern Europe. They also invaded Russia. The Byzantine Church saw the Slavs as people to be influenced for Christ and sought to do so in the ninth and tenth centuries.

Justinian (emperor from 527 to 565) was the most outstanding ruler of this period. In the role of absolute monarch, he reasserted the power of the empire and the power of the emperor, especially in Church affairs. His armies regained Italy, northwest Africa, and several of the Mediterranean islands; and they also gained a foothold in Spain. Justinian oversaw a codification of Roman law. He appointed the patriarch (the leader of the Greek Orthodox Church), decided matters of doctrine, and enforced Church discipline.

Hagia Sophia served as a church from its construction until 1453. After the Ottoman capture of Constantinople in that year, it was converted to a mosque (as shown in this photo from the early 1900s). After World War I, the Republic of Turkey replaced the Ottoman Empire. Hagia Sophia was opened to the public as a museum in 1935.

Greek Orthodox leaders allowed the Slavs to conduct services in their native tongue instead of using the customary Greek. Church scholars even adapted the Greek alphabet to the Slavic language, creating the Cyrillic alphabet (named for Cyril, leading missionary among the Slavs). The branch of the Church in Russia became the Russian Orthodox Church. Russia became the easternmost nation that was influenced by Byzantium.

Civilization in Transition

The Early Middle Ages saw many changes in Europe. Cities such as Rome, Athens, and Jerusalem were not as important and influential as they once had been. Society was more rural based. Kingdoms and nation states were not as significant as large estates owned by nobles. Population growth was not large, and it even declined for a time with a serious outbreak of bubonic plague that affected the Mediterranean rim and Western Europe in the sixth century.

Central and Western Europe, the cultural ancestors of America, were seeing the creation of a new civilization. Like any civilization, it was built on what had come before: Roman culture, European tribes, and a strong Christian presence. The resulting European culture has influenced not only that area but the entire world from that time until today.

For a child will be born to us, a son will be given to us;
And the government will rest on His shoulders;
And His name will be called Wonderful Counselor,
Mighty God, Eternal Father, Prince of Peace.
Isaiah 9:6

Assignments for Lesson 66

In Their Words Read the hymns by Columba and Andrew of Crete and the excerpt from *Beowulf* (pages 95-98).

Literature Continue reading *The Imitation of Christ*. Plan to finish it by the end of this unit.

Student Review Optional: Answer the questions for Lesson 66.

Lesson 67 - Key Event

The Rise of Islam

This story begins hundreds of years ago, but it is as relevant as today's headlines. It is an illustration of why we need to understand history and why understanding only European and American history is not sufficient to be knowledgeable of today's world.

The Life of Muhammad

Arabs are a people who originated in the Arabian peninsula. They speak the Arabic language and maintain Arabic culture. In the sixth century AD, some Arabs lived in cities and conducted trade; most were nomad shepherds. The Arabs believed in many gods and spiritual beings. In the city of Mecca was a shrine called the Kaaba that housed the idols of many pagan gods as well as a sacred black stone believed to have fallen from heaven. Sometimes Arab worship involved infanticide. The level of morality was not high.

Muhammad was born about 570 in Mecca, a trading city in western Arabia. Orphaned as a child, he was reared by a grandfather and uncle. He became a merchant. At age twenty-five, he began working for a rich widow. Impressed by his character, she proposed marriage, and Muhammad accepted. She was forty.

In his trading activity he learned about Judaism and Christianity. When he was about forty years old, Muhammad left the business world and became a spiritual thinker. He believed that he received revelations from Allah, whom he considered the one true deity. Muhammad believed that he was supposed to tell others what Allah told him.

The central truth of his message was that Allah was the only deity and that he, Muhammad, was the last true prophet of Allah. This message was not popular in Mecca, where Muhammad was denounced as a blasphemer. In 622 Muhammad and his few followers fled north to Yathrib (the Arabic word for flight is *hegira*, pronounced ha-JI-rah). Here he was more warmly received and began building a movement. He changed the name of the city to Medina, which means City of the Prophet. The year we number 622 is in Muslim history Year One.

Muhammad wanted to unite the Arab world in one faith, wipe out paganism, end tribal feuds, and guide people to live upright lives. The way to accomplish this, he thought, was for everyone to submit to him as the prophet of Allah. The Arab word for submit is *islam*; a submitted person is a *muslim*.

Lesson 67 - Key Event: The Rise of Islam

This medieval Persian illustration depicts Muhammad praying with Abraham, Moses, and Jesus. According to a Muslim tradition, Muhammad traveled to heaven one night and met various people from the Bible. Allah wanted Muhammad and his followers to pray fifty times per day. Moses told Muhammad that he didn't think people could handle that many prayers. Moses encouraged Muhammad to negotiate with Allah to get the requirement down to five prayers per day, and each one would count for ten prayers.

The movement went beyond mere persuasion. Muhammad believed that he received a revelation allowing the use of force to convert unbelievers if necessary. This cause is called a *jihad,* or holy war. Thus Muhammad became a military leader as well as a spiritual leader.

Muhammad's followers began raiding caravans (a profitable form of evangelism) and taking the lives of those who refused to submit. Six hundred Jews were killed in one year alone. The city of Mecca finally yielded to Muslim forces in 630, and Muhammad returned in triumph. The Muslims destroyed the idols in the Kaaba but kept the Black Stone as a

symbol of the new religion. Desert nomads flocked to the new faith as well. When Muhammad died in 632, most of Arabia was under his control.

Muhammad married often but produced no male heir who survived childhood. His followers chose Muhammad's father-in-law as his successor (*caliph*) and continued the jihad. By 720 the Muslims controlled an area that extended from the western border of India across the Middle East, along northern Africa and southern Italy, and into Spain. Jerusalem fell to the Muslims in 638. Generally speaking, the Muslim empire tolerated Jews and Christians if they paid a tax and refrained from warfare. Many Christians became Muslims; and nearly all of the countries which fell to Islam in its first century are still predominately Muslim.

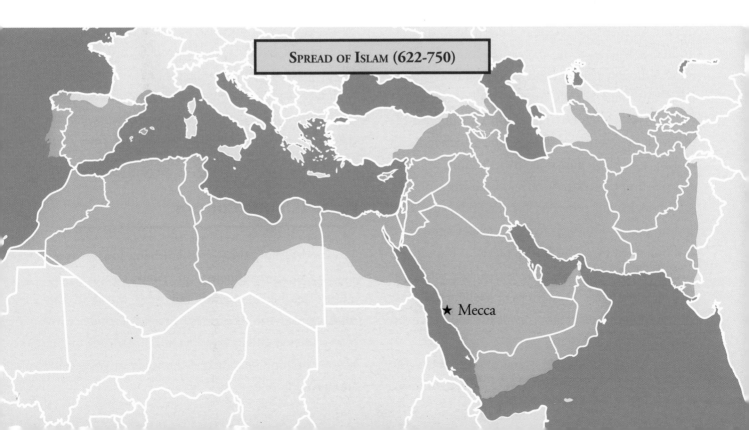

SPREAD OF ISLAM (622-750)

★ Mecca

The Qur'an and the Bible

The Qur'an refers to many people mentioned in the Bible, including Adam, Eve, Cain, Abel, Noah, Abraham, Joseph, Moses, Saul, David, Goliath, the Queen of Sheba, Jonah, Zechariah, John the Baptist, Mary, and Jesus. The illustration at right of Musa (Moses) holding a cane is from a 15th-century Persian manuscript. Several of the stories told about these people agree with what is in the Bible, but there are several changes, too. A son of Noah is said to have refused to go into the ark and was swept away when he took refuge on a mountaintop. Zechariah was said to be speechless for three days, not nine months, when he was told that John the Baptist would be born to him and Elizabeth. Muhammad apparently believed that Jesus died a natural death and that the Jews crucified a man who looked like Him.

Muhammad did not claim to be divine. He accepted the Old and New Testaments as revelations from Allah and believed that Jesus was a prophet. Muhammad's thinking was influenced by the Bible. He taught that the Arabs were descended from Ishmael, son of Abraham by Hagar. He was opposed to idolatry and the eating of pork, and he believed in angels. However, he shaped other teachings on his own.

Muhammad encouraged people to do good but did not emphasize self-denial the way Jesus did. He limited polygamy to no more than four wives to a man, although Muhammad himself was exempted from this limit thanks to a special revelation he received. No limit was placed on concubines. He believed in rewards and punishments after death and in a kind of purgatory for Muslims. Paradise offered sumptuous banquets and beautiful women.

Islam has no provision for images of any kind and no priests, although religious scholars (*mullahs*) and holy men (*ayatollahs*) hold places of respect and authority. The only assembly is a prayer service at midday on Fridays. The sayings of Muhammad were written down shortly after his death and compiled in the Qur'an (or Koran).

Within decades after Muhammad's death, the movement he founded broke into several factions.

The Sunnis favored an elected leader as the successor to Muhammad and accepted traditional practices as well as the Qur'an as their authority. The Shi'ites believed that their leader should be related to Muhammad and accepted only the literal reading of the Qur'an as their guide. Other groups included mystics and free-thinkers.

After a few years of conflict between groups, the Umayyad family gained control. They moved the political capital of the Muslim Empire to Damascus, Syria (Mecca was always its spiritual center). In 750 the Abbasid family took control, named a distant relative of Muhammad as their leader, and moved the capital to Baghdad, where they reigned in increasing splendor over the next few centuries. Other groups rose from time to time and established their own caliphates in different locations.

Arab-Islamic Culture

The Muslim faith was the driving force behind significant developments in Arab culture. The culture reached its zenith (an Arab word) in the ninth and tenth centuries. Increased trade with places such as Russia and equatorial Africa brought new wealth and encouraged the study of geography and navigation.

The Five Pillars of Islam

Most Muslims acknowledge five basic requirements, or pillars of their faith. These are not described in the Qur'an, but in the Hadith of Gabriel. A hadith is an additional collection of sayings or acts attributed to Muhammad.

1. The belief that "There is no god but Allah and Muhammad is his prophet."

2. Daily prayer offered five times per day (at dawn, midday, midafternoon, sunset, and nightfall); a formulaic prayer in Arabic, said while kneeling and bowing toward Mecca.

3. Giving to the poor, which became a routine tax in Islamic countries for helping the poor and for building and maintaining mosques.

4. Daylight fasting during the month of Ramadan (when Muhammad supposedly received his revelations)

5. If possible, a pilgrimage to Mecca and the performing of certain rituals while there. Most Muslims are not able to make this pilgrimage, but it has had a unifying effect on those who have.

A minaret is a tower or spire on or near an Islamic mosque. It is used to call Muslims to prayer five times per day. Pictured below are minarets from around the world.

India (1200s)

China (1300s)

Indonesia (c. 1549)

Hungary (1600s)

Yemen (1914)

Brazil (1972)

UK (2003)

Switzerland (2009)

Ibn Sīnā (commonly known by his Latinized name Avicenna) was a Persian scholar (c. 980-1037). One of his famous works, The Canon of Medicine, summarized medical knowledge of his day. It was translated into Latin, Chinese, Hebrew, German, French, and English, and used in medical training into the 1600s. A page from a 16th-century edition of the book is pictured at left.

The encouragement of learning led to the establishment of universities and advancements in medicine (such as discovering the nature of smallpox, developing antidotes for poisons, and building teaching hospitals) and science (sulphuric acid, nitrate of silver, and the processes of filtration and distillation). The Arabs introduced to the West the number system they discovered in India, which is why it is called Arabic numerals. Arabic mathematicians gave us the zero, the discipline of algebra, and advancements in trigonometry.

Their literature took many forms. The *One Thousand and One Nights* is a collection of Middle Eastern and Asian stories written in Arabic. It was compiled in different versions from the ninth century onward. The famous stories about Aladdin, Ali Baba, and Sinbad the Sailor are from the same cultural setting, but they were evidently not part of the original collection of stories. Omar Khayyam was a Persian scholar (1048-1131) who studied and wrote on a variety of subjects, including mathematics, astronomy, and philosophy. *The Rubaiyat of Omar Khayyam* was published in 1859 by Edward FitzGerald. It purports to be a translation of short poetic quatrains attributed to Khayyam,

The Selimiye Mosque was completed in 1575 in Edirne, Turkey. This is the interior of the dome.

but FitzGerald evidently supplemented Khayyam's work with his own imagination.

Islamic scholars preserved ancient Greek texts including those by Plato and Aristotle. Muslim schools were established in Cairo, Egypt; Toledo, Spain; and Palermo, Italy. European Christian scholars eventually attended these schools and rediscovered ancient writings assumed to be lost.

While European artistic endeavors were few, Arabs were exploring rich forms and colors in tapestries, beautiful architectural forms including elaborate palaces, domes, and minaret towers (the pinnacle being the Taj Mahal tomb from 17th-century India). In an effort to prevent idolatry, Islam has generally discouraged the creation of images of people and animals. Much Islamic art features elaborate geometric and floral designs.

Arabic trade stimulated European commerce in the 12th and 13th centuries. Medieval Gothic architecture was influenced by Muslim accomplishments. Versions of stories from the Arabian Nights found their way into European literature, including Chaucer's *Canterbury Tales*. Many Arabic words have come into the English language, such as traffic, bazaar, alcohol, muslin, tariff, check (the Arabs pioneered its use in trade), and magazine.

The Alhambra in southern Spain was built as a fortress in the ninth century. Muslim leaders in the 14th and 15th centuries expanded it into a palace complex. After Catholic Spanish rulers took over the area in 1492, the buildings were maintained for a while but eventually fell into disrepair. Renovations began in the 19th century, and it became a major tourist attraction. The window above is an example of the Islamic architecture on display there.

Conclusion

The Islamic movement had the impact it did because of the internal motivation of the faithful's beliefs. They believed that they were right and that other people needed to believe as they did. Muslim warriors were convinced that they would be rewarded with riches in this life and paradise in the next.

Several external factors were involved as well. The drive for geographic and financial gain was strong. The Byzantine and Persian empires were weak. Europe was suffering from poor leadership and the effects of plague. Some of the peoples that the Muslims conquered welcomed a change from the rulers under whom they had been living. The Islamic Empire declined after the Crusades and the Mongol invasions that came later. The last major Islamic caliphate, which was controlled by the Ottomans, collapsed after World War I.

Not all Muslims today advocate violent jihad against those who believe differently, but Muslims believe that Islam should be and will be the dominant force in the world. Current statistics suggest that nearly one in four people in the world adhere to Islam. Indonesia, Pakistan, India, Bangladesh, and Egypt have the highest populations of Muslims, and their presence and influence are growing elsewhere in Africa, in Europe, and in the Americas.

During the annual Hajj, the pilgrimage to Mecca, about three million Muslims throng the al-Haram Mosque to walk around the Kaaba (the black structure in the middle of the photo) and perform other rituals.

And there is salvation in no one else [but Jesus];
for there is no other name under heaven
that has been given among men by which we must be saved.
Acts 4:12

Assignments for Lesson 67

In Their Words   Read the excerpts from *The Conquest of Egypt* (pages 99-101).

Literature   Continue reading *The Imitation of Christ*.

Student Review   Optional: Answer the questions for Lesson 67.

Alfred the Great

The Vikings, seafaring bands from Norway, Sweden, and Denmark, were on the move in Northern Europe, from Ireland to Britain to France to Russia. Some made quick raids and returned home. Others stayed where they landed and built new homes. This was the world into which Alfred was born about the year 849. He is the only English monarch to be remembered as "the Great." If that title is fit for any man, Alfred's life and conduct suggest that it is fit for him.

Conflict with the Danes

Alfred was born to King Ethelwulf of Wessex and his wife Osburga. His father took him to visit Rome as a boy. Alfred's mother and father died when the boy was still young, and his older brothers ruled in turn after Ethelwulf.

In the 860s, warriors from Denmark invaded England. The Danes found great treasure in the churches and monasteries, and they met little effective resistance among the unprepared Saxons. As the Danes spread out in the north and east, Ethelred, who was then king, prepared to face them with his brother Alfred at his side.

The first major confrontation came in 871. The Danes approached for battle while King Ethelred was still praying. Alfred was a devout man, too, but instead of waiting for his brother, he decided to lead the Saxons against the foe. Ethelred eventually joined Alfred in the lengthy fight, and they forced the Danes to retreat. Though it was only the beginning of a long struggle, this battle checked the Danish advance and proved that the Saxons were able to field a victorious army. Ethelred became ill and died that year. The Saxons looked to Alfred, still in his early twenties, as their new king.

After a difficult period that saw several defeats for the Saxons, Alfred made a treaty with the Danes. He had to pay heavy tribute, but at least his army was not destroyed. A few years of peace ensued until Guthrum, a new Danish leader, began his assault on Wessex. Alfred attempted to renew peace with Guthrum, but the Danes were ready for combat. In January 878 a surprise attack crushed the Saxon army. Those who were not killed fled. Alfred and a few followers went into seclusion as he tried to rebuild his army.

Alfred has been memorialized in many ways, as shown above (from left to right): as a Byzantine-style saintly icon, as a courageous military leader in a 19th-century history of England, and as a regal ruler in a stained glass window.

A later medieval legend says that while Alfred was regrouping, he visited a peasant woman who did not know who he was. She asked him to watch the cakes she was cooking while she was out. When she returned, she found the cakes burned, and she upbraided the king. A ball-shaped fungus in England is known by the nickname King Alfred's Cake.

After the Danes failed to capture a Saxon stronghold, Alfred called out the fyrd, the local militia. His subjects still respected and admired him, and they were ready to stand with him against their enemies. Alfred marched against the Danes. They met in a great contest, and this time the Saxons forced the Danes to flee. Guthrum and his men asked for peace.

Instead of seeking to destroy his opponents or even asking for hostages, Alfred wanted Guthrum to accept baptism. He hosted Guthrum in his camp, acted as godfather at his baptism, and called him his son. Alfred wanted to establish peace in the land between Saxon and Dane, and they had fourteen years of relative calm.

Building a Kingdom

As he led his people well in war, so Alfred led them well in peace. He was a devout man who recognized the importance of Christianity. He sought to insure justice for the poor. Alfred compiled a book of laws that combined Biblical principles with traditional customs.

Alfred also promoted education. He learned to read and write as king, and he personally translated works from Latin into English. He established a

school featuring scholars from Britain and other countries; and he developed the Anglo-Saxon Chronicle, an historical record that was continued for many generations after him.

Part of his peacetime work included preparations for war. He divided the militia into two groups so that some could stay home while the others were in the field. He encouraged the construction and maintenance of fortifications. He also tried with limited success to establish a navy.

Continuing His Work

Guthrum died in 891, and another Viking army invaded England in 892. Alfred's health was not good, but his twenty-two-year-old son Edward followed in his footsteps as an able commander. Alfred attempted to negotiate with the opposing leader, Hæsten. Hæsten accepted money from Alfred and allowed his two sons to be baptized; but a major clash of arms still threatened. As the threat grew, Edward and his brother-in-law attacked and routed the Danish army. They struck again at a fortified Danish position and won a great victory.

Coin from the Reign of Alfred

What Else Was Happening? (500-1000)

1 The Maya civilization of central America had reached a high point of cultural and technological development (see pyramid from Uxmal at right) when it suffered a mysterious setback around 900.

2 Dorset culture is a name applied to a society that flourished in northern Canada and Greenland from about 500 BC to 1500 AD (see carved polar bear at right). A small number of their descendents apparently survived into modern times. Disease brought by visitors had killed all of the remaining members living on Southampton Island by 1903.

3 The surrender of Jerusalem to the Muslims included a special provision. Sophronius, Patriarch of Jerusalem, gave the key to the Church of the Holy Sepulchre to the Muslim caliph Umar, with the understanding that the church would not be turned into a mosque. Except for a few decades during the Crusades, Muslims have controlled daily access to the church to this day. The Nuseibeh and Judeh families have passed the responsibility down for centuries.

4 The Chinese had been building artificial waterways for a thousand years when Emperor Yang of the Sui dynasty expanded and combined them in the early 600s. Known as the Grand Canal, it is the longest artificial river in the world at 1,100 miles long. Improved over the centuries, it remains in use.

5 The Kingdom of Tondo flourished for several centuries in the Manila Bay area of the Philippines. The earliest known written reference is from the Laguna Copperplate Inscription (c. 900, see replica above right). Along with other Filipino kingdoms, Tondo was subdued in the 1500s by the Spanish, who established their capital at Manila.

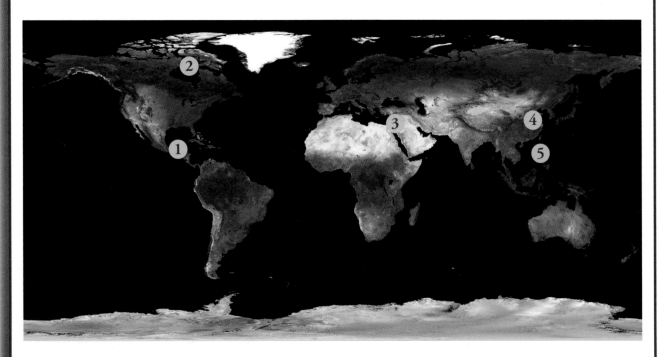

Statue of Alfred in his Birthplace of Wantage

In this battle, the Saxons captured women and children the Danes left behind, including Hæsten's wife and two sons. Alfred could have held them as hostages, but he returned them to Hæsten in a generous gesture of charity. The war continued until 896, but Hæsten apparently did not participate.

His Legacy

Alfred and his wife Ealhswyth had five surviving children as well as others who died in infancy. Alfred died in 899, and his son Edward took up his mantle. His daughter, Ethelfreda, became Lady of the Mercians after her husband died; and she and her brother worked together to resist the Danes. Alfred's legacy of noble leadership continued for many years through his descendants.

English society has undergone many changes in the centuries since Alfred, but his life remains an impressive example of a man who sought to do good.

The king gives stability to the land by justice . . . .
Proverbs 29:4

Assignments for Lesson 68

In Their Words   Read the excerpts from the Anglo-Saxon Chronicle and "O God, Our Maker, Throned on High" (pages 102-104).

Literature   Continue reading *The Imitation of Christ*.

Student Review   Optional: Answer the questions for Lesson 68.

Lesson 69 - Everyday Life

The Vikings

The term "Viking," first used in the 11th century, probably comes from the Swedish word *vik*, meaning bay. The Vikings originated in what is now Sweden, Norway, and Denmark. They were farmers, traders, and warriors. The first mention of these people in the literature of southern Europe was about 800 AD.

Viking society was ruled by chieftains. Free Vikings could carry arms and speak at assemblies. They were divided into *jarls* (or earls) and farmers. Viking slaves were called thralls. Vikings developed their shipbuilding skills and were able to travel to other lands, sometimes for trade and sometimes to wreak havoc.

Viking Life at Home

Families of three generations or more lived in long farmhouses that were built of stone and turf or stone and timber. Roofs were thatched. The main room was used for cooking, eating, and sleeping. The houses also had a storage room and a dayroom, where women wove on looms and sewed.

Vikings grew grain and vegetables and kept cows, which were milked for making butter and cheese. They cooked meat stew in huge iron cauldrons supported by a tripod. They had bowls and plates, usually made of wood. They ate with a knife and spoon. Spoons could be made of wood, horn, or bone and were often carved. Horns were used for cups. Sometimes these had metal tips and rims.

One way we learn about everyday life is from Viking graves. Women were often buried with tools for making flax into thread. Viking men were usually buried with a sword, shield, spear, ax, arrows, and sometimes blacksmithing tools. Great quantities of weapons have been found in Viking graves.

Viking Re-enactors in Germany

Viking women wore a long linen shift, which was sometimes pleated, under a pinafore of wool or linen. Women wore two large ornate bronze, silver, or iron brooches on their pinafores. Wealthy women might wear beads between the two brooches. The shift was usually embroidered at the top and often at the hem as well. Viking men wore trousers and a tunic made of wool or linen and an undershirt made of linen. Sometimes these garments were decorated with embroidery sewn with wool, linen, silk, gold, or silver thread. Viking sagas indicate that clothes for both men and women were brightly colored.

This reconstruction of a Viking house was built near Hobro, Denmark.

The Carta Marina ("map of the sea") from 1539 is the oldest known detailed map of the Nordic countries (Norway, Sweden, Denmark, Iceland, and Greenland). It was created by Olof Månsson, a Swedish scholar who lived in Rome. He also authored the 1555 book History of the Northern People.

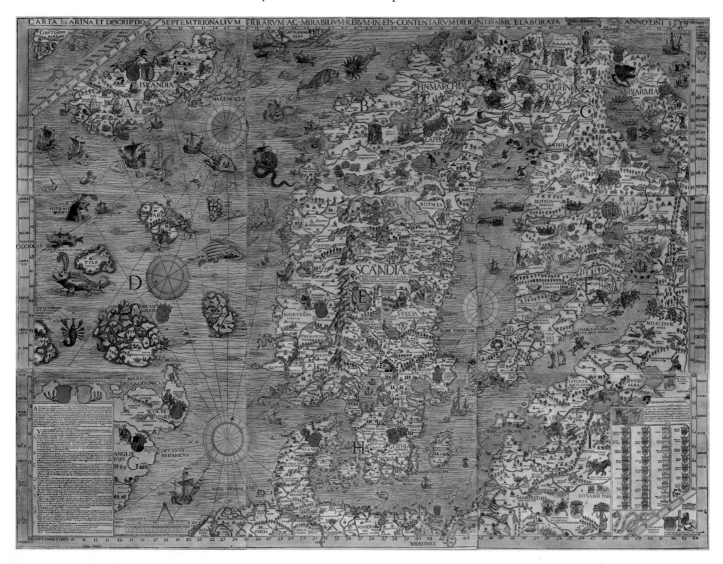

The Stenkvista runestone in Sweden features an image of Thor's hammer, named Mjölnir.

Vikings practiced good personal hygiene, combing their hair and washing their faces and hands at least daily. Some combs were made of bone and occasionally of imported ivory. Some had two opposing rows of teeth, with one row of large teeth spread slightly apart and one row of thin teeth close together. Perhaps they removed tangles with the large teeth and lice with the small ones. Men were buried with a comb and a comb case; women had a comb, but no case. Viking women carried an earspoon for removing wax, a tool for cleaning fingernails, and tweezers. Sometimes these were ornamented and hung on a chain from one of the pinafore brooches.

Viking chieftans served as priests. They sacrificed horses. Their epic poems or sagas told myths about their pagan gods and their relationship with giants, dwarfs, and men. Their most powerful god was the one-eyed Odin, god of death, justice, poetry, warfare, and wisdom. Their most popular god was the slow-witted but strong Thor. Many people wore amulets shaped like Thor's hammer, which was supposedly made by dwarfs. Also important were the fertility gods Frey and Freyja, a brother and sister. Vikings wore amulets, which were religious jewelry. Surviving amulet designs include a key, a heart, and Thor's hammer.

When Vikings built colonies in Normandy, Ireland, and the British Isles, many became Christians. Some Viking women traveled to the new lands, but often Viking men married local women. Also, German and Anglo-Saxon missionaries went to Viking lands. Christian churches were well-established in Denmark and most of Norway by the 11th century and in Sweden by the 12th.

The community of Heddal has the largest wooden stave church in Norway. Originally built in the 13th century, it fell into disrepair after the Reformation. It was restored in the 19th and 20th centuries.

When Christianity came to the Vikings, it frequently was promoted through coercion rather than persuasion. Today a majority of Scandinavians are officially members of the national churches, but a minority believe in a god of any kind, and only a tiny fraction attend church regularly.

The Gokstad ship was discovered in 1880 in a burial mound in Norway. It is 76 feet long and 17 feet wide, with room for 32 oarsmen and a total of 70 men. A replica of this ship was sailed in 1893 from Norway across the Atlantic to Chicago via the Hudson River, Erie Canal, and Great Lakes for the World's Columbian Exposition.

Viking Life at Sea

The Vikings were good shipbuilders. They built fast wooden longships with overlapping planks. The ships were between 57 and 117 feet long and were outfitted with both sails and oars. The ships were able to travel not only on the sea but also on rivers and streams because their draughts were shallow.

The ship crews numbered between twenty-five and seventy-five. They sat on benches on open decks. Some of the largest ships might have carried up to one hundred men. They also carried provisions and even packhorses if needed. Ships had fierce figureheads at the bow and stern. Shields were mounted on the ship's sides.

For three hundred years, Vikings went on voyages to raid and to explore. Raids were often conducted with a single ship, but sometimes ships sailed in fleets of as many as one hundred. Vikings usually fought on or near land with spears, swords, and shields. Battles at sea were rare. When fighting at sea, the Vikings roped their ships together to create a floating island. Vikings tried to capture rather than destroy enemy ships.

The Faroe Islands, located between Norway and Iceland, are a self-governing territory of the Danish Realm (along with Greenland). The local Postverk Føroya issued this set of stamps in 2005 titled "Everyday Life in the Viking Age."

Lesson 69 - Everyday Life: The Vikings

The typical picture of a Viking warrior in a helmet with horns is a myth. This helmet, discovered in Norway and dating from the tenth century, is the most complete Viking helmet found. Metal helmets might have been worn only by the leaders.

Some Viking warriors were called "berserks." They would work themselves into a frenzy. Reportedly, they bit the edges of their shields and could ignore pain. They might have been called "berserks" because they wore bearskin.

The sea-faring Vikings raided coastal lands. They raided many churches, likely because churches were wealthy and had poor defenses. Sometimes the raids were seasonal. Warriors would usually either go back home to farm or settle in the land they raided.

Vikings made their mark over a wide area. Swedes penetrated Russia down to the Black and Caspian Seas in the east. Norwegians skirted the British Isles and moved west to Iceland, Greenland, and likely Canada. The Danes moved into England, France, and around Spain into the Mediterranean.

Sing to the Lord a new song,
Sing His praise from the end of the earth!
You who go down to the sea, and all that is in it.
You islands, and those who dwell on them.
Isaiah 42:10

Assignments for Lesson 69

In Their Words Read the excerpt from *Eirik the Red's Saga* (pages 105-107).

Literature Continue reading *The Imitation of Christ*.

Student Review Optional: Answer the questions for Lesson 69.

Senty Church, Greater Caucasus Region of Russia (Tenth Century)

Lesson 70 - Bible Study

Methods and Motives in Evangelism

Jesus commanded the apostles:

"As you are going [participle expressing habitual action],

"make disciples of all ethne ["make disciples" is the main verb of the sentence, imperative form; ethne is the word for nations from which we get ethnic],

[the next two phrases are participial, explaining what is involved in making disciples:]

"baptizing them in the name of the Father and the Son and the Holy Spirit, [the beginning step of making a disciple]

"teaching them to observe all that I have commanded you, [the long-term process of making disciples]

"and behold, I will be with you all the days, unto the end of the age" [indicating the power whereby they would be able to do what He had commanded] (Matthew 28:19-20, literal translation).

The Lord commanded the apostles to carry the gospel to the world (see also Mark 16:15-16, Luke 24:46-47, and Acts 1:8). The word evangelism is not used in the New Testament, but some men are described as evangelists (Ephesians 4:11, Acts 21:8). Paul was God's chosen instrument to take the message of salvation to the Gentiles (Acts 9:15). After the execution of Stephen, those who were scattered from Jerusalem went about "evangelizing" (proclaiming the goods news).

God wants all people to be saved (1 Timothy 2:4). He does not want any to perish but wants all to come to repentance (2 Peter 3:9). The way that God has chosen for people to learn the message of good news is by individuals telling the gospel to others. Although God could speak the message directly from heaven, He instead instructs His people to tell the message. Even in the cases of Saul and Cornelius, God did not tell the good news from heaven but directed the hearer to listen to another person tell the story.

Over the centuries, the church has grown through the teaching of the gospel to people who have not known the Lord. Missionaries have taken the good news of Jesus to every continent. In doing so, evangelists have used many different approaches. Some have gone as individuals, whereas in more recent years many missionaries have formed teams of workers to encourage and support each other. Some have been strictly teachers, while others have tried to meet the needs of the people (such as providing health care or teaching farming skills) as a way to establish contact and encourage interest in what the evangelists have to say and why they are there.

The period of the early Middle Ages saw important evangelism take place in many parts of Europe. Patrick, for example, took the gospel to Ireland. He was born into a Christian family in Roman-held Britain. At 16 he was kidnapped and sold into slavery in Ireland. There he became deeply committed to following the Lord. He eventually escaped, studied in Europe, and in 432 was ordained a bishop and sent back to Ireland.

Patrick taught the gospel to all. Members of the royal family as well as many everyday people came to faith in Christ. He trained native Irishmen to be priests, and he established monasteries. Through his influence, monks became copyists who preserved ancient literature—Christian and secular—in monasteries across Europe.

Augustine (not the bishop of Hippo) was born in Rome. The pope sent him to England in 597 to convert the Anglo-Saxons. Soon after he arrived, Augustine brought Ethelbert, the Saxon king of southeastern England, to faith (his wife was already a believer). Augustine led in the evangelization of England and became the first archbishop of Canterbury (that is, the leader of the Church in England).

Boniface was born in England but devoted much of his adult life to teaching the Saxons in Germany starting in 719. The area had already seen considerable teaching of the gospel; but many had

Saint Patrick's Memorial Church in Saul, County Down, Ireland, was built in 1932 to commemorate the 1500th anniversary of Patrick's mission. This is the traditional site of the first church in Ireland, a barn donated by Dichu, the first convert.

fallen back into paganism. Some religious practices mixed Christian and pagan traditions. The story goes that Boniface cut down a large oak tree sacred to the Saxon god Thor and built a Christian chapel from the wood. When no thunderbolt came from Thor, many people decided to follow Christ. Boniface was supported by Charles Martel and his son, Pepin. After serving as an archbishop and overseeing the Church hierarchy in his area for several years, Boniface returned to evangelism but was murdered by pagans in 753.

These are some of the most prominent people who were involved in evangelizing Europe, but the task involved many people in many different ways. Even monasteries, ostensibly withdrawn from the world, had an impact as non-believers wondered what motivated such service and self-sacrifice.

The goal of evangelism is to bring a person to a saving faith in God as the one true God and in Jesus as Savior and Lord and to start that person on the road of faithful discipleship. Two common questions that arise concerning evangelism involve (1) the most effective means of evangelism and (2) what a person has to give up from his old life in order to be faithful to God.

This detail from a 1905 work by German painter Emil Doepler shows Boniface cutting down the tree.

This painting by Jan Joesten van Hillegom (Dutch, c. 1530) depicts four men involved in mission work in the middle ages: Boniface; Pope Gregory I, who sent Augustine to England; Adalbert of Egmond, an Anglo-Saxon missionary in Holland and Frisia; and Jeroen van Noordwijk, a Scottish missionary to Holland.

Obviously a person has to be instructed in the basic truths of the gospel, who Jesus is, and what it means to follow Him. In some places in the world and at some periods in history, preaching on the street corner or in some other public place has been an effective means of evangelizing. However, in 21st century America and Europe this might not be as effective. Christians have tried printed gospel messages, radio and television broadcasts, and other means of delivering the gospel using media.

A person must be taught in some way, but how to help a person be willing to be taught is an essential part of what has been called pre-evangelism. Seeing a Christian's life of faith or receiving help from a Christian can lead an unbeliever to be interested in the gospel. This is how every Christian can be involved in evangelism: not only knowing the truth and being able to share it, but having a life that backs up the message one wants to teach.

The stereotype of the Christian warrior from the Middle Ages is someone who tried to make a pagan believe in Jesus at the point of a spear.

This happened sometimes, but it was not the pattern of the medieval Church. When it did happen, it was the unfortunate result of trying to carry out the Great Commission through the world's ways of warfare.

Christians must be careful not to use worldly methods in trying to carry out the Lord's will. It is often the case that when someone is pressured into making a confession of faith (whether at the end of a spear, through slick salesmanship, by the overly-dramatic appeal of a preacher, or in an emotion-charged group setting), the person's faith does not last very long.

The second issue involves what a person has to give up in order to become a faithful Christian. Someone who is converted to Christ must put away the old man of sin and put on the renewed person who has been made alive in Christ (Romans 6:3-11, Ephesians 4:17-24). The Christian must not do what the Bible says is wrong. A life of immorality, dishonesty, anger, filthy language, lust, and many other sins cannot characterize the Christian (Ephesians 4:25-5:4).

An immoral person must give up immorality, but a farmer does not have to give up farming.

This painting from Qocho, China, might represent a Palm Sunday procession (c. eighth century).

Other Medieval Mission Work

- Euthymius was an Armenian missionary in Palestine in the fifth century. He taught Aspebet, the leader of a Bedouin tribe, who became a Christian. Aspebet took the name Peter and became a bishop among the Arabs.

- Missionaries from Persia spread the gospel in Arabia, Central Asia, India, and China in the 500s and 600s. The Nestorian Stele is an eighth-century monument that describes the coming of Christianity to China. According to this text, the early missionaries seemed to focus on gaining favor with the rulers rather than spreading the gospel among all citizens.

- The spread of Islam led to a decline in the influence of Christianity in northern Africa, but Christians did not completely disappear. In the eighth century, Charles the Great sent money to help poor Christians in Africa. In the ninth century, the church in Alexandria, Egypt, sent missionaries to Kairouan, a major Islamic city in Tunisia.

- Cyril and Methodius were brothers from Thessalonica, Greece, who lived during the ninth century. They are best known for their mission work among the Slavic people of Eastern Europe, including translating portions of the Bible.

Cyril and Methodius are still remembered in public festivals in several European countries. This parade took place in 2006 in Khanty-Mansiysk, Russia.

The days of the week have been linked with celestial bodies, each of which was associated with a pagan deity, since ancient times. The 19th-century Italian cameo below has images of the Greco-Roman deities connected with each day of the week.

Except for Saturday, which comes from the Roman deity Saturn, our English names come from the old Scandinavian days of the week, named respectively for Sunna, Máni, Tiw, Wodan, Thor, and Fríge. The Scandinavian name for Saturday, Lørdag, means "washing day".

Despite widespread conversion of Europeans to Christianity, elements of paganism such as these names remained. The Church decided not to make it an issue as people were turning to Christ.

What the Bible does not condemn as wrong does not have to be given up to follow Christ. In the first century, Jewish Christians continued to have scruples about clean and unclean foods and, at least for a time, continued to observe Jewish festivals. Christian evangelists in medieval Europe did not press converts to eliminate every aspect of their pagan lives when they became Christians.

People who come to Christ have major decisions to make and often a deeply-entrenched lifestyle and belief system that they must give up. The more strongly that Biblical faith in Christ is instilled in people's hearts, modeled by other Christians, and taught in the home, the more likely it is that the faith will be adopted by new converts from the heart and continue from generation to generation. Sharing the gospel with unbelievers, especially those from a different culture, can be difficult; but the struggle is worth it to help other people be saved.

I have become all things to all men,
so that I may by all means save some.
I do all things for the sake of the gospel,
so that I may become a fellow partaker of it.
1 Corinthians 9:22-23

Assignments for Lesson 70

Bible   Recite or write Acts 4:11-12 from memory.

In Their Words   Read the Memorial of the Diffusion of the Illustrious Religion in the Middle Kingdom (pages 108-111).

Literature   Finish reading *The Imitation of Christ*. Literary analysis available in *Student Review*.

Project   Complete your project for the unit.

Student Review   Optional: Answer the questions for Lesson 70 and for *The Imitation of Christ* and take the quiz for Unit 14.

15

The Late Middle Ages

Summary

In this unit we look at five countries in Europe to see the political changes that were underway between 1000 and 1500. We take a closer look at the feudal system that gave structure to medieval society. The Crusades affected Europe in many ways, but not in the ways their organizers intended. We consider the thinking of Thomas Aquinas as he tried to reconcile faith with the new emphasis on reason. Finally, in the Bible study we look at the difficult choice of obeying God or obeying men.

Lessons

71 - A Changing World
72 - Everyday Life: Feudalism and the Rise of Cities
73 - Key Event: The Crusades
74 - Key Person: Thomas Aquinas
75 - Bible Study: Obeying God, Obeying Men

St. Vitus Cathedral, Prague, Czech Republic (14th Century)

403

Learn James 3:16-18 by the end of the unit.

The Bible
In Their Words

1) Write 300 to 500 words on one of the following topics:

- Write a position paper in which you either defend the feudal system or criticize it. See Lesson 72. Acknowledge arguments from the opposite position, but come down firmly one way or the other.

- Write a letter to the editor of a fictional newspaper in which you express either support for or opposition to the First Crusade. See Lesson 73.

2) Research the foods that would have been included in a feast during the Middle Ages. Prepare a medieval feast for your family including several of these foods.

3) Create an illustrated timeline of the Middle Ages (476-1300). You can do this as a poster, on several sheets of paper, or on a long strip of paper. Include at least 20 key events and illustrate several of them. Make your timeline not only factual, but beautiful as well, reflecting the artistic value of the illuminated manuscripts created during the Middle Ages.

Lesson 71

A Changing World

Changes in culture do not happen overnight. What begins as an exception becomes a pattern and then a tradition, but this process takes many years and happens at different speeds in different places.

The turn of the millennium saw increasing changes in Europe. Costly wars decreased as time passed. The feudal manor economy worked well for those who benefited from it, but changes in the world would soon weaken that time-honored system. Trade grew as war decreased and as contact with Islamic and Byzantine societies increased. The educational opportunities provided by monastery schools stimulated intellectual activity. The growth of cities energized society, business, and education.

England

In January of 1066, the English king Edward the Confessor died. Harold Godwinson, Edward's brother-in-law, claimed the throne by a decision of the council of nobles. William, Duke of Normandy in France and Edward's second cousin, claimed the throne because of his kinship to Edward and on the basis of Edward's promise some years earlier that William would inherit the throne. Supposedly, Harold had given an oath of allegiance to William at some earlier date, but then he reneged and took the throne himself.

To stake his claim as rightful king of England, William of Normandy invaded southern England on September 28, 1066, to march on London. Three days earlier, Harold had met and defeated another invading army in York to the north led by his exiled brother Tostig and the king of Norway. Harold then rushed south and engaged William's forces on October 14 near the town of Hastings. In the all-day battle, the exhausted Saxon forces eventually collapsed before the Normans, Harold was killed, and William, Duke of Normandy, became William the Conqueror, first Norman king of England. He was crowned at Westminster Abbey in London on Christmas Day.

The new government was strongly French. William put Norman lords in place in England who swore allegiance to him. The official language of the

The Bayeux Tapestry is an embroidered linen cloth about 230 feet long that illustrates the chain of events which culminated in the Battle of Hastings. The original was likely created in the 1070s and is now on display in Normandy, France. A group of English women embroidered a replica of it in the 1880s so that England would have its own copy.

court was French. However, the language of England continued to be spoken in everyday life; and over the years the French presence was absorbed into the English ways.

William's son, Henry I, further consolidated royal power by making government offices a matter of appointment rather than heredity; thus those who filled the offices owed allegiance to the king who appointed them. Henry also created the Exchequer, the central government treasury, that gave the king financial strength without having to depend on the nobles.

Beginning in 1170, however, the English throne lost some of its power and prestige. Henry II had appointed his friend, Thomas Becket, to be archbishop of Canterbury. But Becket began to oppose some of Henry's policies. The king became frustrated with Becket; and some knights, thinking they were carrying out Henry's wishes, murdered Becket in the Canterbury Cathedral on December 29, 1170. Henry was blamed for the assassination and lost almost all respect in England. In addition, his two sons turned against him.

One son, Richard I (called the Lionhearted) was out of the country for all but a few months of his ten-year reign. He led the Third Crusade and fought many battles in Europe trying to maintain or expand his kingdom that included much of France. His younger brother, John, who reigned after him, was a true rascal. He quarreled with the pope over naming the archbishop of Canterbury, and as a result the pope excommunicated him. John had to do penance and declare that England belonged to the pope as papal property, a move which did not please the English barons. In addition, John raised taxes on the barons to finance a war with France; then he lost the war and considerable land in France.

In the last year of his reign, on June 15, 1215, a large group of English barons forced John to sign a large document (the Magna Carta, or Great Charter) listing limitations on royal power, making guarantees of the rights of barons and other citizens, and declaring the Catholic Church to be free to make appointments in England without any royal interference. The Magna Carta also said that the king would not impose new taxes without consulting a council of high officials, barons, and bishops. This

The English Language

One of the reasons English is such a complex language with numerous synonyms for many words is that England was invaded so often—by Saxons, Angles, Vikings, and the French—and the invaders added their languages to what was already in use (not to mention the earlier Celtic languages of Welsh, Irish, and Scottish). This combination, along with the many English words of Greek and Latin origin, makes for a rich and expressive language whose many syntactical exceptions cause problems (difficulties, hardships, trials, adversities, challenges, tough rows to hoe) for a non-English speaker trying to learn it.

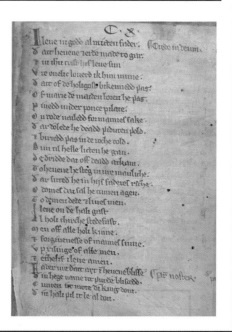

The page shown at right from a 12th-century manuscript includes the Apostle's Creed and the beginning of the Lord's Prayer. Here is the beginning of the Creed in the English of that time period:

I leue in Godd almicten fader datt heuene & erðe made to gar

document is important in the heritage of British and American constitutional rights because it is a written document; because it asserts the principle of limited government; and because it says that the law, not the king, is supreme. However, true to his character, John violated the promises he made in the Magna Carta before his death a few months later.

The power struggle between the English king and the English nobles continued. The king called meetings of the Great Council (which included high officials, barons, and bishops) to obtain their endorsement of new taxes. Some of these meetings also included lesser knights and representatives of towns. The French word for talk is *parle*, so these meetings of the council came to be known as Parliament. In 1295 King Edward I needed money for the war with France, so he called Parliament into session to get new taxes. The gathering

included the nobles and bishops, two knights from each county and two citizens from each town. This assembly is called the Model Parliament because it was the model for the later development of the English Parliament.

At first the nobles and clergy made the decisions. The lesser knights and commoners stood at one end of the hall and could only listen. They could speak only when allowed to do so. Later, the two groups met separately. These groups became the House of Lords and the House of Commons. Parliament increased its powers by demanding concessions from the king before agreeing to new taxes. This government system, in which an assembly puts restraints on the powers of the king, is called a limited monarchy. The king and Parliament jockeyed back and forth for many years defining the role and power of each, but the basic pattern of the government of Britain was set.

France

When the last descendant of Charlemagne died in the western part of his former empire in 987, the feudal lords of France elected Hugh Capet, Count of Paris, to be king. The Capetian dynasty lasted for three hundred years. The Capet family had strong and able leaders who were not sidetracked with family quarrels or weakened with personal failings. These kings consolidated power by adding more French land to their domain through strategic marriages and through successful warfare. When Hugh Capet became king, he ruled only a small area around Paris. By 1328 his successors controlled most of central and southern France.

The coat of arms of the House of Capet is shown at left. Direct descendants of Hugh Capet have continued to rule various European countries. Among these are Juan Carlos, King of Spain (r. 1975 - present), and Henri, Grand Duke of Luxembourg (r. 2000 - present).

The French kings also profited when growth in trade led to increased tax revenues. They appointed a bureaucracy to carry out the work of government in Paris and throughout the country. These bureaucrats answered to the king and not to the nobles.

The first step toward a representative body came in 1302. When Philip IV was embroiled in a controversy with the pope over the king's plan to tax the French clergy, the king called a meeting of the three estates (classes) of French society: the nobility, the clergy, and the *bourgeoisie,* or townspeople. This meeting was called the Estates General and was intended to endorse the king's plan. It was only an advisory board and did not have the power to levy taxes, but it began the movement toward representative government.

The Valois dynasty began ruling in France in 1328, when Philip VI, a relative of the Capets, became king. At that time England controlled much of the land in France, a situation which caused great bitterness among the French. English king Edward III even declared that he should be king of France. In 1337 war broke out between the two countries. This war lasted until 1453 and is known as the Hundred Years' War. English forces were successful at first, in large measure because of new weapons such as the longbow (which superseded the crossbow), gunpowder, and cannons (which could effectively assault castles and fortresses).

Then French forces rallied behind the teenage girl Joan of Arc in 1429. Joan claimed that she had a vision from God telling her to lead the French armies. The French royal family let her do so, and the French forces began winning. When Charles VII was crowned king of France in 1430, Joan was by his side. Joan was captured by allies of England. The English convicted her of heresy and burned her at the stake in 1431. Her martyrdom inspired the French even more. When the war ended in 1453, the English only held the area around Calais in the northeast corner of France along the English Channel.

The only known portrait of Joan of Arc made while she lived no longer survives. This painting was produced around 1485, some fifty years after her death.

The French were bursting with national pride over their victory. The French king was now in a stronger position, and the citizens were gladly loyal to him. The end of the war actually helped England as well, since the monarch could now concentrate on domestic issues. However, a civil war between the Tudors and the Lancasters, two families of the nobility, soon broke out. It was called the War of the Roses because the two sides used different color roses as their symbols. In 1485 Tudor Henry VII led his forces to victory over the Lancasters. Henry became king, thus beginning the Tudor dynasty.

Germany

The eastern portion of Charlemagne's empire became a patchwork of small areas ruled by local dukes. However, in 936 the dukes elected Otto I of

Saxony as king to provide more stability and defense. Otto wanted to increase his power over the other dukes and to control more land. To do so, he allied himself with the papacy and defended the pope's lands from attack. In response, in 962 the pope crowned Otto Emperor of the Romans, successor to Charlemagne, leader of Christendom, and ruler of what was called the Holy Roman Empire. As one observer noted, the Holy Roman Empire was neither holy, nor Roman, nor much of an empire; but the title served to give Otto more prestige in the lands he ruled.

However, a controversy developed between a later Holy Roman Emperor and the pope. The German king took it upon himself to put in office bishops and other officials of the Church in his realm without deferring to the pope. This practice was called lay investiture. Pope Gregory VII banned

The Imperial Crown of the Holy Roman Empire dates from the tenth century. The cross and arch were added in the 11th century. The red velvet was added in the 18th century.

the practice in 1075; but the Holy Roman Emperor at the time, Henry IV, refused to obey. He wanted to appoint Church officials in order to have their support in any controversies with the German dukes. The pope then excommunicated Henry and encouraged the German dukes to elect another king. Henry trudged over the Alps to Rome in repentance to beg the pope for forgiveness, which the pontiff gave.

After Henry returned home, though, he continued the practice of lay investiture. The pope excommunicated him again, but this time Henry invaded Rome with an army and forced Gregory into exile. The controversy was finally settled in 1122 with a concordat (agreement) signed in the city of Worms. The concordat said that the Church would appoint men to Church positions, but the emperor could grant any land and secular powers that went with the ecclesiastical position. For example, sometimes bishops held posts in the government. Many bishops owned huge tracts of land that they had received through gifts and bequests.

The Holy Roman (actually German) Emperors became preoccupied with issues in Italy. Frederick Barbarossa (which means "of the red beard") controlled Italy in 1152, and as a result the pope felt that his control over the papal states was threatened. While the German ruler's attention was diverted to Italy, dukes in Germany ruled their own duchies with little regard for the Holy Roman Emperor. The tradition of weak national leadership in Germany and Italy continued for centuries, and only in the 1800s did each become a unified nation.

Spain

Like other areas of Europe, Spain was not a unified country during the Middle Ages. In addition, Muslims had gained control of many parts of Spain as a result of their conquests in the eighth century. Over time, Christians had regained most but not all of these areas; and the Muslim presence continued.

Wedding Portrait of King Ferdinand of Aragon and Queen Isabella of Castile (Spanish, 15th century)

Russia

Spain took a huge step toward unity in 1469, when Isabella, heir to the throne of the Castile region of Spain, married Ferdinand, who was prince of the Spanish region of Aragon. The power and influence of the Roman Catholic Church was strong during their reign. In 1478 Ferdinand and Isabella agreed to begin the Inquisition. The Inquisition involved Church courts of inquiry that put alleged heretics on trial. Hundreds of people were executed because they did not see the Christian faith in the way that the Roman Catholic Church did.

In 1492 a Spanish Catholic army captured Grenada, the last Muslim stronghold in the country. Also that year, Jews were required to convert to Catholicism or leave Spain. A similar decree was issued to Muslims a few years later.

During this time of national unity and a strong central government, Christopher Columbus approached the monarchs about sponsoring him in a voyage to sail west to reach Asia. We will talk more about this venture in a later unit. Over the next decades Spain became a dominant power in Europe and in the New World.

In 1240 Mongols invaded Russia from the east. They took control of the capital of Kiev and ruled there for some 250 years. The Mongols imposed heavy taxes on the people and cut Russia off from contact with the rest of Europe. During the next century, the princes of the city of Moscow increased their power as Mongol rule weakened. In the fifteenth century, Moscow became the center of the Russian state. The headquarters of the Russian Orthodox Church moved there from Kiev.

Ivan III, who ruled from 1462 to 1505, is considered the founder of modern Russia. He refused to pay taxes to the Mongols, and their rule was so weak by then that he was able to get away with it. Ivan also expelled German nobles who had taken lands in western Russia. He took the title of Czar and called Moscow the Third Rome after Rome and Constantinople.

Influenced by the Byzantine pattern, the czar ruled both the state and the Church. A successor, Ivan IV, who ruled from 1533 to 1584, killed many nobles who might have contended for power. He also established a secret police to gain information about any disloyal activities. Because of his approach to power, he is known as Ivan the Terrible.

A system of feudalism developed in Russia even as the feudal system was declining in the rest of Europe. Russia has always been part of Europe in some ways but not exactly European in others.

When the righteous increase, the people rejoice,
But when a wicked man rules, people groan.
Proverbs 29:2

The Cathedral of the Protection of Most Holy Theotokos on the Moat (commonly known as St. Basil's Cathedral) is located in Moscow. Ivan the Terrible commissioned its construction in 1555 to commemorate his military victories. Napoleon's troops ransacked the cathedral during their invasion of Russia, but it was restored later in the 1800s.

Assignments for Lesson 71

In Their Words   Read the excerpts from the Magna Carta and the Hawaiian story "Lonopuha" (pages 112-119).

Student Review   Optional: Answer the questions for Lesson 71.

Feudalism and the Rise of Cities

Feudalism is a modern term given to the social structure of the Middle Ages that guided economics, politics, warfare, and class interaction. It also influenced religious practice. In many parts of medieval Europe, every person was a cog in one way or another in the system of feudalism.

Background to Feudalism

The background for the system in Europe came from two sources. First, in the late Roman Empire, large landowners in Italy gathered wealth and power to themselves as the Roman government was crumbling. These estates operated as little kingdoms without their lords wanting any help—or any interference—from Rome.

A second forerunner to feudalism was found in the Germanic tribes. A king, supported by a council of chiefs, led each tribe. The chiefs in turn had their armies of warriors whom they would commit to fighting on behalf of the king. The chiefs gave their loyalty to the king, and the king promised to protect the chiefs. The ideals of loyalty, honor, and service were important to the members of these tribes. Germanic kings and chiefs led to medieval kings and nobles.

When Charles Martel, grandfather of Charlemagne, wanted to build an army to face the advancing Muslims in the early eighth century, he turned first to the Church, hoping that the Church would finance a defense force out of its vast holdings of property. When Church officials refused, Charles simply seized Church property and distributed it to nobles in exchange for their service. This was the basis for the feudal arrangement.

After developing in France, feudalism in various forms spread to England, Germany, and the Netherlands during the 1100s and in Russia in the 15th and 16th centuries. Some areas, such as Eastern Europe, never developed a strong feudal system.

The Structure of Feudalism

Feudalism involved issues related to the ownership of land, regardless of whether the land was owned by a king, a baron (or lord, noble, duke, count, or viscount; the list of titles is long), a knight, or the Church. A fief was the right to control a tract of land, often called a manor. The owner of a fief had the right to govern that land. He had authority over the peasants who lived there. The peasants had no say in how they were governed.

412

The governing of the land rested upon a feudal compact, which was at first unwritten but later usually put into writing. The practice of a feudal compact meant that even those who had the power of governing were subject to law and had limited, not absolute, sovereignty.

At the top of the feudal pyramid was the king, who claimed to own all the land in his kingdom. Everybody the rest of the way down the pyramid only had use of land through the king's permission. This would appear to make the king the most powerful person in the system. In actuality, however, the most powerful people were the nobles who oversaw the large estates. The king depended on the nobles to serve in his army, provide defense against invaders, and support him financially with the fees and taxes that came from the use of the land. Nobles could withhold their service or their payments if they opposed an action of the king or wanted to influence a decision of the king.

A lord could grant the use of portions of his fief to lesser lords, who in turn granted land to knights. Usually the smallest fief would support one knight and his family and would not be divided. Anyone down the chain who was responsible to someone higher was called a vassal. A lord was a vassal to the king. A knight was a vassal to a lord.

A vassal committed to giving his superior a set number of days per year (often forty) in military service plus carrying out other tasks the superior might require. The vassal paid a fee for use of the land and promised to ransom his superior if he were

taken captive. The oath of loyalty was called a fealty. The master of an estate was expected to administer justice for everyone on his fief through courts that he created.

At the bottom of the pyramid were the serfs or peasants who lived on the land. They were to work for the master of the fief a set number of days, often three days per week. They planted and harvested crops, cleared forests, repaired manor buildings, and laid roads. In return, the master allowed the peasant to live in a hut on the property and work a small tract, usually about an acre, for his own family.

Serfs were bound to the land and could leave only if they paid a fee. It was not exactly slavery, but it was a hard life that was pretty close to it. On the other hand, a master provided housing and assistance when a serf was ill or old; and the peasants did not usually have to go to war. Some who worked

A member of the French royal family, Jean de Berry, commissioned an illustrated book in the early 1400s. In addition to a collection of prayers and readings, it features a calendar with one illustration for each month. From left to right on the previous page are a feast on New Year's Day (January), a winter scene (February), a couple's engagement (April), and hunting with falcons (August). At right peasants work in the fields around the Château de Lusignan, one of the duke's homes (March).

for a master were freemen who had fewer obligations and could leave a manor on their own initiative. A skilled laborer or artisan might be a freeman.

The Roman Catholic Church played an important role in feudalism. Kings and lords depended on educated clergy to fill responsible administrative positions. This allowed bishops and other high-ranking clergy to exert influence in political affairs. In addition, the Church owned a great deal of land. Bishops were often feudal lords as well as Church officials.

The *Domesday Book,* compiled by the Normans after their conquest of England, is a detailed record of who (king, churchmen, or nobles) owned what land and how much the property was worth. The Normans in southern Italy created a similar document, the *Catalogus Baronum,* a few decades later. It focused on the military duties owed by vassals to their superiors.

A fief would often have a monthly assembly of all free males. On such occasions those who had information about issues being considered would give their testimony. These practices led to representative assemblies and to juries. The French word for being sworn under oath was *jure,* and this practice also contributed to jury trials. At first, the jury was the group of people who gave testimony about a case for the judge to use in reaching a verdict. Later, a distinction was made between witnesses who gave testimony and a jury of one's peers that decided guilt or innocence.

Women, even in families of the nobility, had few legal rights. A woman could inherit a fief, but if she did the property would be overseen by a male family member. A woman's primary responsibilities were to rear the children and oversee the household.

Life on a Feudal Manor

The centerpiece of a feudal manor was the manor house where the lord's family lived. It was much bigger and more comfortable than the peasant huts. The manor almost always had a church building where the lord's family and all who lived on the manor attended services. The priest was supported financially by the lord.

In more uncertain times, or in strategic locations, or if he were wealthy enough, a lord might build a castle as a fortified home. The castle would usually be placed on a hill or beside a river. When his land was attacked, all of the peasants and others associated with the fief could come into the castle for safety. A castle had thick walls and an elevated walkway around the top from which defenders could ward off attackers. The structure was usually surrounded by a moat, a large ditch filled with water. A drawbridge could be lowered across the moat to let friends in and pulled up to keep foes out. A thick iron gate in the castle wall provided further protection. Castles were subject to attack by battering ram, catapults, and siege in addition to assaults by enemy soldiers. The development of the cannon made castles much more vulnerable.

Castles were not comfortable places in which to live. They were fortresses made of stone, which meant they were often cold and damp. Before rugs came into common use, floors were covered with straw. Tapestries on the walls helped rooms to be warmer.

The earliest mention of the Trécesson family is in a 13th-century document. The fortified home known as the Château de Trécesson probably dates from the early 1400s. It remains in use as a private residence.

The lord's family lived in the most strongly defended part of the castle, called the keep. The great hall in the keep was the scene of lavish banquets. Castles were busy as blacksmiths, butchers, carpenters, clerks, and other workers carried out their responsibilities.

Manors were often self-contained villages, with all of the needed resources produced there and all of the needed workers living there. Crop rotation left one-third of the tillable land fallow each year to keep from wearing out the land. Work on the manor was helped by several inventions during this time, including the horseshoe that prevented injury to the horse's feet, an improved horse collar to make controlling the animal easier, the addition of an iron tip on the wooden plow, the use of water mills and windmills for grinding grain and other functions, and improved methods of iron production.

Work on the manor was hard and constant, however there were some breaks. The period from harvest to planting was not as demanding. Labor ceased when the lord declared a feast for the wedding of his child, to celebrate a military victory, or for some other reason. Work would also stop for the many Church holy days (the origin of our word holiday) during the year.

The Development of Towns

As time passed, the feudal system became complex and cumbersome. Land changed hands through marriage, debts, inheritances, and other reasons. Some vassals were beholden to more than one lord, and the lord of one fief might be a vassal to another lord elsewhere. Kings became stronger and less dependent on vassal lords and knights. As the monarchs gained wealth from taxes and conquest, they could pay standing armies. Armored knights became outdated with the invention of new weapons such as the longbow and cannon. As a cash economy grew, even peasants had more money; and lords greedy for money allowed serfs to buy their freedom more easily.

Many European towns retain medieval features and architecture. Rothenburg ob der Tauber in Germany has an extensive wall around the city center.

Towns grew up near castles and monasteries as the population grew and as tradesmen wanted a permanent location for their work. A strategically located castle would likely be on a lucrative trade route. Townspeople asked for a charter in which the lord promised that he would give the people of the town certain rights. Taxes would be spelled out, and the lord promised to create courts to settle disputes and guaranteed that he would not seize the property of townspeople.

Many towns were surrounded with thick walls for defense. The church building and larger homes would be built at the town square in the middle of the village. As a town grew, people still wanted to live within the walls; so five- and six-story structures to house families would be typical. To utilize every foot of space, the upper stories would sometimes extend out over the street.

Medieval towns offered an array of shops, exciting festivals, and fascinating trade fairs; but life was not always pleasant. Overcrowding was common. Water often came from a common well, and there was usually no sewer or sanitation systems. Refuse was often thrown from windows into the street. The smell of a medieval town was overpowering, and the risk of fire with the many wooden structures was great.

As towns grew into cities, merchants and artisans developed guilds to protect their businesses. A guild included all the people who practiced a particular trade or engaged in a particular business (such as merchants). A person usually had to be a member of a guild to do business in a town. The guild set standards of workmanship and often determined prices for goods and services. They also took care of members who were ill or elderly. Some guilds were so powerful that they actually governed the town in which they were located.

The pattern of training new members of a guild involved a boy of seven or eight becoming apprenticed to a master craftsman who carried on business in a town. The master provided room, board, and instruction but no wages. An apprenticeship usually lasted three to seven years (more often the longer period), at which time the young man became a journeyman (from the French *journee*, a day's work or travel) who received pay for his day's work.

A journeyman might roam from town to town to find work or settle in one place. When the guild masters approved a journeyman's work, usually judging one particular item called a masterpiece, the journeyman became a master craftsman. The master could then open his own shop, train new apprentices, and begin the cycle anew.

Trade fairs developed in France in the 1100s. In these fairs, nobles rented out booth spaces to merchants and artisans and collected sales taxes on purchases made. Moneychangers made transactions easier (for a fee) between buyers and sellers from different jurisdictions. Local residents learned about the products, languages, and customs of other parts of the world. Sometimes these fairs lasted for weeks, and the location became a more or less permanent marketplace.

Local fairs were hurt by the development of the Hanseatic League, a group of some eighty cities in northern Europe. This league of cities controlled prices and product availability in the commerce that

Vernacular Literature

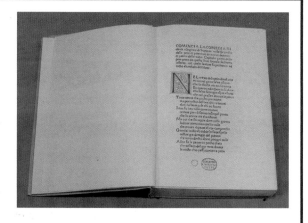

Significant developments took place in European literature during this time. Dante Alighieri wrote The Comedy *(also called* The Divine Comedy*) in the early 1300s. In his work, Dante is guided by the ancient Roman poet Virgil through hell, purgatory, and (without Virgil) heaven. The* Comedy *is a profound consideration of life, death, faith, and sin. Dante dared to describe some of the popes as being in hell. In an important move, Dante wrote the poem in Italian, not Latin. This was the first major piece of what was called vernacular literature—literature in the language of everyday people (whom Dante wanted to reach), not the more scholarly Latin. A printed edition from 1472 is pictured above.*

Later in the same century, Geoffrey Chaucer published his Canterbury Tales. *A varied group of pilgrims going to Canterbury, the most sacred site for the Church in England, exchange stories along the way. Chaucer brilliantly describes the individuals in the group and expertly conveys the stories (some of which are rather bawdy). Like Dante, Chaucer wrote his poem in the vernacular of English. With these two works, literature began to be accessible to a wider audience.*

was carried out on the North and Baltic Seas and in overland trade in that region.

As foreign trade increased, people with enough money were able to acquire fine clothes, spices, and other expensive items that were available through international trade. Spices were used to enhance the flavor of foods, as preservatives, and as ingredients in medicines. Perfumes became greatly desired in societies where baths were rare. Lords became jealous of merchants and other townspeople, who were sometimes richer than the lords were.

Money became more common, and lords began to demand rent payments in coin, not grain, to have the cash for buying goods they wanted. The use of coins from different realms created the job of moneychangers, who made the correct coins available for a fee. Moneylenders often sat on a bench in the marketplace. The Italian word for bench is *banca*. Banks became businesses that loaned money to traders.

When a trader did not want to carry cash, he could make a deposit in a bank and receive a letter of credit or bill of exchange. He carried this document to a distant town, received money from another bank in that town, and made his purchase. Lending money at interest was called usury, and the Church opposed it at first. Bankers charged a fee for their services instead of interest. Later, the pope decided that a moderate interest rate was acceptable.

The growth of cities had an impact on social structure. Merchants and others who conducted business in the towns were neither nobles nor peasants. They were a middle class of businessmen, artisans, and freed serfs. In the city, a person's status depended on the wealth he acquired from his work and accomplishments, not on his family connections or background. A late Latin word for a fortified place or incorporated city was *burgus*. This became, in various languages, burg, bourg, and borough. The business class of cities and towns came to be called burgesses in English, burghers in German, and bourgeoisie in French.

The Palazzo Salimbeni in Siena, Italy, houses the headquarters of Monte dei Paschi di Siena. Founded in 1472, it is the oldest banking business in the world that has been in continuous operation.

Cities were able to get out from under feudal obligations that limited their growth. They became centers of intellectual activity, especially with the formation of universities. Cities also contributed to cultural, artistic, and economic change. Palermo, Italy, was estimated to have a population of 300,000 in the 13th century while Paris had about 240,000. At the same time, London, a latecomer to urban life, probably only had about 45,000.

Unfortunately, cities were also often unhealthy places to live. Townspeople suffered the most from plagues such as the Black Plague or Black Death of the mid-14th century. The disease caused a sufferer's skin to turn dark before he died, hence the name given to the plague. The illness was bubonic plague, carried by the fleas that lived on rats and spread by the filth that characterized medieval cities. The plague probably came to Europe by way of goods brought on trade routes from Asia.

Trade collapsed and farming fell off as so many people died, were ill, or moved into the countryside to try to avoid the plague. It has been estimated that about one-third of the population of Europe died in the plague. Full recovery from the effects of the disease did not come until a century later.

A false balance is an abomination to the Lord,
But a just weight is His delight.
Proverbs 11:1

Assignments for Lesson 72

In Their Words   Read the excerpts from *The Diary of Murasaki Shikibu* and *The Jew in the Medieval World* (pages 120-127).

Student Review   Optional: Answer the questions for Lesson 72.

The Krak des Chevaliers, Syria

The Crusades

. . . This royal city [Jerusalem], however, situated at the center of the earth, is now held captive by the enemies of Christ and is subjected, by those who do not know God, to the worship of the heathen. She seeks, therefore, and desires to be liberated and ceases not to implore you to come to her aid. From you especially she asks succor, because as we have already said, God has conferred upon you above all other nations great glory in arms. Accordingly, undertake this journey eagerly for the remission of your sins, with the assurance of the reward of imperishable glory in the kingdom of heaven . . . .

So spoke Pope Urban II in 1095, urging his European listeners to become Crusaders, which means bearers of the cross, to liberate Palestine from the Muslims. A few months later, the First Crusade departed for the Middle East.

Background to the Crusades

The area of Israel was considered by Europeans to be the Holy Land. From the fourth century on, some Europeans had undertaken pilgrimages to visit the lands of the Bible in order to see sacred sites and relics. Followers of Islam had taken control of the area in the seventh century, but Christians living and visiting there were generally tolerated.

However, a band of Muslim warriors known as the Seljuk Turks had swept over the Holy Land in the 11th century. They captured Jerusalem and reportedly tortured Christians. In addition, the Seljuks threatened Byzantium, the great Christian empire of the east.

The Roman Catholic Church was no friend of the Byzantines. The final division between the Roman Church and the Orthodox Church, ending centuries of conflict, had come in 1054. The two Church traditions had become quite different. Services of the Roman Church were spoken in Latin; the Orthodox Church used Greek. Orthodox clergy were allowed to marry, whereas Catholic priests were required to be celibate.

A Kurdish settlement was located on the hill shown above as early as the 11th century. The Knights Hospitaller, a group of Crusaders, built a fortification there in the mid-12th century, and it developed its current appearance in the 1200s. The crusaders lost control of the castle in 1271.

More central to the conflict, however, was the fact that the pope ruled the Western Church and much of Europe, while the emperor in Byzantium ruled the Eastern Church. The pope did not recognize the emperor's authority, and the emperor did not recognize the pope's authority. A specific controversy developed in the eighth century over the use of icons. The Byzantine emperor banned them, but the pope supported their use and excommunicated the emperor.

As the Seljuk Turks increased their dominance in the Middle East, the emperor in Constantinople appealed to the pope for assistance in defending the Byzantine empire. Pope Urban II decided to respond favorably, probably for several reasons. First, he hoped to reunite the Church under himself as savior of the Christian world. Second, he hoped that the Church itself would be seen as more powerful by the European kings and nobles whom the pope sought to rule. Third, Urban was weary of the almost constant

Medieval Warfare

The feudal system began in response to invasions by foreign armies, but eventually lords fought each other because of disputes over land rights, family feuds, and simple greed. Most battles were relatively small. Knights wore into battle armor that weighed about thirty pounds. Sometimes the horses wore armor as well. Knights were not usually killed by the enemy if taken captive. More often they were held for ransom money.

Warfare was more common in the early Middle Ages than in the later period. The Church exerted its influence to lessen the fighting, banning conflict on certain days each week and during the harvest and Christmas seasons. Kings and lords became more effective in controlling their warrior vassals. During the later Middle Ages, tournaments between knights became popular entertainment. These mock contests helped warriors train for real fighting and also re-directed male energies away from the desire for genuine conflict.

Warriors of the Frankish army who rode horses into battle were called chevaliers, a term which became cavalry in English. Another word derived from this term was the code of conduct expected of medieval warriors: chivalry. The practice of chivalry promoted Christian values and the honor of warriors. Knights were expected to be brave, generous, and loyal and to defend their lord's and their family's honor. When a battle was approaching, the

enemy was expected to wait until the opposing knights had donned their suits of armor. Women were to be treated with great respect and were placed on a pedestal in the code of chivalry. This was encouraged by the poetry and songs of the troubadours that were written during the period. The code of chivalry did not include any provisions for the treatment of peasants.

A boy who showed promise could be selected to serve as a page (largely an errand boy) for a knight. After a few years, he might become a squire and be expected to carry out greater responsibilities. Finally, in a ceremony with his lord, he could be declared a knight. The fighting ability of knights greatly increased with the invention of the stirrup during this period, which allowed the knight to use heavier armor and weapons.

Massacre of Jews in Metz during the First Crusade
Auguste Migette (French, 19th century)

Jews were generally accepted in European towns until the emotion surrounding the Crusades led to persecution. Many cities passed laws forbidding Jews from owning land, they were forced out of many guilds, and others were beaten and killed by mobs. Church leaders generally condemned these attacks on the Jews. As they were expelled from parts of central Europe, many Jews went either to Spain or to Eastern Europe, including Russia.

warfare in Europe; and he might have hoped that an external enemy could divert the attention of warring lords from each other.

At a Church council at Clermont in southern France, the pope issued a stirring summons for people to respond to the call of God, take up arms, and drive the infidel from the Holy Land. When the pontiff had finished his appeal, the crowd responded, "It is the will of God! It is the will of God!" In addition to the many who saw it as a holy cause, some Europeans developed ulterior motives. The possibility of acquiring riches had a strong appeal. Others dreamed of carving out kingdoms in the Middle East. It didn't hurt that the pope offered the Crusaders exemptions from certain debts and taxes.

Before this Crusade could be organized, however, a spontaneous, grassroots crusade formed under the mesmerizing preaching of the barefoot Peter the Hermit. Thousands followed him across Europe,

but the mob looted towns and killed Jews as they went. When they finally arrived in Constantinople, the emperor saw them as troublemakers and sent them into the Turkish wilderness, where they were decimated by the Seljuks.

Taking the Holy Land

The First Crusade departed in early 1096. When the warriors arrived in the Middle East, they won victories in Asia Minor and Syria before taking Jerusalem in 1099 and exacting bloody revenge on the Muslims. The Europeans established four Crusader states in Palestine and Syria, which lasted in some form for two hundred years. However, these states were heavily dependent on Italian merchants supplying them with food and armaments.

When one of the crusader states fell to the Muslims in 1144, Bernard of Clairvaux, a French monk, urged a second Crusade. His words were no less inflammatory than those of Pope Urban II:

Will you allow the infidels to contemplate in peace the ravages they have committed on Christian people? . . . Fly then to arms; let a holy rage animate you in the fight, and let the Christian world resound with these words of the prophet, "Cursed be he who does not stain his sword with blood!" . . . Christian warriors, He who gave His life for you, today demands yours in return. These are combats worthy of you, combats in which it is glorious to conquer and advantageous to die.

However, this Crusade failed; and its participants were scattered in the barren lands of Asia Minor.

The skillful Muslim warrior Saladin led the army that recaptured Jerusalem in 1187. He offered to negotiate free access by Christians to the city, but the pope refused. The Third Crusade, led by Richard I (the Lionhearted) of England, took place from 1189 to 1192. It failed to gain control of Jerusalem.

Salāh ad-Dīn Yūsuf ibn Ayyūb (known to Europeans as Saladin) was a Kurdish leader who founded the Ayyubid dynasty, based in Egypt. Saladin and Richard I developed a mutual respect for each other during the battles of the Third Crusade. This statue of Saladin is pictured in the Military Museum in the Saladin Citadel in Cairo, which was built during the rule of Saladin.

the way were sold into slavery by merchants at the French port of Marseille.

In 1291 Muslims conquered the last of the crusader states; and the much-sought-after Holy Land was back in Muslim hands. The Church later sponsored smaller crusades in Europe against Muslims in Spain and against supposed heretics such as the Albigenses, who are discussed in Lesson 75.

Assessing the Crusades

The Crusades were a key event in the late Middle Ages because they affected the lives of many thousands of people in Europe and the Middle East. The efforts, however, were badly managed and poorly led. In the Holy Land, the Europeans were surrounded by a much larger hostile population. The mixed motives of many Crusaders also hurt their cause.

The fleets of ships built to transport Crusaders came to be used for trade, which helped to stimulate the European economy. The nobles of Europe increased their purchases of goods from India, China, and the Middle East and were able to sell European goods in return. The Crusades weakened the power of European nobles, who had to bow to the influence of the Church. The vassals of the nobles began to realize that they did not have to answer only to the nobles, and they began to look at the world differently as a result.

Europe gained a broader view of the world during this time period. Marco Polo of Venice (c. 1254-1324) was one of the earliest European

Richard accepted a truce that left the city in Muslim hands but gave Christians access to it.

A fourth Crusade was promoted by the merchants of Venice, Italy, who urged Europeans to attack Constantinople, a trading rival of Venice. As thinly disguised as this economic aggression was, an army was organized and attacked Constantinople in 1204. The result only served to weaken Byzantium and to give the Church a black eye for its support of such an unholy cause.

The Crusaders did not gain permanent control of the Holy Land. One theory that developed to explain this failure was that it was punishment for the sinfulness of the participants. It seemed logical to some that innocent children should be able to do what adult warriors could not. In 1212 thousands of French and German children set out for the Middle East, expecting the Mediterranean Sea to part for them. Instead, many of those who did not die on

What Else Was Happening? (1000-1500)

1. Murasaki Shikibu (c. 978-1014), a Japanese noblewoman and lady-in-waiting, wrote one of the world's first novels, *The Tale of the Genji*. Murasaki, depicted at right in an 18th-century illustration by Suzuki Harunobu, also wrote a diary and a collection of poems.

2. The Sultanate of Mogadishu (modern Somalia) was a major trading center that sent merchants across the Indian Ocean from Mozambique to Vietnam. It flourished from the 10th to the 16th century. The Almnara Tower, pictured at right, is a fortified lighthouse from the 1400s.

3. A Scottish army led by Andrew Moray and William Wallace defeated the English at the Battle of Stirling Bridge in 1297. Moray died later that year, and Wallace became Guardian of Scotland until his defeat by King Edward I of England at the Battle of Falkirk in 1298.

4. Tenochtitlan, founded in 1325, became the dominant city of the Aztec civilization in the 1400s. Built on an island in Lake Texcoco, it was larger than most European cities of the time. The royal palace featured zoos, gardens, and salt and fresh water aquaria.

5. Machu Picchu, pictured at right and on the front cover, was built around 1450 by the Inca in what is now Peru. The Inca abandoned the site a century later, and it remained largely unknown to the outside world until 1911. It thus survived as an excellent example of Incan architecture, but its current popularity as a tourist attraction threatens its preservation.

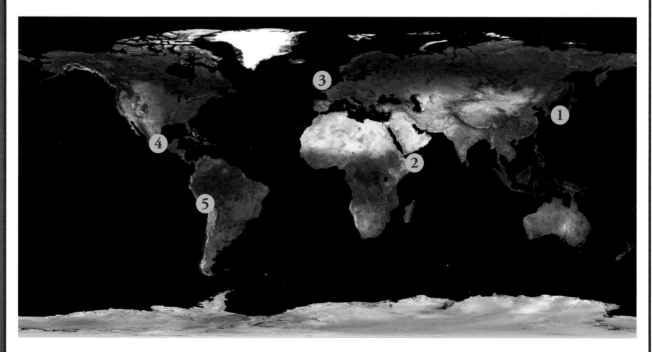

explorers in Asia, but he got there over land. Marco's father and uncle had traveled to China as merchants in the 1260s. The elder Polos returned to China with seventeen-year-old Marco, arriving at the palace of the Mongol emperor in 1275.

Marco became a court favorite and traveled around China for seventeen years in service to the emperor. He finally received the emperor's permission to leave in 1292. After fulfilling a diplomatic mission to Persia, Polo returned to Venice in 1295.

Marco Polo became a prisoner of war during a conflict between the city-states of Venice and Genoa. While in prison, he dictated an account of his travels to a well-known writer. When *The Travels of Marco Polo* was published, many people simply did not believe that it could be true. His narrative was confirmed by other writers, however, and became a stimulus for increased trade and exploration.

Kublai Khan, the Mongol emperor of China who met Marco Polo, asked for scores of priests

This illustration is from a medieval edition of Marco Polo's memoirs.

to come to China to teach the people about Christianity. Sadly, the pope sent only two teachers, who never reached China. How world history might have been different if European believers had undertaken this Crusade instead of the ones they did!

Then Jesus said to him [Peter], "Put your sword back into its place; for all those who take up the sword shall perish by the sword."
Matthew 26:52

Assignments for Lesson 73

In Their Words   Read "O Sacred Head, Now Wounded" and the excerpts from *Annales Herbipolenses* (pages 128-130).

Begin reading *Everyman* (pages 136-142).

Student Review   Optional: Answer the questions for Lesson 73.

Detail from Faith and Reason United, *Ludwig Seitz (German, c. 1885)*

Lesson 74 - Key Person

Thomas Aquinas

What do you know to be true?
How do you know it to be true?
What is the best way to learn what is true?

These deep philosophical questions might not be ones that you ask often, but it is helpful to ask them at some point. We want our lives to be based on the truth. Nobody wants to base his one life on ideas or beliefs that are not true. But how can we know that what we believe to be true is actually true?

Intellectual Pursuits

In the late Middle Ages, an increasing number of scholars began asking these questions. Two main developments influenced this inquiry. First, contact with Muslim culture brought to Europe knowledge of the writings of Aristotle and other ancient philosophers that the Muslims had copied. These works, which predated the New Testament, approached the world from a different viewpoint. Aristotle did not approach the world with a faith in God and a belief in the Judeo-Christian Scriptures. Nevertheless, he appeared to express ideas that were true based on his logical observations of the world. Christian scholars, who were used to beginning their studies with God's revelation in Scripture, found Aristotle's work challenging and somewhat troubling since it did not fit into an intellectual framework with which they were already familiar.

Second, universities began developing in a number of European cities. Scholars in the Roman Catholic Church attracted students who wanted to be trained for high clergy or government positions. One of the earliest universities (groups of scholars in the same place) developed in Paris. Some English students who had to leave Paris because of war between England and France began a university in Oxford, England. Later, a group of students from Oxford began another university at Cambridge. Similar centers of learning grew up in cities across Europe. The students and faculties in these universities were not content to memorize accepted Church doctrine as though they were moving through a catechism. Instead, they wanted to investigate, learn, and go beyond what they already knew.

Pope Leo XIII issued an official declaration in 1879 referring to Thomas Aquinas as "the special bulwark and glory of the Catholic faith." He commissioned a set of paintings at the Vatican, including the one above that shows Thomas Aquinas teaching a group of children in the background on the left side.

This stained glass depiction of Thomas Aquinas is from the Cathedral of Saint-Rombouts in Mechelen, Belgium. The book has words from his hymn Pange Lingua Gloriosi Corporis Mysterium ("Sing, My Tongue, the Mystery of the Glorious Body").

He died when he was about fifty years old, having produced a wealth of commentaries on Scripture and other works. His best known book, *Summa Theologica* (*Theological Summary*), an analysis of how we know what we know, was unfinished at his death.

Thomas believed that the universe is ordered and has a purpose: to fulfill God's plan of salvation in Jesus Christ. The purpose of the universe, our lives, and anything we do in our lives is and should be to honor God. He believed in revelation, and he believed in reason. Rather than seeing Aristotelian logic as a threat to revealed truth, Thomas adopted the logic of Aristotle and used it to defend the faith.

God's revelation of truth and human knowledge of truth, Thomas maintained, are facets of the same body of knowledge. Because truth is truth regardless of its source, he felt comfortable appealing to truths in Aristotle and in Jewish and Muslim writings as well as those in Scripture. Revelation does not conflict with reason that is properly applied. If something appears to conflict with revelation, our perception is mistaken. God is rational and the universe He created is rational, so man should be able to approach it on a rational basis and learn the truth of the universe from both reason and revelation.

For example, God's revelation says that He exists. Thomas developed a series of logical proofs for the existence of God that we discussed in Lesson 10. Thus, revelation and reason do not conflict; instead, they complement each other and arrive at the same conclusion. Some matters that we know through revelation, such as the reality of the Trinity, the incarnation of Christ, and the resurrection of Christ, cannot be proved by reason. However, since what is revealed through Scripture is supported by

In the Catholic Church, the traditional process of learning started with God. According to the Catholic view, the mind of man is unreliable, sinful, and given to prejudice. God revealed truth to man in the Scriptures. By God's Word, we can know what is true. Aristotle, on the other hand, started with man. He believed things to be true based on the logical conclusions that he reached with his ability to reason. He did not rely on divine revelation to decide what was true.

Contributions of Thomas Aquinas

Was Aristotle right? Was revelation the means to knowing truth, or was reason the means to knowing truth? The scholar who best addressed this dilemma was Thomas Aquinas. Born into a wealthy family in southern Italy in 1224, Thomas decided to become a Dominican (over the protests of his parents) and proved to be a brilliant student. He studied in Paris and Cologne and then taught in Paris and in Italy.

logic as far as logic goes, we can logically conclude that such theological "mysteries" as he called them are true as well. This combining of revelation and reason was called Scholasticism. It was a breakthrough in letting students use reason to investigate truth instead of simply relying on the traditional Catholic understanding of the world.

Limitations of Reason

The ability of man to reason is undoubtedly a gift from God. It does help us in understanding the teaching of Scripture and the world around us. However, reason is not ultimate in the universe. God is ultimate. God is reasonable, but His mind does not answer to our reason. God is not irrational, but He is above reason. Some truths must be revealed by Him, and we must accept them by faith whether our reason comprehends them or not. We can never logically conclude from evidence in the world, for instance, that Jesus died on the cross for our sins. That is a truth from God which we must accept by faith. This does not make that truth any weaker or less important, but it is a truth we can only accept on the basis of faith.

Another limitation on human reason is that it is imperfect. We perceive the world through sin-stained glasses. For instance, Thomas believed that man has free will but cannot choose to follow God without assistance. This is why, he concluded in his logic, we must have the sacraments to bring grace and clearer spiritual vision into our lives. But this is not the only conclusion possible from the evidence in Scripture. Thomas also logically concluded that extreme punishment is necessary to protect the soul from heresy. Thus he gave his endorsement to the Inquisition. This conclusion was logical to him, but he was prejudiced by his preconception that the Roman Catholic Church was always right in what it did. His logical conclusion was actually a rationalization for Church practice.

Observation and Experimentation

Thomas did not pursue observation or experimentation as means of acquiring truth. This was the contribution of an English philosopher who was a contemporary of Thomas, Roger Bacon (c. 1214-1294). Bacon believed that all knowledge should enhance theology, the study of God. Experiments, measurement, and observation were essential, he said, in knowing what was true. What appeared logical to the human mind might not actually be true. Aristotle might have been wrong in some of his logical conclusions about the world because he did not or could not conduct scientific experiments.

It might have seemed logical to Aristotle that worms spontaneously generated from spoiled meat. Experimentation, however, showed that the maggots came from eggs laid by flies. It might have seemed logical that the sun revolved around the earth. That was the accepted doctrinal position of the Roman Catholic Church. However, scientific calculations proved that the earth orbited the sun.

Roger Bacon predicted flying machines and horseless carriages. He also studied lenses and magnification and might have invented a simple microscope. This statue of him is located at Oxford University, where he studied.

The Age of Cathedrals

With the increased prosperity of the late Middle Ages, the Church wanted to honor God through the construction of beautiful and majestic cathedrals. Civic pride also played a part in these projects, as towns started competing with other towns to outdo one another. The word cathedral is from the Latin word for chair. A cathedral could only be built in a town where a bishop sat in his authority, and a town could only have one cathedral.

Earlier cathedrals were of the Romanesque style, which included vaults and domes and rounded roofs. Since walls had to be thick and strong to support the ceilings, only narrow slits could be cut for windows. In general, Romanesque cathedrals were somewhat plain.

Advances in architecture allowed for more ornate cathedrals to be built. These newer cathedrals were built in the Gothic style, so called because critics thought the first cathedrals built in this style were things the barbarian Goths would have done. Gothic cathedrals had taller walls, high pointed arches, and larger windows, creating a more impressive visual effect inside and out. To support the taller walls, some cathedrals had flying buttresses on the outside. A typical cathedral had a floor plan in the shape of a cross. The altar area was at the top, most of the seating was at the bottom of the longer section, and additional seating or smaller chapels were on the sides.

Gothic cathedrals were intricately decorated with statues and stained glass representations of Bible stories and church history. Relief sculpting inside the cathedral also portrayed Biblical events. These artistic works helped the largely illiterate population become familiar with what the Bible taught.

Cathedrals took many years to be completed. For instance, work on the Cathedral of Saint Stephen in Metz, France, began in 1220; it was consecrated in 1552. A craftsman or stone mason might spend his entire life working on a cathedral and not see it finished. The cathedral became the center of town life, and the area in front of it usually became a marketplace or town square.

The Difference It Makes

We have outlined three ways to acquire knowledge: truth revealed by God, truth arrived at by human reason, and truth discovered through scientific experimentation and observation. The difference that all of these seemingly obscure ideas makes relates to what we believe and what we reject in determining the basis of truth for our lives.

God's revelation must come first. He is above us and we are subject to Him. His truth is unchanging and essential. However, we must differentiate between God's revealed truth and human interpretations of that truth. God has told us that He made the world. He did not tell us that the sun revolves around the earth. That was a human conclusion accepted by the Church for many years, but it turned out to be wrong. We must not accept religious traditions as having the same level of authority as God's Word. We can accept truth wherever we find it as giving honor to God and providing us with greater insight so that we can serve Him more effectively. What we believe and why we believe it make a difference in how we live.

We are destroying speculations and every lofty thing raised up against the knowledge of God, and we are taking every thought captive to the obedience of Christ.
2 Corinthians 10:5

Assignments for Lesson 74

In Their Words   Read the excerpt from *Summa Theologica* (pages 131-132).

Continue reading *Everyman* (pages 143-148).

Student Review   Optional: Answer the questions for Lesson 74.

Monument to Jan Hus in Prague, Czech Republic

Lesson 75 - Bible Study

Obeying God, Obeying Men

Around 1200 the Roman Catholic Church was at the height of its power. Across Europe the pope appointed powerful bishops and either endorsed or excommunicated kings. The pope influenced the domestic political affairs in the developing nations of the continent. The Church intended to root out heretics through the Inquisition. Church offices were sometimes sold to the highest bidder in a practice called simony (after Simon Magus in Acts 8:9-24). Some monasteries became wealthy through receiving donations of land or money. Some of the clergy, especially higher-ranking members, engaged in a lavish lifestyle, wearing expensive clothes and at times indulging in immorality.

On the other hand, sometimes a king exercised power over the pope. In 1294 King Philip IV of France tried to impose a tax on the clergy in his country. The pope ordered the clergy not to pay. Philip then had the pope kidnapped. The king later engineered the election of a French pope and had the papal headquarters moved to Avignon in southern France. During this period, from 1305 to 1378, the pope was a pawn of the French king. The period was dubbed the Babylonian captivity of the pope.

In 1378 two popes were elected by two different bodies, one in Avignon and one in Rome. The schism with competing popes lasted until 1417, when a Church council decided in favor of the pope in Rome. The French king proceeded to tax the clergy. Edward I of England declared that his country was no longer a papal fief. The Church lost some of its power and prestige because of this controversy.

The Sacraments

The Roman Catholic Church declared seven sacraments, or avenues through which grace was dispensed to individuals. These were:

- baptism (soon after birth)
- confirmation (of young children)
- communion (the weekly observance)
- marriage (when performed in the Church with the couple promising to rear their children as Catholics)
- penance (upon confession of sin to a priest who assigned works of penance)
- holy orders (the vows taken by priests, monks, and nuns)
- last rites or extreme unction (administered to a dying person)

The Church thus claimed the ability to give grace to its members from birth to death. Anyone who dared to contradict Church practice and teaching faced the threat of being excommunicated, or being declared ineligible to receive communion, which they believed to be the weekly dispensation of grace. A decree called the papal interdict could even cut off the sacraments from an entire area until the king there repented of a sin. This put great pressure on the king to stay in line with the pope. The system of sacraments threatened to make Christian practice a mechanical ritual because the Church insisted that, when the sacraments were observed, grace was administered regardless of the lifestyle or dedication of either the priest or the supplicant.

Attempts at Reforms

At various times the Church implemented reforms to clean up some of its practices. In 1059 the College of Cardinals was organized for the purpose of electing popes. It began with the high-ranking clergy of Rome but later was broadened to include the highest Church administrators wherever they served. The College was an attempt to remove any political or worldly influences from the selection of a pope.

The Cluny movement encouraged reforms in monasteries. In addition, two new groups attempted to improve the image and work of the Church. Francis of Assisi (a town in Italy) began a monastic order dedicated to helping those in need. This group came to be known as the Franciscans. Dominic of Spain founded an order (the Dominicans) which took as its mission the responsibility of teaching Church doctrine to avoid heresy. Some friars (from the Latin word for brothers) lived in towns, not in monasteries, and tried to be a visible and positive presence for the Church.

Protests Against Church Authority and Practice

Some believers decided that they would not simply accept the authority of the Roman Catholic Church over their lives. In the late 1100s, Peter Waldo began a movement in southeastern France that extended across northern Italy and into Germany. He began preaching publicly even though he was not an ordained priest. This violated Catholic orthodoxy. Waldo translated or obtained a translation of portions of Scripture, which was also a violation of Church doctrine.

Waldo taught that one did not have to follow the practices of the Roman Catholic Church in order to be saved. He denied the authority of the pope and priests; refused to do reverence to a crucifix or other icons; and rejected the doctrines of purgatory, veneration of saints, and infant baptism as well as other Catholic beliefs. Waldo appealed to the pope for his group to be accepted by the Church, but the request was denied. The Waldensians were branded as heretics in 1215 and persecuted by Church authorities.

Members of the Waldensian movement were largely absorbed by the Reformation, but some groups maintained a distinct identity. This Waldenserkirche in Gottstreu, Germany, was built in 1730. A museum about the Waldensians is located nearby.

Wycliffe Giving 'The Poor Priests' His Translation of the Bible, *William Frederick Yeames (English, 19th century)*

The Waldensians were sometimes lumped together with the Albigenses, who were an heretical group about the same time with roots in gnosticism and other errant doctrines. The Albigenses (named for Albi, a town in southern France) believed that the physical world was evil. They denied that Jesus was actually incarnated in the flesh, since that would have made Jesus evil. They wanted nothing to do with the physical world, including the procreation of children. The pope ordered a crusade against this group, and a ruthless persecution of them continued for several years. The Waldensians and Albigenses were a major reason that the Church began the Inquisition, which supposedly was a way to help heretics save their souls and to purify the Church from false teachers.

John Wycliffe was a scholar in Oxford, England, in the late 1300s. He organized a group of lay preachers called the Lollards, who went from town to town preaching the Bible to all who would listen. Wycliffe questioned the role and necessity of the priesthood. He said that God and the Scriptures were the only true spiritual authorities. He denied monasticism, transubstantiation, and the sale of indulgences. The Church sold indulgences, teaching that the purchase of these would release loved ones from purgatory.

Wycliffe believed that the Bible should be available to all and not just to those who knew Latin. He and his followers undertook a translation of Scripture into English, completed and published after his death. Wycliffe was excommunicated and forced to retire from his teaching position, but he was not put to death by the Church. Many of the Lollards were executed, however. Wycliffe is called the Morning Star of the Reformation.

The ideas of Wycliffe were picked up by a reformer in Bohemia, Jan Hus. A professor in Prague (now in the Czech Republic), Hus also strongly attacked Catholic authority and the corruption that existed in the priesthood. Hus was tried on charges of heresy, convicted, and burned at the stake in 1415. In response, Bohemia erupted in a revolt against the pope and against German rule (it was part of the Holy Roman Empire at the time), a revolt which was brutally suppressed. At the same time, Church officials ordered Wycliffe's remains to be exhumed and burned, and the ashes scattered over water.

Diebold Schilling the Elder was the Swiss author of three illustrated chronicles, including the Spiezer Chronik *(1485) that featured this illustration of Jan Hus being burned at the stake.*

"We Must Obey God"

When Peter and the other apostles were brought before the Sanhedrin and were reminded that the Jewish authorities had forbidden them from teaching in the name of Jesus, the apostles replied, "We must obey God rather than men" (Acts 5:29).

In general, the New Testament teaches obedience and submission to authorities (Romans 13:1-2, 1 Peter 2:17). Christians are to obey and submit to those who must give an account for the oversight of their souls (Hebrews 13:17).

Leaders should guide the church on the basis of their wisdom and mature faith. Younger or newer church members may not have those perspectives. Leaders deserve the benefit of the doubt. Christians should not make every question, practice, or matter of opinion the subject of controversy. However, leaders—even in the church—can be wrong. They can make mistakes, or be motivated by fear, or misunderstand a passage of Scripture. When it comes to a matter of truth or faithful practice, Christians must obey God rather than men.

This places heavy responsibility upon both leaders and members. Leaders must humbly and prayerfully analyze their shepherding of the church to make sure that they are not insisting on a mere tradition or following the world. At the same time, members must humbly and prayerfully consider their reaction. They need to be sure that they are not resentful of the leaders or wanting to call the shots themselves. Both parties need to ask whether the issue at hand is something Jesus would care about. Both parties must be open to learning and correction—even from each other—and must be willing to accept those whose faith does not look exactly the same as their own (Romans 14:19, 22).

Certainly the Golden Rule should apply in handling church problems. We must lay down our lives for one another (1 John 3:16). But the faith of a disciple should not be held hostage by someone simply because that person is in a position

Dominic (1170-1221) was a Spanish priest who founded the Dominican Order. According to later tradition, he was an early leader of the Inquisition in Spain; however, evidence from the time of his life is unclear. An auto-da-fé (act of faith) was the required act of public penance before a condemned heretic was executed. The painting above is Saint Dominic Guzmán Presiding Over an Auto-da-fé *by Pedro Berruguete (Spanish, c. 1495).*

of leadership. If this were true, the great reforms in church history would never have taken place.

The world needs to see Christians living in harmony and getting along with each other despite our differences. Unity is a more convincing testimony to unbelievers than the splintered Christian world that exists. This fellowship of love in spite of our differences is also better for the church. We are more likely to learn and grow if we respect and listen to those whose faith is not already exactly like our own.

So then each one of us will
give an account of himself to God.
Romans 14:12

Assignments for Lesson 75

Bible Recite or write James 3:16-18 from memory.

In Their Words Read "All Creatures of Our God and King" and "On Penance" by John Wycliffe (pages 133-135).

Finish reading *Everyman* (pages 149-155). Literary analysis available in *Student Review*.

Project Complete your project for the week.

Student Review Optional: Answer the questions for Lesson 75 and for *Everyman*; take the quiz for Unit 15; and take the third history, English, and Bible exams.

Autumn Colors on the Qiao and Hua Mountains, *Zhao Mengfu (Chinese, c. 1295)*

Credits

Images

Images marked with one of these codes are used with the permission of a Creative Commons Attribution or Attribution-Share Alike License. See the websites listed for details.

CC-BY-2.0   creativecommons.org/licenses/by/2.0/
CC-BY-2.0 FR   creativecommons.org/licenses/by/2.0/fr/
CC-BY-2.5   creativecommons.org/licenses/by/2.5/
CC-BY-3.0   creativecommons.org/licenses/by/3.0/
CC-BY-SA-2.0   creativecommons.org/licenses/by-sa/2.0/
CC-BY-SA-2.0 DE creativecommons.org/licenses/by-sa/2.0/de/
CC-BY-SA-2.5   creativecommons.org/licenses/by-sa/2.5/
CC-BY-SA-3.0   creativecommons.org/licenses/by-sa/3.0/
CC-BY-SA-3.0 DE creativecommons.org/licenses/by-sa/3.0/de/

The World Map used in the "What Else Was Happening?" sections is from the NASA Visible Earth Project / NASA Goddard Space Flight Center Image by Reto Stöckli (land surface, shallow water, clouds). Enhancements by Robert Simmon (ocean color, compositing, 3D globes, animation). Data and technical support: MODIS Land Group; MODIS Science Data Support Team; MODIS Atmosphere Group; MODIS Ocean Group Additional data: USGS EROS Data Center (topography); USGS Terrestrial Remote Sensing Flagstaff Field Center (Antarctica); Defense Meteorological Satellite Program (city lights).

Uncredited images are in the public domain in the United States, taken from Wikimedia Commons and other sources.

iii   Samantha Beddoes / Flickr / CC-BY-2.0
iv   Rajeev kumar / Wikimedia Commons / CC-BY-SA-2.5
v   Andreas F. Borchert / Wikimedia Commons / CC-BY-SA-3.0 DE
vii   cjuneau / Flickr / CC-BY-2.0

x   Miami University Libraries - Digital Collections
1   NASA
3   A. Sparrow / Flickr / CC-BY-2.0
4   Arian Zwegers / Flickr / CC-BY-2.0
5   George M. Groutas / Flickr / CC-BY-2.0
7t   Ian Mackenzie / Flickr / CC-BY-2.0
7b   Trees ForTheFuture / Flickr / CC-BY-2.0
8   Yosomono / Flickr / CC-BY-2.0
9   R/DV/RS / Flickr / CC-BY-2.0
11   Number Six (bill lapp) / Flickr / CC-BY-2.0
13   Ronnie Macdonald / Flickr / CC-BY-2.0
15   emilio labrador / Flickr / CC-BY-2.0
17   Feed My Starving Children (FMSC) / Flickr / CC-BY-2.0
20   NASA
21t   USER:Gx872op / Wikimedia Commons / CC-BY-SA-3.0
21b   Georges Jansoone JoJan / Wikimedia Commons / CC-BY-SA-3.0
23   PretoriaTravel / Wikimedia Commons / CC-BY-SA-3.0
25   Charlene Notgrass
27   Olga Kruglova / Flickr / CC-BY-2.0
31   Stained Glass: Selbymay / Wikimedia Commons / CC-BY-SA-3.0
34tl   Charlesjsharp / Wikimedia Commons / CC-BY-SA-3.0
34ml   SElefant / Wikimedia Commons / CC-BY-SA-3.0
34mr   Merbabu / Wikimedia Commons / CC-BY-SA-3.0
34bl   NewPapillon / Wikimedia Commons / CC-BY-SA-3.0
34br   Pentocelo / Wikimedia Commons / CC-BY-SA-3.0
36   Jack Versloot/ Flickr / CC-BY-2.0
38l   newberry library
40   NPS (Kristen M. Caldon) / Flickr / CC-BY-2.0

Also Available from Notgrass Company

Exploring America by Ray Notgrass

Your child can earn one year of credit in American history, English (literature and composition), and Bible. Engaging history lessons, combined with primary sources, provide a rich understanding of our nation's past. High school.

───────────────

Exploring Government by Ray Notgrass

With a special emphasis on the U.S. Constitution, lessons cover Federal, state, and local government and also contemporary issues in American government. This one-semester course provides a half-year credit. High school.

───────────────

Exploring Economics by Ray Notgrass

This one-semester course provides a half-year credit. It gives a practical and thorough overview of economic terms and concepts to help the student understand how our economy works and grasp contemporary economic issues from a free market perspective. High school.

───────────────

America the Beautiful by Charlene Notgrass

This one-year American history, geography, and literature course combines the flexibility and richness of a unit study with the simplicity of a textbook-based approach to history. Ages 10-14.

───────────────

Uncle Sam and You by Ray and Charlene Notgrass

This one-year civics and government course has daily lessons that teach your child about the foundations of American government, the elections process, and how Federal, state, and local governments work. Ages 10-14.

───────────────

For more information about our homeschool
curriculum and resources, call 1-800-211-8793 or
visit www.notgrass.com.